791.43　　　　　　　　　109120
Tal

Talbot.
Moving pictures.

The Library
Nazareth College of Rochester, N. Y.

The Literature of Cinema

ADVISORY EDITOR: **MARTIN S. DWORKIN**
INSTITUTE OF PHILOSOPHY AND POLITICS OF EDUCATION
TEACHER'S COLLEGE, COLUMBIA UNIVERSITY

THE LITERATURE OF CINEMA presents a comprehensive selection from the multitude of writings about cinema, rediscovering materials on its origins, history, theoretical principles and techniques, aesthetics, economics, and effects on societies and individuals. Included are works of inherent, lasting merit and others of primarily historical significance. These provide essential resources for serious study and critical enjoyment of the "magic shadows" that became one of the decisive cultural forces of modern times.

Moving Pictures

Frederick A. Talbot

ARNO PRESS & THE NEW YORK TIMES
New York • 1970

Reprint Edition 1970 by Arno Press Inc.
Reprinted from a copy in The Museum of Modern Art Library
Library of Congress Catalog Card Number: 71-124038
ISBN 0-405-01638-7
ISBN for complete set: 0-405-01600-X
Manufactured in the United States of America

MOVING PICTURES
HOW THEY ARE MADE AND WORKED

Frontispiece

TRICK CINEMATOGRAPHY—THE AUTOMOBILE ACCIDENT.

The producer giving instructions to the principal actor and his double, the legless cripple. The dummy legs in the foreground.—*See page* 211.

CONQUESTS OF SCIENCE

MOVING PICTURES
HOW THEY ARE MADE AND WORKED

BY

FREDERICK A. TALBOT

AUTHOR OF
"THE RAILWAY CONQUEST OF THE WORLD," "THE NEW GARDEN OF CANADA,"
"THE MAKING OF A GREAT CANADIAN RAILWAY," ETC.

ILLUSTRATED

PHILADELPHIA: J. B. LIPPINCOTT COMPANY
LONDON: WILLIAM HEINEMANN
1912

Printed in England

PREFACE

THE marvellous, universal popularity of moving pictures is my reason for writing this volume. A vast industry has been established of which the great majority of picture-palace patrons have no idea, and the moment appears timely to describe the many branches of the art.

I have endeavoured to deal with the whole subject in a popular and comprehensive manner. I have been assisted by several friends, who have enabled me to throw considerable light upon the early history of motion photography and the many problems that had to be mastered before it met with public appreciation :—MM. Weiss and Bull, the Director and Assistant-Director respectively of the Marey Institute in Paris; M. Georges Demeny; Messrs. Frank L. Dyer, the President of Thomas A. Edison, Incorporated; W. F. Greene, Robert W. Paul, James Williamson, Lumière & Sons, Richard G. Hollaman, the Eastman Kodak Company, Dr. J. Comandon, F. Percy Smith, Albert Smith, and the numerous firms engaged in one or other of the various branches of the industry.

I am indebted especially to the editor of *L'Illustration,* the well-known Parisian illustrated weekly newspaper, in conjunction with the Société des Établissements Gaumont, for permission to publish the photographs illustrating Chapters XIX., XX., and XXI., as well as the frontispiece; also to Mr. A. A. Hopkins, the author of "Magic," and to Messrs. Munn & Co., the proprietors of *The Scientific American*, of New York, U.S.A.

The book makes no claim to being a practical manual, because thereby intricate technicalities would have been unavoidable. The information respecting the various mechanical aspects of cinematography are set forth in a readable manner, so that the broad principles may be understood.

While the most popular features of motion photography are described fully, I have not omitted to introduce the reader to the educational and scientific developments, which are more wonderful and fascinating. Indeed, the cinematograph will probably achieve greater triumphs in these fields than it has accomplished already as a source of amusement.

FREDERICK A. TALBOT.

CONTENTS

CHAPTER		PAGE
I.	WHAT IS ANIMATED PHOTOGRAPHY?	1
II.	THE FIRST ATTEMPTS TO PRODUCE MOVING PICTURES	10
III.	THE SEARCH FOR THE CELLULOID FILM	23
IV.	THE KINETOSCOPE: THE ANIMATOGRAPH: THE CINEMATOGRAPHE	30
V.	HOW THE CELLULOID FILM IS MADE	50
VI.	THE STORY OF THE PERFORATION GAUGE	57
VII.	THE MOVING PICTURE CAMERA, ITS CONSTRUCTION, AND OPERATION	65
VIII.	DEVELOPING AND PRINTING THE PICTURES	76
IX.	HOW THE PICTURES ARE SHOWN UPON THE SCREEN	88
X.	THE STUDIO FOR STAGING MOVING PICTURE PLAYS	103
XI.	THE CINEMATOGRAPH AS A RECORDER OF TOPICAL EVENTS: SCENIC FILMS	116
XII.	THE CINEMATOGRAPH THEATRE AND ITS EQUIPMENT	130
XIII.	HOW A CINEMATOGRAPH PLAY IS PRODUCED	146
XIV.	MOVING PICTURES OF MICROBES	161
XV.	SOME ELABORATE PICTURE PLAYS AND HOW THEY WERE STAGED	169
XVI.	PICTURES THAT MOVE, TALK, AND SING	179
XVII.	POPULAR SCIENCE AS REVEALED BY THE CINEMATOGRAPH	190
XVIII.	TRICK PICTURES AND HOW THEY ARE PRODUCED.— I. THE FIRST ATTEMPTS AT CINEMATOGRAPH MAGIC AND THE ARTIFICES ADOPTED	197

CONTENTS

CHAPTER		PAGE
XIX.	TRICK PICTURES AND HOW THEY ARE PRODUCED.—II. DANCING FURNITURE: STRINGS, CORDS, AND WIRES: "THE MAGNETIC GENTLEMAN": THE "STOP AND SUBSTITUTION": "THE AUTOMOBILE ACCIDENT": REVERSAL OF ACTION	207
XX.	TRICK PICTURES AND HOW THEY ARE PRODUCED.—III. MANIPULATION OF THE FILM: APPARITIONS AND GRADUAL DISAPPEARANCES BY OPENING AND CLOSING THE DIAPHRAGM OF THE LENS SLOWLY: "THE SIREN": SUBMARINE EFFECTS	218
XXI.	TRICK PICTURES AND HOW THEY ARE PRODUCED.—IV. LILLIPUTIAN FIGURES: "THE LITTLE MILLINER'S DREAM": THE "ONE TURN ONE PICTURE" MOVEMENT: HOW SOME EXTRAORDINARY INCIDENTS ARE PRODUCED: "THE SKI RUNNER"	231
XXII.	TRICK PICTURES AND HOW THEY ARE PRODUCED.—V. "PRINCESS NICOTINE" AND HER REMARKABLE CAPRICES	242
XXIII.	TRICK PICTURES AND HOW THEY ARE PRODUCED.—VI. SOME UNUSUAL AND NOVEL EFFECTS	254
XXIV.	ELECTRIC SPARK CINEMATOGRAPHY	264
XXV.	THE "ANIMATED" NEWSPAPER	277
XXVI.	ANIMATION IN NATURAL COLOURS	287
XXVII.	MOVING PICTURES IN THE HOME	301
XXVIII.	MOTION-PHOTOGRAPHY AS AN EDUCATIONAL FORCE	312
XXIX.	RECENT DEVELOPMENTS: THE GROWTH AND POPULARITY OF THE CINEMATOGRAPH: SOME FACTS AND FIGURES: CONCLUSION	319

LIST OF ILLUSTRATIONS

To face page

Trick Cinematography—The Automobile Accident . *Frontispiece*	
Dr. E. J. Marey's Famous Experiments—Photographic Gun of 1882	16
Consecutive Pictures of a Gull Flying, taken with the Photographic Gun	16
Chronophotographic Apparatus for taking Consecutive Pictures upon a Single Glass Plate	16
Dr. Marey's Animated Pictures made in 1884–6 for the Analysis of Motion	17
Edison's First Kinetoscope	32
Edison Film made about 1891 for the Kinetoscope . .	33
Edison Film made in 1911 for the Cinematograph . .	33
Paul's Camera showing Mechanism for moving the Film intermittently past the Lens	36
The First Kinetoscope Film made in England . .	36
The " Black Maria," the First Edison Studio for making Kinetoscope Films	37
The Dissolving Room	52
The Mixing Barrel	53
A Battery of Celluloid Mixers	54
The Liquid Celluloid Storage Room	55
Paul's Rotary Perforator	60
The First Cinematograph Studio-Stage . . .	60
The Williamson Film Perforator	61
The Perforating Room of the Cines Company in Rome .	66
The Film-moving Mechanism of a Cinematograph Camera .	67
Paul's Complete Developing, Printing, and Drying Outfit .	70
The First Developing Room in Great Britain, at Robert Paul's Pioneer Film Factory	70
After Development and Washing the Films were transferred from the Racks to the Cylinders	71
The Drying Room, showing Films wound on the Drying Drums .	71

LIST OF ILLUSTRATIONS

To face page

The Developing Room at the Pathé Works	78
The Drying Room at the Pathé Works	79
A Row of Printing Machines in the Rome Works of the Cines Company	82
The Williamson Printing Machine	83
The Projector and Mechanism	100
The Complete Projecting Installation	100
The "Chrono" Projector	101
Outstripping the Human Eye	101
An Early Open-Air Studio-Stage for producing Cinematograph Plays	104
The Scene-Painters' Shop at a Pathé Studio	105
Battle Scene from "The Siege of Calais"	108
Exterior of the Modern Edison Film-Play-Producing Theatre	109
Building a Solid Set for "The Two Orphans"	109
Building a Scene on one of the Pathé Studio-Stages for a Film Play	112
The Wardrobe Room at the Selig Film Factory	113
The Selig Stock Company at Los Angeles	113
The First Topical Film	118
The White Man's Child	119
Arizona Bill	119
The Luxury of the Modern Picture Palace	134
The Lantern Room of a Modern Cinematograph Theatre	135
How the Sound Accompaniments to Pictures are Produced	140
The Trial Scene from "Rachel's Sin"	141
The Film-Play Producer at Work	148
Taking Three Picture-Plays Simultaneously	149
The Fatal Duel Scene from "The Two Orphans"	152
The Colleen Bawn	153
The Lost Freight Car	153
Sorting, Examining, and Joining the Strips of Film	156
Preparing the Titles	157
Dr. Comandon's Apparatus for taking Moving Pictures of Microbes	164
The Phenomenon of Agglutination in a Fowl's Blood	165
The Blood of a Fowl suffering from *Spirochæta Gallinarum*	165
A Remarkable Instance of Picture-Play Enterprise	172
The Gigantic Horse being Hauled by the Greeks under the Walls of Troy	173
"The Fall of Troy"	173
Building an Elaborate Interior Scene for a Picture-Play	176

LIST OF ILLUSTRATIONS xiii

To face page

A Scene from the Picture-Play representation of Tasso's poem, "Jerusalem"	177
An Episode from "The Bride of the Nile"	177
Nature and the Cinematographer—Mr. Percy Smith at Work	192
Fly Seated in a Diminutive Chair Balancing a Cork	193
An Unfamiliar Juggler—Bluebottle Balancing a Piece of Vegetable Stalk	193
Fly Lying on its Back Spinning a Wheel	194
Juggling Flies	194
The Fly Walking Up the Turning Wheel	194
The Life of the Butterfly	195
The Magic Sword: A Mediæval Mystery Explained	200
A Christmas Carol: How Scrooge saw Bob Cratchit's Home	201
"Ora Pro Nobis," and How it was Produced	202
The Secret of the Haunted Curiosity Shop	203
Motoring Round the Ring of Saturn	204
The Car Circling the Sun	204
The Animated Swords	205
The Travelling Bed	208
The Magnetic Gentleman	209
The Pursuing Man-hole Cover is a Wooden Property	210
The Lamp-Post is a Stage Article Hinged in the Centre	210
The Trick Picture—The Automobile Accident: The Actor being replaced by the Legless Cripple with the Dummy Legs	211
The Taxi-cab Running over the Sleeper and Apparently Cutting off his Legs, but in Reality Displacing the Legless Cripple's Property Limbs	212
Observing the Effects of the Disaster, the Doctor Proceeds to Replace the Severed Legs	213
The Limbs Replaced, the Patient and Doctor Shake Hands	21
The Roysterer, after being run over by the Taxi-cab, Sitting up and Brandishing his Severed Limbs	214
The Legless Cripple being Prepared for the Act	214
The Fountain of Youth	215
Pumpkins Running Up-hill	215
The Revolving Table	220
The Secret of the Fairy's Disappearance: While a Length of Film is being exposed the Diaphragm is closed slowly	221
The same Length of Film is re-exposed after the Fairy has entered the Picture, under a slowly opening Diaphragm	222
The Effect of Double Exposure under closing and opening Diaphragm	223

LIST OF ILLUSTRATIONS

To face page

The Mystery of "The Siren"	226
The Mystery of "The Siren" revealed	227
A Workshop in which Tools move without Hands	238
The Skater approaching the Factory Chimney	238
The Result of the Collision with the Chimney	239
The Ski-runner Disappears into Space	239
Princess Nicotine—A Dainty Trick Film	246
The Fairy, Buried in the Heart of the Rose, Smoking a Cigarette	247
The Diminutive Form of the Fairy on the Table	247
The Fairy Imprisoned in the Bottle. This effect is obtained by double exposure	250
The Fairy, after Coquetting with the Bachelor, is driven away by the Smoke from his Cigarette	250
The Fairy proceeds to Build a Bonfire with Matches	251
The Fairy, her Accomplice, and Properties, which are Enlarged Reproductions of the Actual Articles	251
The Dissolution of the Government	258
The Latest Craze in Trick Cinematography: Silhouettes with Models	259
A Quaint Advertisement Film	260
Mr. Asquith in Cartoon	260
A Novel Curtain Idea	260
The Human Butterfly: How are the Effects Obtained?	261
M. Lucien Bull's Complete Apparatus	270
The Novel Camera showing Stereoscopic Lens	270
A Bee cinematographed in Full Flight	271
A Dragon Fly in Flight	274
Cinematograph Film of a Bullet Fired through a Soap Bubble	275
Preparing the Pathé Colour Films	288
The Pathé Colour Machine-Printing Room	289
The Kinora Camera	302
The Mechanism of the Kinora Camera showing Paper Negative Film in position	302
The Reel of Positive Prints	303
The Kinora Reproduction Instrument	303
The Cinematograph Attachment removed from Camera, showing Mechanism	308
The Interior of the Camera showing Film Threaded ready for use	308
The Birth of a Flower	309
Waging a Health Campaign by Moving Pictures	309
Cinematographing Africa from a Locomotive	314

LIST OF ILLUSTRATIONS

To face page

Mount Etna in Eruption: looking into the Crater of the Volcano	315
The Plumes of Smoke as seen from the Observatory	315
The "Cradle of Cinematography": The Marey Institute in Paris	322
The latest marvel in Moving Pictures: Combining the X-rays with the Cinematograph	322
After Fifty Years. This Film won the First Prize of 25,000 Francs at the recent Turin Exhibition	323

CHAPTER I

WHAT IS ANIMATED PHOTOGRAPHY?

FROM the day when it was found possible (by the aid of sunlight) to fix a permanent image of an object upon a sensitised surface, inventors steadily applied their ingenuity to the problem of instantaneous photography. In other words, they strove to realise the possibility of photographing an object in motion.

In our days the idea of "snapshot" photography is such a commonplace that we can no longer realise the proportions of the task which confronted the early inventors. Probably most of us are unacquainted with the conditions under which the first photographs were taken. The writer has often heard a member of his family relate the amusing story of an ordeal which, as a lad, the latter underwent at the hands of the Frenchman, Daguerre. He was seized upon by the inventor as an experimental subject and was forced to sit in the brilliant sunlight for a long time. It seems incredible, but it is true, that when photography was in its infancy, an exposure of six hours was required to secure a recognisable impression of an object—a circumstance which left practically nothing but still life as feasible subjects for photography.

The problem which confronted the pioneers of instantaneous photography was the reduction of the period of exposure from about 20,000 seconds to a mere fraction of a second. Considering the magnitude of this difficulty, it is not surprising that the average person was sceptical as to its solution. The possibility of fixing a horse in the act of jumping, a bird in the act of flying, or an orator's lips at the moment of uttering a word, must have seemed nearly as remote as the discovery of the Philosopher's Stone. It is interesting to imagine the sensations of the sceptic of one hundred years ago, to whom instantaneous photography appeared a chimerical idea, should he be recalled to life to-day and be shown first a procession passing down the street, and a few hours afterward the same procession repeating itself before his eyes upon a screen in a darkened room, with all the semblance of reality in colour and animation.

In the end, it was the chemist who solved the problem of instantaneous photography, without which animated photography as we know it to-day would never have been even conceivable. He carried out innumerable laboratory experiments for the purpose of rendering the sensitised surface more and more susceptible to light—accelerating its actinic speed, as it is called—until at last he revolutionised photography, as he has changed nearly every other field of our modern industrial life. He succeeded in preparing a surface, or emulsion, so sensitive to light that it can take a picture clear, distinct, and full of detail, not merely in the space of one second, but in less than a thousandth part of a second—a picture equal, if not superior, to those which in the early days of photography required an exposure 20,000,000 times as long!

The wonderful achievement of instantaneous photography assumed at first a scientific rather than a commercial value. Many a "snap-shot" is taken which does not betray whether the plate has been exposed for six hours or only one-thousandth of a second; but, on the other hand, a "snap-shot" of a quickly moving subject may seize upon and fix an interesting or characteristic motion. It was this fact which led certain ingenious minds to perceive in instantaneous photography a valuable means of analysing motion. If a single photograph reproduced the exact posture of a moving subject at any given instant of time, they argued that a series of such photographs, if taken in sufficiently rapid succession, would form a complete record of the whole cycle of movements involved, for instance, in the jump of a horse or the flap of a bird's wing.

Here, again, the inventor encountered a difficulty almost as great as the initial one of instantaneous photography. Not only had the chemist to devise a new sort of sensitised plate with a gelatine coating better and more convenient to handle than the medium before employed, but the mechanical engineer, the optical instrument maker, and the lens maker had to co-operate on a special sort of camera which should minimise the interval between successive exposures.

As earlier inventors had reduced the duration of the period of exposure, modern ones have succeeded in their turn in reducing the interval between exposures to a minute fraction of a second. When this result was achieved, animated photography became a reality.

It was possible to secure a long series of consecutive snap-shots, or instantaneous pictures depicting motion, recorded at such brief intervals that when they were passed swiftly before the eyes they produced the *illusion* of movement.

At this point it is best to consider the physiological basis upon which animated photography rests. The word illusion, as used above, correctly describes what takes place. The eye sees a swift succession of instantaneous photographs; but it is deluded into believing that it sees actual movement.

We have all marvelled at the magician who causes bottles, eggs, birds, and animals to appear and disappear mysteriously before our very eyes. We know that it is trickery, pure and simple: that the eye is being deceived. The camera is a far more perfect trickster than the most accomplished illusionist that has ever lived, and moving pictures are the most cunning illusion that has ever been devised.

In order to convey this delusion, the photographer has taken advantage of one deficiency of the human eye. This wonderful organ of ours has a defect which is known as "visual persistence." Briefly defined, this means that the brain persists in seeing an object after it is no longer visible to the eye. I will make this clear by further explanation.

The eye is in itself a wonderful camera. The imprint of an object is received upon a nervous membrane which is called the retina. This is connected with the brain, where the actual conception of the impression is formed, by the optic nerve. The picture therefore is photographed in the eye and transmitted from that point to the brain. Now a certain period of time must elapse in the conveyance of this picture from the retina along the optic nerve to the brain, in the same manner that an electric current flowing through a wire, or water passing through a pipe, must take a certain amount of time to travel from one point to another, although the movement may be so rapid that the time occupied on the journey is reduced to an infinitesimal point and might be considered instantaneous. When the picture reaches the brain a further length of time is required to bring about its construction, for the brain is something like the photographic plate, and the picture requires developing. In this respect the brain is somewhat sluggish, for when it has formulated the picture imprinted on the eye, it will retain that picture even after the reality has disappeared from sight.

This peculiarity can be tested very easily. Suppose the eye is focussed upon a white screen. A picture suddenly appears. The image is reflected upon the retina of the eye, and transmitted thence to the brain along the optic nerve. Before the impression reaches the brain the picture has vanished from the sight of the eye. Yet the image still lingers in the brain; the latter persists in seeing what is no longer apparent to the eye, just as plainly and as distinctly as if it were in full view. When the image does disappear, it fades away gradually from the brain.

True, the duration of this continued impression in the brain is very brief. In the average person it approximates about $2/48$ths of a second, which appears so short as not to be worth consideration. Still, in a fraction of time a good deal may happen, and in the case of animated

I WHAT IS ANIMATED PHOTOGRAPHY? 5

photography it suffices to bring a second picture before the eye ere the impression of the preceding image has faded from the brain. The result is that the second picture becomes superimposed in the brain upon the preceding image; and being stronger and more brilliant, it causes the disappearing impression to merge or dissolve into itself.

Indeed, one might go farther, and say that the brain acts in the same manner as a dissolving lantern. This apparatus is very familiar to us all, and in its most approved type one view is dissolved into another. For the purpose two lanterns are required, placed either side by side or one above the other, and both focussed upon the screen. For the purpose of illustrating our complex point we will consider that they are one above the other. A slide is projected brilliantly from the uppermost lantern. Presently the moment arrives to change the slide. If the operator withdrew it from the upper lantern and inserted another there would be a defined break or blank interval upon the screen betraying the change. So he inserts the new slide in the lower lantern, at the same time increasing the volume of light emitted from that lantern, and diminishing the volume thrown from the upper lantern. The result is that the picture projected from the upper lantern becomes fainter and fainter, while that shown by the lower lantern becomes stronger and stronger, until only the latter is seen upon the screen—the former has merged or dissolved into the latter.

The same action takes place in the brain in connection with cinematography. A picture is thrown upon the screen, and remains visible for 1/32nd part of a second. It is then eclipsed by the shutter, and—supposing that the photographs are taken at the rate of sixteen pictures per second—for the next 1/32nd part of a second the screen is darkened owing to the passage of the shutter. This division of time is not strictly correct, as we shall see later, but for present purposes I have considered the intervals of exposure and eclipse to be of equal duration.

Now as a picture will linger in the brain for 2/48ths of

a second after it has vanished from the sight of the eye, the brain retains the impression during 1/32nd part of a second, while the shutter is passing across the lens. The second picture now comes before the eye, and although the previous picture still will remain in the brain for another 1/96th part of a second—the difference between 1/32nd and 2/48ths—the new picture, being the more brilliant, becomes superimposed upon that already obtained, and consequently causes the former dying image to merge into the later and brighter impression. This successive dissolution of one picture into the other continues until the whole string of snap-shots is exhausted. It will be noticed that every picture remains on the screen for 1/32nd of a second, followed by a period of darkness of nearly equal duration, the pictures thus being projected at the rate of sixteen per second.

The illusion of movement is enhanced by the fact that all fixed and stationary objects retain their relative positions in each succeeding image. Suppose, for instance, that a series of pictures, depicting a man walking along a street, are being shown upon a screen. In the first picture the man is shown with his left foot in the air. This remains in sight for 1/32nd of a second, and then disappears suddenly. Though the picture has vanished from the eye, the brain still persists in seeing the left foot slightly raised. One thirty-second part of a second later the next picture shows the man with his left foot on the ground. The shops, houses, and other stationary objects in the second image occupy the positions shown in the first picture, and consequently the dying impression of these objects is revived, while the brain receives the impression that the man has changed the position of his foot in relation to the stationary objects, and the left foot which was raised melts into the left foot upon the ground. The eye imagines that it sees the left foot descend. Another 1/32nd part of a second passes, and the right foot is seen elevated, but the fixed objects retain their positions still, and so on. The brain only notices the difference in the position of the moving objects, and thus secures an illusory idea that movement is taking place. I have taken a very simple example to illustrate the idea. As a matter of fact, moving pictures of men walking are seldom perfectly successful, generally having a jerky movement.

Thus we have seen what we describe as animated photography is not animation at all. All that happens is that a long string of snap-shot photographs, taken at intervals of 1/24th or 1/32nd part of a second, are passed at rapid speed before the eye. If the pictures are projected at the rate of one per second they resemble ordinary magic lantern projections. As the operator slowly and gradually increases the speed, the figures shown in the pictures assume a spasmodic motion, as if their limbs were moved jerkily by means of strings; this action becoming less and less pronounced as the speed is accelerated, until, at last, when the operator gains the requisite rate of projection, the jerky movement becomes resolved into steady rhythmic action.

In the early days it was difficult to convey the impression that motion was being shown, because the movement of the shutter cutting off the picture was so emphasised as to convey a distinct sense of blankness between the successive images. This regular intermittent occurrence of invisibility, described as "flicker," caused tremendous strain to the eyes, and provoked nauseating headache. When the flicker was eliminated the strain ceased; the illusion was rendered more perfect as well.

In order to satisfy one's self that the semblance of animation is an illusion, one has only to compare the projection of a moving object upon the screen, and its appearance in the *camera obscura*. In the latter case absolute continuous motion is shown. It may be said that complete animation by photography is quite out of the question with the single camera and projector. How it can be avoided and a more perfect *camera obscura* effect produced upon the screen is described later. Mechanical ingenuity has not succeeded yet in achieving such a result by means of a single lens.

As a matter of fact, only one-half or less of the movement that actually takes place is recorded upon the film. What is lost occurs during the period the shutter is closed after exposure, in order to permit a fresh area of sensitised surface to be brought into position behind the lens. However, the lapses are equal in point of time; and when sixteen pictures are taken per second, the interruption in the movement is not detected by the brain.

It may be asked why the operator confines himself to photographing at a speed of about sixteen pictures per second. This question is governed for the most part by economical motives. Film is expensive, and therefore the obvious point is to consume the minimum of material to secure the illusion. When Edison produced the kinetoscope, at least thirty pictures per second were necessary to bring about the illusion, but Messrs. Lumière and Paul, by means of their apparatuses, which were the first commercial cinematographs, reduced the number to sixteen pictures per second. If twenty-four photographs were taken and projected per second the result would be practically no better than when only sixteen pictures were made in the same period, so that the additional eight pictures and their requisite length of film represent so much wasted effort and material.

This law in regard to visual persistence concerning the number of pictures per second holds good only so long as pictures are taken and projected in monochrome or black and white. When animation in colour is introduced, the illusory effect produced upon the brain becomes disturbed, as is explained in the chapter dealing with this latter development of the art.

An interesting illustration of the fact that the eye is deceived may be narrated. A film of a train passing through a tunnel was required. Two trains were secured for the purpose, and at the rear of the leading train the camera was mounted in order to photograph the one following, care being observed to keep them an equal distance apart. In the darkness of the tunnel the question of illumination for the purposes of the exposures was somewhat perplexing. Various expedients were attempted, but all to no avail, and it appeared as if the task would have to be abandoned.

One of the party thereupon suggested a novel solution of the difficulty. A section of the track was marked off, and subdivided into short sections. The train was brought to the first mark and there stopped, when a flashlight photograph was made. It was then advanced to the next mark, and another flashlight instantaneous picture was secured. This process was repeated several times, the train being moved forward about eighteen inches between each exposure. About fifty exposures were made in this manner, and the length of exposed film thus obtained was multiplied to form a continuous picture of great length. When projected on the screen several hundred photographs were passed before the audience at the speed of sixteen pictures per second, and the semblance of motion was perfect, the train having the appearance of travelling through the tunnel at express speed.

This is one of the most interesting examples known to me of illusion by animated photography, and although it was not motion at all that was recorded, still it sufficed to convey the impression of movement to the public. In the course of the following chapters, however, various successful illusions caused by this means are described, especially in regard to "trick pictures."

CHAPTER II

THE FIRST ATTEMPTS TO PRODUCE MOVING PICTURES

The idea of producing apparent animation by means of pictures is by no means new. The origin of the most primitive form of moving picture device is lost in the mists of antiquity; but it is certain that long before photography was conceived animated pictures were in vogue, and constituted a source of infinite amusement among children. The illusion was secured by a simple device known as the Zoetrope or the "Wheel of Life." It consists of a small cylinder, mounted on a vertical spindle in such a way that it is free to revolve horizontally. A band of thin cardboard, or thick paper, on which is painted a series of pictures, generally in colour, depicting successive stages in a particular movement, such as a horse jumping, a child swinging, or two youngsters playing see-saw, is placed horizontally around the inside of the lower half of the cylinder. The upper half is pierced at regular intervals by long narrow slits or vertical openings, which come opposite the pictures and extend only about half-way down the length of the wall. When the cylinder is rotated sharply and one looks through the slits, the pictures portray apparent motion—the horse rises and falls in the jump, the swing moves to and fro, and the see-saw goes up and down—in accordance with the laws of visual persistence.

Each successive picture, it must be pointed out, is interrupted by the space in the surface of the wall between two consecutive slits through which one peeps into the cylinder. We have, in fact, a cinematograph in the most primitive form; the space between the apertures corresponding to the opaque sector of the shutter of the camera and the projector, whereby one picture is eclipsed from view on the screen to permit the next to be brought before the lens. Indeed, one can easily convert the zoetrope into a cinematograph if, instead of painted pictures, prints of a cinematograph film are mounted in the same way. As a matter of fact, some ingenious person followed this practice years ago, thus unconsciously producing the first animated pictures by photography, and in a crude way anticipating the kinetoscope.

From time to time the zoetrope was modified and revived in the praxinoscope, phenakistoscope, zoopraxinoscope, and a number of other forms with awe-inspiring names. In every instance, however, it was merely our old friend in a new guise. One of these modifications created a flutter of excitement in France in 1877. It was called the "praxinoscope," and its creator, M. Reynaud, for the first time enabled a large audience to see animation upon the screen.

In this case projection was carried out in a highly novel manner. The front, or proscenium opening, of the stage was occupied by a large white screen, such as is used for magic lantern projection, the operator and his apparatus being on the stage behind, out of sight. Accordingly the audience saw the picture through the sheet. At the back of the stage a limelight lantern was set up, from which a still life picture was thrown, filling the greater part of the surface of the screen. The picture thus shown formed as it were the setting for the animated picture, in just the same way as the scenery comprises the environment for a stage play.

Below the level of the stage was a large rectangular table, at each corner of which were placed small vertical rollers. At one end of the table were two large spools, fitted with handles which were revolved horizontally. One spool carried a long band of transparent material, on which were painted at regular intervals silhouette figures in colour in successive stages of movement. The band led from this spool round the vertical roller immediately adjacent, then along the side of the table to the next corner, on to the next corner, on to the third corner, back to the fourth corner, and then to the empty reel, on which it was wound. By simultaneously rotating the loaded spool with the left hand, and the second reel with the right hand, the transparent picture band was passed round the table from one spool to the other.

Centrally with the sheet, and on a level with the table, there was a second limelight lantern, the back of which was towards the audience. This lantern threw its rays upward at an angle of forty-five degrees or so. As the band of pictures travelled along the table edge from the first to the second corner roller, it was passed through this second lantern, which projected the silhouette picture into a mirror hung overhead at the back of the stage, which in turn reflected the image on the screen. The figures on the band thrown from the second lantern appeared in the scene of the slide shown by the first lantern. As the band was moved forward, bringing successive phases of action upon the screen, apparent motion was produced. In fact, animated pictures were shown, and it was possible with a number of spools of painted bands to produce a comedy, tragedy, or other stage play in pictures. This crude apparatus was the first attempt to portray moving pictures upon a sheet before a large audience.

As instantaneous photography developed and efforts were made to adapt photographic records instead of painted pictures to the praxinoscope, great difficulty was experienced in securing the consecutive pictures sufficiently close to one another so as to reduce the loss of action between two successive pictures to the minimum. The cameras available were not suited to this work. Too much time was lost in removing the exposed sensitised surface to permit another unexposed area to be brought before the lens.

About 1872 Mr. Muybridge, an ingenious Englishman, resident in San Francisco, conceived a novel means of obtaining snap-shot photographs in rapid succession. He maintained that such photographs taken at regular intervals, reproduced in such a manner as to simulate natural animation, would reveal the peculiar attitudes of animals in motion and would prove of invaluable service to artists. He approached Governor Stanford and unfolded his scheme. Stanford was so impressed that he placed every facility at Muybridge's disposal for the completion of the experiment, including the use of his valuable stud of horses and exercising track.

As it was impossible to secure the desired end with a single camera, Muybridge built a studio beside the track, in which twenty-four cameras were placed side by side in a row. On the opposite side of the track, facing the studio, he erected a high fence, painted white, while across the track between the studio and the screen twenty-four threads were stretched, each of which was connected with a powerful spring, which held in position the shutter of a camera.

When all was ready, a horse was driven over this length of track at a canter, gallop, trot, or walk, as desired, and as the animal passed each camera, it broke the thread controlling its shutter, so that the horse photographed itself in its progress. In these experiments, however, Muybridge made no effort to secure detail. The photographs were taken in brilliant sunlight, and the white screen threw a dazzling reflection, causing the objects to stand out in bold relief, so that the record appeared in silhouette. As these photographs were taken for a specific purpose—the analysis of movement—the screen was subdivided into panels, whereby it was possible to determine the distance between each successive picture. (Fig. 1.)

As Muybridge's experiments were carried out upon a somewhat private basis, the information about them that reached Europe was of a very meagre description. In France, however, they aroused a strong curiosity and peculiar interest, especially in artistic and scientific circles. They appealed especially to one man—Meissonier. The great artist, whose accuracy in the most minute detail was proverbial, was fascinated. He had observed very closely the curious attitudes that horses assume when in rapid motion, and had committed the observations to his canvases,

14 MOVING PICTURES [CHAP.

FIG. 1.—THE FIRST MOVING PICTURES. [*By Permission of "The Scientific American."*]

Twelve successive photographs, by Mr. Muybridge, of a horse in full gallop. In the last figure the horse is seen standing still. The speed of the horse was about 1,142 metres (3,746 feet) per minute.

only to meet with strenuous hostile criticism from his colleagues and the public. So when Governor Stanford, while visiting Paris, displayed some of Muybridge's photographs, the great painter spent hours in studying them, and characterised them as an incalculable aid to art. Through Governor Stanford, he extended an invitation to Muybridge.

In the following year the Anglo-American experimenter —who might be described as the father of animated photography—visited the French capital, and received a warm greeting by Meissonier. The artist had been criticised for his views concerning muscular action, as displayed by the animals on his canvases, yet here was a man who could demonstrate, by the conclusive evidence of photography, that his views were correct. Meissonier arranged a private demonstration, which ranked as one of the most important social events of the year in Paris. Among those who accepted the invitation to witness the new wonder were Gerome, Goupil, Steinheil, Detaillé, Alexander Dumas, and Dr. Mallez. Muybridge had brought a representative collection of photographs with him, showing horses in movement, dogs, deer, and other animals running and jumping, as well as men wrestling, leaping, and performing other athletic exercises.

The pictures were examined at great length individually. Then by means of the zoopraxoscope, a form of the wheel of life, whereby pictures in action could be thrown upon the screen, they were displayed in animation, thereby conclusively demonstrating the fact that what appeared so incredibly singular an attitude in a painting or an individual photograph was in reality part of a graceful harmonious natural movement.

There was one feature of Muybridge's work which must not be overlooked, and which decidedly restricted its application. A battery of cameras had to be employed, placed side by side. It was as if a number of photographers, standing in a row, pressed a button the instant the object in motion was opposite their respective cameras. All the photographs were broadside views, and taken from the same relative position. The results were not as the following eye of one person saw them, but as the eyes of twenty or thirty persons standing side by side grasped a glimpse of motion during the five-thousandth part of a second. If Muybridge had attempted to take 900 photographic impressions, such as the cinematograph camera records in the space of a minute to-day, he would have required nine hundred cameras for the purpose.

Of course, such a plan had no commercial possibilities. Its real value lay in the fact that it stimulated the ingenuity of a host of inventive brains towards the solution of animated photography. One and all were bent upon securing the same result that Muybridge had achieved, but with a single camera and from one point of view. Among these experimenters the names of Greene and Evans, Acres and Paul stand pre-eminent in Great Britain, while France and the United States had an equal number of contemporaneous investigators engaged upon the problem. Even Muybridge himself attempted its solution, for he realised only too well that a battery of cameras was impracticable to ensure the commercial success of animated photography.

It appears to be a sorry trick of fortune that every great invention, or development, should produce a bevy of claimants for the honour of being the "original inventor." The word "original" is somewhat obscure and ambiguous, but it is employed frequently. As a matter of fact, it is a wise invention that can single out its creator. Animated photography has been no exception to the rule. Lawyers and the courts have reaped a rich harvest from protracted litigation in the effort to settle the question once and for all, with the inevitable result—the law has left the matter in a more hazy condition than ever.

The claim to the discovery of animated photography can scarcely be sustained by any one man. Desvignes devised an apparatus in 1860; Du Mont formulated the first tangible scheme of chronophotography, as it is called, in 1861, which Donisthorpe put into practice in 1876, while a host of other experimenters contributed to the problem in some particular detail. It was not invention, for the simple

DR. E. J. MAREY'S FAMOUS EXPERIMENTS IN CINEMATOGRAPHY.

1. Photographic gun of 1882, to photograph birds in flight. 2. Consecutive pictures of a gull flying, taken with the photographic gun.
3. Chronophotographic apparatus for taking consecutive pictures upon a single glass plate, showing mechanism.

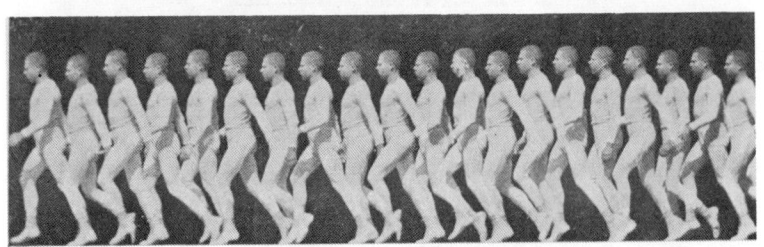

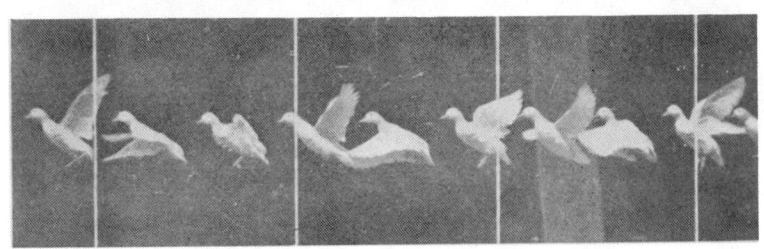

DR. MAREY'S ANIMATED PICTURES MADE IN 1884-86 FOR THE ANALYSIS OF MOTION.

1. A man jumping.   2. A man walking   3. A duck flying.   4. A man leaping. The objects, clothed in white, passed before a black screen, and the exposures averaged about $\frac{1}{2000}$ of a second.

reason that there was nothing to invent; it was merely evolution and the perfection of details. As we have seen, what the experimenters had to accomplish was the reduction of the length of time occupied in bringing one sensitised surface before the lens after the preceding sensitised surface had been exposed. This was a matter of mechanical detail, for the chemist accelerated the speed of the sensitised surface more and more, and finally evolved the celluloid film. Various means of bringing successive sections of a sensitised surface before the lens were evolved, and produced a plethora of patents; but the perfection of details does not affect the fundamental principle of animated photography. In Great Britain many investigators were energetic in the quest, but the great majority never succeeded beyond the model stage; that is to say, their apparatuses never possessed any practical value, and only served to emphasise once more the truth of the well-worn axiom that there is a great gulf between the creative mind of the inventor and the commercial world with its enormous capacity for development and exploitation.

Among the early British experimenters was W. F. Greene, who, like others, was handicapped by having to make use of glass plates. In 1885 he displayed his first apparatus for taking and producing moving pictures, and two years later exhibited some pictures taken on glass in the window of his premises in Piccadilly. This unusual display created such interest, and the curiosity-provoked public so crowded the pavement that traffic was impeded, and the police called upon Greene to remove his pictures.

In France even greater things were being accomplished. Dr. E. J. Marey took up Muybridge's work at the point where the Anglo-American abandoned it. Marey followed rather the lines laid down by the astronomical investigator Jansen, who in 1874 evolved a photographic revolver to secure records at short intervals of the transit of Venus across the sun's disc. Marey constructed a photographic gun in 1882, with which he studied the flight of birds, and which worked on the principle elaborated by Jansen eight years before. The object of his quest was the analysis of motion. It will be seen, therefore, that in its very earliest stages the value of animated photography was conceded to be rather in the field of science than that of amusement. This celebrated French experimenter realised the inestimable value of "chronophotography" for the study and investigation of moving bodies, the rapidity in the changes of the position or form of which was impossible to follow otherwise. Marey, however, made no effort towards synthesis or reproduction of the motion thus obtained; he did not seek projection upon a huge scale upon the screen, but regarded chronophotography rather as a means of enabling photographic results to be resolved into diagrams for examining and elucidating obscure points incidental to motion.

Special apparatus was evolved and was set up at the Physiological Station in Paris, and some wonderful results were communicated by this industrious scientist to the French Association for the Advancement of Science at Nancy in 1886. Investigations were being carried out upon a large and advanced scale in France while the English were merely dabbling with the idea. Marey secured records of action intermittently from a single point of view by the revolution of a handle, and to a pronounced degree anticipated the present-day cinematograph.

Marey's camera was successful in its details, especially considering the extreme difficulties attending the use of glass plates. He ascertained that in order to secure continuous motion it was imperative to cut off the light from the plate at regular intervals; and he accomplished this interruption by rotating an opaque disc, pierced with small radial slots, which permitted the light to reach the plate only intermittently. The general design of Marey's camera is shown in Fig. 2. The camera, of the ordinary bellows type, was mounted in the upper part of a wooden frame clamped to a special support. Beneath was the handle, which rotated the shutter through gearing. This shutter moved at the back of the bellows, occupying the same position relatively as the focal plane shutter used in very rapid still-life instantaneous photography. By means of this shutter, the passage of a body across the field of the lens was split up into a number of consecutive units. The interval between two successive images, and the time of the exposure, could be altered merely by varying the revolving speed of the shutter. As a rule, the exposures were made at the rate of ten per second, but in some cases the length of the exposure was only 1/2,000th part of a second, with an interval of one-fifth second between two

FIG. 2—MAREY'S CAMERA, SHOWING SHUTTER WITH RADIAL SLOTS.

consecutive pictures. Marey used a black background, and his figures were clothed in white.

There was an important reason for this reversal of Muybridge's procedure. In the latter the shutter of each camera had to be opened as the horse or other object passed the lens. In Marey's system the sensitised surface of the plate is directed against a dead black screen, and the lens may be left open without exercising any ill effect upon the photographic plate, because the latter receives no light. When a man clothed in white passed across this black surface in full sunlight, only his figure was recorded upon the sensitised surface, and thus was thrown in strong relief against the black background.

Special arrangements, however, had to be made to ensure the success of the result. A flat plane black background did not suffice, as a certain amount of light was reflected therefrom into the lens, resulting in the plate becoming fogged. The black screen employed was in reality a black cavity, known as "Chevreul's black." The cavity may be likened to a shed, the front wall of which is removed, and the whole interior blackened. In the screen used by Marey at the Physiological Station in Paris, the back of the shed was hung with black velvet, the floor was covered with pitch, while the sides and ceiling were treated with a dead black medium.

These arrangements enabled Marey to secure more useful results than were possible to Muybridge. From the scientific point of view they proved of incalculable value. His marvellous pictures widened our knowledge of animal motion to a remarkable extent, and provided incontrovertible records of action. Professor Marey ultimately recorded the sum of his experiments in a volume, *Movement*, which is now regarded universally as a classic in physiological science, and even to-day is consulted freely for the purpose of elucidating complex and obscure phases of motion.

Other investigators at about this time were General Sebert, M. L. Soret of Geneva, and Ottomar Anschütz of Berlin. Soret succeeded in analysing some very intricate movements, while Anschütz produced a curious "wheel of life," which was called the "electrical tachyscope." A special camera was evolved whereby photographs were taken in rapid succession. From these negatives glass transparencies similar to lantern slides were produced, and mounted in sequence around the rim of a large wheel, which had to be of sufficient diameter to contain the whole series of pictures. It was mounted upon a massive iron pedestal, and was revolved from the rear by means of a handle.

Behind the wheel, and at the highest point, which corresponded to the level of the eyes of the average person while standing, a small box was placed. The front of this box was open, the size of this aperture corresponding exactly to the dimensions of the transparency. It was fitted with a small electric light—a Geissler tube, in fact, through which a current was passed from a Rhumkorff coil—and this light was switched on and off by each picture as it passed before the front of the lamp box. As each picture came into position before the aperture a contact was established, and an impulse of electricity was discharged through the lamp. It was a mere flash, but it served to illuminate the transparency immediately in front, so that the people gazing at the wheel received a brilliant and well-defined impression of the picture, which was shown in an apparently stationary position, though, in fact, the wheel was revolving continuously. When the wheel was rotated with sufficient speed, the flashes occurred in such rapid sequence that, in accordance with the phenomena of visual persistence, the illusion of animation was secured.

This was an extremely ingenious apparatus, but was too complicated, expensive, and elaborate to command any commercial value. It was regarded generally as a scientific toy. It was on view in London, in the Strand near Chancery Lane, for a little while, but failed to arouse very marked enthusiasm. However, the "inventor's fiddle," as the Anschütz tachyscope was popularly called, was adopted by several other inventors with certain modifications, but its application was naturally extremely limited. Comparatively speaking, only a very few pictures could be carried in the rim of the wheel, and as the travelling speed was somewhat high in order to convey a tangible impression of continuous motion, a subject was exhausted in a few seconds.

Associated with Dr. Marey in his experiments was another indefatigable spirit, M. Georges Demeny. He displayed considerable ingenuity in breaking down the peculiar difficulties associated with this work. Unfortunately the value of M. Demeny's efforts have never been appreciated; but he brought his mind to bear upon the subject at a critical period, and devoted all his energies, time, and thought to the solution of complicated problems that defied contemporary experimenters. He proved an indispensable colleague to Professor Marey, which the author of *Movement* did not fail to acknowledge. So far as France is concerned, he rightly deserves to be regarded as the pioneer in cinematography. He not only photographed motion, but he reproduced it upon the screen, and devised an ingenious camera and projector to achieve his end.

M. Georges Demeny was forestalled in Great Britain by Messrs. Greene and Evans, who produced a chronophotographic apparatus which they patented in June, 1889, wherein the film was drawn intermittently before the lens for exposure. Two months previously, in April, 1889, another inventor, Stern, had filed a patent also, and these constitute the first intimation at the British Patent Office of the pending developments in cinematography. Neither issued beyond the experimental and model stage, for the simple reason that they were not reliable in their operation. There was no satisfactory mechanical means for moving the sensitised surfaces forward an equal distance after each exposure, and this omission of an indispensable feature proved fatal to their success.

CHAPTER III

THE SEARCH FOR THE CELLULOID FILM

IN the struggle towards the perfection of animated photography the use of glass plates was a great hindrance. Investigators were hampered very seriously; they were thwarted at every turn. True, the appearance of the dry plate somewhat facilitated their efforts, but nevertheless the inevitable glass was bulky, heavy, fragile, and awkward to handle. Finally, the number of pictures obtainable upon a single surface was limited.

Realising the restrictions incidental to this sensitised medium, the energies of many investigators were devoted to the discovery of a less bulky, lighter, and more convenient substitute. Gelatine appeared promising at first sight, but failed to give the anticipated results because it lacked stability, and when immersed in the developing solution precipitated a variety of unexpected disasters which placed it out of court completely. The next expedient was the use of transparent paper, similar to what we call grease-proof paper, covered with the gelatine emulsion, invented by Morgan and Kidd, of Richmond. When the exposures were made, the paper was opaque and resembled ordinary bromide paper, the essential transparent effect being secured by an operation after development and fixing. This failed to give a clear, distinct positive, and the grain of the paper so broke up the resultant picture that this alternative was abandoned. A suggestion advocated by the Rev. W. Palmer also was attempted. The picture, after development and fixing, was stripped from its opaque support, and attached to a stiff sheet of insoluble gelatine. This gave a somewhat better effect, but it was a round-about method, and the stripping operation was one of great delicacy, involving extreme care, and uncertain in its results.

These substitutes failing one after another, the hopes of the experimenters became centred upon celluloid, which from every point of view appeared the most suitable medium. The application of celluloid to photographic purposes had been advocated many years previously, but there were many obstacles of a technical character which prevented its use at the time. The investigator, however, continued the struggle towards bringing the celluloid film into the realm of practicability.

He was baffled in one particular direction. Celluloid could not be employed with the collodion process, for the collodion which constituted the sensitive surface in the old wet process with glass plates, and which in itself is a solution of pyroxyline, a kind of guncotton—one of the basic constituents of celluloid—dissolved the celluloid which was coated with it. The perfection of the gelatino-bromide process removed this defect.

Then another difficulty loomed up. Celluloid at that time was not made in sheets sufficiently thin to render it applicable to photography, and the manufacturers of the commodity could not be prevailed upon to prepare the substance in this form. They argued that there was no promise of a sufficiently remunerative market to warrant the design of special machinery for the manufacture of such a product. Consequently, the experimenters were forced to prepare their own film bases.

The experiences of those who grappled with this question and faced trials and tribulations innumerable in this particular phase of operations make interesting reading. One reduced the celluloid to a liquid consistency and poured the plastic mass over large glass plates, rolling it out to form a thin skin. The surface of the glass previously was cleaned carefully to prevent the mixture adhering thereto. The pouring had to be carefully done so as to secure an even thickness, and to avoid the formation of air bubbles.

SEARCH FOR THE CELLULOID FILM

In this way a thin sheet was secured—a decided forward step. In the dark room this "base," as it is called, had next to be covered with a thin layer of sensitised emulsion, and the whole left to dry. Afterwards the sheet was cut into strips of the width required for the camera and apparatus. Unfortunately, in drying, the celluloid was found to play many sorry tricks. It buckled, twisted, and shrank into strange contortions, and the films thus produced were still somewhat too substantial, being, in fact, very similar to those used in the pack-film camera of to-day.

Another worker was more fortunate. By dint of importunity he succeeded in inducing one manufacturing firm to produce sheets of celluloid no thicker than drawing paper for his experiments. But when the sheets were delivered they were far from being satisfactory, being deficient in uniformity of thickness. Before the surface could be coated with sensitised emulsion a tedious task had to be performed. The inequalities had to be scraped and pared off, and finally the whole sheet had to be made thinner by being rubbed down with emery cloth and sandpaper. Hours were occupied in this process, and often a maddening accident happened in the final stages which irreparably injured the sheet and wasted not only time, but costly material. Even when sensitising was carried out successfully, it was found extremely difficult to keep the material flat. It is not surprising that after a prolonged experience of these disadvantages, this particular investigator abandoned his experiments for a time.

In the majority of these efforts the pictures obtained were about four inches in width by three inches deep, while the modern cinematograph film is only $1\frac{3}{8}$ of an inch in width by three-quarters of an inch deep, and almost as thin as a shaving. The celluloid made at that time was not very transparent, and as the pictures were somewhat dense, the results were far from being satisfactory.

It began to look as though celluloid were doomed to follow in the wake of the other expedients that had been tested and found wanting. Such would have been the case but for the indefatigable efforts of one man who persevered with his experiments in the face of heartrending failures and disappointing results. This was Mr. Eastman, of Rochester, in the State of New York, who worked in conjunction with Mr. Walker. These two gentlemen had established a dry photographic plate manufacturing process, which had developed into a conspicuous success, and become known as the Eastman Dry Plate Company, now familiar as the Eastman Kodak Company.

The story of their innumerable experiments and ultimate success constitutes a fascinating chapter in the story of animated photography. As early as 1884 Mr. Eastman realised that a substitute for glass was in demand to facilitate ordinary photography. Accordingly he set out to discover a system of photographing on films. As he admits himself, it was by no means a new idea. From time to time spasmodic attempts in the same direction had been made by enterprising inventors, the earliest known dating back as far as 1854, a year or two before the invention of Parkesine, now known as celluloid, by Mr. A. Parkes, of Birmingham. All of these experimenters, however, had been baffled by the technical difficulties confronting their quest, and Mr. Eastman had no tangible assistance to aid him in his work of research. He was compelled to create the foundation upon which to carry out his developments, and to reap success from mortifying failures.

In 1884, when Messrs. Eastman and Walker commenced operations, the problem to be solved in the production of a suitable film, and the evolution of the means to handle it in the camera, were formidable obstacles. The mechanical part of the work proved the easier, and in 1885 roller photography, which has revolutionised the art of photography, at any rate from the amateur point of view, was invented and put on the market. This principle is now well known. A length of film, wound upon one roller, is passed behind the lens in sections for exposure, and then rolled up on a second roller, until the whole has been exposed. The device simplified the process very appreciably, and it may fairly be accused of being the parent of the modern "Kodak fiend."

SEARCH FOR THE CELLULOID FILM

Though the mechanical part of the problem had thus been solved successfully, the film question was perfected only partially at this time. The film itself was far from satisfactory, but it sufficed to meet the requirements of the day, and to enable roller photography to come into vogue.

To meet the peculiar demands of roller photography, Mr. Eastman had set himself the task of producing a transparent base or support for the sensitised emulsion. That is to say, he sought and produced a stable substitute for the glass plate upon which the sensitised emulsion to record the image could be mounted. It was no easy search, as he speedily found to his cost, for it involved scores of experiments, one after the other, all of which resulted in heartrending failure. He sought to build up such a base as he had in mind by means of successive layers of collodion and rubber, but the result did not possess sufficient substance and strength.

Then he had recourse to paper, which he used merely as a temporary support. The roll of paper was first coated with soluble gelatine, and afterwards with the sensitised emulsion, which was rendered insoluble in itself by the addition of chrome alum. This produced a substantial film which was exposed by means of the roll holder attached to the ordinary camera. The image was developed and fixed. Then, still attached to the paper, the film was placed while wet, immediately after washing, upon a piece of glass coated with a thin solution of rubber.

As soon as the surface had dried, hot water was applied to the paper, which as the gelatine dissolved became detached, leaving the film adhering to the surface of the rubber-coated glass. In place of the paper a moistened thin sheet of gelatine was substituted. When the whole had dried thoroughly it was detached from the glass, and the result was a perfectly transparent negative.

The process was necessarily somewhat intricate and occupied some time, but the results obtained were sufficiently practicable to render it commercially exploitable. Mr. Eastman, however, soon recognised the fact that the trouble of transferring the image from the temporary paper base to the gelatine support decreased the practical value of the process. He decided to dispense with the paper support entirely, and in his search for a suitable substitute his thoughts turned toward celluloid. He communicated with the various manufacturers of that material, but not one was prepared to supply him with the substance in sheets of sufficient size and thinness. Consequently he was compelled to devise ways and means to supply the deficiency; and this was achieved partially by accident.

In the early part of 1889 some experiments were being made to discover a varnish to take the place of the gelatine sheets. One of his chemists drew Mr. Eastman's attention to a thick solution of gun-cotton in wood alcohol. It was tested to prove its suitability to take the place of the gelatine, but was found wanting in practical efficiency. However, Mr. Eastman recognised the solution as one which might prove to be the film base for which he had been searching. He had had such a medium in mind when engaged in his first experiments in 1884, which resulted in the production of the stripping film. He decided to utilise this solution of gun-cotton in wood alcohol and to fashion it into the foundation for the sensitised emulsion, so that stripping and other troublesome operations of a like nature might be avoided. He was moved to this experiment because this solution could be made almost as transparent practically as glass. Accordingly he set to work to devise a machine to prepare thin sheets such as he required from this mixture. Success crowned his efforts, and in 1889 the first long strip of celluloid film suited to cinematograph work appeared in the United States.

Messrs. Eastman and Walker had not been alone in their quest. In England experiments were being carried out in the same field. Curiously enough, the main idea in this instance was to evolve a form of roller photography, the British experimenter being Mr. Blair. He likewise met with success; and the film was manufactured at St. Mary Cray in Kent. Though this film was far from being perfect, showing considerable variation in thickness, it served to assist the experiments in animated photography to a marked degree. The celluloid strip thus produced was about twice the width of that now used in cinematography, and as in the early attempts towards moving pictures, no effort was being made towards projection—the illusion was received by looking into an instrument through which the film travelled, and behind which a light was placed—it was made with a matt surface, so that it closely resembled ground glass, upon which the images stood out distinctly and brilliantly. The width of the film was gradually decreased; but this film-manufacturing industry never got a firm foothold in England. The Blair company was merged in that of the Eastman company in America, and it was not until many years had passed that another bid for participation in the manufacture of celluloid film for moving picture purposes was made by a British firm.

So soon as it leaked out in America in 1889 that Mr. Eastman had succeeded in his difficult search, and that a film with a transparent rigid support which was no more difficult to handle than a glass plate, and yet which was flexible and free from fragility, was commercially available, another experimenter appeared on the scene. He had been labouring in the field for some years, but, realising the futility of glass plates, had postponed his investigations until such time that a substitute could be obtained. His apparatus was ready, but the film was the missing link. Immediately it was available he secured some of the material and completed his apparatus. That man was Thomas Alva Edison, and his "Kinetoscope," was the first commercial appliance to show pictures in natural movement. Animated photography was lifted from the realm of experiment into that of commercial practicability.

CHAPTER IV

THE KINETOSCOPE : THE ANIMATOGRAPH : THE CINEMATOGRAPH

The Kinetoscope

THE World's Fair at Chicago drew huge crowds from all parts of the world in 1893. The innumerable and varied side-shows evinced keen rivalry to obtain popular patronage. But there was one building sheltering a small instrument which made a particularly bold bid for public favour. It was a novelty, something that the man in the street had never seen before.

The announcement ran that "Edison's Kinetoscope, showing photographs in motion, was to be seen for the first time." It worked automatically, and to investigate the new wonder the curiosity-provoked sightseer dropped a nickel—a coin equal in value to $2\frac{1}{2}d$.—into the slot, and applied his eye to the peep-hole, when he was treated to a new sensation for about 30 seconds. He saw photographic pictures flit before his gaze in such rapid succession that they appeared to be imbued with life. Children skipped, the lips of an orator moved in speaking, and so on. It certainly was a marvellous device, and those who availed themselves of the opportunity to see it in operation by means of the nimble nickel, expressed undisguised wonderment; to many it appeared uncanny.

The Kinetoscope, Fig. 3, was housed in a wooden cabinet with a hinged door at one side. Within was a wooden frame A, which carried a series of small reels B and B^1 arranged in two horizontal rows at either edge of the frame. At the top of the frame there were two larger

CH. IV   THE KINETOSCOPE   31

wheels *C*, between which was a magnifying lens *D*. Behind the latter there was a small electric lamp and reflector *F*. In front of the magnifying lens there was a disc having a narrow radial slot near its edge, which constituted the shutter. This was rotated continuously, and completed one revolution during the passage of each image across the eye-piece or magnifying lens.

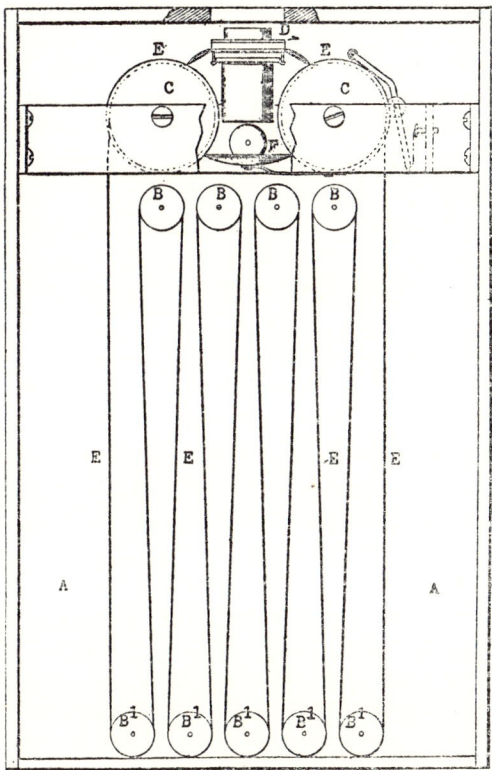

Fig. 3.—Edison's First Kinetoscope.

The ribbon of pictures, printed as transparencies upon a strip of celluloid film, somewhat dense so as to bring out the detail, formed an endless band *E*, 40 feet in length. This was threaded over the various reels in the manner shown in the illustration, and finally passed over the first large wheel *C*, thence to the second large wheel *C*, and back once more on to the reels B B^1. Though 40 feet constituted the average length of film employed, longer ones could be used within certain limits, by increasing the number of reels on the frame. As the film passed from one of the large wheels C to the other, it had to traverse the field of the magnifying lens, and the light, striking through the transparency, gave the person looking through the eye-piece a slightly magnified view of the picture.

The cabinet stood on end, so that one had to bend over the instrument to peer through the small eye-piece. When the coin dropped into the slot, an electric motor was started, setting the film and shutter in motion. The film travelled from left to right, while the shutter rotated in the opposite direction, cutting up the band of pictures into separate images, so that only one was seen at a time. The band travelled continuously, and each image was momentarily rendered visible by the light flashing through the radial slot in the shutter, the effect being the same as if the electric incandescent lamp were extinguished and relighted intermittently, at very brief intervals.

The shutter had to be revolved at sufficient speed to bring the radial slot near its edge centrally over an image; in other words, the shutter had to complete its revolution with sufficient speed to bring the opening over the picture at the moment the latter on the travelling celluloid film came into the centre of the field of the lens. When this operation was carried out with sufficient velocity, the images were seen in such rapid succession as to convey the idea of continuous motion, by virtue of the principle of visual persistence.

One point must be borne in mind. The band of pictures travelled *continuously*. It did not, as in the machine of to-day, make a momentary pause as it came between the light and the lens. The movement to-day is intermittent, not continuous, though, curiously enough, all the early experimenters strove first towards the perfection of the latter arrangement. Continuous motion of the film has proved to be impossible, because the shutter must

EDISON'S FIRST KINETOSCOPE.

This machine, completed about 1890, was very crude. It was known as the "peep-hole," because one peered into the cabinet through the eye-piece at side.

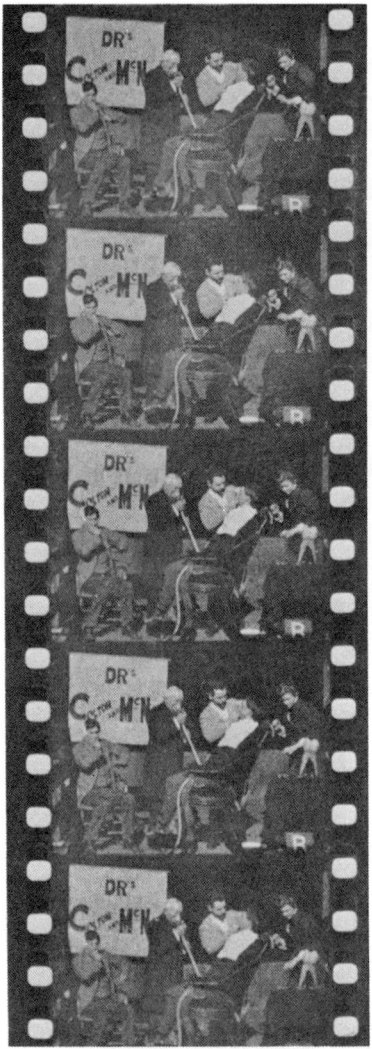

Edison Film made about 1891 for the kinetoscope.

Edison Film made in 1911 for the cinematograph.

TWENTY YEARS' HISTORY OF MOVING PICTURES IN FILMS.

The only difference between the two films is that the kinetoscope film had to be made very dense. The size of the picture, 1-inch wide by ¾-inch deep, and perforation gauge, are identical.

revolve at such a speed that the illumination is not sufficient to produce a bright impression upon the screen.

In order to prevent the film slipping in any way while travelling over the smooth reels by friction, a toothed sprocket was introduced to ensure the film being fed regularly and steadily before the lens; and to secure a purchase upon the film the latter was perforated uniformly along the margin to engage with the sprocket teeth. Edison found, as a result of his experiments, that four perforations per picture, on either side of the film, gave the best results, though in his earliest investigations he confined himself to perforating only one edge in this manner.

Although many years have passed since the Kinetoscope first startled the public, the film has undergone but little change. The width remains the same; the dimensions of the picture are identical; and the perforation gauge has never been revised in regard to the number of holes per picture. The only salient difference between two Edison films, taken at intervals of twenty years, relates to the density of the picture, which nowadays, being projected upon a screen instead of being followed through a magnifying glass at short range, is thinner and lighter.

Brilliant as the Kinetoscope was, it made no great impression upon the public. It became known as the "peep-hole machine," and was regarded, like the telephone in its early days, as a scientific toy. Edison appears to have failed to grasp its possibilities and the important part it was destined to play in our complex life, for he did not patent it in Great Britain.

The Animatograph

Among those who saw the instrument at the World's Fair were two Greek visitors from London. One was a greengrocer, the other a toy-maker. With shrewd business instinct they perceived here an opportunity to make a fortune in England. The Kinetoscope was known only by name in London, and the search for novelty in regard to new forms of amusement inevitably brings a rich reward to the ingenious exploiter. The two men acquired a machine and brought it home with them, their intention being to make duplicates and instal them in public places, to work upon the penny-in-the-slot principle.

The two Greeks evidently were not animated by very lofty ideas of business integrity, for they did not trouble to ascertain if the Kinetoscope were patented in Great Britain.

Upon arrival in London they sought for a man who could duplicate the machine they had brought with them; and they approached Mr. Robert W. Paul, an electrical engineer and scientific instrument maker, who at that time had his workshops in Hatton Garden. They brought the Kinetoscope to him. He had never seen it before, and was deeply interested in its operation. When, however, they suggested that he should produce copies of it to their order, he declined, for he felt sure that Edison never would have omitted to secure its protection in Great Britain. He pointed out to the Greeks that reproduction would probably be illegal, and that both he and they would expose themselves to litigation and heavy damages for infringing a patent.

His clients expressed dissatisfaction at this decision and departed with the instrument. After they had gone, Paul was prompted to make a search at the Patent Office, and to his intense surprise he found that Edison had not protected his invention by taking out British patents. He was thus at liberty to build as many machines as he desired, and forthwith he set to work, not only for his Greek visitors, but also for his own market.

The experience with the Kinetoscope in the United States was duplicated in Great Britain, as, indeed, it was in every other country where it was placed on exhibition. Several machines were set up at apparently suitable points, but the public failed to respond. Two factors contributed to this result. In the first place, the machines were weighty, and as the electricity for driving the motor and lighting the incandescent electric lamp was drawn from accumulators, the whole apparatus was somewhat bulky and awkward to move from place to place. Besides, it was difficult to secure the necessary films; sufficient variety could not be supplied for the machines. Only one company was engaged at the time in their production—the American Kinetoscope Company—and the only studio in operation was at Orange in New Jersey, the output of which was relatively small. Under these circumstances public curiosity could not be sustained.

The difficulty with the film supply presently became still more acute. The American company learned that the Kinetoscope was being manufactured in England, and that American films were being used with English machines. As manufacture could not be prevented, owing to Great Britain being an open market, and as, consequently, Paul was perfectly justified in his action, the American company decided on a novel method of frustrating Mr. Paul's efforts. Two agents, Maguire and Baucus, came to London and endeavoured to corner the English market. They secured the output of Kinetoscope films from America, and declined to sell them to anyone in Great Britain who did not possess an American-built machine. The result was that all the purchasers of the Paul Kinetoscopes found themselves unable to secure further films; even Paul himself could not obtain supplies.

The Americans regarded the outlook with complete self-satisfaction. They believed that the English market was within their grasp. But they reckoned without their host. Paul was determined not to be vanquished so easily, especially as he had sold Kinetoscopes to customers in all parts of the world, and had a steady stream of buyers flocking to his workshops from points as remote as Tokio, South America, and New Zealand. Many of these early purchasers of the British-built Kinetoscopes have since become famous in the world of cinematography either as producers or manufacturers, notably Monsieur Charles Pathé, the founder of the celebrated French cinematograph film manufacturing establishment, who was one of Paul's first customers.

Now although Paul had manufactured several Kinetoscopes, he realised the disadvantages of the instrument. Only one person at a time could see the picture in animation. What was required in order to popularise moving pictures was to devise a way to enable several hundreds, or even thousands, of people to witness the same subject simultaneously.

Paul's first idea was to convert the ordinary Kinetoscope into a projecting apparatus. While he was quietly considering the feasibility of this scheme he was introduced to another inventor, Mr. Birt Acres, at that time in the employment of a firm engaged in the manufacture of dry plates and bromide papers. Acres had conceived a mechanical means of printing on bromide paper from glass negatives a number of copies of a subject at a very rapid rate, and had committed to paper his crude suggestion. He submitted his drawing to Paul. The negative was to be set in a frame, beneath which the bromide paper travelled over rollers in a continuous length. The coil of paper was to move a certain distance—the length of the negative, in fact—and then to pause; when a flat pad, carried at the end of a lever beneath the paper, was to rise up and press the latter flatly and tightly against the negative. When the exposure had been made the clamping device, as it was called, fell back, and permitted the paper to travel another short distance to bring a fresh unexposed surface beneath the negative, when the same cycle of operations was repeated.

When Acres brought his sketch to Paul, the latter was wrestling with the problem of photographing objects in motion. It was imperative to perfect a camera in order to defeat the machinations of the Americans bent upon the capture of the English film market. In this task, however, the most satisfactory means of securing intermittent motion was the stumbling block. He thought for a time that Acres's ingenious method of printing bromide prints might offer a clue. Being a mechanical engineer, Paul recognised the inefficiency of Acres's idea as far as its application to cinematography was concerned, because

THE FIRST KINETOSCOPE FILM MADE IN ENGLAND.

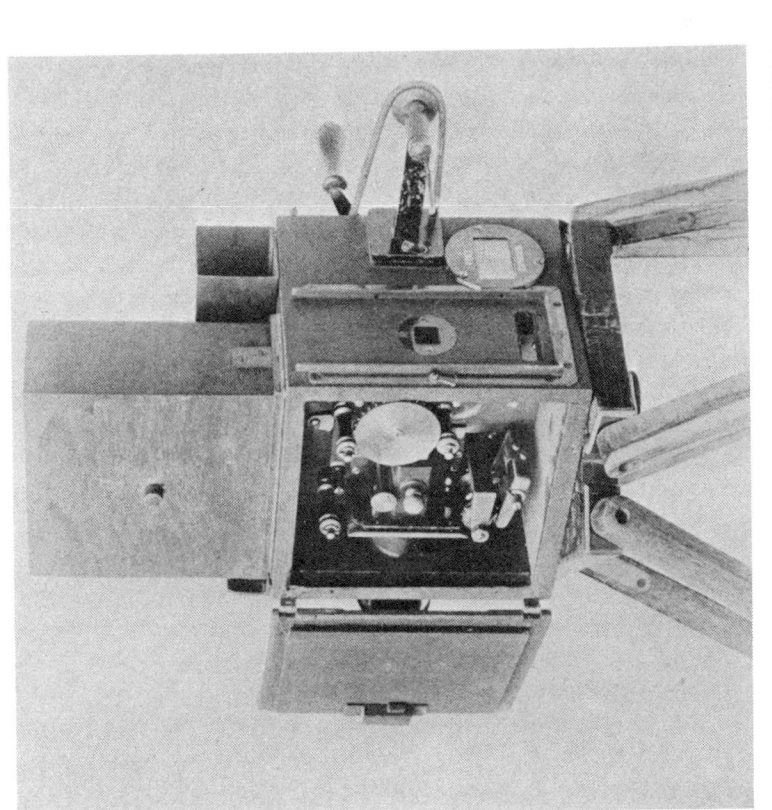

PAUL'S CAMERA SHOWING MECHANISM FOR MOVING THE FILM INTERMITTENTLY PAST THE LENS. THE FILM WAS CARRIED IN DETACHABLE DARK BOXES.

The manufacture of films was commenced in England by Robert Paul to thwart the American attempt to corner the British market.

THE "BLACK MARIA," THE FIRST EDISON STUDIO FOR MAKING KINETOSCOPE FILMS.

It was a rambling building of cheap construction mounted centrally upon a pivot. It revolved upon a circular track to face the sun.
See page 105.

the clamping device was not actuated by a positive drive. But the rough drawing which Acres had made of his bromide printing process set Paul thinking, and gave birth in the end to an entirely different project.

His efforts were accelerated by the tactics of Maguire and Baucus, and it was not long before he produced a camera working with an intermittent motion. With this camera some excellent films were obtained, and in the first instance these were employed with the Kinetoscope. The purchasers of the Paul machines consequently experienced no difficulty whatever in getting all the films they wanted, and the American product was ignored. It was not comparable with the English films in excellence or variety; and Maguire and Baucus retired from the scene completely discomfited. The attempt to obtain possession of the English market was a dismal failure owing to the unexpected enterprise of Robert Paul.

Paul had already attempted to apply the principle governing the operation of the Kinetoscope to the projection of a picture upon the screen. He had contrived a special lantern through which the film was run continuously, the revolution of the shutter serving to cut out each picture on the film, and throw it individually upon the sheet, thereby bringing it into a stationary position for a minute fraction of a second. But the projecting efforts were somewhat disheartening. The illusory effect was produced; but the picture was so faint as to render the result of no commercial value. The conditions attending the watching of the pictures at a range of about six or eight inches, as in the Kinetoscope, and at one of ten times as many feet, when thrown upon a whitened wall or screen, were vastly different. The shutter had to revolve at such a rapid rate to prevent blurring that a sufficient volume of light could not be passed through each picture in the short interval the shutter was open—less than 1/1,000th of a second—so the resultant image was faint and ill-defined.

It was evident that the film would have to be brought momentarily, by some means or other, into a fixed position behind the lens, so as to enable sufficient light to pass through to the screen, to yield a picture comparing with that of a slide projected from a magic lantern; and, further, that the picture would have to be moved during its eclipse by the shutter, in order to allow the next image to be brought into place. In other words, instead of the film moving forwards continuously, it would have to advance with a jerky or intermittent motion while the shutter was passing across the lens, and cutting off the light from the screen.

Paul concentrated his energies upon this problem. It was by no means a simple undertaking, for there were no previous efforts in the same direction to assist him. The great point was how to bring successive pictures into position before the lens. He thought out a clamping device, which is known as the "gate," and which he attached behind the lens. This gate was formed of two parts, one fixed and the other having a swinging or opening movement. The fixed part was pierced with an aperture which could be reduced by a sliding diaphragm. The aperture of the second part was of the same shape and dimensions as the picture on the film. The film was wound on a spool, and from this it passed through the gate and thence over a sprocket, the teeth of which engaged with the perforations in the edge of the celluloid band.

The sprocket had to move intermittently, in such a way that a length of film corresponding to the depth of a picture was drawn through the gate at each movement, while the shutter momentarily cut off the light, otherwise there would have been a confusion of two consecutive pictures projected at the same time. How this movement was evolved is described in Chapter VII. It seems a simple task, but it proved exasperatingly difficult to secure accuracy, smoothness of motion, and the steadiness of the picture when thrown on the screen.

About three o'clock one morning, in the early months of 1895, the quietness of Hatton Garden was disturbed by loud and prolonged shouts. The police rushed hurriedly to the building whence the cries proceeded, and found

Paul and his colleagues in their workshop, giving vent to whole-hearted exuberance of triumph. They had just succeeded in throwing the first perfect animated pictures upon a screen. To compensate the police for their fruitless investigation, the film, which was 40 feet in length and produced a picture 7 feet square, was run through the special lantern for their edification. They regarded the strange spectacle as ample compensation, and had the satisfaction of being the first members of the public to see moving pictures thrown upon the screen.

In February, 1896, the first public demonstration with this projection apparatus, described as the "Theatrograph," was given at the Finsbury Technical College, and it caused a thrill of excitement and interest. A few days later, on February 28th, 1896, the apparatus was shown in the library of the Royal Institution. Again it stirred enthusiasm, and Mr. Robert Paul was congratulated warmly upon the success of his work by many of the leading British scientists of the day. This was the first demonstration of animated photography before a scientific institution in Great Britain. The films displayed were those which had been taken by the patient experimenter and his collaborators for the Kinetoscope, and included, among other things, a "Shoeblack at work in a London street," and of "A Rough Sea at Dover."

The fact that the display was given before one of the foremost scientific bodies in the world stamped it as being a development of signal importance. The interest it created was universal. Among those who saw the demonstration was Lady Harris, the wife of the famous impresario, Sir Augustus Harris, who evinced the keenest enthusiasm in the apparatus, and who plied the experimenter with searching questions as to how the apparent animation was obtained.

Next morning Paul received an urgent invitation from Sir Augustus Harris to join him at breakfast. The latter had heard from Lady Harris all about the remarkable exhibition at the Royal Institution, and, with a showman's keen instinct, desired to glean further details without delay.

He said that he had heard in Paris of a French invention similar to Paul's. This took the English experimenter by surprise, for he had been labouring in absolute ignorance that other men were at work in the same field. However, the impresario was on business bent. He saw the possibilities of the Theatrograph as a form of amusement, and Paul was asked if he were willing to permit its being exploited at Olympia, which Harris had acquired.

"Well, I don't know," rejoined the experimenter. "I have no idea of its value from the public point of view." He thought that the indifference of the British public to the Kinetoscope did not augur well for the new development.

"Now look here," continued Sir Augustus Harris. "It won't draw the public for more than a month. They soon get tired of these novelties. Are you prepared to come in on sharing terms, say, 50 per cent. of the receipts? Do you agree?"

Paul was somewhat doubtful of the results, but he acquiesced, and the agreement was drawn up there and then. The sequel showed how ill-founded his apprehensions had been. The Theatrograph caught the popular fancy, and proved the most powerful amusement-magnet at Olympia. It was the first picture palace in the world, that is to say, the first establishment devoted exclusively to the projection of moving pictures as a complete entertainment. From it the whole modern development of cinematography may be said to have sprung.

Indeed, it is difficult to realise the effect produced upon the world at large, through the skill and industry of Robert W. Paul. So far as Great Britain is concerned, he certainly fathered the enterprise of animated photography, as is evidenced by the fact that in British cinematographic circles he is known popularly as "Daddy Paul." The lapse of time has not effected any essential change in the construction of the apparatus. The camera and projector as used to-day are fundamentally the same as those Paul first employed. Modifications have been made in details of the mechanism, but they are of slight importance. When the outcry against the danger of the cinematograph was raised in the early days of the industry, as a result of the fire at the Charity Bazaar in Paris, it was found that Paul had realised the danger and had endeavoured to guard against it, though his idea, being somewhat premature, was disregarded at the time.

The success of the "Theatrograph" at Olympia caused a wholesale demand for the new marvel. People wanted to attach the device to existing magic lanterns, so that animated pictures could be produced upon the screen whenever desired. Paul still cherished such little faith in his invention that he sold the projector attachment for the small sum of £5 ($25), and it could be fixed to any lantern. He was inundated with orders from all parts of the world. Many enthusiasts acquired a complete projecting outfit, the price of which at that time was about £80 ($400). The capacity of the workshop in Hatton Garden proved quite inadequate to the demand. The men worked night and day turning out the projecting apparatus, and the sale aggregated several hundreds sterling per week during the years 1896 and 1897. Provincial showmen lost no time in acquiring the novelty, or arranged with the inventor to provide such an item in their programmes. Within a short time twenty machines were being operated under Paul's personal direction in the provinces.

London was by no means backward in following up the development. The first to introduce moving pictures to a metropolitan vaudeville audience was Mr. Moul, the energetic manager of the Alhambra Theatre. Like Sir Augustus Harris, however, he regarded it merely as a nine-days' wonder, and did not think that the sensation it had created could be sustained for more than a week or so, which shows how even the most astute showman may sometimes err in gauging the public taste, and also parenthetically the professional estimation of the idea. An arrangement was made whereby Paul undertook to give a display with the "Animatograph"—this name had been substituted for the original "Theatrograph"—at the Alhambra Theatre, for a fortnight from March 25th, 1896. According to the terms of the contract, if the display proved popular, it was to be prolonged upon the same terms until moving pictures fell from public favour. That engagement of fourteen days grew into one of four years! For over 1,000 nights Paul personally superintended his moving pictures at the Alhambra; and then retired only because of pressure of work in other directions. Of course, other music halls in the metropolis acquired the apparatus. Operators were scarce, and they could not be trained rapidly enough to meet the demand. As a rule, men manipulating the limelight in the theatres were found to be the most suitable for the purpose, and they readily accepted an opportunity to earn £4 ($20) per week for a few minutes' work every day. Times have changed since then, and to-day operators can be secured for about half that sum as weekly wage.

At one time in the early days Paul had no less than eight theatres in London demanding his personal attendance, involving a nightly journey of twenty miles. It is significant of the tremendous enthusiasm that was aroused by the moving pictures that the managers of the various halls had to arrange their programmes to suit the convenience of the operator, so that there might be no interference with his carefully prepared time-table of his evening's movements from one place to another.

The exigencies of the manufacture of apparatus and films became at last of such a character that Paul found the strain of operating to be intolerable, so he retired from active work in the projecting world. His film manufacturing business attained considerable proportions, and this was continued until the latter part of 1908, when he abandoned all active participation in the industry he had initiated, to devote himself to his work on precision instruments for electrical measurements. His association with cinematography to-day is very slight, being confined mostly to collaboration with eminent physicists and scientists in illustrating scientific subjects by the aid of motion photography.

The Cinematograph.

While Robert W. Paul was busy in his laboratory, problems identical with his own were engaging the attention of French experimenters, and notably of Messrs. Lumière and Sons, of Paris and Lyons, a firm famous in the manufacture of photographic apparatus, dry plates, and paper, whose efforts to solve the problem of natural colour photography are well known to the world. Their attention, like Paul's, was first directed to this new field by the Kinetoscope, which made its appearance in France about 1893. Messrs. Lumière instantly realised its drawbacks and limitations, the greatest of which, from their point of view, was the fact that the long ribbon of instantaneous pictures was visible to one person only. Then again they considered the number of pictures shown per second—thirty—to be too high.

They sought to devise an apparatus operating with an intermittent action, whereby a short length of film corresponding to the depth of a picture was jerked into position behind the lens while the light was eclipsed by the shutter, and afterwards to project the same pictures by a similar mechanism.

With the Kinetoscope as a basis they set to work, and, by means of a reciprocating motion given to a hook frame under the movement of a triangular piece of mechanism, they succeeded in stopping and starting the film alternately with such a degree of nicety that the successive sections of film were brought into position before the lens without damaging the guiding perforating holes or films. This constituted the salient feature of the Lumière device and the fundamental principle of the patent.

The Lumière camera was distinctly ingenious, simple and positive in its action, as well as being light and compact. The mechanism whereby the film was jerked down sufficiently after each exposure to bring another section of sensitised surface before the lens, may be likened to two projecting fingers which engaged with a hole on either side of the film. These two pins, or hooks, by the revolving action of a triangular eccentric, were brought forward towards the film and engaged with the perforations. When the shutter swung across the lens, thus cutting off the light, this pair of fingers dropped down, smartly jerking the film with them. The latter was then gripped and held firmly in position during the next exposure, when the two fingers withdrew from the perforations, rose sharply upwards, and clutched the film once more by the next pair of perforations.

While the Lumière experimenters adopted the width of film used in the Kinetoscope and secured pictures of the same dimensions, yet they made an important deviation from Edison's idea. Instead of making four perforations per picture on either side of the film at regular intervals, they made just one round hole on each side of the image. These perforations were placed 20 millimetres—approximately 4/5 inch—apart. The reason for this deviation from the Edison method was that they had refrained from the use of toothed sprockets such as Edison and Paul had adopted, and which had to mesh with the film so as to feed it regularly and steadily forward before the lens in both the camera and the projector. From the mechanical point of view theirs was a preferable method, inasmuch as the comparative closeness of the perforations in the Edison gauge somewhat weakens the strength of the film, and can easily result in tearing.

There is every reason to believe that Messrs. Lumière were in ignorance of the efforts of Paul, in just the same way as the British investigator was oblivious of the work of the Frenchmen. In France the Kinetoscope failed, as it did in England and the United States. From the French point of view a unique opportunity existed to establish a new industry; accordingly they manufactured several films upon their principle.

The original bands of pictures were 17 metres—nearly 56 feet—in length. Unfortunately for the Lumière firm, the Kinetoscope had, thanks to Paul, been purchased more generally than was at first thought possible; while Paul had marketed in England a considerable number of films carrying the Edison standard perforation. The result was that they could not dispose of their films to people who were already possessed of the moving picture machine, and who demanded films of the Edison gauge. Messrs. Lumière ultimately abandoned the single perforation on either side of the picture in favour of that which had come into vogue through the Kinetoscope and the work of Paul.

The early Lumière projector was very interesting. Realising the high inflammability of the celluloid film, and the intense heat produced by the focussing of the electric arc light through the condenser upon the film, the experimenters sought to remove the danger of fire by

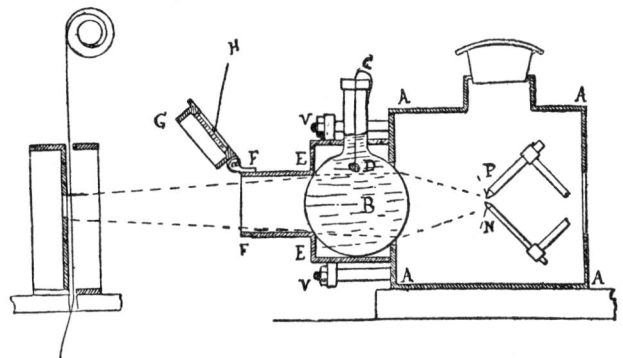

FIG. 4.—THE EARLY LUMIÈRE PROJECTING SYSTEM SHOWING WATER CONDENSER B.

counteracting the heat production of the rays of light. A spherical bottle, filled with water, was placed between the electric arc and the lens to act as condenser, Fig. 4. The bottle B was encased in a metal cylinder E, fixed to the front of the lantern A by four rods, each terminating in a screw V. The metal cylinder E was continued forwards in the form of a tube F, the end of which was fitted with a hinged shutter G carrying a small piece of ground glass H. When the film was set in motion this hinged shutter was lifted and laid back upon the top of the tube to which it was attached.

The spherical bottle, which was filled with distilled

water to which a few drops of acetic acid were added, acted in exactly the same way as the glass condenser of to-day. But it possessed this advantage. The luminous rays were concentrated, and there was no loss of luminous light; only the heat rays were absorbed almost entirely by the water. Another beneficial result was that the light thrown through the picture, and thence on to the screen, was whiter, because the condenser glass is greenish, and imparts that tint to the light passing through it.

In the course of about 30 or 40 minutes the water under the action of the heat rays commenced to boil, but no inconvenience resulted. A piece of coke D, attached to a short length of wire C, was suspended in the decanter and placed just below the surface of the water, thus causing it to boil with complete evenness; there was no spurting of the contents, and no bubbling to interfere with the light. If the sphere of water were removed or broken during the operation of the lantern, as the condensation of the light rays immediately ceased there was no danger of the film being set alight. It may be pointed out, in passing, that Edison introduced a bulb of alum water between the electric lamp and the film as a heat absorbent in his Kinetoscope.

Although highly efficient, this expedient possessed certain drawbacks, and consequently in the course of time it was superseded by the glass condenser. Mechanical ingenuity succeeded in devising a means of minimising the danger of combustion or provided some method of smothering it in its incipient stage.

Although the Lumière invention proved a great success in France, and was the first commercial apparatus produced in that country, it did not get a foothold in Great Britain, owing to the contemporaneous work of Paul. The Lumière apparatus was a well-built mechanism, typical of French workmanship, but if anything rather too light for general wear and tear. It was introduced to the English public by Professor Treuwé, the famous French conjurer, at the Regent Street Polytechnic in 1896, but failed to provoke a sensation, because Paul's "Theatrograph" had already been seen at Olympia and held first place in public esteem. On the other hand, it created widespread interest in the United States, where, at the time of its arrival, projection upon the screen was unknown. Paul's machine had not penetrated to North America, because the British market demanded his whole attention. It is a curious irony of fate that, although animated photography was first made possible in America by the ingenuity of an American inventor, and the only films then available were the product of the Edison "Black Maria" at Orange, yet it was a French apparatus which laid the foundations of the cinematograph industry in the United States. The product of Messrs. Lumière was introduced mainly through the enterprise of one man, Mr. Richard G. Hollaman, the energetic president of the Eden Musée Company.

Mr. Hollaman saw the Kinetoscope at the Chicago World's Fair in the summer of 1893, but as it was crude and did not arouse great enthusiasm, he took no especial interest in it. In the following year, however, he acquired an improved Kinetoscope from Berlin, which had been made by the celebrated electrical engineering firm, Siemens and Halske. This machine was circular in shape, and showed the pictures in movement in much the same way as Edison's contrivance. Two of the machines were installed in the Eden Musée and remained there for six months. At the end of that time they were abandoned for the reason that no new films could be obtained.

In the spring of 1896 an exhibition was given in a shop in Park Row, New York City. In this instance the pictures were thrown upon the screen. The machine had been devised and built by an experimenter named Latham, but it was exceedingly faulty. The pictures shown depicted two prize fighters, but the images vibrated so violently on the screen, and were so scratched and imperfect, that the eyes of spectators were subjected to a fearful strain, and the apparatus was commercially valueless. Mr. Hollaman sought out the inventor with a view to the perfection of the device for his theatre, but learned that lack of capital prevented Latham from perfecting his apparatus.

A little later the president of the Eden Musée received a communication from a firm named Raff and Gammon. They offered him the State rights for a moving picture machine which had been designed by Edison, and of which they were empowered to dispose on his behalf. They invited Mr. Hollaman to a demonstration at Koster and Bial's theatre, where they threw a picture upon the screen which measured about 10 feet in width by 6 feet in depth. Mr. Hollaman has told me that he recalled very vividly two of the films he saw there. One depicted "Mammy washing her child," while the other was "The Gardener playing the Hose." Both these films were made by Lumière and Sons at Lyons.

In the autumn of 1896 the Lumière apparatus appeared in the United States. It was introduced by Mr. Hurd, acting as agent for the French manufacturers, and this was the first practical cinematograph apparatus to be seen in North America. A demonstration was given, and Mr. Hollaman, realising the tremendous strides it represented in the projection of moving pictures, made a contract for its installation at the Eden Musée. The picture thrown on the screen by this projector measured 22 by 16 feet. From the day the "Cinematographe" was first shown to the public in the Eden Musée in 1896, it has constituted a permanent feature of the place. In fact, Mr. Hollaman has been the pioneer of all developments in the field of cinematography in North America. The French machines had been in use for some time, when Lumière's agent, who had let them out on lease, suddenly called in all the projectors and retired from active operations in the United States. Another machine had to be secured for the Eden Musée, and for three months a Joli instrument was used, followed by an American apparatus operated by its maker, Eberhard Schneider.

Another change was made in September, 1897, when Mr. Charles Urban, now identified with Kinemacolor, but at that time acting as salesman for Maguire and

Baucus, who had endeavoured in vain to oust Paul in London and who had retired from the scene after meeting with failure, approached the Eden Musée with a new projector, which was installed. Some time later Urban introduced a new machine which he had made himself, and as it possessed several improvements it was adopted. This was the first "Bioscope," as it was called, that was ever shown to the public.

Shortly afterwards Maguire and Baucus, in company with Urban, left the United States for London, to establish an English cinematograph firm under the name of the Warwick Trading Company. In 1900 Mr. Hollaman secured the services of Frank Cannock, an expert operator and mechanician, for his cinematograph department, which had now become of paramount importance; and since that date the latter has manufactured all the machines required by the Eden Musée.

I have given a brief outline of the most interesting chapter in the story of cinematography, the epoch in which experimenters in different countries were struggling to perfect the same idea, independently of one another, and by different methods. Several other investigators were engaged in the quest, but their work was not of such importance as that of Edison, Paul, or Lumière. The first evolved the crude idea, and the latter two, in their respective countries, produced successful apparatuses entirely different from one another. The work of Robert Paul should command the greatest appreciation; for the Bioscope, which amuses the multitude from morning to night every day between the two Poles, is fundamentally the same as that which he introduced to the theatrical world for the first time on March 25th, 1896.

CHAPTER V

HOW THE CELLULOID FILM IS MADE

I HAVE already shown how the perseverance and ingenuity of Eastman and Walker aided in solving the problem of animated photography. Their film was used for the first time experimentally in the United States as far back as 1889, although it did not enter the general market until about two years later. From that time there was an increasing demand from the host of experimenters for large quantities of the narrow, thin sensitised strip of celluloid. As the demand increased the chemists associated with the subject redoubled their efforts; their product was still far from perfection, and even to-day they will admit that many abstruse problems remain to be unravelled.

Although the present-day consumption of celluloid film for cinematograph purposes is enormous, aggregating several million feet per week, the manufacturing process is of such a peculiar character that the number of firms identified with its production can be counted upon the fingers of one hand. In the United States it is controlled by the Eastman Kodak Company, who have extensive factories at Rochester in the State of New York, and a large establishment at Harrow in England. In France Messrs. Lumière and Sons, and in Germany the Gaevert firm, have large factories. British effort is represented by the Austin-Edwards Company, which produces an excellent film, but the home industry is in its infancy. The three first-named firms supply almost the entire demand. The Eastman firm has the largest output, about 3,500,000

CH. V HOW THE CELLULOID FILM IS MADE 51

feet per week, which is due to the fact that in the United States there are over 14,000 picture palaces open every day from morning until midnight, and many large firms engaged in the preparation of the film subjects. Most of the Eastman supply is used in the United States and Great Britain. Aside from it and the French and German products, some of the large European film producers prepare their own stock, as the celluloid base is called. If all these totals were added together, the sum of them would show something like 6,000,000 feet of film, in both negatives and positives, consumed every week.

Each country has millions of pounds invested in the enterprise. It is difficult to gauge the proportions of the entire industry. If all its varied branches are taken into consideration, it probably ranks as one of the largest in the world. And the whole of this development has taken place within twenty years.

In order to gain an idea of one branch of the industry, the manufacture of the film, one must pay a visit to the extensive works of the Eastman Company, the plant of which is able to turn out no less than 7,200,000 lineal feet of film for moving pictures every week—truly a tremendous output. This capacity has not been taxed to the utmost yet, but when the requisite machinery was laid down, the company decided to anticipate the future. Should the present pace of development be maintained, there is no doubt that, before the end of another twenty years, this firm will find its present installation barely sufficient to meet the demand. Continued chemical research and improvement of processes is tending to reduce the cost of the material, and while at the same time the moving picture business itself is expanding on all sides, fresh markets are constantly being opened up for the products of the manufacturers.

At the Eastman works is to be seen a striking illustration of the growth in the manufacture of celluloid film. In the room where the ingredients are mixed together there is a small barrel, which will hold 500 pounds of the film mixture. This little barrel, together with another of the same capacity, sufficed to meet all requirements in the year 1891. In the same building is a battery of fifty huge barrels, each with eight times the capacity of the small one, and these are run night and day to meet the present demand for the material. The little barrel is no longer used; but it is preserved as an honoured relic of the past and an eloquent witness of the tremendous growth of the film-manufacturing industry for cinematography.

The ingredients for the film are gun-cutton, known technically as pyroxylin, and wood alcohol. The pyroxylin is prepared by treating cellulose devised from such vegetable materials as flax or cotton waste, with a mixture of sulphuric and nitric acids. The ingredients are associated in large cylindrical tanks ranged in long rows upon the upper floor, and discharged through trap doors into the barrels beneath. The gun-cotton is then dissolved in the alcohol by mechanically rotating the huge barrels. It is possible to treat in this way some 200,000 pounds of material at one time. The mixing process reduces the gun-cotton and wood alcohol to a viscous liquid of the consistency of extracted honey, which substance forms the base of the film, or support for the sensitive emulsion, and is known technically as cellulose-nitrate.

When the gun-cotton has been dissolved to the requisite degree, the syrup-like mixture is drawn from the barrels and stored in cylindrical tanks.

The next step is the conversion of the mixture into sheets of the requisite thinness. It is not rolled out, but poured upon suitably polished supports, and spreads out, like varnish, in a thin film. The Eastman patent specifies three distinct kinds of receptacle for the pouring process: a long sheet of polished glass, an endless polished metallic belt, and a revolving drum having a highly polished surface. Any of the three will produce the result; and in each case the deposit has to be permitted to dry to a certain degree.

When the drying is achieved, the thin coating of transparent flexible material, resembling a skin, is stripped from its support and coated with the sensitive emulsion. The latter is of two degrees of sensitiveness, according to

THE DISSOLVING ROOM.

The ingredients for the celluloid film are dissolved in large tanks. The liquids are drawn off and led through the trap doors into in-mixing barrels.

[*By permission of the Eastman Kodak Company.*]

[*By permission of the Eastman Kodak Company.*
THE MIXING BARREL.

This picture conveys a striking impression of the growth of the film manufacturing industry. Two small barrels, each holding 500 pounds, made all the film base or "dope," as it is called, in 1891. The larger barrel behind holds 4,000 pounds.

whether the film is to be used as a negative or a positive. The former is of the very highest sensitiveness to light that it is possible to obtain, since under normal circumstances it is only exposed for the fraction of a second; while the film required for the positive, which is used for projection, is rendered less sensitive, as it can be given a longer exposure in the printing operation.

The base, with its sensitised coating, is now permitted to become dry and hard. At the conclusion of this operation the length of thin celluloid sheeting, technically called a web, which is about $3\frac{1}{2}$ feet wide, is slit into strips of the standard width now used in all cinematograph cameras and projectors—$1\frac{3}{8}$ inches wide.

Extreme care has to be taken to secure a uniform thickness. The plant at the Rochester works has reached such a degree of accuracy that the thickness of the film which is taken from the polished rolls, although the web measures 2,000 feet in length, does not vary above the standard by more than 1/4,000th part of an inch.

As I have already said, however, after all this care, the product is far from being perfect, and it sometimes displays strange caprices. They are most pronounced in the tropics. Owing to the volatile character of the ingredients employed in its manufacture, the film undergoes considerable shrinkage in hot climates owing to evaporation. I have seen film shrunk so much that it failed to conform with the standard gauge, and the teeth of the sprocket in the printing machine, instead of engaging with the holes, played upon the outer smooth edges of the film. To maintain the prime condition of the film it is necessary to keep it somewhat moist, and accordingly the packing boxes carry a certain amount of damped material. But in tropical countries where the heat is intense, it is by no means a simple matter to keep the film in condition; and for this reason it is often difficult to secure satisfactory pictures of scenes in tropical countries. A firm which dispatched an operator to Central America to secure a series of scenic and industrial films failed to obtain a single length of pictures worth showing. I saw the results of the expedi-

NAZARETH COLLEGE LIBRARY

tion. The film was badly distorted, and the pictures in some instances were so thin or indistinct as to defy projection. £500 ($2,500) had been expended without result.

There is another eccentricity displayed occasionally by some films in tropical climes, which is difficult to explain. An operator will expose several hundred feet of film, which, when developed, fails to show the slightest sign of exposure. I have seen the results of a first-class cinematographer working between the limits of Capricorn and Cancer. His films when developed were as clear as if they had never been exposed to the action of light. The firm took one section of the exposed film and re-exposed it on a London street. It showed on development the image of London traffic, being as bare of any other image as if it had never seen the jungle. Heat and dry atmosphere seem to exercise some obscure chemical action, which prevents the sensitive surface of the films from being affected by exposure; yet when the film is returned to a naturally moist climate, like that of England, it appears to recover its original qualities.

As the component parts of a cinematograph film are of an inflammable nature, the resultant fabric is naturally also highly inflammable. This danger in the early days severely menaced the development of the industry, especially since those occupied in projection were careless of the most elementary precautions. The film, after passing through the lantern, fell a dishevelled mass into a basket, where it formed a tangled heap of thin combustible material, as inflammable as petrol-soaked shavings. Celluloid emits a vapour of an explosive nature, and it is always dangerous to use a naked light in its close proximity. Yet custom rendered the operator heedless of the danger. The outcome was inevitable. Legislation stepped in and ordained that the projector should be encased in a steel fire-proof chamber for the protection of the public. The result was that the cinematograph was barred from many places where the magic lantern was used.

Moving pictures could not be shown at such establishments as schools, merely because they did not possess a

A BATTERY OF CELLULOID MIXERS. [By permission of the Eastman Kodak Company.

Fifty barrels, holding 200,000 pounds of the "dope," are run continually day and night.

THE LIQUID CELLULOID STORAGE ROOM. *[By permission of the Kodak Eastman Company.*

When the ingredients are mixed thoroughly the syrup-like mass is stored in cylindrical tanks until required by the machines to be made into the film. Each vessel is of five tons capacity.

v   HOW THE CELLULOID FILM IS MADE   55

fire-proof chamber in which to operate them. A non-inflammable film was, of course, the next demand. To attempt to render celluloid non-combustible was akin to rendering gunpowder non-explosive. An absolutely new film-base had to be found. Cellulose as a basic constituent could not be dispensed with—in fact, chemical research has not yet succeeded in discovering an efficient substitute. Efforts were concentrated upon the treatment of the cellulose in such a manner as to prevent it being readily combustible, with the resultant production of the preparation known as cellulose-acetate, which is practically non-inflammable. But while this substance complies with the letter of the law and does not burst into flame, it does melt, however, under the influence of heat, and in so doing sometimes emits copious clouds of smoke, which are capable of producing panic in an audience quite as readily as an outburst of flame.

Under ordinary circumstances, this non-inflammable film is quite safe to handle, and from that point of view is adapted for the purpose of exhibiting in buildings where a special chamber is not provided. The heat produced by the focussed rays in the lantern, or the inadvertent contact of a naked light, do not promote combustion. The cellulose-acetate merely chars or melts, the action being purely local.

The celluloid film is supplied generally in lengths of 165 feet, which is approximately the capacity of the average film box. The actual picture itself upon the film measures one inch in width by ¾ of an inch in depth.

The question naturally arises as to what becomes of the films which have passed through their allotted span of life. When the celluloid film was first placed on the market this material was of a certain value. The sensitised gelatine emulsion was stripped off, and the base was converted into varnish. But this practice has fallen into disuse. Practically speaking, old films have no economic value. As a rule they are burned. If the junk film is obtained in sufficiently large quantities, a slightly remunerative by-product can be obtained in the form of metallic silver from the ashes, but the yield is so small and silver is so cheap that the trouble involved does not pay unless the waste is destroyed in tremendous bulk.

This is the era of the profitable utilisation of waste products, and no doubt a large fortune is awaiting the chemist who succeeds in evolving a cheap process for turning the useless cinematograph film to commercial account. Newspapers, old iron, and other metals, rubber, sawdust, and even garbage, possess a certain economic value, and there is no reason to suppose that used celluloid film is an exception to this general rule of utilising waste products. One by-product, as we have pointed out, is certain of reclamation—the silver—but the other constituents might prove just as valuable if a cheap, inexpensive method were contrived for their commercial reclamation.

CHAPTER VI

THE STORY OF THE PERFORATION GAUGE

WE have seen that before the film can be used in the camera it has to be perforated on either side in order that successive areas of film $\frac{3}{4}$ of an inch deep—the equivalent of a picture—can be seized and brought into position behind the lens. This perforation has become standardised in accordance with what is known as the "Edison Standard Gauge," which is 64 perforations per foot on either side. This perforation is of an elongated form, measuring about 1/8 of an inch in width by approximately 1/16th of an inch in depth.

The preliminary operation is carried out with a machine, which stamps the holes by means of specially hardened steel punches. Extreme care has to be taken to carry out the task with mathematical accuracy, in order that the film may be used with any type of camera and projector. Without it steadiness of the picture upon the screen is absolutely impossible.

It seems strange that all films should have to be perforated according to the Edison system, when it is remembered that the first commercial cinematographic apparatuses for the projection of pictures upon a screen were made, not by Edison, but by Paul and Lumière, who, one might think, would have established their own gauges. This important point involves an interesting little story.

In the very earliest days of cinematography, when a film of greater width was used than at present, it was advanced by friction. Rollers, or clutches, gripped the edges of the film tightly, and moved it forward the desired extent. But their action was uncertain. Sometimes the rollers became slack and the film slipped, the celluloid ribbon varied in thickness or was a trifle slippery, with the result that the forward movement was irregular, and the pictures did not appear in rhythmic succession. Some were askew, others were overlapped by the preceding or succeeding image, or a wide gap was left between consecutive pictures.

In order to overcome the drawback, attempts were made to devise a system of moving the film forward by the aid of pins engaging with holes in the sides. But the apparatus employed was mechanically defective. The film dragged, and the holes were either torn or became so worn that they did not engage accurately. Square holes were first tried, but the wear and tear set up by the pins or sprocket teeth soon gave them a circular or elongated shape. Then circular perforations were adopted, but they soon became elliptical. The number of perforations per picture was varied also in the hope of securing steadiness of the film both in the camera and more especially in projection, but every effort appeared to refuse to remove the difficulty.

One of the early investigators was discussing the subject one night with Lord Kelvin. The eminent scientist became deeply interested in this trouble with regard to the perforations, and the disadvantages of the respective shapes shown to him. After a few minutes' reflection, he remarked, "Why not use perforations of triangular form? They will not wear round or square. They will always retain their shape more or less, and at all events will give improved steadiness in running." The advice of Lord Kelvin was followed, and the triangular holes were found to give the best results achieved up to that time.

Meanwhile the shape of the perforations and the gauge had settled itself in a curious manner. The kinetoscope appeared with small rectangular perforations, numbering four to each picture, on either side of the film. Edison had settled on this plan for his apparatus, finding that it afforded him the best results. The machines were made

VI STORY OF THE PERFORATION GAUGE

and despatched to various parts of the world. To maintain the interest in the novelty, a number of films were prepared and sold to various customers possessing the kinetoscope.

When Messrs. Lumière brought out their projecting apparatus, only one brand of film available for demonstration purposes was on the market—that made for the kinetoscope. When Paul first entered the manufacturing field, he, of course, prepared films for use with the kinetoscope of his own manufacture, and he naturally adopted Edison's gauge. As already narrated, Lumière made an attempt to set up an independent gauge, with one hole each side per picture, but the Edison and Paul films with an identical gauge had become too firmly established, especially as the famous American inventor commanded the situation in the United States. There was no market for either machines or films deviating from Edison's gauge. Exhibitors who had bought kinetoscopes and films, when they acquired a Lumière projector, demanded that it should be so designed as to use the films which they owned already, and which were highly expensive. When other film-picture manufacturers entered the arena they followed in Edison's footsteps, because there was no market for their wares if they did otherwise. Consequently the Edison perforation gauge became more and more firmly established as time progressed, until at last it became regarded as the standard. It must be pointed out that this result was largely attributable to Paul, who became the largest manufacturer of kinetoscope films in the world.

Yet it must not be thought that the settlement came about smoothly. There has been a battle of the gauges in the cinematographic as in the railway world. The Edison standard gauge has its admitted drawbacks, the greatest of which is that there are too many holes per picture, which weaken the film and tend to precipitate tearing. Two, or even one, hole per picture on either side would suffice, as demonstration has conclusively proved.

An American rival attempted to swerve from the

standard in another direction, using a film $2\frac{3}{4}$ inches wide —double the width of the kinetoscope film. He eventually abandoned the wide band, partly on economic grounds, as a ribbon half the width produced pictures in every respect equal to those obtained from the wider film. On one or two occasions the gauge has been revised slightly, but the variations merely affected the dimensions of the hole to a microscopic degree. Fundamentally, the gauge as set by Edison for the first commercial apparatus for showing photographs in motion prevails to-day, and is universally accepted.

The film is received from the manufacturers in a plain ribbon, and the perforation has to be done shortly before the film is taken in hand for exposure. The film manufacturers cannot possibly supply it perforated, because the celluloid base undergoes continuous physical change while in storage. Under varying climatic conditions it shrinks and expands to an extent which may not be observable to the eye, but becomes pronounced when the picture is projected upon the screen.

The necessity for mathematical precision in the matter of perforating is somewhat obscure to the uninitiated, but its effects may be demonstrated very easily. Compare the vibrating or oscillating flickering picture of 1896 with that shown upon the screen to-day, in which the effect produced comes very close to that of the *camera obscura*. If the perforation errs the hundredth part of an inch, steadiness in the picture is forfeited. The films have to be punctured with the same mathematical accuracy that goes to the production of a tiny screw intended for the most delicate piece of mechanism.

This is especially the case in regard to the perforation of the negative film. If this is not absolutely true to gauge, the existing error will be magnified in the passage of the film through the camera; and should the latter be ever so slightly at fault, the defect becomes intensified still more. By the time the picture reaches the projector the infinitesimally small defect in the first instance becomes increased fourfold or even more. The picture will jump

PAUL'S ROTARY PERFORATOR.

To punch the holes in the margins of the film before it is exposed.

THE FIRST CINEMATOGRAPH STUDIO-STAGE.

Built by Robert Paul, at New Southgate, London. It faced north. The camera and operator were mounted on a platform which travelled upon rails.

See page 104.

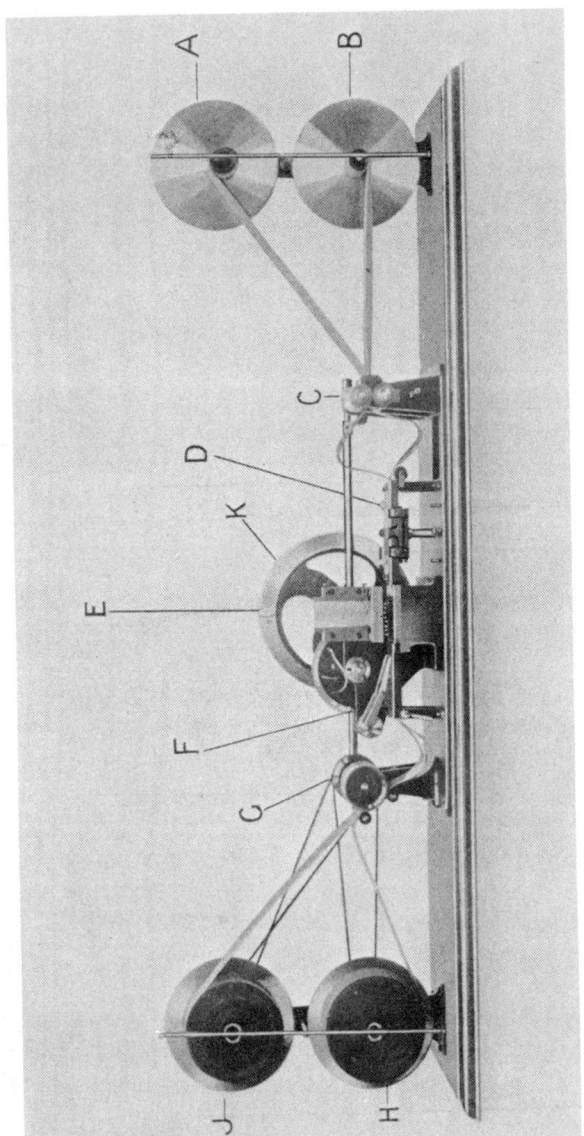

THE WILLIAMSON FILM PERFORATOR.   *For explanation of design and operation see page 62.*

VI STORY OF THE PERFORATION GAUGE   61

and flutter in the most distressing manner, and no matter how dexterous the operator may be, and despite the excellence of his projector, he cannot by any means rectify or mitigate very appreciably defects arising from indifferent perforation.

The contribution of imperfect perforation to unsteadiness in projection was recognised in the earliest days; and great technical skill was devoted to the elaboration of machines to puncture the film with scientific precision. Marvellous appliances have been produced for this purpose; but despite the infinite labour bestowed upon their production the possibility of error is ever present. Still, it has been reduced to infinitesimal proportions, and, given a careful operator, a film can be perforated with the holes varying not a thousandth part of an inch from the gauge.

The very earliest type of perforating machine was known as the "Rotary Perforator," Paul leading the way in this, as in several other ramifications of the industry. The machine was driven by a mechanism identical with that utilised in the camera and projector; because the film had to be advanced intermittently beneath the punches, which were provided with an oscillating movement. This type of machine is shown in the illustration. Paul's first appliance has always ranked as more simple, efficient, and reliable than any other.

During recent years the rotary perforator has fallen from favour, on the plea that it soon becomes imperfect in working; but such an accusation cannot fairly be brought against Paul's machine, since its designer used it continuously for four years, during which time it punched millions of holes, and to-day is as correct in its work as when first used.

It is impossible within the scope of this book to describe all the various types of perforation apparatus now in vogue, more especially as their interest lies mainly in highly technical details. I will content myself with describing three machines which exemplify the three most important methods of perforation.

As this operation has to be carried out in the dark room

in the dim light of a ruby lamp, it is imperative that the machines should be of the most simple design and operation, demanding the minimum of labour on the part of the operator.

In the Williamson perforator, four holes on either side of the film are punched at one time, and two films are perforated simultaneously, the sensitised surfaces being face to face. This arrangement obviates the danger of scratching or rubbing the sensitised surface during the operation. One coil of plain film is mounted on the spool A, and another on the lower spool B. The leads from these two spools are taken between the rollers C on to a small platform or guide gate D, where the two superimposed films are brought accurately together to pass under the punches. These are mounted in two rows, the requisite distance apart, in a moving head piece E, which descends at the critical moment, the punches piercing the films cleanly and sharply, the pieces of detached celluloid falling into a receptacle on the floor beneath.

When the head containing the punches rises, the two hooked fingers or claws F engage a hole on either side of the films, and pull them forward ready for the punching of the next four pairs of holes. In addition to carrying four pairs of punches, the head E carries four pairs of projecting pins, set to the same gauge, and before the punch descends these guide pins engage with the four preceding pairs of holes, so that the distance between the sets of four holes on either side is bound to be exactly the same as between any two consecutive holes made simultaneously. The result is that the holes are perforated with absolute mathematical accuracy.

As the film emerges from the perforator proper, it is passed between two guide rollers and a toothed sprocket G, which meshes with the perforations, and thence the lower film passes to the re-winding spool H, and the upper film to the spool J. Between the perforating plate and the respective rollers C and G, small loops will be observed. These are provided for the purpose of obviating any pull upon the film while in the guide gate, and beneath the punches, which might otherwise destroy the alignment and accuracy of the gauge. These loops remain constant, but they can be altered at will while the machine is running without disturbing the actual perforation. The Williamson perforator can be run under power at a relatively high speed, the wheel K being capable of 400 revolutions per minute without impairing the accuracy of the work in the slightest degree.

A different type of machine is represented in the "N.-S." perforator, Fig. 5. In this instance the coil of plain film A is

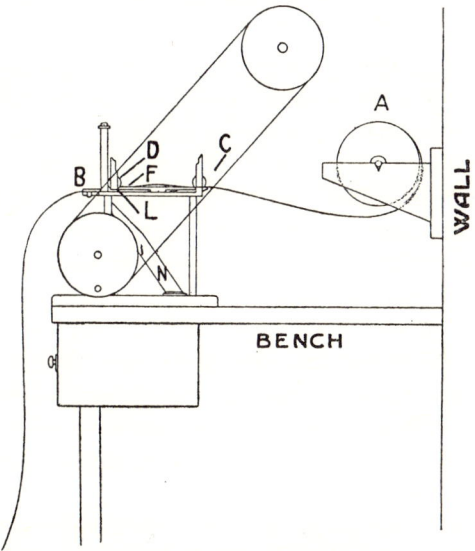

Fig. 5.—The N.S. Film Perforator.

set up in a convenient position away from the machine, but in such a manner that the feed thereto is in an easy curve. The film enters the machine through two roller guides, C and D, to a channel F, and then under the dies in the top plate L. The punctured pieces of film fall away clear of the instrument through the tube N, so that there is no probability of such particles fouling the mechanism and thus possibly upsetting the accurate working of the apparatus. After being perforated the film is moved forward by means of guide pins, and finally issues through a guide *B* to be re-coiled. This apparatus is very convenient for driving by power, is simple, efficient in its operation, and owing to the solidity of its construction there is little possibility of the precision of the gauge being upset by wear and tear, or by other external influences. The gauge, moreover, can be altered, if desired, to as small a degree as 1/100th of an inch per foot. As the positive film shrinks somewhat after development, it is an advantage to be able to compensate for the contraction when perforating. When the film is dry, although it may have shrunk a trifle, it is found that the gauge is perfectly accurate.

In the Urban-Joy perforator, only a single pair of holes is punched at a time—one on either side of the film. At first sight this method appears somewhat slow, but there is the distinct advantage that the holes are made with incontestable scientific precision, and after all this is the all-important factor. This machine is capable of the very finest adjustment, it being possible to vary the stroke of the punch to the millionth part of an inch. Its simplicity of operation is another distinct point. All strain upon the film is avoided for the simple reason that it is passed through the machine by the pendulum action of the punches. When these are disengaged the film is held in position by a clamp working in opposite step to the action of the punches.

Years of labour have been expended upon the evolution of the perforator. The fruit of these efforts, however, is a material improvement in the steadiness of the picture upon the screen.

CHAPTER VII

THE MOVING PICTURE CAMERA, ITS CONSTRUCTION, AND OPERATION

ALTHOUGH it was as far back as 1894 that the first commercial moving picture camera appeared in Great Britain, the years have not produced many marked departures from the design as elaborated by Paul. Time has proved his plan to be the most reliable and efficient. But as the art has developed and many minds have been concentrated upon the apparatus, it has undergone modification and improvement in minor details, all tending towards greater excellence in the ultimate results.

Paul's camera was a small wooden cabinet, measuring only about six inches each way. It contained merely the requisite intermittent mechanism to bring successive depths of the film before the lens, and the tube to enable focussing to be carried out easily from the back, and in such a way that it was impossible for the film to become fogged when the tube was left open inadvertently.

This instrument was a model of simplicity, compactness, portability and convenience. The film was carried in separate dark boxes of a size to hold 160, 350, or 700 feet, according to requirements. These were detached from the camera itself, the box of unexposed film slipping into a device on top of the camera in such a way as to ensure a light-tight joint, and locked into position to prevent accidental detachment. From this box the film was led through the camera mechanism, past the lens and into a second box, similarly detachable. The apparatus therefore was resolved into three main parts—the camera, and the unexposed and exposed film boxes.

The modern cinematograph camera is completely self-contained; the film boxes are incorporated within the case that carries the mechanism for moving the film forward. Further improvement is hard to imagine. Bulk and dimensions are reduced to the minimum, with, at the same time, the maximum of efficiency.

The cinematograph camera, unlike most machinery, is called upon to face exigencies, and to perform exceedingly hard work under the most adverse conditions. To-day it may be in the broiling sun on a tropical desert; a few weeks hence it is plunged into the extreme cold of the Arctic circle; a little later it is well-nigh submerged in a reeking swamp or vapour bath. Such varying conditions subject the material and workmanship of the instrument to a supreme ordeal. Consequently the greatest care has to be exercised in the selection of material, the fashioning of the component parts, and their fitting together. Only the best seasoned mahogany can be utilised to withstand the strains of warping, shrinking, and expansion under extremes of heat and cold, and climatic fluctuations.

In the ordinary stand camera used for still-life work, there is a bellows which can be racked to and fro to enable the subject to be focussed sharply upon the ground glass screen. The cinematograph camera has no bellows, and there is no fixed screen for focussing purposes. In the simpler and cheaper cameras, suited to amateur use, the operator is not troubled with focussing details at all, the lens being of a fixed focus as in certain types of snap-shot hand cameras; but in the more expensive instruments, designed for producing the finest classes of work, focussing facilities are incorporated.

In order to grasp the operation of the camera, we will open the hinged door with which it is provided on one side, and gain access to its interior mechanism. It would be invidious to select any special type of camera, inasmuch as they all work more or less upon the same principle, the differences being only in minor details.

By reference to the illustration it will be seen that the apparatus is in three main parts. The rear half of

THE PERFORATING ROOM OF THE CINES COMPANY IN ROME.

The operation has to be carried out in ruby light.

THE FILM-MOVING MECHANISM OF A CINEMATOGRAPH CAMERA.

The spool of unexposed film is carried in dark box A. From this it is led over sprocket D, through the "gate" between the lens and the focussing tube C, where it is exposed. The film is then jerked down the depth of a picture through the gate by claws F, over sprocket and into exposed film box B, where it is wound on a bobbin. E is the eyepiece of the focussing tube.

the cabinet carries two square compartments, A and B, one above the other. These are for the two film boxes, A carrying the unexposed, and B the exposed film. It will be noticed that the cinematograph works upon the system of roller photography. Indeed, it might be described almost as a semi-automatic application of the familiar snap-shot camera using roll-films.

The lens is set centrally in the front face of the camera, and carries a screw, by means of which focussing is effected by moving the lens itself to and fro a short distance within a horizontal tube, which corresponds to the bellows in the ordinary camera. In addition, it is fitted with stopping facilities working upon the well-known Iris principle, whereby the size of the aperture may be increased or diminished by a rectilinear movement. Behind the lens, and on a line with it in the interior, a tubular connection C extends transversely through the width of the camera to the rear, and through the outer wall to the external face of the case. This is the focussing tube, into which the operator looks through the small circular orifice E in the back face of the camera, known as the eyepiece.

The mechanism by which, with an intermittent motion, the film is jerked forward three-quarters of an inch after each exposure, is of the simplest design. The film as it issues through a narrow slit from the unexposed film box A, is passed under a small guide roller, having a smooth face. Thence it passes upwards over a second roller and down under the sprocket wheel, the teeth of which engage with the perforations in the edges of the film, and thus guide it forward. As the film passes upwards from the sprocket wheel, it is kept in mesh by another guide roller, which maintains an easy pressure upon the film to keep it in contact with the wheel, this grip being ensured under the tension of a spring. The roller is mounted on the end of a small lever, which can be moved slightly so as to release the grip upon the sprocket wheel in order to insert the film. The arrangement adopted enables the contact roller to ride over any variations in the thickness of the films should such exist—a remote possibility in view of the wonderful mathematical accuracy with which the films are made to-day. It is impossible for the film to jump the sprocket wheel, even when the machine is run at a very high speed. The contact roller is so mounted, however, that it offers no resistance to the free passage of the film.

The film now passes behind the lens for exposure, travelling through what is known as the "gate," which consists of two parts, one fixed and rigid, the other having a slight swinging movement. By means of the gate the film is guided evenly into position, and held rigidly behind the lens during exposure. The swinging part of the gate is clamped to the fixed section by means of a spring catch, so that when the gate is closed the film is imprisoned between two sheaths which hold it firmly, and keep the surface flat and even during exposure. The end of the focussing tube C presses against the moving part of the gate and tends to hold it rigid.

The film is pulled through the gate by an ingenious plan. There are two claws or hooks F, the points of which engage with a perforation on either side of the film. These two fingers are controlled by an up-and-down cam movement attached to the bottom sprocket. As the latter revolves, the hooks are lifted and carried upward. Reaching the limit of their upward travel, they drop upon the film, clutching it by the perforations, and as the claw action has a sharp downward movement, the gripped film is pulled down suddenly and smartly through the gate three-quarters of an inch at a time. The extent of the downward travel reached, the claws are lifted so as to disengage with the film, are swung upwards once more, and the same cycle of operations is repeated until the whole length of film has been exposed.

After the exposure is made, the film passes downwards and through mechanism which is almost a duplicate of that immediately above the lens. It passes under the rocking contact roller, which keeps the perforations meshed with the teeth on the sprocket wheel, after pass-

VII THE MOVING PICTURE CAMERA

ing round which it continues under a guide roller, and enters the lower film box B, where it is wound on a bobbin.

Action is imparted by the rotary movement produced by the turning of the handle through suitable mechanism, which is carried in a small space on the opposite side of the camera to that containing the film. The handle, however, not only supplies the drive to the inter mittent film moving action, but also rotates the shutter steadily and continuously, through gearing. The shutter is mounted in a small special compartment behind the lens and in front of the film. It is adjustable; that is, the opaque sector can be increased or reduced in area so as to increase or diminish the size of the opening; thus the period of exposure can be varied according to the light, and as a supplement to the stopping down of the lens. The gearing is practically the same in all English cinematograph cameras, namely, 8 to 1, and the turning speed should be two revolutions per second, which is practically the slowest speed permissible.

The preparation of the camera for exposure is as follows The operator has selected his working position, and the camera has been set up rigidly and firmly on its tripod, so that no oscillation can occur during exposure. The side of the camera is opened, and the loaded film box, from the slit in the bottom of which the end of the film protrudes, is slipped into the upper compartment.

Next the subject is focussed. The eye-piece of the focussing tube is made telescopic, as a rule, so that it can be extended a slight distance from the back face of the camera case to facilitate focussing; it is fitted invariably with a light, tight screw cap or gravity fall shutter, which closes over the eye-piece so that no light may enter through the tube to fog the film. For focussing purposes a piece of transparent film with a rough "Matt" surface is used. This is inserted in the film gate to act in the same way as the ground glass screen in the ordinary stand camera. The object is focussed by turning the screw, which racks the lens forward or backward as desired. When the picture appears sharp and clearly defined the matt film is removed, the cap is replaced on the eye-piece, and the latter is pushed home flush with the surface of the wood casing.

The film is now threaded. It will be observed that a slight loop is made at either end of the gate. This is necessary in order to give sufficient play to the film to enable the latter to be jerked down without any strain with each movement of the hook-claws behind the lens. If it were pulled directly off the top sprocket the film would be torn. The loops are kept constant, the upper being connected to the lower sprocket through mechanism so that they revolve simultaneously. Consequently three-quarters of an inch of film is fed into the top loop gate at the same time as three-quarters of an inch of film is jerked through the lower side of the gate.

In loading, care must be taken that the sensitised surface is brought towards the lens, and that the object is not taken through the thickness of the celluloid base. In order to thread the film through the gate the focussing tube is pushed back slightly—it is made telescopic for the purpose—the spring catch of the gate is released, and the moving part swung back. The film is now slipped into the gate, care being taken to see that the hooks of the device whereby it is intermittently pulled down after each exposure engage with the perforations. The gate is now closed, and the focussing tube under the action of a spring returns to its original position. Finally the film is led into the unexposed film box, where it is secured by a clip to the spindle of the reel. The box is shut, the handle is given a turn to make sure that the mechanism runs evenly and smoothly, and then the camera is closed, all being ready for taking the pictures.

There is a popular impression that the operation of the cinematograph camera is as simple as turning a coffee-mill or a barrel-organ, and that the cinematographer has nothing else to do but to revolve the crank. Never was there a greater fallacy.

Turning the handle appears remarkably easy at first sight, but a short trial proves that appearances are decep-

PAUL'S COMPLETE DEVELOPING, PRINTING AND DRYING OUTFIT.

THE FIRST DEVELOPING ROOM IN GREAT BRITAIN, AT ROBERT PAUL'S PIONEER FILM MANUFACTORY.

See page 77.

AFTER DEVELOPMENT AND WASHING THE FILMS WERE TRANSFERRED FROM THE RACKS TO THE CYLINDERS.

[Photos by permission of Robert Paul.

THE DRYING ROOM, SHOWING FILMS WOUND ON THE DRYING DRUMS.

See page 77.

VII THE MOVING PICTURE CAMERA

tive. It is essential that the handle should be rotated at uniform speed, and occasionally it is no easy matter to resist the desire to slow down. For instance, when a funeral is passing, there is an almost irresistible inclination to slacken speed. The amateur responds to this desire, and is astonished at the dislocated character of his pictures when projected upon the screen. As a matter of fact, the slowest funeral procession has to be taken with the same number of revolutions per second, and the same number of exposures—sixteen pictures per second—as an express train travelling at 60 miles an hour; the crawl of the tortoise has to be photographed just as rapidly as a horse race, in order to secure natural motion. If a subject has been photographed too slowly it cannot be corrected by accelerating the speed in projection. The judgment of the actinic value of the sunlight, and the requisite stop for the lens, as well as the adjustment of the shutter, are factors which only can be determined from experience.

Possibly the box A contains a roll of film measuring 300 feet, whereas the subject photographed only demands the exposure of 60 or 100 feet. Then one makes a few punch marks on the film by the manipulation of a small brass knob projecting from the outside of the camera, and marked "film punch." When the film reaches the developing room, the operators working in the ruby light can tell by these marks the ends of a series of exposures.

When the upper box has been exhausted of film, the lower box, now charged with exposed film, is removed, the empty upper box is slipped out of its compartment and re-inserted into the lower recess, to serve in turn as a receptacle for film after exposure, and a fresh loaded film-box is placed in the upper space, the mechanism being threaded as before. The operator can ascertain at a glance how much film still remains to be used, because on the outside of the case is a dial which registers in feet the amount of film exposed, and which is set to zero whenever a fresh box of film is inserted.

The task of the operator is increased in difficulty where the subject being taken is moving at great speed horizontally and vertically at the same time, when the object passes in a very short while beyond the field of the lens, and in order to secure a good record the operator must follow the movements steadily and smoothly in such a way as to keep the object near the centre of the picture. The development of aviation has taxed the capabilities of the cinematographer to a supreme degree; for in photographing moving objects in the air the camera has to be trained in two directions at the same time.

For this work a special tripod is required. It has a flat table, but by means of two gear wheels the camera can be swung round panoramically, that is, in a horizontal direction, while another wheel will move it up or down through as large a vertical arc as required. Rigidity and freedom from oscillation are essential to secure sharp, well-defined pictures, and consequently this moving table has to be of massive construction, while the worm and wheel gearing has to be heavy to ensure steady movement. The camera is fitted with a direct view finder, whereby the operator can train his instrument so as to keep the subject well in the picture. Both horizontal and vertical training movements are carried out by means of hand-wheels.

One of the finest examples of the operator's skill that I have ever seen was a film of Wilbur Wright's flying exploits in France, on the occasion of his first visit to Europe. The camera was manipulated by two men. One concentrated his energies on the revolution of the photographing handle, while the other, with his eyes glued to a special direct view-finder devised for this particular operation, kept the camera steadily and regularly trained both horizontally and vertically upon the aviator as he described his evolutions in the air. Their joint efforts were so successful that they produced a film free from that dislocated or jerky action which as a rule characterises the lateral or vertical movement of the camera while exposures are being made; the results were just as if the camera had been kept stationary during the whole time.

The ordinary tripod is used generally for outdoor work. Many American and Continental film producers, however,

VII THE MOVING PICTURE CAMERA 73

resort to a special type of support for the camera in the studio or for indoor operations, such as the filming of plays. This is a solid metal pillar, recalling a machine-gun mounting, fitted with wheels to facilitate movement from point to point, and other adjusting devices. It is an excellent support for indoor work, as it ensures a solid foundation for the camera, free from vibration. In many instances the camera is driven by an electric motor.

It is sometimes desirable to secure two negative records of an important event or subject, so that, should one film prove defective, the mechanism break down, or the film be damaged or destroyed, the duplicate is available and prevents a total loss. For this purpose the camera is in duplicate, though contained within a single case, with two lenses mounted side by side as in a stereoscopic camera. Both sets of mechanism are operated by the single handle, and one person suffices for the operation of the instrument.

Within a few years, cinematography has widened its sphere of usefulness in a novel and unexpected way. Forty years ago no expedition of importance set out without some member who possessed artistic ability, that pictorial records of the life and character of the new country might be brought back to civilisation. As photography developed, the artist of palette and brush was superseded by a man armed with a camera. To-day the latter gives way in his turn to the cinematographer, who brings back to us marvellous animated pictures of the remote and unknown corners of the globe.

An ingenious camera has been devised for this especial field of enterprise. It contains a unique feature that had not been previously applied to the art. Two investigators, Newman and Sinclair, by dint of considerable experiment and labour, have succeeded in producing a moving-picture camera with a reflex attachment, and this without increasing the size of the case, or interfering with the action of the short-focus lenses. By means of this apparatus focussing can be accomplished in fifteen seconds, without disturbing the film in the gate, which is threaded up, ready for use, before the camera is taken from the dark room. In this way the camera can be operated in much less time than is possible by means of the ordinary cinematographic apparatus.

As may be seen from the diagram, Fig. 6, the internal mechanism of this handy little camera differs radically from the description given in the first part of the present chapter. The two film boxes are placed side by side instead of one above the other. The film goes into and out of them through narrow mouths, which, when the camera is closed and light-tight, are automatically increased in size to facilitate the passage of the film, and automatically decreased again when the camera is reopened. In order to see, arrange, and focus the picture,

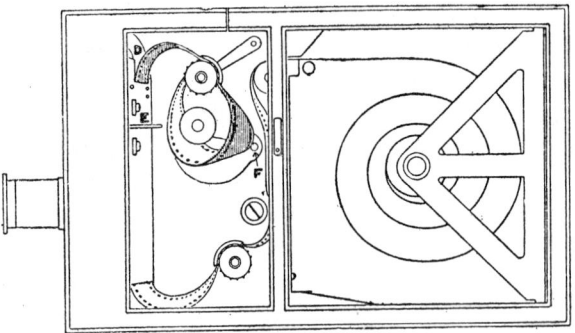

FIG. 6.—THE NEWMAN-SINCLAIR REFLEX MOVING PICTURE CAMERA.

it is only necessary to raise a knob on the top of the camera, which renders the image visible by means of a magnifying eye-piece without disturbing the film. The shutter is also adjusted from the outside of the camera, and can be closed to give an exposure of 1/100th of a second.

This camera is one of the most compact, portable, and lightest cinematograph instruments yet evolved for the purposes of hard work. It is designed to carry either 400 or 500 feet of film, and, when a picture is finished, the end of the subject on the film is indicated by a device which cuts a tongue-shaped opening in the film, and which can be readily detected by touch when the film is uncoiled in the dark room. It is an ideal instrument for travellers, explorers, scientists, and others to whom quick work is imperative. Its many excellent qualities received recognition from Captain R. Scott, R.N., who included it in the scientific equipment for the latest British Antarctic expedition.

For special work, the usual form of camera is altered in certain details, or equipped with special devices. Such modification is emphasised particularly for the purpose of taking trick pictures, to which subject reference is made in subsequent chapters.

CHAPTER VIII

DEVELOPING AND PRINTING THE PICTURES

THE history of the cinematograph impresses upon us at every turn the necessity which experimenters were under of devising special facilities and improved apparatus in all of the numerous fields that impinged upon their work. They were obliged to break ground in every direction. For instance, besides securing the right kind of film, they had also to find the best means of developing it. A thin, narrow ribbon of pictures 40 feet in length is a vastly different thing to handle from a rigid glass plate. Its flexibility presented many perplexing obstacles which had to be overcome. Those who used the old roll film with the snapshot hand-camera of the early days, can relate pathetic and humorous stories of the trials and tribulations they suffered in passing the awkward length of film through the developing and other baths. When it was unwound from the roller preparatory to immersion in the developing solution, it persisted in buckling and twisting into strange contortions. Development was carried out in an uneven or patchwork manner, some parts of the film being fully developed before others had betrayed the slightest sign of yielding the latent image.

The plight of the animated photographer was even more unenviable; the handling of sensitised celluloid about as thick as a substantial wooden shaving, was infinitely more exasperating than that used in the ordinary hand camera, for the latter was wider, thicker, and far shorter.

The developing methods at first advocated were of the crudest nature possible. Messrs. Lumière tried to assist

CH. VIII DEVELOPING AND PRINTING PICTURES 77

the tyro by comprehensive explanation of a very simple way to carry out the task. They suggested suspending the coil of exposed film upon a rod slipped through the centre of the bobbin to form a kind of spindle, upon which the coiled film was free to revolve over the bath. The operator was then told to unwind the coil very rapidly by hand, passing it into the bath between the fingers, which acted as a guide.

It appeared an absurdly simple operation, but without considerable practice it defied success. One had to be extremely careful not to damage the delicate sensitised emulsion of the film while uncoiling it; that no greasy

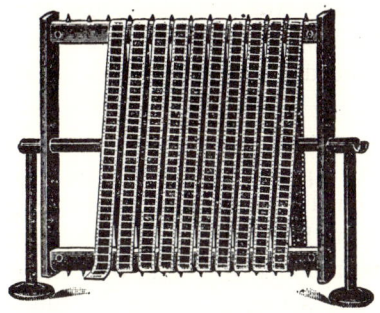

By courtesy of Messrs. Butcher & Sons, Ltd.
FIG. 7.—HOW THE FILM IS WOUND UPON THE WOODEN FRAME FOR DEVELOPING.

matter, such as perspiration from the fingers, might come into contact with the gelatine surface; and no bubbles must be produced while feeding the slippery strip into the bath. Mr. Robert Paul experienced these troubles, and displayed considerable ingenuity in the evolution of special means to avoid them. The efficiency of his method is proven by the fact that in the main it is practised to this day.

His solution of the problem was simple, safe, and satisfactory from every point of view. He took a light, square wooden frame, similar to that in Fig. 7, which rested loosely upon two uprights in such a way that it could revolve. The free end of the film was fixed to one side of the frame, and the film was then passed from one side to the other, as if being wound upon a wheel, as it was uncoiled from the spool, the inner end of the film being likewise secured to the frame. This rack was dipped first into a vertical tank to soak the film, and then was placed in a flat tank or trough to be developed in the same way as an ordinary glass plate. By this means every part of the exposed surface was developed equally. Development carried to the requisite degree, the frame was withdrawn, washed, and finally immersed in the fixing tank, which was of the same horizontal design. When the image was fixed it was placed in another tank and received a thorough washing, to remove all traces of the fixing solution, as in the ordinary developing process. This task completed, the film was uncoiled from the flat rack to be re-coiled upon a wooden drum, which was suspended from the ceiling in the drying chamber, until the film was dry and hard.

As may be supposed, different factories practise different methods of carrying out this operation. Nowadays a film may be as much as 300 or 400 feet in length, and consequently special methods have to be employed. I have been in some establishments where development is carried out upon an extensive scale, in which the films, as withdrawn from the camera film box, are wound at once upon a large wooden reel, seven feet or so in length, suspended upon brackets above the developing bath. When the drum has received its full length of film it is lowered into a deep tank containing the desired solution, and there kept revolving slowly and steadily until the treatment has been completed. Then the reel is withdrawn by two men and lowered into the next bath; and so on until at last the reel finds its way into the drying room, where the film is uncoiled from the developing drum and re-wound upon the drying reel. The disadvantage of this process is that two men are required to handle the reel, whereas, when a frame is used, one pair of hands is sufficient.

The developing and printing rooms in a large film-picture factory are highly interesting hives of activity. Large troughs and tanks containing the various solutions

THE DEVELOPING ROOM AT THE PATHÉ WORKS.

The films are wound upon wooden frames and immersed in large tanks containing the various solutions.

THE DRYING ROOM AT THE PATHÉ WORKS.

This illustration shows the wooden frames upon which the lengths of film are wound and the overhead racks from which they are suspended.

VIII DEVELOPING AND PRINTING PICTURES

are on every hand, together with adequate supplies of running water. Everything, of course, is carried out in semi-darkness, the only light available being that emitted from ruby lamps. The fixing solution after it has served its purpose is not thrown away, but is subjected to a chemical treatment to recover the bromide of silver which the hyposulphite of soda has dissolved from the sensitised emulsion on the film. The silver in suspension is precipitated by chemical action in a thick sediment. In large works this recovery process is profitable, several pounds of this metallic silver being secured every week.

The solution employed for development is either a combination of hydroquinone and metol, or a bath of rodinal, developing agents which are familiar to the amateur photographer, while the fixing bath is a solution of hyposulphite of soda. The developing formula is modified by various firms as a result of individual investigation. The drying operation is one that has to be carried out very carefully; the temperature of the chamber must be evenly maintained, and the air which is circulated through the room must be filtered before admission, in order to arrest all particles of dust which otherwise might settle upon the gelatine surface and wreak appreciable damage.

In the early days the fickle character of the film was a serious difficulty. If it were dried too rapidly it evinced a tendency to curl, and severe shrinkage often ensued. To guard against this trouble the film was glycerined before being dried, by being passed through a bath containing a solution of glycerine and alcohol. The improvements effected in the manufacture of the film, however, have enabled this subsidiary treatment to be dispensed with. In cases where a topical film must be rushed out quickly to catch the public in the height of its interest, however, drying is accelerated by subjecting the film to a bath of alcohol in some form or other.

Although a spool of film, measuring perhaps 300 feet in length, is handed over for development, possibly that 300 feet carries two, four, or more exposures, *i.e.*, different sections were exposed at different times, on different days, or under different conditions of light, &c. The camera operator has indicated the end of each exposure by means of the camera punch. When the developing operator receives the spool, he first searches for such marks as he uncoils the film, and the latter is severed at those points, and each exposure is developed separately. When the developing process is completed, therefore, the film relating to one subject is in a fragmentary condition. These odds and ends have to be sorted out, all useless parts cut away, and then arranged in sequence and joined together to form a continuous band containing, in the ordinary case, the whole subject. If the series of pictures runs into two or three thousand feet, the aggregate will be divided into 1,000 feet sections, which is the approximate capacity of the spool mounted on the projector. The sections are united by means of a transparent cement, known as amylacetate.

When the negative is dry and the gelatine surface has hardened enough to permit the sections to be handled and joined together, the next stage is taken in hand. This is printing the positive. Obviously a printing frame, such as the amateur uses for printing from a single glass plate, is quite out of the question with a negative several hundred feet in length. Invention born of necessity has met this question in a novel manner, and the printing process is one of the most interesting phases in the preparation of a picture. Considerable mechanical ingenuity has been displayed, and various types of printing machines produced; but for the purposes of explaining the subject most lucidly and comprehensively two typical machines will suffice. Before printing, however, the raw film or stock intended for the purposes of the positive or transparency must be perforated, an operation which is similar to that followed in perforating the negative film.

Printing is carried out by contact; that is to say, the sensitised surface of the positive film is pressed tightly against the emulsion side of the negative film at the instant the exposure is made. One image is printed at one time. The two films are given an intermittent action, the con-

VIII DEVELOPING AND PRINTING PICTURES

secutive images on the negative film and the corresponding sections of sensitised surfaces on the positive film being brought before the illuminant during the brief period that the light is cut off from the printing box by the passage of the shutter.

In the Newman-Sinclair apparatus, Fig. 8, the negative-film is wound upon spool 1, while the positive film is carried on spool 2, both being supported upon the projecting bracket 3. The negative passes over the guide roller

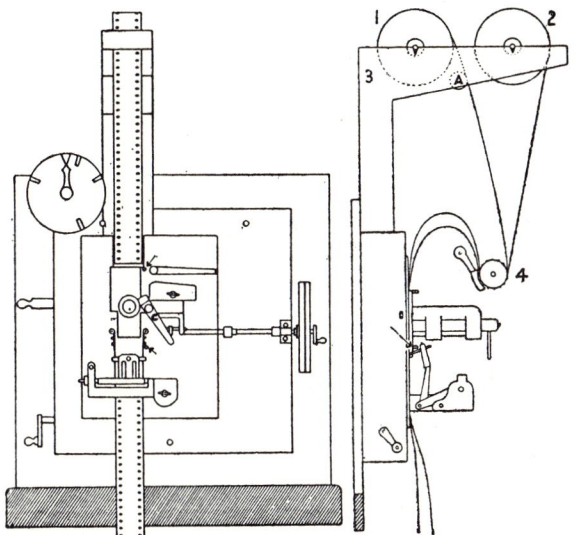

Fig. 8—Front and Side Views of Newman-Sinclair Printing Apparatus.

A, and descends with the positive film to the toothed sprocket 4. At this point the two films are brought together with the gelatine surfaces inside, while the teeth of the sprocket mesh with the perforations in each. The two films pass from this sprocket, form a loop, and together enter the gate, which clamps them tightly and flatly together, with their respective perforations exactly coinciding.

At the point where the two films come opposite the aperture through which passes the light from the lamp, there is a mask, by which the position of the picture relative

G

to the exposure hole is corrected. The mask also determines the shape of the positive picture. It may be rectangular, oval, circular, or have rounded corners as desired. Immediately behind the film, in line with the exposing aperture, is a red screen, over which a shutter slides. When this shutter is opened, the operator can see the negative image through the positive film, and thus can ascertain that the position of the picture is correct in relation to the exposure aperture, and also that the perforations on the two films are in synchrony. The light by which the exposure is made is contained in a light-tight box, or may be placed on the outside of the wall of the printing room, an aperture being cut in the partition to admit the light to the printing apparatus, which is screwed to the wall. Between the light and the film there is a revolving shutter, as in the camera, which cuts off the light intermittently, enabling the succeeding negative image and area of positive film to be brought into position before the exposure orifice.

The film is drawn through the machine by a pair of fingers or claws which engage with the perforations of the two films and pull them downwards together. As the pictures are printed, the negative and positive films pass into boxes or other suitable receptacles to be re-wound on their respective spools. The machine can be operated either by hand or power according to the requirements of the establishment. As the sensitised surface of the positive film is slower than that of the negative, printing is carried out at a reduced speed, the average recommended with this apparatus being about five pictures per second.

Another printing machine has been recently produced which is regarded as the simplest, most mechanically perfect, most compact, and self-contained apparatus yet devised for this work, and which compels attention as much from its efficiency as from the point of view of mechanical excellence. This is the Williamson printer. It is a complete unit, and can be moved from place to place with facility.

It comprises a large rectangular box or cabinet, standing on one end. The front face carries the printing mechanism,

A ROW OF PRINTING MACHINES IN THE ROME WORKS OF THE CINES COMPANY.
This establishment is able to print 100,000 feet of film per day.

THE WILLIAMSON PRINTING MACHINE.

For making the positive films.—*For explanation see page* 82.

VIII DEVELOPING AND PRINTING PICTURES

while the interior, divided into two compartments, contains the driving mechanism and the illuminating agency for printing. The apparatus is so designed that after printing the films are wound upon separate spools at once, thus saving time, and dispensing with the necessity of a box or basket to gather the loose films, which is both a dangerous and an unsatisfactory process, inasmuch as the films are liable to become damaged by curling and cracking, and through the surfaces rubbing against one another.

The negative film is placed upon the spool A immediately below which is the positive film spool B. The sensitised surfaces of the two films face one another, and the two are brought together as they pass under the grip rollers and over the toothed sprocket C, where the teeth mesh with the perforations in the respective films. Issuing from this sprocket a loop is formed, and then the films enter the gate D over the printing aperture. This gate is side-hinged, and when closed it presses evenly upon the whole surface of the films under exposure, ensuring a perfect even contact. There is a small red screen E, which, when released by means of a small lever, drops down, thus enabling the negative to be examined without danger of the positive film being fogged in the operation. By this means the printer can satisfy himself that the picture is central to the exposure hole.

As the picture is printed, a simple claw device F, resembling two hooked fingers, engages with the perforations in the two films and draws them downwards. This claw device is of very simple construction, working on a cam, so that when the film has moved downwards the proper distance—sufficient to bring the succeeding picture and its area of unexposed positive film before the printing aperture —the fingers disengage themselves from the films, rise, and move upwards to drop into other perforations and repeat the operation.

As the film descends, it forms a loop, and passes under a double smooth-faced roller and a toothed sprocket G, at which point the two films part company, the positive to be wound upon the bobbin H, while the negative film is wound upon the lower bobbin I. These lower spools are driven by belt and pulleys from a bevel gear wheel, which carries a spindle actuating the claw giving the intermittent movement to the films, and which by means of another spindle rotates the upper and lower sprockets C and G so that the loops above and below the gate remain constant. By this arrangement no pull or strain is imposed upon the films by the sprockets, which act merely as guides and not tractive devices.

The compartment J is lined with asbestos, and contains the illuminant by means of which the printing is done. An electric lamp of 50 candle-power, having a filament in the form of a grid, is placed directly opposite the window through which the exposures are made. This lamp is mounted upon a slide controlled by a lever on a quadrant on the face of the machine, by means of which it may be moved as required from 2 inches to 10 inches from the printing window. The power of the light may be varied according to the density of the negative by means of a controller, which increases or decreases its intensity in much the same way as a gas jet can be turned up or down, it being possible to secure six variations in light intensity ranging between 16 and 50 candle-power. When the door of the chamber is closed the compartment is perfectly light-tight, though ample ventilation is secured.

The lower compartment K carries the electric motor by means of which the apparatus is driven, and the speed of printing is altered at will by means of a controller. The motor is of 1/12 horse-power, and six direct speeds can be obtained. The drive is communicated to the mechanism through a system of cone pulleys, which enable three speeds to be obtained; and as each of these three speeds can be given one of the six speeds of the motor by means of the regulating switch or controller, the apparatus can be driven at eighteen different speeds, according to requirements. Wide range of action, combined with simplicity of control, characterise this apparatus. The printing speed varies according to the density of negative and the intensity of the light, but the average speed in printing from a

VIII DEVELOPING AND PRINTING PICTURES

normal negative is about 500 exposures of pictures per minute.

The positive film, after being exposed, is developed by a method similar to that used for the negative. Both these developing processes demand considerable skill and experience in order to ensure the best possible results. An accomplished developer, like his colleague working with glass plates, can rectify many deficiencies arising during exposure. The camera operator often has to work under the most adverse conditions concerning light, and it is the task of the man in the dark room to obtain the utmost from a poor negative. By care and attention, combined with experience and knowledge, he will be able to improve, make up for under-exposure, and mitigate the evils due to over-exposure. It will be realised that development is the most critical stage in the whole operation, for upon the manner in which it is carried out much of the excellence and merit of the projected picture depends.

The fact that the cinematograph camera is being regarded more and more as an indispensable unit in the impedimenta for travelling and exploring expeditions has resulted in attention being devoted to the perfection of a small portable developing outfit to enable films to be developed at once, instead of sending them home for treatment, as hitherto has been the case. The "N.S." developing apparatus is an excellent appliance of this character. It has been taken by Captain Scott, R.N., upon his Antarctic expedition, and forms part of the photographic outfit carried by Mr. Cherry Kearton upon his travels. The developing apparatus consists of a rotating cylinder and two or more semi-circular troughs. The film is wound spirally upon the drum, being held in position by means of wire staples, and the apparatus is so designed that the drum with its film can be moved from one trough to the other by the simple movement of a lever. The design of the apparatus ensures economy in the quantity of developer required. Three pints of solution are sufficient to treat 75 feet of film, and the bath can be thrown away when work is finished or bottled for further use.

After washing, the film is wound upon a collapsible drum, which folds into a small space when not in use. The outfit is made of pine, with waterproofed joints, the whole of the woodwork being treated with paraffin wax to render it impervious to the action of chemicals and moisture. When packed, the apparatus, capable of dealing with 50 feet of film, measures $3\frac{1}{2}$ feet in length, by 26 inches wide, and 18 inches deep. The outer packing constitutes the support for the apparatus when in operation.

Waste is absolutely unavoidable in the cinematograph industry, and no matter how carefully operations may be conducted, it is bound to assume impressive proportions. In a travelling expedition the operator records pictures of what he deems to be sufficiently interesting from various points of view—scenic, ethnographic, historical, or merely anecdotal and humorous. When the films are developed and a trial positive is struck for projection before the powers that be, to receive official approbation and sanction to enter the market, the critics in the private projecting room sometimes fail to see eye to eye with the cinematographer, and deem this and that to be lacking in the essentials which render a film attractive to the public. Accordingly, these sections are eliminated. From 300 to 3,000 feet may be destroyed in this manner.

The waste is still greater in the filming of picture plays. Sometimes a scene, occupying 100 or 150 feet of film, will have to be photographed three or four times. I once saw a scene, taking 200 feet of film, recorded six times before it gave satisfaction. It was a picture involving the movements of a large crowd, and in five instances something went wrong at one point or another, despite the fact that rehearsals had been prosecuted with such energy and persistence that at last everything appeared to move with the precision of the wheels of a watch. A thousand feet of film were spoiled in this particular case, which, at an average of $1\frac{1}{2}d$. (three cents) a foot, represented a waste of £6 or $30 in film alone. Yet this is by no means an isolated instance; the proportion often approximates 20 per cent.; that is to say, 200 feet out of 1,000 feet are useless.

VIII DEVELOPING AND PRINTING PICTURES 87

The bigger the production being recorded, the heavier the waste in this direction.

When the positives have been dried and hardened sufficiently to enable them to be handled, they are sent to a room where the different sections are identified and allotted to their positions in the subjects to which they belong. The sections are joined together, the lengths of film bearing the explanatory sub-titles are inserted in the proper places, and the whole subject, after a final examination, is wound upon a spool ready for the market. The examination of the films is carried out rigorously, those suffering from the slightest blemish or coming below the firm's standard being discarded.

It has been seen from the foregoing that the preparations for developing and printing are somewhat elaborate, and demand expensive apparatus in order to insure the most satisfactory results. These considerations react against the amateur cinematographer. But should one fall a victim to the fascinating glamour of cinematography, one need not apprehend difficulties in connection with developing and printing. There is no necessity to acquire perforators, to establish a complete developing room, or to invest in a printing machine. The majority of cinematograph manufacturing establishments undertake to develop negatives, and to supply positive prints ready for projection at a nominal figure. It is far better to entrust the work to a skilled staff, who can be trusted to handle the film successfully, than to attempt to wrestle with unknown difficulties with a serpent-like film 200 feet long, in the murky gloom of the dark room.

CHAPTER IX

HOW THE PICTURES ARE SHOWN UPON THE SCREEN.

HAVING obtained the positive film, with its string of consecutive pictures, we now proceed to reproduce upon a large scale the animation which has been, so to speak, harnessed by the camera. For this purpose three essentials are necessary—a projecting apparatus, a powerful and brilliant illuminant, and a white surface or screen, upon which the pictures are thrown.

In its general appearance the projector resembles the magic lantern, which before the advent of the cinematograph held the field as a favourite source of amusement. It has the small box or cabinet in which the light is placed, and the condenser whereby the rays from the illuminant are converged into a powerful beam to be thrown through the picture and the lens upon the screen. This part of the apparatus is practically the same as that required for the purpose of showing still-life lantern slides. It is the mechanism required to bring the consecutive pictures singly before the lens in rapid succession that constitutes the real difference between the modern projector and the old stereopticon.

The projecting mechanism has the same task as the camera for securing the pictures. That is to say, a small section of film corresponding to the dimensions of a picture has to be brought into position before the lens in such a way as to permit the powerful concentrated beam of light from the lantern to pass through it and throw an enlarged, brilliant, and clearly defined picture upon the screen. The image rests on the screen for the fraction of a second, to be followed by the next picture. One does not observe the change from one picture to the other, as there is a revolving shutter, the opaque blade or blades of which cut across the screen at regular intervals. While the shutter is passing the lens, thereby interrupting the passage of light to the screen, the succeeding picture is brought into position; and when the opaque blade has passed, it is exposed in its turn and makes way for the next picture, this alternate action continuing until the end of the film is reached. It will be seen that an intermittent motion has to be given to the film in projection, in precisely the same manner as is required in the camera for exposure.

Although the evolution of a smooth-working and perfect camera taxed mechanical ingenuity to a high degree, the proportions of the task were not to be compared with those involved in the design of the projector. Many factors had to be taken into consideration. In the first place, it was imperative that each picture should be superimposed exactly upon its predecessor, that when the image reached the sheet it should stand as steadily and as still for the minute fraction of a second as if it were a lantern slide, and that the change from one picture to the other should be carried out in such a way as to render the change as imperceptible as possible to the spectator. In short, every effort had to be made to reproduce by intermittent motion the effect obtainable with the *camera obscura.*

The perfection of this illusion has demanded years of unremitting experiment and research. When animated pictures first came before the public they had a violent flickering, oscillating, and jumping motion, which proved exceedingly painful to the eyes. The effect was somewhat similar to that produced by gazing at a picture which is vibrating, and blinking rapidly meanwhile, or when a flicker-disc is rotated very rapidly before the limelight centred upon a stage scene and actors.

By dint of persistent effort and the perfection of mechanical details, this serious flickering and jumping effect has been eliminated; that is, so far as is possible with an apparatus designed to convey the impression of continuous motion by intermittent action. The projecting mechanism is of substantial design, while the moving parts subjected to wear and tear are made of the strongest metals. The wear and tear, however, is tremendous, and as all the moving parts are liable to displacement they must be fitted with adjusting devices whereby all slackness can be taken up and the apparatus be kept tuned to a high pitch of efficiency. Great ingenuity has been displayed in the conception and manufacture of these details, and the cinematograph projector of to-day is a wonderful piece of mechanism.

The optical principle of the cinematograph is exactly that of the magic lantern. Reference to Fig. 9 will explain it fully. The illuminant is represented

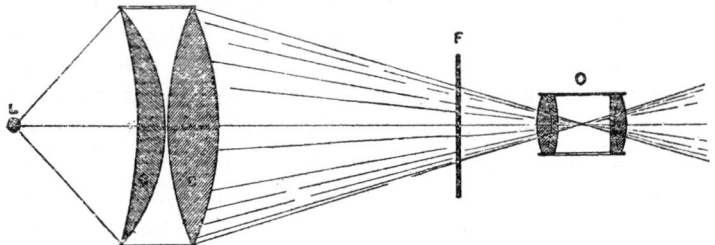

[*By courtesy of Messrs. Butcher & Sons, Ltd.*

FIG. 9.—THE OPTICAL PRINCIPLE OF THE CINEMATOGRAPH.

by L and the centre of the light is opposite the centre of the condensers C C, which receive the rays and condense them, the point of convergence being in the lens or objective O, from which they pass out in the form of an expanding cone of light to fall upon the screen. The rays in passing from the condensers penetrate the picture F on the film in position before the lens. It will be seen that the lens has to be mounted so that its longitudinal axis is level with the light. The distance of the light L from the condensers, and similarly the distance of the lens or objective O from the picture F is governed by the focus of the objective.

It is obvious, therefore, that the picture to be projected must be brought to a stop in a position central to the lens,

HOW PICTURES ARE SHOWN

and for this purpose there is a film trap or gate, where it makes a momentary halt, in precisely the same way that the unexposed film is arrested in its progress through the camera.

The film to be projected is carried upon a spool mounted on an arm or bracket above the mechanism, with the pictures upside down as in the ordinary magic lantern. The spools used are of the open or the closed type. The former is permissible in countries where there is no rigid legislation governing cinematograph displays, or where non-inflammable films are used; but in Great Britain the film must be wound upon a spool enclosed in a metallic case, to provide protection against fire. The best spool boxes are lined with asbestos, which ensures a greater degree of safety.

From the spool the film is threaded over a toothed sprocket, which engages with the perforations, and also under a spring grip roller which keeps the film in contact with the sprocket. A loop is then formed, and from this the film passes into the gate behind the lens. This gate consists, as in the camera, of two pieces, one rigid, the other swinging and hinged to the first, so that it may be opened to enable the film to be introduced. When closed, the film is held flat and rigid. As the shutter passes across the field of the lens, cutting the picture off the sheet, the film is given a sharp jerk downwards to bring the next picture into exactly the same position in the gate before the lens as that occupied by the preceding image. The descending film passes round a second toothed sprocket, with its grip roller, and thence into the second spool box, where it is coiled upon the bobbin. The machine is operated either by hand or by power and belting passing over a pulley.

I have described the broad principle upon which the projector operates; the details of the mechanism vary according to the ideas of various makers. There are several excellent projecting mechanisms on the market, each possessing departures in detail, to some of which reference is made later.

The great difficulty was to impart intermittent motion

to the mechanism which feeds the film to the lens at regular intervals from a continuous rotary drive, the handle being revolved at uniform speed. It occurred to Paul, who was the first man in England to attack the problem scientifically, that it might be feasible to employ the type of intermittent gear used in watches, known as the Geneva stop. He decided to adopt this mechanism.

The driving wheel when it completes a revolution falls into a notch of the driven wheel, and in continuing its rotary movement moves the latter forward the extent of one notch, but no more, owing to the convex space between each notch, or concave rim of each tooth, which coincides with the curve of the driving wheel and fits closely against its circumference. When the driving wheel makes its second revolution it engages with the second notch, and so on, with the result that in this case the driving wheel makes seven revolutions to one of the driven wheel. Each notch coincides with a picture; that is to say, each time the driving wheel forces the second wheel forward one notch, a picture on the film is brought before the lens for projection.

This novel gear gave the desired result, but it underwent considerable modification, the number of teeth in the driven wheel being ultimately reduced to four. The driving wheel was also altered. Instead of being notched as in the Geneva stop movement, it was fitted with a pin, which, when the wheel made a complete revolution, fell into one of the deep notches in the driven wheel, and so moved it forward. By this modification the gearing was reduced to 4 to 1; the driving wheel made four revolutions to one of the driven wheel, and each notch of the latter corresponded to a picture. Owing to the fact that the notches in this driven wheel resemble a Maltese cross in form, the device became known as the "Maltese Cross" movement. It is in use to-day. The notched Maltese cross wheel is attached to the spindle of the sprocket wheel below the lens, and the movement forward of one notch suffices to jerk the film down smartly three-quarters of an inch or the depth of one picture.

The advantage of this movement is that the film is pulled

down very quickly, and as a result the flicker is reduced to a negligible quantity. The gear is noiseless and enables a very steady picture to be obtained upon the screen. On the other hand, not being a true mechanical movement, the forward motion of the film is accompanied by a certain degree of shock, which not only imposes a strain upon the fragile film, but at the same time sets up great wear and tear in the mechanism itself.

For these reasons another system of bringing the film into place was evolved. A wheel having an eccentric movement is introduced below the film gate. This wheel carries a projecting roller, and with each revolution the roller strikes the film which passes over the wheel, and pulls it down the depth of a picture. This type of action is known as the "dog" movement, and is incorporated in a variety of ways for the purpose of facilitating the smooth and regular movement of the film through the gate. Its disadvantages are that it is noisy; and secondly, that it is almost impossible to secure a steady picture upon the screen, as the dog strikes the film so smartly as to set up a vibration which is communicated to the picture in the gate. But it is simpler than the "Maltese cross" movement, while the wear and tear upon the mechanism itself is so slight as to be almost non-existent.

These two movements have divided the cinematograph world into two camps, one adhering to the "Maltese cross," the other staunch in its support of the "dog" movement. But the former appears to be increasing in favour, despite its acknowledged defects. Some years ago Paul indicated an improvement on it which demands attention because it converts an indifferent mechanical movement into one scientifically correct. The principle is shown in Fig. 10. Instead of having four notches or slots in the driven wheel, as in the Maltese cross, he has only three slots. The driving member A has an arm C carrying a roller E at its outer edge. The driving member A when it completes a revolution, enters the slot c in the driven wheel B, and at the moment of entering the slot is at a tangent to the circular path a of E, with the result that the roller E enters the slot without setting up any shock whatever, carries the wheel B round, and leaves the slot at a similar tangent to its path, at the same time bringing the next slot tangent to the path of the roller E on arm A. Thus the film is given increasing speed without the slightest strain, and as the movement enables the images to be changed rapidly without jarring, it is possible to reduce the period of eclipse to almost nothing. For this reason, the opaque sector of the shutter can be cut down to one sixteenth of the area of the

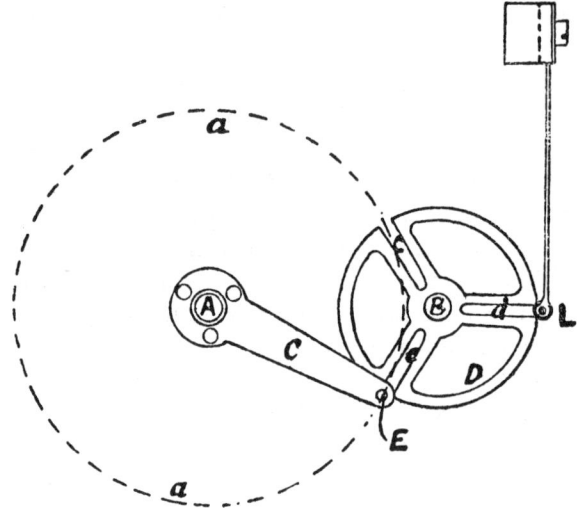

FIG. 10.—PAUL'S IMPROVED "CROSS" DRIVING MECHANISM.

circle described by the shutter. With the other movements the sector of the shutter must cover at least one-quarter of the superficies. In other words, the three-slot wheel cuts down the period of eclipse to less than one-quarter of that possible by any other mechanism, and as the sector only covers one-sixteenth of the circle, the period of light thrown through the film on to the screen is increased, with an accompanying increase of brilliancy and a complete absence of flicker.

The shutter is one of the most important features of the

HOW PICTURES ARE SHOWN

projector. In the majority of cases it is placed before the lens, but in the Gaumont "chrono" machine it is placed between the condenser and the picture. In order to secure the best results, the area of the opaque surface covering the lens while the next picture is brought into position should be reduced to the minimum, and the eclipsing action should be so carried out as to reduce the flicker, which is directly due to the cutting off of one picture to enable the next to be brought into position. In the early days the shutter had one blade only; when a brilliant light was used, the alternate periods of light and darkness could be easily distinguished, and the eyes suffered accordingly. An effort to remedy this disastrous effect was made by the introduction of a violet-coloured sector of similar area to the opaque sector, and set opposite to the latter, which gave the shutter the appearance of a two-bladed propeller. This is effective to a certain degree; but it has been superseded by a shutter having three blades. The shutter is mounted upon a spindle in front of the lens, the distance therefrom being determined by the focus of the objective.

The heat concentrated upon the film by the converging rays of light from the condenser is tremendous. The effect is identical with that produced by focussing the sun's rays with a lens upon a piece of paper. If the rays are permitted to play upon one part of the celluloid film for four or five seconds it will become ignited. So long as the film is moving little apprehension need be entertained; the danger arises when the film is stopped to attempt focussing with a stationary picture, or the film breaks during projection and stops in the gate. Several disastrous catastrophes have arisen from the firing of the film during projection. It is impossible to lay too great a stress upon the danger, for the average operator is little more than a cog in the machine, and fails to concentrate attention upon the work in hand so as to anticipate and meet emergencies.

Manufacturers have tried to remove the danger by the evolution of what is known as an automatic safety cut-off. This is a second shutter, which, when the projector is at rest, drops between the light and the lens. The shutter is connected to the balls of a governor. As the revolving speed of the governor is increased by the turning of the driving handle, the balls assume a horizontal circle of rotation, and in so doing, lift the shutter until it rises clear of the aperture in the gate, through which the light strikes the picture. In the same way, as the revolving speed of the governor is decreased, the balls fall and the shutter descends.

The introduction of this automatic cut-off is somewhat to be deplored. It makes the operator less careful; he trusts blindly to his automatic friend, which, though it functions admirably, is, like all such mechanisms, liable to fail at a critical moment. When such a breakdown does occur, the average operator is invariably caught napping, and the film is fired before he realises what has happened. The older system, whereby the cut-off, a shutter working upon a hinged flap principle, had to be operated manually, was far safer. Its opening or closing constituted a part of the cycle of operations in the preparations for projection, thus calling for a definite movement on the part of the operator.

The most efficient safety appliance yet associated with the projector itself is the Urban-Joy-Harris anti-firing device, Fig. 11, a very simple arrangement, whereby the rising and falling gate is converted, to all intents and purposes, into a fire-proof box. When the film is threaded through the gate, only that part before the lens, upon which the light rays are converged, is exposed to the air on the side nearest the light. On the opposite side the exposure hole is contained in a tube, holding the lens, which consequently forms an air-tight chamber upon that side. Should the film catch fire while stationary in the gate, the air contained in the lens chamber A becomes heated suddenly, and expands, so that the products of combustion are discharged through the exposure hole of H into the air. The fire cannot creep up and down the film, as small bars exactly above and below the exposure hole successfully prevent such action.

In addition there is the Harris safety shutter, which in the event of the film breaking below the gate, and thus preventing its own passage owing to the interruption in the driving effort, shuts off the light from the film, and also stops the electric motor, should the machine be driven by electricity. This safety-shutter B holds a semi-circular flap D, which is connected by a small lever to a rectangular

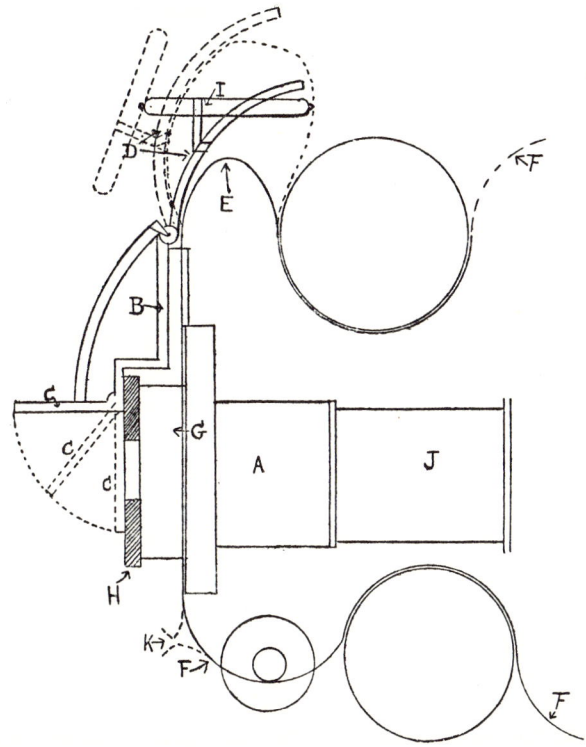

FIG. 11—THE URBAN-JOY-HARRIS ANTI-FIRING DEVICE. THE DOTTED LINES SHOW ACTION OF MECHANISM CLOSING SHUTTER C WHEN FILM F BREAKS AT K.

flap C. The flap D is so adjusted as to hang over the loop in the film E between the sprocket and the entrance to the film gate. Under normal conditions the loop E does not come into contact with the shutter D, but when the film F becomes broken below at K, the loop E is enlarged suddenly owing to the film not being able to pass through the gate, with the result that it forces the flap D to a vertical

H

position, and this in turn throws the flap C down over the exposure hole. There is a tube I which contains about half-an-ounce of mercury with an electrical contact at either end, the object of which is to change the centre of gravity of the flap D, and also to cut off the supply of electric energy to the motor. When the machine is running smoothly this tube I is in a horizontal position making the electrical connection at either end, but when the flap D rises, owing to the enlargement of the loop E in the film, the weight of mercury is thrown to one end of the tube, causing it to cant in such a way as to retain the flap D in a vertical position. If the film should take fire, only the picture before the lens is consumed. Even the perforated edges remain untouched, so that the film is not severed, and can continue its travel through the machine when the breakdown is repaired.

To supply the light necessary to projection, acetylene, the oxy-hydrogen limelight, and the electric arc have all been used; but the last is the illuminant most generally favoured. It enables the maximum amount of light to be collected by the condenser. When the projection of moving pictures was first attempted an arc light was unavailable, because that form of lighting had not been adapted to the magic lantern. The late T. C. Hepworth, the eminent authority on the lantern, was wrestling with the problem, but there was no commercial apparatus suited to the cinematograph. In using electric light a resistance is required to absorb or dissipate in the form of heat the current over and above that required for the light. Many types of resistances have been devised for this purpose, to suit varying requirements. This method of dealing with the surplus current is, however, distinctly wasteful, and accordingly, where picture projection is being carried out on a large scale, a motor generator is adopted. The current derived from the supply main is utilised to drive an electric motor, which in turn actuates a dynamo, whereby current is furnished for the light. This seems a roundabout process, but it effects a great economy in the consumption of electricity.

The mounting for the lantern is also important. As there is continual movement in the mechanism owing to the communication of driving effort, either by hand or by power, the mounting chosen must be of a sufficiently massive character to absorb all the vibration set up. Paul devised an iron pillar, to one side of the top of which the lantern was fixed, while the projector was attached to the other. The principle was similar to that used for the mounting of a machine gun, and although the idea met with considerable criticism, yet Paul succeeded in producing steadier pictures than were possible with other forms of mounting. That his idea was sound is witnessed to-day, for the principle he advocated has been resuscitated in the Brockliss Motiograph, which is mounted on a rigid pillar, and undoubtedly throws a steadier picture than is possible from any other system of supporting the projector.

In the majority of projecting mechanisms a second lens is mounted upon the frame, in line with and beside the cinematograph objective. This second lens is used for the projection of lantern slides for the illustration of a song, title announcement, or other purposes. In order to bring the light of the lamp into line with this second lens the lantern is moved bodily sideways the requisite distance; the projector itself is not touched—it remains a rigid fixture.

Paul also adopted a driving system which might be revived profitably to-day where manual operation is practised. Instead of the small handle placed somewhat high, calling for quick rotation and fatiguing wrist movement, he used a large wheel mounted at such a height that the operator, when standing beside, had the lowest travel of the handle almost at arm's length. The wheel being of large diameter, a slow, steady revolution was sufficient, which caused no fatigue, the drive being transmitted through a pulley or chain to the projector. In many of the latest picture palaces, however, the apparatus is driven by an electric motor, which yields a more uniform speed and conduces to steadier projection.

I will now take up the distinctive features of some of the

best known makes of projector. A comparison of the latest Edison model, the "B Underwriter," with the first kinetoscope, affords a striking illustration of the advance of cinematography in twenty years. The new machine is constructed throughout of metal, is wonderfully compact, and the mechanism has been reduced to the acme of simplicity. All moving parts subject to heavy wear and tear are made of lignum vitæ. The shutter is of the three-bladed type, while the intermittent action is conveyed by the Maltese Cross movement. Being rigidly mounted upon a heavy stand, the picture projected is very steady and free from all disconcerting lateral and vertical movement.

In the "Gaumont Chrono" projector, the salient characteristic, as I have mentioned already, is the position of the shutter, which is placed between the film and the condenser. The film-trap is worthy of notice because it conduces very materially to the steadiness of the picture thrown with this machine. The edges of the film are gripped by means of burnished steel runners or vertical clamps, and they secure it in position during exposure with the exact degree of tension required to obtain steadiness, yet without hindering the travel of the film through the gate, or inflicting injury upon the celluloid. The trap is fitted with an asbestos shield, which serves to insulate the film while passing through the trap from the intense rays of the light, which is continually playing upon the metal around the exposure hole.

The dog movement has been adopted in this apparatus, but upon an improved principle. Instead of striking the film one smart blow to jerk it through the gate, it imparts a steady pushing action. The result is that the film does not suffer any injury. A massive dog striking the film heavily is apt to produce cracks across the perforations at the points of impact, which in time become weak spots in the film. This well-conceived machine has met with remarkable popularity among moving picture theatres in this country; it is an excellent example of French engineering skill, wherein lightness is combined with strength and simplicity.

The Ernemann "Imperator" projector commands deserved attention. It is built stoutly so as to last and

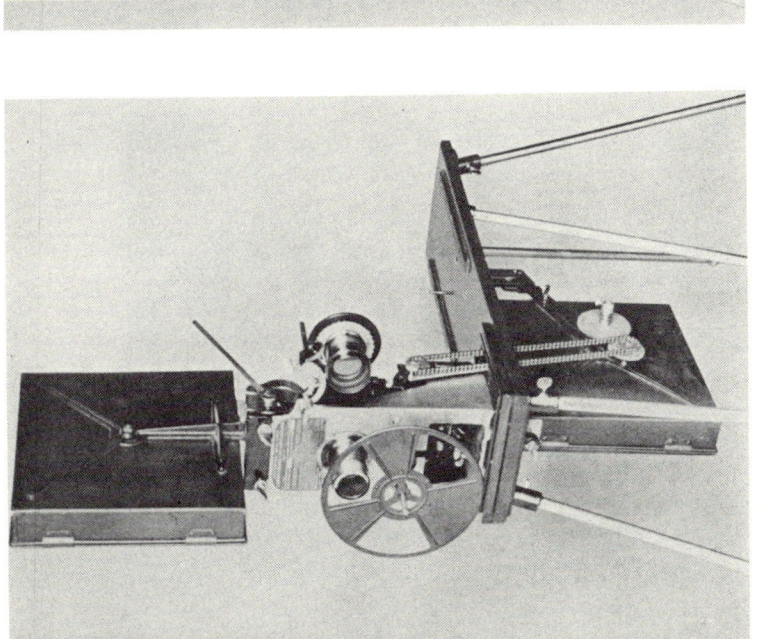

The projector and mechanism. The complete projecting installation.

THE LATEST EDISON DEVELOPMENT IN CINEMATOGRAPHY.

This outfit is in striking contrast to the original "peephole" machine facing page 32.

OUTSTRIPPING THE HUMAN EYE. *See page* 319

The Greene di-optic projector which shows on the sheet what the organ of sight misses during blinking.

THE "CHRONO" PROJECTOR.

The main feature of the Gaumont lantern is the position of the shutter between the film and the light, instead of outside the lens.

withstand rough usage. Steel forms the constructional material throughout, and a noticeable feature is that motion is communicated to all driving parts through heavy gearing. In this machine the "Maltese Cross" movement has been brought to its highest pitch of perfection, being of large substantial construction, and so designed as to obviate the objections to its use. The driven part is made of hardened silver steel, and there are means of taking up all slack arising from wear directly it becomes manifest. Instead of the cross being struck by a pin on the driving wheel, the latter carries a roller which picks up the slotted wheel without jar or noise. The mechanism is kept cool by running in an enclosed oil bath, which tends to reduce the wear and tear to a minimum, while at the same time the machine is light and easy running, a feature which appeals to the operator.

Another machine which possesses many interesting points is the "Silent Knight," its chief claim to attention being, as its name implies, quietness in running, combined with easy operation and steadiness of the pictures projected. It has the fire-proof gate already described, and also aluminium fire-proof spool boxes. The movement is the Maltese Cross. Simplicity has been studied to the last degree, and the necessity to withstand hard wear and tear, as well as rough handling in inexperienced hands, has not been overlooked. All the vital parts are made of chilled steel running in an oil bath, with the necessity for adjustments reduced to the minimum, though capable of being carried out easily when the necessity arrives.

The foregoing by no means exhausts the variety of machines on the market. There is the Pathé machine, a masterpiece of French manufacture; the Kamm projector, the "Empire," remarkable for its many ingenious devices to secure protection against fire, the chief of which is a contrivance whereby the light is cut off automatically in the event of the film breaking, although the machine is still running, and so on. In every instance the direct aim is the evolution of a projector which will produce an absolutely steady picture, free from flickering and fluttering, and as noiseless in operation as human skill can contrive. In this particular field England and the Continent are ahead of the United States manufacturers. Except in one or two instances the American product is distinctly inferior. It looks attractive, but its results fail to stand comparison with the British and French machines. The projecting features of the moving picture industry in the United States have not advanced to the high state of excellency attained in Europe.

In projecting, the pictures have to be thrown upon the screen at the same speed as that at which they were taken by the camera, that is, if steady continuous motion is to be secured. The average speed is, as I have said, about sixteen pictures per second, and it is essential that the handle should be rotated at a regular uniform pace. Outside influences appear to exercise a distinct effect upon this manual action, just as we have seen them do in the process of taking the original picture. The musical accompaniment is likely to induce the inexperienced operator inadvertently to accelerate or retard the speed of projection. For this reason, power driving is coming more and more into use, the motion being communicated to the mechanism by means of a small electric motor. The results are far superior to those produced by the average operator, though not comparable to projection by a practised and intelligent hand. The latter can tell the approximate speed at which the pictures were taken, and can adjust his speed to a far greater nicety than is possible by a mechanical agency which maintains a constant speed.

CHAPTER X

THE STUDIO FOR STAGING MOVING PICTURE PLAYS

When the cinematograph made its bow to the public the latter were satisfied with the reproduction in animation of scenes and incidents associated with every-day life—rather trivial unrehearsed incidents which were void of newspaper interest. There was the shoeblack at work, the firing of a big gun, athletes at practice, and so on. Humour was presented in Mammy washing her young hopeful, a great favourite for many years, likewise in a set of films depicting a mischievous youth indulging in pranks with the garden hose.

But the popular taste changed in the course of time. The audience became fastidious, and demanded novelty. There was a clamour for picture-plays. The man in the street saw no reason why dramas, tragedies, comedies and farces should not be reproduced in pantomime upon the screen. This popular demand was by no means easy to meet. Obviously plays could not be photographed upon the ordinary stage in the theatre owing to difficulties of lighting. Special arrangements would entail a certain outlay, to be entered upon without knowing whether the results would justify the expense incurred. A further complication lay in the attitude of the showmen themselves. They wanted plays, but not with actors and actresses, or "anything theatrical"; and they protested against the incursion of the "legitimate" into their field.

Robert Paul decided to test the public taste with a little comedy which he called "The Soldier's Courtship." The roof of the Alhambra Theatre, in Leicester Square, was extemporised as a stage, and Mr. Moul, the manager, who had realised the possibilities of the cinematograph, acted as stage manager. Scenery and properties were brought up from the theatre below, and the assistance of one or two actresses and actors were enlisted. With much difficulty a film measuring 40 feet in length was obtained —the standard length of the time, though it appears insignificant in comparison with the films of to-day, which vary between 500 and 3,000 feet in length. In 640 consecutive pictures a pretty little "tabloid" comedy was expressed.

Some apprehension was entertained as to the reception the effort would receive. However, all doubts and anxieties melted instantaneously when the picture was shown for the first time. The audience gave it a hearty welcome, and a new era dawned in the history of cinematography. This initial effort—the first animated "picture play" produced in Great Britain—tempted Paul to more ambitious undertakings.

A plot of land was acquired at New Southgate in North London, and here the first building was erected designed essentially for the staging of picture plays. It was a combination of a theatre with an ordinary photographic studio utilised for portraiture, in a commodious lofty hall, with a proscenium opening measuring 18 feet in width by 13 feet in height. The stage level was about 8 feet above the ground, the under part being available for working effects from below, such as bridges, stage traps, and other artifices of the playhouse. The front wall, which faced the northern sky, was divided vertically so as to permit the sections to be opened out on either side to any required extent to reveal the interior. The front roof, set at a sharp angle was glazed to give top light.

A special platform, running on a wheeled carriage and track, the deck of which was level with the floor of the stage, was laid opposite and at right angles to the proscenium opening, to accommodate the camera and operator. Looking into the studio from this point, one saw a familiar theatre stage, with wings, flies, and other facilities. Such

AN EARLY OPEN-AIR STUDIO STAGE FOR PRODUCING CINEMATOGRAPH PLAYS. [*By courtesy, "The Scientific American."*]

It was on the flat roof of a building in New York City. The camera and operator were accommodated in the small hut. The whole revolved on a massive iron turn-table so that the stage faced the sun throughout the day.

THE SCENE-PAINTERS' SHOP AT A PATHÉ STUDIO.

The back-cloths and flats of canvas are stretched like carpets upon the floor for the artists.—*See page* 109.

STAGING MOVING PICTURE PLAYS

was the earliest venture in what is now one of the most important branches in the cinematographic industry. Upon that stage Paul himself produced several hundred plays of infinite variety, comedy, tragedy, melodrama, farce, and magic.

In the United States a crude attempt in the same direction was made by Thomas A. Edison in order to produce films for his kinetoscope. His building was unpretentious in the fullest sense of the word.

It was of the flimsiest character, with a movable top, and covered externally with roofing material. It became known colloquially as the "Black Maria," a singularly appropriate name. A notable feature was its central mounting upon a pivot, and a circular track for wheels placed under the extreme edges of the building. The structure could thus be rotated in either direction like a turn-table, according to the position of the sun, so that the studio could be used at any time of the day. As the kinetoscope failed to arouse public enthusiasm, work in the studio was abandoned, until Edison, who had seen the tendency towards projecting pictures upon an enlarged scale before audiences, was able to perfect his projector.

At about the same time another American firm commenced work in the same field—the American Mutoscope Company. Their studio was open-air in the fullest sense of the word; the stage was the roof of their own building in New York City. A heavy network of steel beams was laid down, upon which the stage was erected. Opposite was a small hut built of corrugated iron, which housed the camera, its accessories, and operator. The stage could be swung round upon its track so that the bright sunlight fell squarely upon the scene, and similarly the camera house could be moved over its wheeled track to assume the desired position for taking the pictures.

American enterprise, however, grew dissatisfied with the short lengths of the picture films then produced. Certain interests in New York resolved upon a masterstroke. They cherished the idea of preparing something staggering in its sensationalism: the production of a gigantic film upon some striking subject which should startle the cinematographic world, and completely eclipse all previous efforts in the field. They succeeded to an extent which surpassed their own most sanguine anticipations.

After prolonged discussion it was decided that the "Passion Play" would prove a powerful magnet with the public. But where was the man to be found sufficiently daring to attempt to carry out the project? With the crude facilities available at that time the task was one not lightly to be undertaken. The New York interests approached Mr. Richard G. Hollaman, the President of the Eden Musée, who had been intimately identified with the popularisation of moving pictures ever since the days of the kinetoscope.

Mr. Hollaman was somewhat startled by the proposals, and at first considered the task entirely out of his province, and quite beyond him. However, he deliberated upon the suggestion, and at length consented to undertake the work. He secured the assistance of Mr. John Vincent as stage manager, and Mr. Albert Eaves as costumier. No expense was to be spared in its mounting—it was to be the most gorgeous production of the day. The Salmi Morse version of the "Passion Play" was prepared especially for the cinematograph, and the company was enrolled.

The next obstacle was in getting the play staged. No studio-theatre existed in America at that time, and the open air roof-stages were far from being suited to the work even if they had been available. As a result the producers had to make their own arrangements. The roof of the Grand Central Palace in New York was selected, and in the middle of November, 1897, rehearsals commenced. Several weeks were devoted to the preparation, and no less than \$16,000 (£3,200) were spent upon the preliminaries. The film ran to three reels, or about 3,000 feet, and some 48,000 separate pictures. It was the first three-reel film subject ever produced in the United States, if not in the world.

The first exhibition took place at the Eden Musée, and

required about 55 minutes to project. It created a tremendous sensation. Some idea of its popularity may be gathered from the fact that it ran continuously for six months. Copies of the film were printed off and sold broadcast throughout the United States, the success of the New York display ensuring it a warm reception wherever it was exhibited. Few films have created such enthusiasm as did the "Passion Play," and it has never lost its popularity. As Mr. Hollaman was not associated with the film-manufacturing side of the industry, he accepted the first offer he received for the negative. Thus the "Passion Play" passed into the hands of Edison, who starred the production in his catalogue of films for a considerable period.

Meantime the movement went on in Great Britain. Shortly after Paul brought his studio stage into full swing, a second establishment came into existence at Hove, on the Sussex coast. The promoter of this enterprise was Mr. James A. Williamson, who, as the founder of the Hove Camera Club, had been introduced to the cinematograph in his official duties. He became fascinated with the work, and procured a projector, but at first confined his efforts to showing moving pictures for the edification and enlightenment of his interested club-fellows. Then he decided to participate in the taking of the pictures. The camera at that time, however, was so expensive that he resorted to an ingenious expedient. He took the lantern projector, which is similar in its design and operation to the camera mechanism, and fitted this into a light-tight box carrying the spools for the unexposed and exposed films. With this apparatus he secured many interesting albeit conventional subjects, with which the public was content at that time.

Meanwhile, Mr. Esmè Collings, the well-known portrait photographer, had entered into partnership with W. F. Greene, who produced the first model of a cinematographic or chronophotographic apparatus, as it was called. With his camera Mr. Collings secured an excellent varied series of pictures. But after a time he lost interest in cinematography, when his stock of films was acquired by Mr. Williamson. The latter now decided to enter the stage-picture film field, and a commodious and well-equipped studio was erected on the outskirts of Hove. His films, owing to their high technical or photographic qualities, attracted widespread attention, especially in America. In fact, the United States constituted his most valuable market, the Williamson productions being in great demand. Several of his pictures, as well as those of Paul, created a sensation, and these two producers practically controlled the play-picture film market of the world for many years. The period between 1896 and 1900 was most critical in the cinematograph industry, and it was due mainly to the perseverance of the two pioneers that it became firmly established. Lovers of moving pictures to-day realise little of the innumerable difficulties which confronted Paul and Williamson, and the puzzling obstacles which they had to break down. They were dependent upon their own resources and ingenuity, and had to learn by their own mistakes instead of by the example of others. They had to be photographic artists, scene painters, stage carpenters, and stage managers.

Both Paul and Williamson have now retired from the play-picture producing business, the first-named to revert entirely to his original occupation, and the second to the mechanical side of the industry, the manufacture of perforators, printing machines, and so forth. His studio was acquired for the production of Kinemacolor films, and is in active use to-day during the summer months of the year for the production of plays in natural colours.

Paul and Williamson led the way in the manufacturing of picture films, and for a time controlled the market. They were followed by several others, until about half-a-dozen studio-theatres were scattered over the country. The scope of their work was somewhat limited, yet their products commanded a wide sale. They dominated the American market; Williamson alone furnished some 60 or 80 films a week for the cinematograph theatres of the United States, and he was patronised also by the German

BATTLE SCENE FROM "THE SIEGE OF CALAIS."

This film, produced by Pathé Frères, is the most ambitious ever attempted, 2,500 men and horses taking part therein.

EXTERIOR OF THE MODERN EDISON FILM-PLAY-PRODUCING THEATRE.

This structure contrasts with the "Black Maria." It is a lofty glass building, 100 feet long by 60 feet wide and 45 feet high, and cost £20,000.—*See page* 112.

BUILDING A SOLID SET FOR "THE TWO ORPHANS."

This scene, on one of the Selig open-air stages, shows the care and expense taken to mount a modern film-play.—*See page* 112.

public. Unfortunately, however, the industry in Great Britain did not develop so promisingly as these early achievements augured. The British producer does not appear to be able to gain the confidence of the capitalist; he is still as ambitious and as capable as ever, as witness the production of Tennyson's "Maud," but he is handicapped on every side. He finds it increasingly difficult to compete with his foreign rivals. To-day there are only two fields in which he reigns supreme—popular drama and comedy; and this slight modicum of success is due rather to the fact that the British public is somewhat insular in its tastes; it does not understand foreign humour, and will not tolerate foreign tragedy.

About six years ago the cinematograph play underwent a great change. Up to that time the productions were somewhat conventional both in plot and mounting. The scenery was commonplace, and the *dramatis personæ*, as a rule, comprised only about half-a-dozen persons. Moreover, the pictures betrayed a sad deficiency in stage technique, a result due entirely to the fact that the producers were not conversant with stage-craft.

The French producers saw a unique opportunity, and grasped it promptly. Foremost in the movement was the firm of Pathé Frères, which is to-day one of the largest and most enterprising film-producing establishments in the world. They launched out upon the most elaborate lines. Huge stages or studios, with the latest appliances, which from the technical point of view would rival the famous Drury Lane stage, were constructed at immense cost, eminent stage managers, versed in every phase of the technique of production, were obtained from the theatres, while the services of the foremost French actors and actresses were secured. The scenery was prepared upon an extensive scale, the mounting was lavish, and plays which hitherto had been considered beyond the scope of the picture-producer were taken in hand boldly. If the British producers introduced the stage-play to the cinematograph film, the French certainly perfected the idea, and set the elaborate production upon its feet. Some of the plays which the French producers have filmed are extremely bold in their conception, as well as being wonders of stage-craft, scenery, and photography. At the present moment the Pathé firm has no less than eight stage managers engaged in the production of picture plays of every description; the Gaumont establishment, which is pressing the Pathé hard for first rank, has six producers, while several other firms in the same country have elaborate organisations. Gorgeousness of production is the predominant key-note, associated with acting excellence; and the policy has been attended with merited success.

The triumph of the British and subsequently of the French film producers reached the United States. Like a huge wave the European films overwhelmed the country. In comparison, the American productions were trash. The native firms were confronted with extinction unless they made a bold and united stand, which was hardly to be expected, for at that time the American cinematograph world was in a state of chaos. Litigation was raging on all sides. Edison was engaged in a deadly struggle to maintain his position according to his original, or kinetoscope, patent. As a result of the turmoil, the industry became unsettled, and the money which should have been expended in the furtherance of the craft, simply went to fill the pockets of hungry lawyers. Edison triumphed at last; his claim was sustained by the Supreme Court. The establishment of this contested point cleared the air, and one outcome was the formation of a Cinematograph Trust or community of interests to resist foreign invasion. Several firms enlisted under the banner of the Edison patent—other interests which still disputed his claim combined to form a second trust.

The first move of the combination was to eliminate the foreign competition from which it was suffering so disastrously. Special terms were drawn up which European firms were compelled to observe under threat of their films being forbidden to the country. The European producers, foreseeing the loss of a valuable market, tried desperately to mitigate this drastic policy, but in vain. The American terms were: either limited sale, as stipulated by the trust, or else complete boycott. The British producers saw their most remunerative market eliminated at a stroke. Williamson suffered particularly from the decision, for all standing contracts were cancelled. As he never had made strenuous attempts to cultivate the British market, which was open to producers in all parts of the world without the slightest restraint, but had concentrated his efforts upon pleasing his United States clients, he concluded that retirement from play production was the wisest course, especially as the mechanical side of the industry was so full of attractive promise.

The American producers, entrenched firmly behind the wall of protection, set to work energetically to make up for lost time. The story of the automobile industry, which was similarly hindered in its infancy by patent wars, was repeated. The Americans imitated the French example and embarked upon the most elaborate enterprises. Keen rivalry was displayed between the various concerns to acquire the best managers of the legitimate stage, with the result that the theatre suffered heavily. Several stage managers, seeing the trend of events, and realising that cinematographic picture plays possessed a tremendous future, abandoned their old field and gave their energies to the new one, which offered such great scope for their abilities.

The American stage, like that of Great Britain, France, Germany, and Italy, had regarded the picture play with disdain, and had ridiculed the possibility of its ever becoming a spirited competitor to their particular interests. To-day the American stage is engaged in a struggle for supremacy with the moving-picture theatre. The American picture producers erected huge studio-theatres, with every convenience, capable of producing any type of play demanded, and giving the author greater opportunity for effect than ever the legitimate stage could hope to offer.

It is difficult to realise the proportions which these

American studio-stages have attained, or the work they can carry out. Take the Edison Company for instance. We have seen the humble little "Black Maria" which sufficed to supply the film needs of the Kinetoscope in 1892. The present Edison studio, which cost something like $100,000 (£20,000) to build, is a huge glass building measuring 100 feet in length, by 60 feet in width, and has a height of 45 feet. The stage has a proscenium opening of 30 feet and an area of 2,400 feet. In addition there is a huge water-tank with a capacity of 130,000 gallons, which is used for aquatic spectacles.

The Edison establishment is but one of many. In Brooklyn the Vitagraph Company has a huge building, the Lubin films are produced in spacious studios in Philadelphia, while Chicago boasts the famous Essanay and Selig plants. The latter is especially noteworthy owing to its great size and the remarkable plays which it produces for the delight of moving-picture lovers in all parts of the world. It is devoted exclusively to making films, and finds employment for 400 hands. The main studio, in which are two stages, measures 179 feet in length by 80 feet wide. In addition to this indoor establishment, there are between two and three acres of surrounding land which have been enclosed for outdoor work. This field, if such it may be called, presents a strange sight. It is dotted with little groups of scenery. Here is a mediæval castle with ruined battlements; a few yards away to the right is a modern street; while on the left is the interior of a stately drawing-room. In one corner are a number of artificial hills fashioned by the dumping of earth, criss-crossed with paths and trails. It is an incongruous medley of periods and scenes, but one and all little assemblages of back-cloths and wings represent a stage, and one and all face the southern sun. Upon these little stages the plays are produced.

The Selig organisation is one of the largest in the United States, having, in addition to the Chicago establishment, another theatre at Los Angeles on the Pacific coast, devoted to the portrayal of pictures having a western

BUILDING A SCENE ON ONE OF THE PATHÉ STUDIO-STAGES FOR A FILM PLAY.

The stage is fitted with every possible device, such as overhead bridges, to facilitate the moving and setting of scenery as well as for the working of effects.

THE WARDROBE ROOM AT THE SELIG FILM FACTORY.
Over 7,000 costumes of all descriptions are stored ready for instant use.

THE SELIG STOCK COMPANY AT LOS ANGELES.

The remarkable development of the picture-play industry has resulted in the acquisition of leading actors and actresses by the largest producers. High salaries are paid for the exclusive services of eminent artistes.

setting. There is the Pacific Ocean on one side to form a background for marine incidents; the Sierras, frowning down upon the coast, provide a natural background for subjects set among the mountains; while within easy reach is the vast stretch of Nevada desert, where the atmosphere of the Sahara of Africa, or the great wastes of Australia, can be reproduced. The Chicago studio is provided with an artificial pool of 60,000 gallons, where a lake, lagoon, or swamp environment to a picture can be secured.

The modern cinematograph studio-stage is far more elaborately equipped for the production of effects than its counterpart behind the footlights, while the attendant plant is overwhelmingly extensive. The stage of Drury Lane Theatre in London and of the Opera House at Paris respectively are considered marvellous homes of stage-craft, and regarded as models of equipment. But compared with the great French, Italian, or American cinematograph studio-stages, they are insignificant. Large, well-lighted and spacious rooms are set apart for the stage carpenters and the scene painters to prepare the back-cloths, wings, and flats. This work alone, owing to the high pressure at which production is maintained, affords employment to a large staff. As the average output is three films per week—the Edison establishment produces four or five subjects in that time—the scene painters are kept busily engaged from morning to night. All scenery has to be painted in black and white, and the excellence of the work plays an important part in the effect of the picture, for the camera is ruthless in its exposure of indifferent work. The scene may be the interior of a shack, or a sylvan valley with a river winding like a ribbon of silver among the trees and a stately castle rearing above the foliage. In each instance the same artistic care is demanded, for it must be remembered that by the time the picture reaches the screen it is of the same dimensions as the original, or even larger.

As the picture-play producer roams through all the periods of history in all countries, a large stock of properties and an extensive wardrobe must be maintained.

I

The Selig establishment in Chicago has a wardrobe in which are carefully packed and labelled ready for instant use no fewer than 7,000 costumes, of all countries and peoples scattered between the Arctic and Antarctic circles, and ranging from prehistoric times through the picturesque middle ages to the prosaic twentieth century.

From morning to night the studio-stage echoes the ring of hammers and the shouts of the stage carpenters as they set this scene or strike that. Frowning masonry castles are pulled down, and suburban villas rise up with greater speed than their jerry-built prototypes in bricks and mortar. The numerous dressing rooms are busy hives, where actors and actresses change swiftly from one costume, age, and clime to another, separated from it by centuries.

When the play is cinematographed indoors, a battery of powerful electric lights is placed overhead in front of the stage, corresponding to theatrical top-lights, and throwing a powerful glare upon the scene. They are controlled by switches, so that the light can be concentrated as desired. When the lights are in full blast, more than 80,000 candle-power may be thrown upon the stage. In addition, other lights are disposed for the purpose of producing different effects, so that upon a large studio-stage a body of well-trained electricians is indispensable.

The scene itself occupies but a small space, generally about 12 or 16 feet in width. As a rule the camera is brought within a few feet of the picture, in order that the actors may be photographed as large as possible. On the floor on either side battens are laid to indicate the limits within which actors and actresses must move. Beyond these confines is to vanish from the scene, and the stage manager may be heard over the whirr of the camera shouting peremptorily to one or other of the company to keep in the picture.

The large producer thinks expense is a secondary consideration in the preparation of plays. A simple conventional modern comedy costs about £50 ($250), while a gorgeous production runs well into £6,000 ($30,000). On the average, about 150,000 feet of film are placed on the British market every week, and this quantity is steadily increasing. It is computed that there are some 50,000 picture theatres scattered throughout the world, and as the number thereof is increasing daily the supply of films has by no means yet reached the limits of demand.

CHAPTER XI

THE CINEMATOGRAPH AS A RECORDER OF TOPICAL EVENTS: SCENIC FILMS.

IN spite of the fact that the programme of the average picture palace of to-day is chiefly occupied with film plays, nevertheless the greatest attraction is undoubtedly the "topical picture." British audiences were first introduced to its possibilities by seeing the 1896 Derby re-run before their eyes on the screen in the Alhambra Theatre, creating a tremendous sensation. In fact, the reproduction of this classic British horse-race upon the white sheet twenty-four hours after it was run excited more attention than the actual race itself. In those days cinematography was unfamiliar to the general public, and those who followed the race upon the screen could not resist rubbing their eyes in amazement: it seemed scarcely credible. Certainly, very few items of sensational interest have ever created such a deep impression and brought such heavy receipts to the box-office of this famous vaudeville house as the first Derby film.

The manner in which the film was obtained was typical of Paul's quiet, unassuming methods. His "animatograph" had become established firmly at the Alhambra, and he was always on the alert to secure new and striking subjects. When he decided to attempt the representation of the classic race, he told no one, and sought no favours to obtain commanding positions from which to photograph the contest. On the morning of the race he appeared at Epsom. He chartered a wagonette, upon the seats of which he intended to set up his tripod and camera. He hoped to be able to secure a good position unobserved, but he came near to having his plans upset.

When he arrived on the course, one of the itinerant booth-holders, a pugnacious, gipsy-like individual, thought the vehicle was some form of rival side-show and barred its progress. An altercation ensued, but Paul drove on with the enraged gipsy in pursuit. The latter, seeing that his irate remonstrances were of no avail, threatened to take the law into his own hands and to upset the offending vehicle and its strange contents. Paul thwarted this contingency by tying the wheels of his vehicle firmly to the rails, alongside of which he had taken up his position, and the film was secured without further untoward developments.

From the night on which the Derby was run at the Alhambra, the success of the topical film has been established. Scarcely an item of absorbing public interest escapes being recorded. Probably no topical film has created such enthusiasm as that which Paul secured of the "Prince's Derby" when the late King Edward VII., as Prince of Wales, carried off the blue riband of the British turf. The Alhambra Theatre was converted into a reproduction of the famous course, for the entire audience cheered the moving pictures with as much gusto as if they were following the actual struggle on Epsom Downs, and would not desist until the film had been passed across the screen three times. Paul cinematographed the Derby on no less than six consecutive occasions, and there is probably no established British annual event which he has not recorded.

In the early days, as Paul was practically in full possession of the topical film field, there was an entire absence of that haste of competition. Then it was immaterial whether the film were shown one or two days after the event. The many processes which had to be carried out between the securing of the negative and the production of the positive print for the projector were not hurried, and in fact could not be accelerated very well, if good results were desired. But as other firms appeared on the scene, keen rivalry sprang up. The various establishments left no stone unturned to be first in projection, and the theatres, of course, encouraged the enterprise. Consequently the race against time and rivals became more and more bitterly contested.

As a natural result, great improvements were made in the developing, drying, and printing operations. Whereas twenty-four hours or so had been required to produce a positive ready for use, it now became possible to reduce the time of preparation to about eight hours. To-day a subject can be thrown upon the screen four hours after it has occurred. The topical film appears while the subject to which it refers is still absorbing public interest; and accordingly meets with overwhelming success. The men armed with the camera have the same zeal that animates the reporter bent on securing exclusive information for his paper. No effort or expense is spared to outstrip a rival, as the following incident shows.

An American firm required a film of an event which it thought would be of absorbing interest to the American public. It communicated with its agents in London to "get it, and ahead of anyone else." The outlay was such that the firm could only hope to recoup itself by capturing the entire market for that particular firm. As it happened, only one other firm decided to exploit the same topical subject in the United States. The first firm secured commanding positions for its camera operators, and the films as they arrived were packed and dispatched to New York by special messenger. The competitors failed to show such initiative, and had their films transmitted in the usual manner. Not only did the first firm receive its negatives within the shortest possible space of time, but it found itself in undisputed command of the whole country, for the rival's product went astray in transit! The successful establishment expended £300 ($1,500) in acquiring the negatives, but it proved an excellent investment.

The Americans, however, have not made such a speciality of the topical film as it has become in England, where there are several firms excelling in this particular field of activity. Under energetic management it is one of the most lucrative branches of the industry, success attending those who display the greatest amount of energy and initiative.

The power of the topical picture was demonstrated most

THE FIRST TOPICAL FILM.

The Derby of 1896 cinematographed by Robert W. Paul, and shown the day after the event at the Alhambra Theatre, London.—*See page* 116.

THE WHITE MAN'S CHILD.
Red Indians acted in this production. They delight in performing before the cinematograph camera.

[*By permission Markt & Co. (London), Ltd.*
ARIZONA BILL.
Picture plays dealing with American Indian and frontier life are highly popular. The natural settings heighten the effects of realism.

convincingly by the Coronation festivities of King George V. For some weeks after that event the picture play fell into second position. The Coronation films were in urgent demand on every hand, not only in Great Britain, but in the Colonies as well. Some theatres even found it profitable to give an extended run exclusively to Coronation films and kindred subjects. The most remarkable outcome of the popularity of the Coronation films was the establishment of "Kinemacolor" in the favour of the public. Cinematography in natural colours had not in the earlier stages attracted more than passing interest, and had languished somewhat. But when the royal festivities were reproduced in the full glow and brilliancy of colour, the success of this development of the art became assured.

The Coronation has probably been responsible for more achievements in the work of topical cinematography than any other event. On all sides the keenest competition was displayed among the rival firms. In London, ere the Royal procession left Westminster Abbey after the crowning ceremony, films were being shown of the morning procession to the Abbey; and before the crowds in the evening were gazing upon the illuminated streets, the return journey to Buckingham Palace was being thrown upon the screen of a multitude of theatres throughout the country. Possibly the most remarkable feat was that whereby English residents in Paris and the French nation were enabled to see the ceremony within a few hours of its occurrence. This was an achievement of the English branch of the well-known Gaumont Company, which is probably unexcelled in time-saving ingenuity.

This firm had cameras and operators scattered freely along the route of the Royal procession, and all the films which were secured up to the time of the arrival at Westminster Abbey had been packed and entrusted to a special messenger. The train was due to leave Charing Cross at 2.20 p.m. The clock had barely struck two when the return journey commenced to Buckingham Palace. The operator stationed near the Abbey, in a position to secure one of the best views along the route, was suddenly seized with the idea to set up a new record. A taxi-cab was engaged and held in readiness. At about ten minutes past the hour the procession drew within the field of the camera and the filming commenced. Within about four minutes the coach bearing their Majesties had passed beyond the lens. The film was slipped out of the camera, and the second operator, snatching it up, entered the cab and drove off at full speed to the station. The train was caught in the nick of time, the film was handed over to the special messenger, and before the whole procession had left the precincts of Westminster Abbey, the film bearing the passing of the crowned King and Queen was bound for the French capital, where the pictures were thrown upon the screen late that night.

On the occasion of the investiture of the Prince of Wales at Carnarvon an even more astonishing performance was accomplished by the same firm. A London manager, Mr. Laurrilard, of the Marble Arch Electric Theatre, desired to show the ceremonies on the evening of the day they took place, if that were humanly possible. He approached the Gaumont Company, which decided to make the attempt. A great difficulty was sure to be encountered in dispatching the film, on account of the enormous crowds and the strictness of the traffic regulations; moreover, it was plain that in order to project the film in London the same evening it would have to be developed and prepared on the train. With the greatest difficulty, owing to the abnormally heavy traffic and arrangements already made for a large number of extra trains, the Gaumont firm succeeded in chartering a special train on the London and North-Western Railway. The railway company stipulated that the train must leave Bangor at exactly the time designated by them, in order not to interfere with the departure of trains after the ceremony was over.

Two brake vans (each measuring 50 feet in length) were coupled up and converted into temporary dark-rooms. They were fitted with tanks for developing, fixing, and washing, together with a printing machine and a large drum upon which the films could be dried quickly. A great difficulty was an adequate supply of water for washing the films, 75 gallons at least being required for the purpose. Another quandary was the impossibility of obtaining electric current to use with the printing machine; special lamps had finally to be acquired to enable this task to be carried out. By the time the arrangements were completed over a ton of apparatus had been erected within the two vehicles.

This train was kept under steam at Bangor ready to start at the pre-arranged minute. The distance between Bangor and Carnarvon had to be covered by motor-cars chartered from Chester, 94 miles distant. The police arrangements would not permit these vehicles to approach within one-and-a-half miles of the castle, and the latter stretch had to be covered on foot.

The whole ceremony was recorded by operators posted at convenient points, each of whom had to carry his film-box at top speed to the waiting motor. All worked smoothly. There was some fear lest the final scene in the ceremony would have to be omitted, but by keen judgment and quick work the last operator secured his film and left the scene, the ceremony concluding at 4 p.m. The schedule had been drawn up so accurately that a little delay at any one point would have thrown the whole arrangements to the four winds.

However, the train was caught and punctually to the minute the special drew out. In addition to the cinematograph dark-room on wheels a third dark-room, similarly improvised from a baggage car, was attached for the *Daily Graphic,* in order to enable this paper's photographic correspondents to develop their plates ready for the preparation of the process blocks for the next day's issue. The complete character of the arrangements enabled the developing of the films to proceed without a hitch, despite the fact that the train was making a steady sixty miles an hour. Within two hours the negatives had been developed, washed, and were being dried upon a huge drum. Printing was taken in hand, and a single positive was hurried through its processes. The parts were connected together in proper sequence, and the various titles and subtitles, prepared in both English and Welsh, were duly inserted. By the time the train reached Willesden the film was completed and wound up ready for slipping into the projector. Arriving at Euston seven minutes late, the film was received by a waiting motor-car; and at 10.15 a large audience followed for some twelve minutes a ceremony which had been performed six hours before over 200 miles away. The film was 750 feet in length. As it was the only moving picture record of the Investiture of the Prince of Wales seen in London that night, as may be supposed it created no slight sensation. By working all night the firm made over 100 copies of the subject, varying from 500 to 1,000 feet in length, and by seven o'clock had dispatched them to all parts of the country. Copies were hurried to the Continent, and were seen in the French capital several hours ahead of any rival.

A prize-fight between two famous champions provokes extraordinary energy on the part of the cinematographic artists. Fabulous prices are paid for exclusive rights to photograph the contest, and no expense is spared to secure a continuous record. In order to obtain adequate illumination of the ring, a battery of powerful electric lamps has to be set up, and the glare of tens of thousands of candle-power concentrated upon the combatants. If the battle is short and sharp the results are disappointing both to the cinematographer and his public, but if it be long, requiring several hundred feet of film, he is happy. The prize-fight film, however, is meeting with considerable opposition, which should be welcomed as a healthy sign even by the film-producers themselves. The cinematograph can surely do more elevating, profitable and entertaining work than the recording of a prize-fight. Furthermore, the result has not always paid the speculators concerned, and one or two more heavy losses in the field, combined with popular censorship, will result in the prize-fight being eliminated entirely from the category of "topical" films.

At the present moment the largest film-producing establishments refrain from practising in the "topical" world, as the special requirements necessary to get the films quickly upon the market upsets the arrangements of a well-organised factory, where the day's work must be very carefully scheduled. When a topical subject is under contemplation, it must be decided whether the financial results will compensate for the losses arising from the disorganisation of the film factory. This point of view is responsible for the apathetic American attitude towards the "topical," as it is called in Great Britain.

Topical work, however, not only possesses its fascinations, but is beset with considerable danger at times. A calamity of such dimensions as to send a deep thrill around the world is a powerful topical subject, and in their haste to secure striking films, the operators occasionally run extreme risks. The Messina earthquake was a striking case in point. The first authoritative news of that catastrophe precipitated the rush of a small army of operators and cameras to the spot. Scarcely had the earth ceased its mighty devastating shivers when the cinematographer was among the tottering ruins securing records of the disaster. Now and again there was a rush to a point of safety to escape a collapsing wall. Sometimes the flight was so hurried that the operator had to abandon his camera, and saw it buried beneath thousands of tons of *débris*. Occasionally the operator himself was too slow and was overwhelmed while pursuing his dangerous work.

It is always possible for the film producer to realise large profits on a great national disaster of this kind, provided he displays the requisite energy and initiative. Colliery accidents, conflagrations, railway collisions, are all sources of income to him. He has often to contend with innumerable adverse factors—the weather may be bad, or the lighting conditions unadapted to this work; but the film must be obtained by some means or other. The public sometimes find fault with the quality of such pictures, expecting the brilliance and perfect definition incidental to the average picture play, and ignoring the fact that the film may have been exposed upon a dreary, wintry day in the pelting rain, or when the scene was enveloped in a blanket of fog.

Now and again a stirring item of news enables striking success to be achieved. During the battle with the anarchists in the East End of London, an enterprising firm dispatched its operators and assistants to the scene without loss of time. In the course of an hour a short length of film arrived at the factory, which, upon development, was found to be capable of producing a sensation of the first rank. Instantly telegrams with replies prepaid were dispatched to all customers throughout the kingdom announcing that a film had been secured. Of course, the event constituted at the time the sole topic of conversation in every walk of life. The films were brought in as fast as possible; and by four o'clock in the afternoon eighty copies thereof had been dispatched to all parts of the British Isles; in several instances being shown on the screen that evening whilst the newsboys outside the theatres were shouting out the latest details concerning the episode.

The topical film is a favourite in the British Colonies, for it enables audiences in the most remote parts of Greater Britain to become more vividly familiar with incidents and events in the Home Country than they could in any other way. The Derby may be run in the Antipodes six weeks after the horses have sped over the course at Epsom; a prominent Royal function may have slipped from memory, but the film revives it in all its freshness. When the film shows such subjects as the funeral of King Edward VII., the unveiling of the Queen Victoria Memorial, or the Coronation of King George V., the sale of the films in the Colonies aggregates several thousand feet per subject.

To be successful in the production of topical films one must have not only an extensive and well-equipped organisation, but also facilities for working at high pressure. The business, moreover, is speculative to a degree; for the average topical film is little more than a six days' wonder—many of them are less—and the manufacturer can make a profit only by flooding the market within an hour or two of the occurrence of the incident. Every hour means money, and every day depreciates the value of the film from the showman's point of view.

Some of the firms concerned in the work of topical film production, however, are jeopardising its future by doing work of very indifferent quality. This is partly due to heavy cutting in prices. It is possible to purchase topical films for fifty per cent. less than the price charged per foot for film plays; at which figure the margin of profit is slight and quality must suffer. The public is displaying its disapproval of these tactics, and unless a radical improvement comes, the topical film will be ousted from the picture palace by force of popular opinion. Indifferent workmanship certainly does not assist those who are endeavouring to lift this form of entertainment to its highest level.

If the topical film brings a glimpse of the great world into remote and unsettled corners of the earth, the scenic film, on the other hand, does a like service for the dweller in cities; it brings sweeping panoramas of nature, magnificent and unfamiliar landscapes before his eyes. He has the joys of travel without stirring from his comfortable chair in the cinematograph theatre! In fact, the best scenic film is that taken from the front of a railway locomotive, with the camera and operator mounted upon the cowcatcher or its equivalent. In this instance the illusion is conveyed that the audience are seated in the moving train; the panorama is unfolded on all sides, and there are the gleaming metals and the flitting in and out of tunnels to assist in the illusion of actually travelling. The railway scenic film has been modified recently to conspicuous advantage. Instead of taking the picture from the front or rear of the train, the practice of taking the film from the carriage windows has been introduced with strikingly convincing effects. The camera is mounted near the rear of the train with the lens pointing towards the engine. The result is that when the train swings round a sharp curve a glimpse of the leading carriages is caught, giving a highly realistic result.

When the Urban Trading Company sought to record some of the natural marvels of the Tyrol in order to bring them before large audiences in distant theatres, valuable assistance was extended by the Imperial Austrian Railway

Ministry, which placed a special engine and carriage at the disposal of the cinematographer, so that he might be enabled to obtain his pictures under the best and most advantageous conditions. Similarly when Kinemacolor set out to harness the gorgeous beauties of Nature among the Rocky Mountains of British North America, the Canadian Pacific Railway, which co-operated in the enterprise, provided a special engine attached to a dark-room on wheels. This "Kinemacolor special" moved at leisure among the snow-clad giants, and some very impressive and beautiful pictures were obtained to delight vast concourses.

The cinematographer of to-day acts in the capacity of an explorer. At great risk he ventures into unknown or forbidden territories, and brings back scenes of wonderful interest, though in many instances he has to resort to novel subterfuge to secure his results. For instance, when some films of the country, habits and customs of the peoples of inland China were desired, it was considered too dangerous to entrust a white man with the work. Instead, an intelligent and highly cultured Chinaman was obtained. Months were devoted to initiating him into the mysteries of the camera, and when at last he obtained proficiency he sallied out upon his perilous mission.

Equally daring was the expedition of the Urban Trading Company into Central Africa. The cinematographer followed the route of the Cape to Cairo Railway so far as practicable, securing magnificent film records as he proceeded along the line, and then pushed on into the interior. When the railway was left a number of native porters had to be pressed into service to fulfil the work of the iron horse, the members of this human pack-train bearing the camera and its innumerable accessories, together with the impedimenta of the operator, upon their heads.

The Victoria Falls upon the Zambesi River have proved a happy hunting ground for the cinematographer, and this enormous tumble of water promises to rival the famous Falls of Niagara as a cinematographic centre of attraction.

RECORDER OF TOPICAL EVENTS

Since the bridge has been thrown across the gorge excellent coigns of vantage have been provided to secure impressively beautiful films of this cataract. One of the most powerful pictures of this wonder of Nature, however, was a close view of the Boiling Pot, and the recording of the seething water bubbling and frothing provided a unique and thrilling experience for the operator. There was only one means by which a close view of this awful spectacle could be secured—that was to lower the operator and camera by ropes from the bridge overhead to within a few feet of the raging waters. The ropes were snubbed round friendly posts and the operator with his camera was lowered over the side for a distance of about 400 feet, being steadied as much as possible while in that unenviable position by his comrades on the bridge above. It was an eerie sensation dangling in mid-air, and the cinematographer, after swirling round at the end of the ropes, like a joint on a roasting-jack, gave a breath of relief when he was hauled up and felt his feet touching the roadway of the railway bridge once more.

Possibly the greatest triumph of scenic cinematography is the convincing manner in which the sensitised celluloid band brings before the teeming thousands of the crowded cities of civilisation the terrible difficulties confronting polar exploration. The still-life studies of the interminable wastes of snow and ice which were brought back by Nansen, Jackson, Sverdrup, Captain Scott, and other intrepid spirits who ventured into the silent, cold strongholds around the poles, were indelibly powerful, but they failed to convince the man in the street of the bitter hostility of those icy climes in such a vivid manner as those produced in movement upon the screen, which were taken for the first time during the Shackleton expedition. This daring explorer indicated a new opportunity for motion photography, and since that expedition no other party has ventured into those forbidding wastes without a cinematograph and a few thousand feet of film. Captain Scott has a complete cinematographic equipment, and his films initiated the masses into the inconceivable difficulties, privations, and peculiar existence of the small communities determined to penetrate Farthest South.

Similarly, the Duke of the Abruzzi brought before one and all the topmost heights of the Himalayas. The Roof of the World has been wrapped in much legend, and has been the scene of many remarkable mountaineering exploits, but the task of scaling those dizzy peaks has never been conveyed so realistically to the man in the armchair before as by the films that were taken on this occasion. In a like manner another daring explorer has penetrated the innermost recesses of New Guinea, and in the heart of the unknown has made several exposures, the value of which is not confined to the satisfaction of the curious. The pictures are also of incalculable value to geographical and ethnographical science, as we see how these unknown natives move, live, and have their being, just as vividly as if we were transported to the spot by a magic carpet, and viewed the sights with our own eyes, while we become acquainted with the physical characteristics of the country. Theodore Roosevelt also brought back striking films of life in the lesser-known recesses of the African jungle. It is stated that the cinematographic records of his journey cost no less than £2,000 ($10,000), which affords an insight into the expense incurred to bring the uttermost parts of the earth to the city dweller.

Nowadays an explorer may reap appreciable financial benefit by the display of a little forethought. The manipulation of the moving picture camera does not demand a long course of tutelage to enable pictures to be taken. Accordingly, whereas formerly the hand camera constituted a prominent part of the impedimenta, the cinematograph now occupies the pre-eminent place. The films obtained command a distinct value, which fluctuates according to the popular interest created in the particular exploration achievement to which they refer. Any film manufacturing firm will undertake readily to place the subjects upon the market under a handsome royalty. The Gaumont firm has displayed considerable initiative in this direction; for it introduced the films of Shackleton's famous Antarctic expedition to the masses, and has recently acquired the films of Captain Scott relative to his Antarctic expedition, and also those of the daring journey into the innermost parts of New Guinea.

CHAPTER XII

THE CINEMATOGRAPH THEATRE AND ITS EQUIPMENT

WHEN moving pictures made their first claim on popular interest, they did so in the form of an item to the programme of the ordinary music-hall or vaudeville theatre. In the front rank of this movement was T. J. West; in fact, he might be considered the pioneer of the travelling cinematograph show. He had seen the popularity of the cinematograph feature on the programme of Professor Treuwé, the French prestidigitateur, during his appearance at the Regent Street Polytechnic. The conjurer used a Lumière apparatus and operated it himself. When his engagement was concluded, West decided that the Polytechnic ought not to lose one of its greatest attractions; accordingly he offered a complete entertainment in motion photography. From this small beginning has grown up one of the largest individual cinematographic exhibition businesses in the world. West realised the possibilities of the craft, and with commendable enterprise organised a touring show, with which he travelled not only through the towns and cities of the British Isles, but even in the remote colonies. To-day he has no less than twenty permanent establishments devoted to the projection of moving pictures scattered throughout the British Empire, providing employment for over 600 people.

The touring cinematograph proved conclusively the popularity of entertainments devoted exclusively to animated pictures. Permanent exhibitions were then tried, at first in a somewhat unpretentious way. Empty shops in prominent thoroughfares, which could be rented at a low price, railway arches, and so forth were acquired, and converted at small expense into dark halls. A screen and apparatus were purchased; the seating accommodation comprised hard wooden seats similar to school forms. The show was continuous: it commenced about mid-day and continued without intermission for ten or twelve hours, sufficient pictures being secured to provide amusement for about one hour, and repeated throughout the day. The prices of admission were very low, averaging about one penny, or two cents; and as the expenses were trifling, it did not require very extensive patronage to ensure a substantial weekly profit upon the investment.

In the United States the same practice was adopted. The first steps there were taken just as warily as in Great Britain; empty buildings were hired at a low price and turned into temporary "store" theatres, as they were called. If the enterprise proved unsuccessful, the energetic showman simply closed down, vacated the building, and tried his fortune in a more promising situation. This practice is still followed extensively throughout North America and Canada, and the initiative of the showman knows no limits. He seeks to instal himself in a small community where there is no competition. The experiment invariably proves successful from the financial point of view, because in the outlying townships the cinematograph hall constitutes the sole centre of amusement for miles around. If there is no available empty building, the showman constructs a cheap wooden theatre. Often the frontier moving picture palace is only a shack built of logs, capable of seating 100 people or so, the price of admission ranging between five and ten cents—$2\frac{1}{2}d.$ to $5d.$ The cinematographic entertainment in North America is known colloquially as a "nickel" or "dime" show, from the prices charged for admission. In Great Britain it became known in the early days as a "penny gaff," which contemptuous colloquialism still remains in use, though the price has gone up.

I have seen some very amusing and interesting manifestations of the showman's energy in remote districts of

America. When I visited Cochrane, a town which has sprung up in the wilderness of Ontario within 175 miles of the shores of Hudson Bay, the picture showman had planted himself firmly in its midst. There was only one masonry building in the place, the majority of the 300 inhabitants living in wooden shacks or tents, because the town was in the formative stage. The showman had come up with the first settlers, cannily foreseeing that a little colony 150 miles from the nearest town would need some form of diversion to while away the long evenings. He acquired a site upon one of the main streets, and ran up a cheap wooden building with an attractive arched front, gaily bedecked with small red, white, and blue lamps. There was not a unit of electricity or a cubic foot of gas generated in the place, but the indefatigable showman overcame these difficulties by recourse to substitutes. The theatre was thronged the whole evening, a result due in a great measure to the fact that Cochrane was situate in the Prohibition Area, and the theatre consequently had not to compete with the lures of the liquor saloon. The ranks of the inhabitants were swelled every day by gangs of workmen passing to and from the great railway construction camps, and the theatre was a distinct success and source of profit to the enterprising operator.

I encountered another quaint outburst of initiative at a far more inaccessible spot—the town of Hazelton around the Hudson Bay post at the head of navigation on the Skeena River, in British Columbia. Prince Rupert, 186 miles away, was the nearest town, and that port is 550 miles from Vancouver. A cinematograph showman arrived in Hazelton, which at that time boasted a handful of white men, and several Indians. The operator took over an excavation in the side of the hill overlooking the town, which had been made for storing various goods, but which at that time was empty. In this cramped, unventilated cellar he rigged his screen and lantern. On the wooden door he nailed a large sheet of paper, on which was scrawled the name of the "Theatre" and the programme of films "now being shown."

The preparations demanded only a few hours. Boxes, barrels, and logs sufficed for seats, while a good many patrons sat or sprawled upon the earthen floor. The little vault was packed to suffocation on the opening night. The Indians were amazed and the whites were amused, though the films would not have been tolerated in London or New York, having long since passed their span of usefulness. The show was kept going day after day until the audience became too small to defray the cost of the illuminant, when the "theatre" was closed, and the showman haunted the verandah of the hotel until he received some new subjects. His supply of films was both uncertain and irregular. He had to order them by post from Vancouver, whence they were brought up by boat. If the fates were kind he received an entire change of programme in about a fortnight; if the river were difficult to navigate, a month passed before they reached him, and often the boat came up without his goods, owing to lack of space. Probably no showman ever offered to amuse the public under more difficult conditions. It was doubtful if he would secure any films at all during the winter, as, the river being frozen, communication between Hazelton and Prince Rupert had to be maintained by dog trains, which carried letter-mail only.

In comparison with the luxurious conditions under which the triumphs of the art may be seen in London, New York, or Paris, the "Hazelton Picture Palace" was a half-pathetic, half-laughable spectacle—a strange link between civilisation and the aboriginal. I saw it after being immured for several weeks in the primeval bush; and though the pictures in the cellar danced and flickered on the screen, they seemed to me like a welcome handshake with the great world.

About four years ago the cinematograph theatre underwent a fresh change. The success of the "halls" extemporised from empty shops and railway arches induced a movement in favour of a theatre especially designed for the projection of moving pictures. Companies sprang up on all sides. At first empty buildings of all descriptions, disused slaughter houses, empty factories, roller-skating rinks, chapels without congregations, were taken over. Landlords who had despaired of ever receiving an income again from their vacant property reaped a golden harvest. In the first enthusiasm little discrimination was displayed in the acquisition of premises. The interiors, having been cleared down to the bare walls and ceiling, were redecorated, and provided with comfortable theatre seats.

The converted building was not entirely successful. Moreover, the cinematograph theatre needed established houses in order to compete with the vaudeville and legitimate theatres. Managers became more and more ambitious; and to-day rivalry is being displayed between competitive interests to eclipse one another in the elaborate construction and palatial appointment of the building.

Great improvement was made in the mechanical installations. Hitherto they had been more or less haphazard; but expert electrical knowledge naturally soon entered the field, and the electrical engineer has found a new opportunity for the display of his ability. Every large company retains a highly competent electrical engineer and an efficient corps of assistants, and the success of the twentieth century picture palace is dependent to a very great extent upon electricity.

Improvement in this particular field is probably responsible for the fact that, taken on the whole, the British picture theatre is the best in the world from every point of view, as an inspection of the theatres on the Continent and in North America will readily show.

The picture houses under the control of the Provincial Cinematograph Theatres, Limited, offer a good illustration of my point. This company has studied the tastes of the British public and has set the pace in elaborate and comfortable buildings. The day of the moving picture theatre comprising only the box office and the dark hall screened off from the street by heavy curtains is past; and the comforts and conveniences of the vaudeville house and the legitimate theatre have been incorporated.

Our illustration shows the Picture House at Briggate,

THE LUXURY OF THE MODERN PICTURE PALACE.

General interior view of the Picture House, Briggate, Leeds.

[*By permission of the Provincial Cinematograph Theatres, Ltd.*

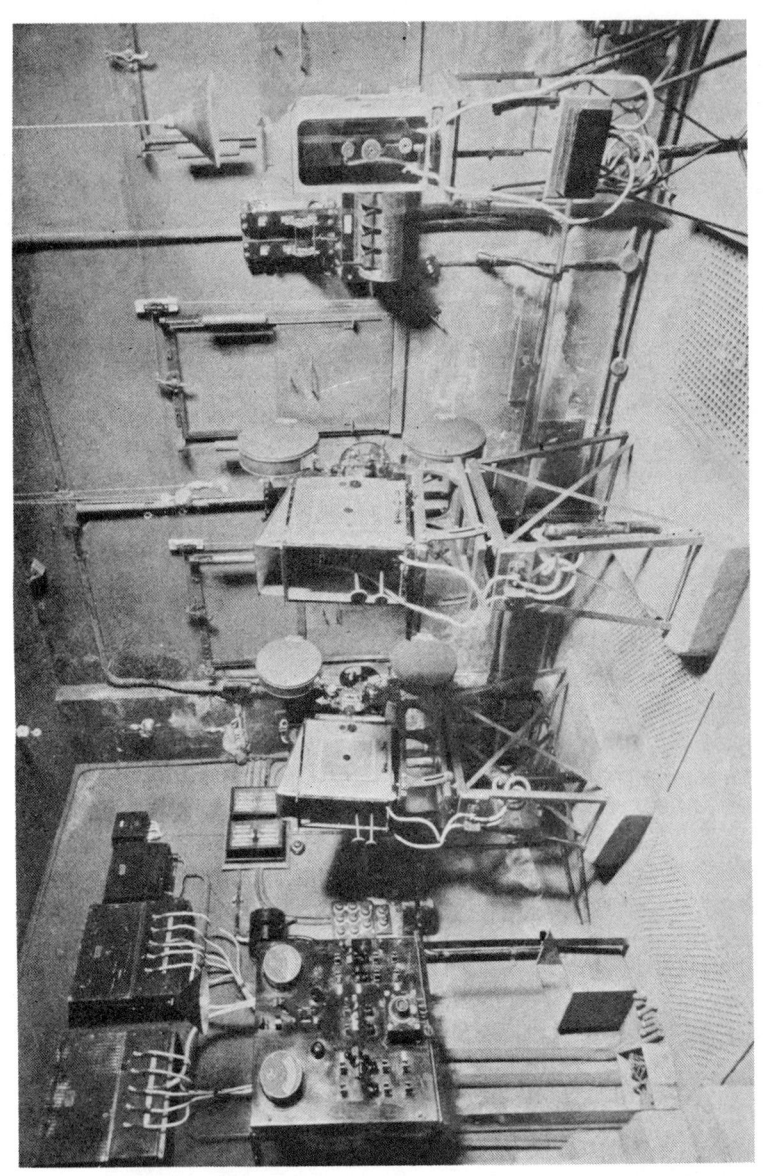

THE LANTERN ROOM OF A MODERN CINEMATOGRAPH THEATRE.
[*By permission of the Provincial Cinematograph Theatres, Ltd.*

The operating room of the Picture House, Briggate, Leeds, showing two film projectors and slide lantern.

Leeds, one of the chain of theatres belonging to the Provincial Theatre Company. The building is of fire-proof construction, as every moving picture theatre should be; the decorative details have been carried out upon a lavish scale, and the seating arrangements have every device of luxurious comfort.

The projecting hall has accommodation for about 600 people, and there is a lounge, a tea-room, and a smoking-room. Such a liberal policy brings the picture theatre on a level with the vaudeville house or legitimate theatre.

British law demands that the operating room shall be insulated by means of steel walls. In the early days a cupboard-like box built of iron met this requirement; but nowadays larger accommodation is necessary, because the compartment has to house far more than the mere projector. When a continuous show is given, and the programme lasts about an hour, the public insists upon full value for its money; consequently the interval between each film must be reduced to the minimum. Under ordinary circumstances $1\frac{1}{2}$ minutes suffice, not only to enable the film to be changed easily, but to give sufficient time for the audience to change.

The projecting apparatus should be in duplicate, not only to provide a reserve apparatus in case of accident, but to permit alternate use, so that the lantern does not become overheated. Moreover, the advent of Kinemacolor has made the 2-lantern plan essential. In colour work the projector requires a special type of shutter with alternate sectors of red and green glass, or screens, with intervening opaque sectors; and thus, obviously, when black and white alternate with colour pictures in the programme, a second projector is essential, to obviate the necessity for repeated detachment and re-attachment of the Kinemacolor shutter. A third lantern is required for stationary projections, such as announcements, titles, and so forth. Under these conditions a commodious lantern room is indispensable.

The front of the operating house is provided with small sliding shutters through which the pictures are projected.

If a film should catch fire these doors, by a single movement, close either from within or without the lantern room, the fire is confined to the lantern house, and the public within the theatre need receive no intimation of the mishap. As the lantern house is provided with an ample ventilating system, no smoke or gases find their way into the main building.

In the modern theatre, however, the lantern room has to fulfil other requirements beside merely housing the projectors. From it control of the various electrical arrangements is effected. The picture palace of to-day, instead of being entirely dark during projection, is suffused with the subdued glow of ruby lamps, which do not affect projection or the brilliancy of the picture to any material degree. Under the old *régime* darkness prevailed from one end of the programme to the other, save, perhaps, during a short interval; but now the lights are turned up throughout the hall while the films are being changed. The conversion from darkness to brilliant light, and *vice versâ*, which is so detrimental to the eyesight, is not, however, carried out instantaneously, but gradually. When the end of the film is reached the hall is filled—for about five seconds—with a soft diffused light, followed by full illumination; darkness comes on in the same gradual manner when the next film is ready.

In the modern picture palace, such as we illustrate, the electrical equipment is of the most elaborate character. The supply of current is derived, as a rule, from the public supply service, and the pressure has to be broken down to meet the requirements of the projector and of the electric lighting arrangements throughout the building. The supply service is generally in duplicate to guard against the failure of one installation, while should the whole service break down some other form of illumination has to be in readiness for use until the fault in the electric system is repaired.

The electrical installation is essentially of technical interest, appealing mostly to the engineer. In many instances the projector mechanism is driven by electric power, a small motor being fitted for this purpose. For natural colour work, indeed, owing to the number of pictures projected per second, a motor drive is imperative to secure satisfactory results.

After a film has been passed through the lantern it must be re-wound upon another reel to bring the first picture into the starting position once more. This operation is carried out with a film-winder. A large number of these devices are on the market, all working upon the same fundamental principle, but the "Empire" winders have achieved a high reputation, being excellent machines for the work and capable of withstanding hard wear. The operation is

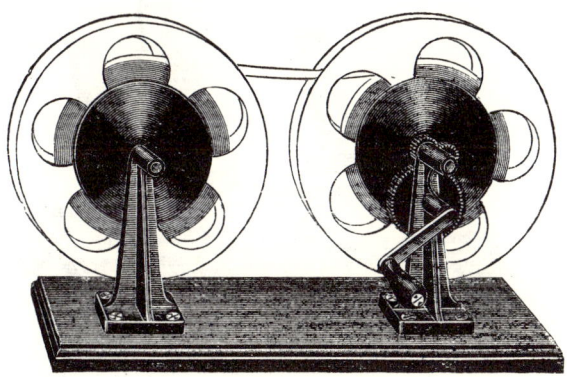

FIG. 12.—THE "EMPIRE" FILM-WINDER
After a picture has been run through the projector it has to be rewound upon its spool for the next display.

so simple that there is no necessity to describe the apparatus, as the illustration, Fig. 12, conveys its design and method of working.

Occasionally when a film is being run through the projector it becomes severed by some means or other. Before it can be used again the break must be repaired by splicing the two parts together. This is a simple task. The broken edge of one film is cut off about one-eighth of an inch below the line dividing one picture from the next. The gelatine emulsion upon this small section is removed with a knife. The other part of the film is trimmed exactly at the dividing line between two pictures, and the two facing surfaces of the film are treated with film cement, applied by means of a brush, the overlapping edges then being pressed tightly together and allowed to dry for about three minutes. This cement is a combination of amyl-acetate and acetone in the proportion of two to one for ordinary celluloid films. When a non-inflammable film is used the constitution of the cement is varied. To facilitate such splicing a small clamping device is used generally, and, although it is not essential to effect a good joint, its use certainly enables the task to be performed more neatly and satisfactorily. Fig. 13.

Though the excellence of a moving picture display

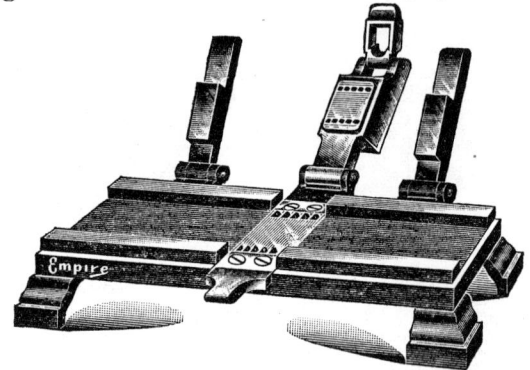

Fig. 13.—The "Empire" Film Mender. The Illustration Shows how a Broken Film is Rejoined.

depends primarily upon the projector and the film, its brilliancy and clear definition can be made or marred by the screen. When the pictures are being thrown from the front of the house and the audience see a reflected projection, the screen must be opaque and prepared from a suitably woven cloth. It is stretched taut, and the surface is treated with a good whitewash or matt white paint. Recently, various preparations have been placed on the market to enhance the brilliancy of the picture. They may achieve the result; but often at the price of introducing other flaws, such as alteration of the tone values and occasionally the impoverishment of the pure whites in the picture.

XII THEATRE AND ITS EQUIPMENT 139

If the audience is viewing the picture through the screen—that is, if the projector is placed at the back of the stage and out of sight—the sheet must be made of transparent material. This practice, however, has fallen into disuse. The screen must be set perpendicular to the horizontal axis of the projector objective and condenser, and if the machine is inclined slightly the sheet must be tilted in a corresponding degree, or it will be impossible to secure a picture which is clear and sharp all over, for the simple reason that some of the rays of light from the projector will be shorter than others. If the former are focussed sharp and clear the latter will be blurred, and *vice versâ*. In hanging the screen a certain amount of care must be taken to secure the best possible results. The edges are covered with a black material—velvet is the best medium—carried for a small distance on all sides of the sheet, giving the appearance of a white surface being set in a deep black frame. Such an arrangement improves the pictures by throwing them into stronger relief.

Within the past two or three years the idea has come into vogue of accompanying movements in the pictures with characteristic sound effects. When a horse gallops, the sound of its feet striking the road are heard; the departure of a train is accompanied by a whistle and a puff as the engine gets under weigh; the breaking of waves upon a pebbly beach is reproduced by a roaring sound. Opinion appears to be divided as to the value of the practice. Some more cultivated motion photography lovers are opposed to it, on the ground that unless every motion is given its distinctive sound, none at all should be audible; others contend that sound imparts an additional realism to the scene. There is no doubt that at times the sound effects come as an unpleasant and disturbing shock, especially when they are neither in time nor harmony with the motion—for example, when the realism of a mediæval battle is heightened by the vigorous rattling of a machine gun, or when horses galloping over the turf make a clatter that only a city pavement could cause.

But, on the other hand, since sound effects are indispensable to the legitimate stage, why should they not be extended to the moving picture theatre? What would Macbeth be without the crashing of thunder, and how could the impression of rattling hail, or the howling and shrieking of the wind, be conveyed without recourse to various devices in the wings? Even if the play be in pantomime, all sound is not suppressed. The players may be mute, but yet one hears the slam of a door, or the crash of an overturned chair as it strikes the floor, and so on. Accordingly it would seem that sound effects are perfectly justifiable in moving pictures, provided they are judiciously managed.

The first attempts to introduce sound effects provoked humorous situations. The boy deputed to the task enjoyed the chance to make a noise, and applied himself with a vigour of enthusiasm which overstepped the bounds of common sense. Nowadays such effects are employed with all the care and discrimination expended on the pictures themselves, and the result is harmonious and pleasing.

Of course, it has been necessary to devise all sorts of contrivances for realistic sound production, from the firing of a 12-inch gun to the squeak of a mouse. The most interesting of these is the "Allefex," invented by Mr. A. H. Moorhouse. It is the most comprehensive and ingenious machine ever made for the mimicry of sound, for although it measures only four feet in height, by about three feet in width and depth, it produces some fifty characteristic sounds, including the howl of a storm, the rushing of waterfalls, the bark of a dog, and the twittering of birds. Every artifice for producing these noises is contained within a small cubical space, and the operation has been so simplified that one man is sufficient for the task.

A general impression of this machine may be gathered from the illustration. It appears to be a maze of levers, cranks, plug-holes, and bulbs, but each attachment performs some definite purpose and produces one or more distinct sounds. Another striking feature is that its operation demands the minimum of practice, for the majority of the effects are produced by straightforward action. It is only

HOW THE SOUND EFFECT ACCOMPANIMENTS TO PICTURES ARE PRODUCED.
The ingenious "Allefex" machine, whereby over fifty distinctive noises can be made.

THE TRIAL SCENE FROM "RACHEL'S SIN." [*Copyright the Hepworth Manufacturing Co. Ltd.*

A striking example of a British picture play. From every point of view this film is equal to the finest foreign work. The English home producers excel in domestic drama of this character.

here and there that a little practice is required, such as, for instance, to imitate the bark of a dog, or the cry of a baby.

It would be impossible to describe in one chapter all the various effects produced by means of this apparatus. I will confine myself, therefore, to some of the more difficult sounds, many of them apparently beyond the reach of mechanical mimicry. The shot of a gun is imitated by striking a drum at the top of the machine, on which a chain mat has been placed, a smart blow with a felt drumstick as near the centre as possible. The same device serves to represent successive shots. The interior of the drum is fitted with three drum-sticks, which are manipulated by the turning of a handle, the number of shots varying, with the speed, according to the picture. At the bottom of the machine is a large bellows worked by the foot. Their manipulation in conjunction with one or other of the handles will produce the sound of exhaust steam issuing from a locomotive, the rumbling of a train rushing through a tunnel, and so on. Running water, rain, hail, and the sound of rolling waves are obtained by turning a handle, which rotates a ribbed wooden cylinder against a board set at an angle from the top of which hang a number of chains. By varying the speed of the cylinder any of the above sounds may be obtained with accuracy. The puffing of an engine is made by revolving a cylinder with projections against a steel brush; the crash of china, pots and pans, &c., is due to the revolution of a shaft on which are mounted a series of tappets striking against hammers, which in turn come into contact with a number of steel plates. The crackling of a machine gun is caused by turning a shaft having tappets which strike and lift up wooden laths, subsequently releasing them to strike smartly against the framework of the machine. The same device also serves for imitating the crash attending the upsetting of chairs, tables, and so on. Pendant tubes serve to produce the effects of church bells, fire alarm, ship's bell, and similar noises; the sound of trotting horses is caused by revolving a shaft carrying three tappets which lift up inverted cups. This shaft is slightly movable, so that by adjustment a trot can be converted into a gallop and *vice versâ*, while distance effects are obtained by a muffling attachment. Thunder is made by shaking a sheet of steel hanging on one side of the machine; the press of a bulb gives the bark of a dog; the bellows and another attachment operate the warbling bird; while the cry of the baby is emitted by the dexterous manipulation of plug-hole and bellows.

A machine like this is a distinct acquisition to the modern picture theatre, for when skilfully controlled it provides a scientific and perfect mechanical apparatus for the production of distinctive sound, correctly, and at the proper moment. At the same time, it is so simple that little practice is demanded to make the operator expert in the art of mechanical mimicry.

During the past two years special attention has been devoted to what is called "daylight projection," *i.e.*, the display of pictures in broad daylight. A method evolved by Quentin for accomplishing this end was adopted at the Cinéma Palace in Paris nearly three years ago. Here the practice was to show the pictures upon the screen with half the lamps in the theatre lighted, the projector being 66 feet from the screen, the size of the picture being 10 by 8 feet, and the arc lamp taking normally a current of 30 amperes from the supply mains of a 110-volt circuit. Another system to the same end was evolved by Antoine and Prosper Poch, the image being projected upon a translucent screen placed between the spectators and the projector. With this apparatus the pictures could be thrown upon a screen measuring about 24 by 30 inches, so as to be clearly visible in the middle of the day by people passing along the street.

For this work the screen demands special treatment. If it is to be used only temporarily, the tracing cloth used by architects is a very satisfactory material. One inventor produced what he called a "rainbow screen," prepared by soaking a suitable white material with fish glue and attaching thereto a thin layer of tinted fabric. Moving pictures "without darkness" have been exploited in the

XII   THEATRE AND ITS EQUIPMENT   143

United States upon a small scale, and on one or two occasions in this country. The object of the plan, however, is not quite clear, for moving pictures can obviously be seen at their best only in total darkness or a very slight suffused red glow. It is claimed by the advocates of the daylight pictures that the eyes are fatigued less under such conditions. The advantage, however, has not been recognised by the public, for daylight projection is no more popular to-day than it was in 1897, when the appearance of a method for accomplishing it appeared and sank into oblivion after causing a passing interest.

A prominent feature of the development of the cinematograph theatre is the formation of "moving picture circuits," or chains of theatres controlled by one organisation. This practice was taken over, of course, from the music hall and the legitimate stage; and its application to the new field has been largely responsible for the improved status of the cinematographic industry. Keen and growing rivalry is displayed between the various circuits. Thus has developed a spirit of healthy competition, resulting in the improvement of the picture theatre as a building, and in the production of superior programmes. When two or more rivals in a single town are making a common bid for popular favour, the public naturally patronises the establishment which offers the most refined pictures combined with comfort in the seating arrangements. The inferior film is being driven from the better class of cinematograph theatre, where a programme is offered which is varied in character, and of the highest excellence from the photographic, dramatic, and educational point of view, as well as from that of sheer amusement.

In the United States the growth of the cinematograph theatre has been phenomenal. The success of the first displays with the Lumière machine at the Eden Musée prompted the proprietors of other places of entertainment to introduce the biograph in their programmes. The news of its success at the Alhambra in the English metropolis doubtless likewise influenced the development on the other side of the Atlantic. The first display in a New

York music hall was at the Union Square Theatre in the Keith vaudeville circuit. It did not meet with an immediately enthusiastic reception; but in a few days it caught the public fancy, and thereafter the house was always well filled. The value of the moving picture machine to this house is reflected by the average weekly receipts. At the time of its introduction the average receipts were £600 ($3,000) per week; a month later they had risen to £1,400 ($7,000)—the cinematograph more than doubled the revenue of the theatre.

Within a year there was not a music hall of repute in the country which did not possess its bioscope. Then came the first movement towards the creation of a moving picture palace, in the same way that it occurred in England. Empty shops were taken on all sides, and within a few years there were no less than 600 of these "store" theatres, or "nickel" and "dime" shows, in New York alone, while about 30,000 similar establishments dotted the country between the Atlantic and the Pacific Oceans, and from the Gulf of Mexico to the Great Lakes.

Men who started with no more capital than was barely sufficient to purchase the outfit and rent the empty shop, found that they had discovered an El Dorado. The more energetic started theatre after theatre, and in a short time possessed "circuits" of twenty or more moving picture shows. One of these pioneers, Marcus Loew, starting unpretentiously in a suburban district, found himself in five years possessed of forty theatres, from which the money rolled into his banking account in forty steady streams. It must be borne in mind that this fortune was accumulated from the public in five and ten cent pieces.

At the present time the moving picture theatre in the United States is in a state of transition. The palatial character of the British cinematograph theatre has spurred ambitious spirits in the United States to like achievements. Loew has built two palaces, spending some $1,000,000 (£200,000) upon the buildings and appointments.

Moving pictures are rivalling all other forms of entertainment in the United States. As suitable buildings fall vacant exorbitant bids are made by rival factions to secure their acquisition, and the rents paid are very high. William Fox, a man very similar in character to Loew, who entered the field a year later than he, startled the cinematographic world by acquiring the lease of a legitimate theatre in the fashionable theatrical centre at a yearly rental of £10,000 ($50,000), and converting it to cinematography. Scarcely had the excitement died down when it was announced that he had rented the Academy of Music at £20,000 ($100,000) per annum. The price he is paying in rental to bring moving pictures before the public continuously throughout the day represents one-third of the original cost of erecting the building, so that the proprietors may be said to have profited handsomely in the transaction. Gambling in sites for the establishment of picture palaces in the United States has reached a far greater climax than was ever attained in Great Britain in the height of the enthusiasm. Here the bubble has been pricked, and the same outcome is anticipated in the United States. Probably the most luxurious picture palaces in the world are in South America; there they are palaces in the fullest sense of the word. That territory has scarcely been touched yet, and is one of the most attractive fields for development. It is in the "land of to-morrow" that animated pictures promise to attain their greatest heights of success.

CHAPTER XIII

HOW A CINEMATOGRAPH PLAY IS PRODUCED

When a stirring drama or uproarious farce is projected upon the screen the actions are so natural, the situations develop so obviously—in fact, the whole thing proceeds so smoothly—that the average person concludes that the production of a picture play is the simplest thing in the world. But the average person was never more mistaken. A visit to a studio-theatre to follow a production from the beginning to the end undeceives him very promptly and thoroughly.

The stage management of a play before the celluloid film is far more exacting than the staging of a play behind the footlights. Situations have to be handled which never develop on the legitimate stage. The picture play is essentially pantomime and the camera is a searching, unequivocal critic. It produces a stern, matter-of-fact representation of what is enacted before it. There is no dialogue to conceal blemishes, or mitigate the deficiencies of the actors and actresses. Words have to be converted into action and gestures. In a picture-play every muscle of the body has practically to be called into use to convey to the spectator a lucid and coherent idea of the progress of the plot, since there is nothing but the action to tell him "what it is all about."

Furthermore, everything must be condensed to the irreducible minimum without forfeiting coherency. The plot must be unravelled without the slightest interruption of the main thread of the story. Once the spectator loses grip of the theme, interest is lost. As brevity is the soul of wit, so terseness is the keynote of success in a picture-play.

CH. XIII   HOW A PLAY IS PRODUCED   147

The producer must be a man of many parts. He must have a keen instinct for dramatic situation, possess wide histrionic ability and experience, have a sharp eye for minute detail, be supplied with unlimited energy, and capacity to extract the utmost from his company. One factor is all-important to him—time. The stage-manager works on a time-schedule, not of minutes, but of seconds; it must be remembered that every second of time is equivalent to twelve inches of film. A producer will spend five minutes in the effort to condense by five seconds the action necessary for a certain situation.

In what form does the picture play reach the stage-manager's hands for production? Does the playwright prepare the contribution in detail complete with dialogue and business, as if for the theatrical stage, or does he supply a bare outline? The answer varies according to the dramatist, and to the stage-manager for whom he is working. Some authors cannot convey their ideas coherently without extensive dialogue. Others can achieve their end in 200 words. Again, one producer fails to see eye-to-eye with the author's idea unless the latter is worked out minutely, while another will grasp the whole situation instantly. As a result, it is impossible to lay down any hard and fast rules, as to how to write a picture-play; but, generally speaking, the briefer the scenario or story of the play, the more likely it is to find favour, all other things being equal.

I have seen both methods in execution. In one case the author's story had been worked out to the smallest detail, the manuscript covering some fifty pages. On the other hand, a friend of mine who has produced many eminently successful picture films, scribbles the bare idea on a single sheet of paper—the back of an envelope suffices sometimes—briefly indicating the progress of the plot step by step, retaining all the stage business in his head, and modifying his ideas as he proceeds, to suit the circumstances.

Equally divergent is the practice followed in production. Among the French producers the general method is to write out all the parts complete with dialogue, and to hand the lines to the members of the company concerned, to be committed to memory in the usual way. Actors and actresses thus become familiarised with the atmosphere of the story, and are left to a great extent to their own histrionic instinct to interpret the character assigned, the producer introducing his ideas as rehearsals proceed.

On the other hand, many producers prefer to keep the members of their company in ignorance of the plot. The story is carried through in brief sections, step by step, the lengths of each section being between 45 and 100 seconds or thereabouts. The actors and actresses are given instructions as to how to make up their characters, and are then marshalled upon the stage. The first situation in the play is taken, the producer showing each character concerned how the part is to be played. The members are put through their paces time after time, rehearsing being continued until the whole company moves like a machine, and then the camera films the incident. Sometimes the producer himself will undertake a part, and shout instructions on the stage as the action proceeds, keeping every actor and actress moving just as he desires. This method is followed very extensively in America. Its advantage is that the members of the company, not knowing what is coming next, are kept acutely expectant in order to fall naturally into the spirit of the parts and plot; they work themselves to a high pitch of intensity; and this gives the play the vim and animation which are peculiarly requisite for a picture-play.

By this method also the stage-manager compels the actors and actresses to interpret his ideas, which he regards as suiting the man in the street. The members of the company have no opportunity to thrust their own impressions before the camera. When the lines are given out beforehand to the members of the company, each naturally forms an individual opinion as to how this or that part should be played, and once this impression has taken root, it is difficult for the producer to modify it upon the lines he has conceived. Another disadvantage of the latter method is that an actor or actress sometimes fails to regard a part

THE FILM-PLAY PRODUCER AT WORK.
Rehearsing at the Edison Cinematograph Theatre.
This picture shows the stage setting, the powerful battery of electric top-lights for illuminating the scene, and the electrically driven camera.

TAKING THREE PICTURE-PLAYS SIMULTANEOUSLY.

This photograph of the Selig Cinematograph Studios, in Chicago, shows how scenes are set side by side. The battens on the floor indicate the boundaries of each stage.

with sympathy, and the result lacks realistic effect. Repeated rehearsals also tend to dull enthusiasm; the members of the company become somewhat lethargic; and there is a marked absence of zest and swing in the resultant picture.

When the play reaches the producer's hands the first point is to settle the length of film to which it shall run. This depends upon the character of the play itself. The average length varies between 600 and 1,000 feet, occupying from ten to sixteen minutes to project upon the screen. If an elaborate or novel production is contemplated of a character able to sustain the interest of the audience, the length may be doubled or quadrupled. The film version of "A Tale of Two Cities," for instance, ran to 3,000 feet, which meant that the screen was occupied for some sixty minutes. That was an exceptional production, however, and there are few plays which could rivet the attention of an audience for an hour.

The actors and actresses, like the producer, are drawn from the legitimate theatre. The majority of the large organisations collect and maintain their own stock companies, ready to produce any character for any description of play. This idea was first practised, and is still continued to a limited extent, in Great Britain, the company averaging six or eight principals. But in the early days the public resented the too frequent appearance of the same face upon the screen; so the studios which were situated in the vicinity of the metropolis began to draw their material from the theatrical market, securing an excellent selection, and at the same time plenty of variety.

Cinematograph studios situated farther afield availed themselves of the touring theatrical companies, whose members benefited appreciably from the introduction of the film-play; as it gave them an opportunity to increase an otherwise meagre weekly wage. The practice is still in vogue in the British provinces, and has been found very profitable to the producer, because the varied experience of the average touring actor or actress is a valuable asset on the picture-play stage.

The film-play does not offer any opportunity to the amateur theatrical individual. The camera emphasises far too acutely any weak points in histrionic ability. The professional is the essential raw material, and the heart-breaking drill of the legitimate stage renders the actor or actress all the better adapted to the exacting requirements of the film play; though at times it demands indescribable patience and perseverance, if not bullying, on the part of the producer to compel the professional to adapt himself to changed conditions and realise the difference between the two phases of the histrionic art. Many producers, in fact, prefer to maintain their own stock company, every member of which can grasp in an instant what the stage-manager demands, thus saving much valuable time. The nucleus is increased as necessity demands for special occasions or particular characters from the ranks of available touring companies, while the supernumeraries are likewise recruited from a wide field.

The selection of the actors and actresses is by no means easy. The cinematographic stage has its own peculiar requirements. The pre-eminent one is that the actor or actress must not only act but look the part. A young man cannot make up to take an old man's part—he must be an old man. A woman of middle age may on the legitimate stage excel in a young girl's rôle; but she may not take it on the camera stage.

Make-up has to be reduced to the minimum, because the huge enlargement which the picture undergoes in projection renders such artifices hideous. Facial make-up is practically out of the question. Nowadays the practice is to abandon general make-up entirely, and to whiten all the faces. Under the glare of many thousand candle-power emitted by several electric lamps it is possible in this way to secure striking contrasts in facial expressions. When the features are torn by malignant hatred, or uproarious mirth, the shadows formed by the wrinkling of the skin as the muscles are brought into operation emphasise the expression. There is another reason for the whitening process. An actor or actress may have a natural high colour, or dark complexion, when the face comes out with a dark or black tone, conveying the impression that the part has been performed by a negro or mulatto. This method of making up, however, it must be explained, applies only to black and white cinematograph production.

There is no dearth in the supply of actors or actresses, consequently the producers are able to carry out a weeding process in order that they may secure the very best histrionic ability. One large American company supplies every aspirant with a form in which to record full particulars of his or her stage career. If the applicant has had no professional experience he or she is told at once that the company needs none but experienced artistes.

Certain American producers have not only acquired a large stock company, but have also, by offering large salaries, attracted old favourites, whom they star precisely as in the legitimate theatre. Posters and photographs of their leading actors and actresses are circulated broadcast, and the public has its favourites on the cinematographic as on the legitimate stage. The Edison Company has fourteen principals at Orange, in New Jersey; and in addition a company of seven stationed in Western America for plays having a western setting. The Selig Company has thirty players permanently attached to its Chicago and Los Angeles establishments. The practice has by no means fallen into disuse in Great Britain. The Hepworth Company, from whose studios come some of the best films prepared especially to suit British and Colonial tastes, maintains two stock companies at Walton-on-Thames; while the Kinemacolor plays are produced by a stock company of twelve players, augmented as occasion demands, which divide their time between the studio-stages at Hove and Nice, frequenting the former during the English summer, and spending the remaining six months of the year in the south of France, being transported to and fro each season.

There has been considerable complaint, to some extent justified, of the indifferent character of the British film play productions. British producers have not received sufficient encouragement to enable them to incur great expense in mounting or in the maintenance of a large and excellent stock company. However, there are signs of a change; and as the technical quality of the picture is improving it should not be long before the British film play industry attains a position of importance. As soon as this happens a wide success will be reaped; for this country possesses unique and extensive opportunities for producing plays capable of making a world-wide appeal, and is rich in the natural settings so much in demand for the attainment of atmosphere.

Let us follow the production of a picture play at a large establishment having between three and six producers at work every day from morning to night. The players upon arrival consult the "call-board" to see when rehearsals commence, upon what stage, and for what productions. One artist may appear in two or three plays in a single day, as a play is occasionally not photographed complete through all its scenes; it may be interrupted for several days from some reason or other.

At the pre-arranged time the company assembles upon its allotted stage. The manager marshals those required in the scene and explains precisely what he wants each artist to do. The business on the stage is demonstrated, and those in waiting are told just how to make their entrances, and all exits are indicated very concisely. The stage-manager rehearses the first episode before those concerned, to convey a general idea of his requirements, and they immediately repeat it. No dialogue is written, but the actors of professional experience realise what words are demanded for different situations, and accordingly extemporise as they proceed. In the reproduction the movement of the lips renders the action distinctly more conclusive and realistic; moreover, the enunciation of suitable dialogue induces the correct facial expression, one of the most important requirements in the picture play, and the audience must at times derive from it the significance of the situation.

In this fragmentary manner the producer carries the company through the incident, and it is now rehearsed time

THE FATAL DUEL SCENE IN "THE TWO ORPHANS."
This magnificently staged and acted film is one of the finest which has been produced in the United States.
[*By permission of the Selig Company, Chicago.*

THE COLLEEN BAWN.

The Kalem Company despatched a company of players from the United States to Ireland to produce Irish plays in their natural settings.—*See page* 158.

THE LOST FREIGHT CAR.

To obtain this scene the American producer purchased a railway goods waggon and pitched it over a high embankment.

after time, little modifications and improvements being made on each occasion to animate the action still further. Those waiting to enter are given the cue, and when an exit has to be made it is announced in an emphatic manner by the manager. The scene is repeated perhaps a dozen times before it goes with the swing that the producer desires. Then what may be termed a dress rehearsal is carried out. Watch in hand, the camera operator follows it through from end to end. The producer has decided the length of film the whole play shall occupy, and has allotted to each incident a certain number of seconds, that is, of feet of film. The final rehearsal completed, the producer inquires, "How long?"

"Seventy seconds," replies the operator.

"Too long," remarks the producer, and forthwith the scene is rehearsed once more, the producer abbreviating it as the action proceeds, by shouting stentorian orders to the players to make a quicker entry, cutting short a situation, or by sharply and unceremoniously telling a member to "get off" if there is a sign of lingering in the exit.

"Fifty-five seconds," remarks the operator.

It is still too long by five or six seconds. The producer sees where he can compress the scene still more, so decides to do this while the camera is working. The operator takes his position, and then a scene of great animation is witnessed.

"Are you ready?" shouts the manager. The actors come to the alert. "Right!" The camera commences its rhythmic purring, and as the first strains of the buzz break out the manager gives vent to a loud "Go!"

The whole time the picture is being filmed the producer is shouting instructions, giving abrupt cues, and sharp orders as to how to improve the business. Although orders and commands are delivered in an endless stream, not a single player loses his head. One and all proceed as if the manager were non-existent. It is a babel of noise; the producer raps out breathless orders such as "Look towards the camera"—"Shout out the dialogue"—"Come towards the front"—"Get off!"—"Look happy"—"Not so quickly"

—"Come in"—"Roll your eyes"—"Don't move your hands as if you were playing the piano"—"Cry!"—"Hurry up!" and so on without ceasing. The actors are worked up to an exciting pitch, each man and woman singling out the comment which concerns him or her. The scene is brought to a climax, and there is a shout of "Stop." The purring of the camera ceases immediately.

"How many feet?" inquires the producer.

"Fifty-three," replies the operator.

"Good! Next scene! Twelve years later," and forthwith every artist receives further explicit instructions.

Perhaps the operator finds that he has not enough film in the box to carry him through the whole of a scene. In such a case, when by reference to the dial on the camera he finds that the film is on the verge of exhaustion, he cries "Stop!" Immediately the actors become rooted to the spot and remain motionless until a new loaded box of film is inserted into the camera and threaded up, an operation which takes half a minute or so. Occasionally the "Stop" call is given at an awkward moment, when the stage hands rush forward to support artists who have been interrupted in the middle of some action, and are caught in difficult positions. When the word "Go!" is given once more, the supporters rush off the stage and the acting is resumed as if there had been no interference. The first few pictures upon the new film are afterwards cut out, and the connection between the two bands is effected so neatly that no evidence of a break in continuity is revealed upon the screen.

As on the legitimate stage, so here also there is a tendency to pay more and more attention to realistic detail. Once upon a time it sufficed for a frontier scene if a shack were painted on the back cloth. Every time an actor touched the cloth a series of undulating waves went across it, with ludicrous effect. A disconcerting ripple of laughter would run through the house, even in the midst of an intensely tragic situation. The public soon lost interest in plays so ill mounted, and their dissatisfaction, of course, generated the necessary improvement.

XIII HOW A PLAY IS PRODUCED 155

Audiences demand nature and realism, and the producer responds. Instead of improvising a railway station in canvas and battens upon the stage the producer transports his company, lock, stock, and barrel, together with all the properties in motor cars or cabs to an actual station to secure the required results in a natural setting. If a scene is laid in a given thoroughfare, the company is sent thither to act the story.

In the United States the demand for realism has developed almost into mania. The American Biograph Company had arranged to produce a film version of the famous Indian novel "Ramona," in which the great scene is the devastation of a white settlement by Indians. The story is laid in California; so the firm assembled a company of sixty-five artists and dispatched them across the continent from New York to the Pacific Coast, where they stayed five months so as to become saturated with the environment. In order that the sacking and destruction of homes might be correct in every detail, a small village was purchased and fired! In another instance the same company wanted a modern fire scene. They rented a plot of land, upon which they built a house of the style required; then they set it on fire and burned it to the ground. But the Selig Company eclipsed even this performance. One day a fire broke out in a large department store in the heart of the city of Los Angeles. It was a unique opportunity to obtain a powerful play; so the producers, after securing over the telephone the sanction of the fire brigade authorities, hurried principals and operators to the conflagration. The film hero was garbed in the uniform of a fireman, and at the head of a squad equipped with a hose, he dashed into the burning building; the whirring of the camera testified that this incident had been recorded. Shortly after, a woman—one of the best actresses of the company—was observed at an upper window surrounded by fire and smoke. She uttered a despairing cry for "Help!" and in response, the pseudo-fireman made a frantic rush up the ladder, broke in the window, and snatched the prostrate form of the actress from the flames. The players ran great risks, but the film producer was satisfied. He had secured a sensational fire rescue in an actual big fire in a crowded thoroughfare, with the fire engines, a towering building, smoking and well alight, and a huge crowd looking on as a setting. It is hard to imagine a stage-manager attempting this feat under similar conditions in London or any other European city.

The feverish clamour for realism has occasionally met the reward of rashness. In South London, in a scene where a railway locomotive played an important part, one of the men in the act was run over and killed; in another case an actor was drowned while engaged in a thrilling water scene. Mr. Edison relates that during the filming of a Boer War play by his company, one of the actors dropped a lighted match into a glass vessel containing gunpowder! He has been picking stray pieces of glass from various parts of his anatomy ever since! In another instance a superannuated cannon was used, which killed one or two actors and injured many others.

An elaborate production, which is a great favourite in the United States, is "Uncle Tom's Cabin," which lends itself admirably to film treatment. On the legitimate stage "Uncle Tom's Cabin" has become to the touring American manager what "East Lynne" is to his English contemporary. It will fill a house; and it has established the same rank for itself in the cinematograph theatre.

As an amusing comment on this fact, I must tell the story of the introduction of the cinematographic version south of Mason and Dixon's line. The stage version had never been played in the Southern States—managers feared it would kindle smouldering fires in the breasts of the white population. An invisible barrier was drawn across the country south of which the play never ventured. The same apprehension was entertained in regard to the moving picture production. However, one manager took the risk and presented the film to a crowded house in New Orleans. It had been announced for a night or two only, but its success was so overwhelming that it held the screen for two or three weeks, the house being crowded at each projection.

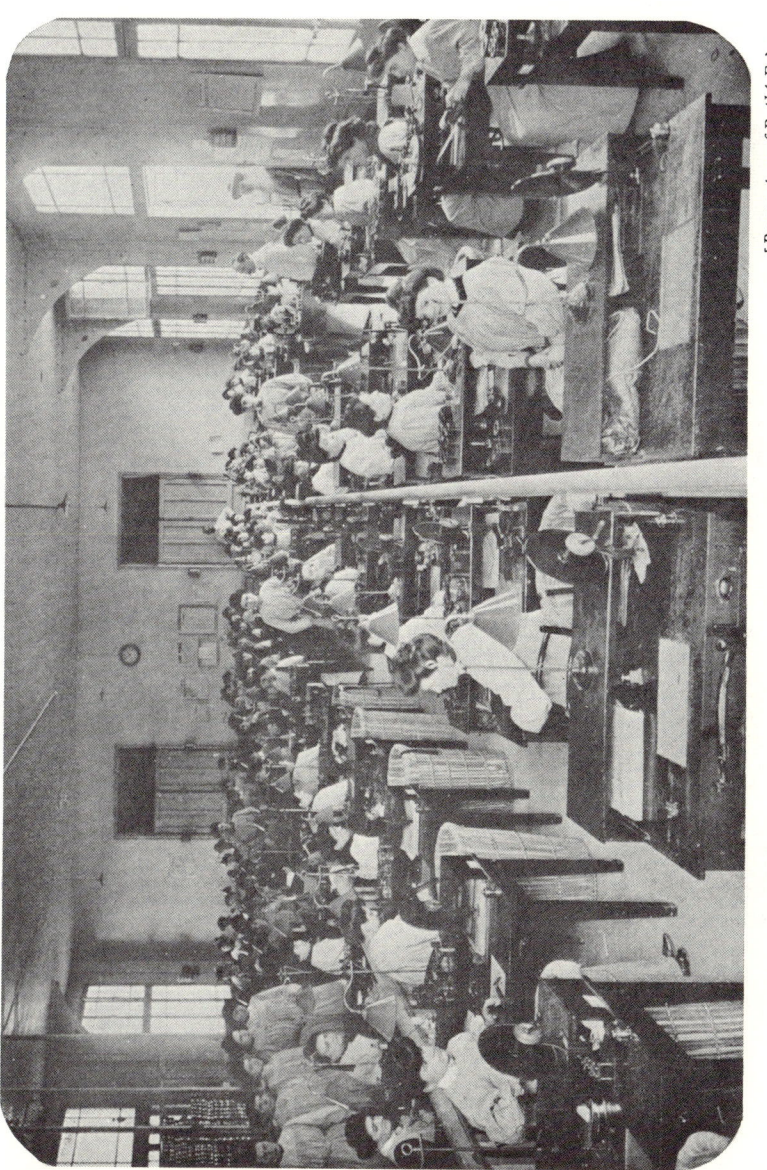

SORTING, EXAMINING AND JOINING THE STRIPS OF FILM. [*By courtesy of Pathé Frères.*

The positives are prepared in varying lengths. The different sections of a subject have to be identified, trimmed, and connected together to form a continuous ribbon.

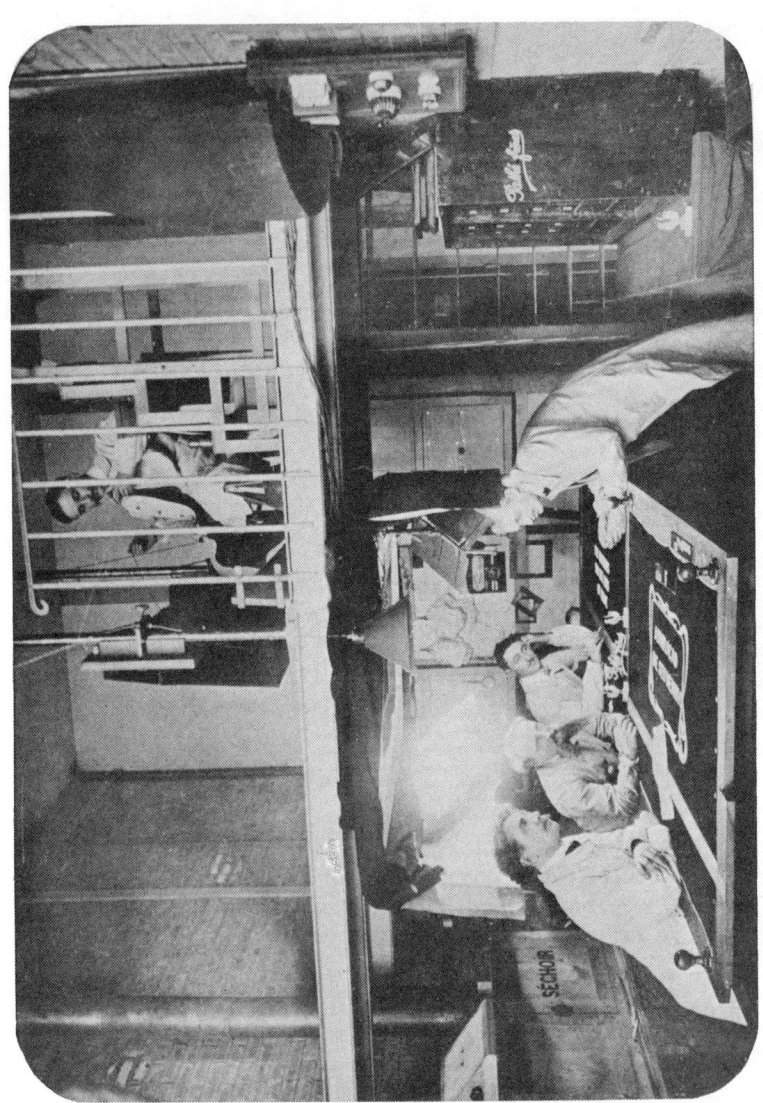

PREPARING THE TITLES.

This is an important operation. The title is designed upon a flat table, and under powerful electric lights is photographed from above, the lens of the camera pointing downwards vertically. The cinematographer may be seen watch in hand, with his instrument.—*See page* 87.

The moving picture producer is even capable of turning to account a disaster to his own plant. While a play was in progress upon a studio-stage in New York the building caught fire, and unrehearsed scenes were enacted. The camera operator seized the opportunity. While the building was blazing, and the company were rushing wildly to and fro, he kept his handle turning lustily, and as a result filmed the whole subject. In order to secure a dramatic automobile disaster the Edison Company drove a motor-car to the top of a lofty cliff. A dummy was seated in the vehicle to take the part of the character who had been acting in the play up to this point, the steering-wheel was fixed in its hand, the car was started up, and it was driven at full speed to the edge of the cliff, over which it plunged. The film operator caught it falling through the air, as well as the splash produced by its headlong dive into the waves. Another company desired to secure a dynamite explosion at sea. For this purpose it purchased an old schooner for £200 ($1,000), stocked it with dynamite, towed it beyond sight of land, where the charge was detonated, and a stirring series of pictures of the disaster was recorded from the deck of a yacht chartered especially for the occasion.

Sometimes the struggle after realism provokes humorous situations. The Edison Company once wanted a riot scene, so they produced one in a quiet country district by the aid of their company and a number of local supernumeraries, who entered into the plot with tremendous enthusiasm. While the mock riot was at its height the myrmidons of the law swept down and arrested all the ringleaders, who, naturally, were the principals of the play, and promptly incarcerated them. The players expostulated that it was all make-believe, but the police were not to be hoodwinked; they had heard that story before. Some time elapsed before the mock rioters were released from gaol; but the manufacturers scored, because the interference of the police imparted additional versimilitude to the whole proceeding.

In Germany an hilarious party was rowing up a river. Suddenly all the gay company were seen struggling in the water—the boat had capsized. There was a rush from all sides to bring help; boats put off hurriedly, while spectators either were rooted to the spot in horror or dived into the water on rescue bent. The scene was intensely dramatic, and it was not until one of the swimmers, while bearing the frail form of a girl to the bank, hearing a strange buzzing near his head, looked round and saw an amused operator a few feet distant, nonchalantly turning the handle of a camera. Then the fact dawned upon every-one that the anxious rescuers had unconsciously contributed to the greater success of a cinematograph play.

The French producers Pathé Frères once disturbed the peaceful life of a sleepy village by acting a scene in the deserted main street. While the work was in progress one of the most prominent citizens hurried up. He was bursting with righteous indignation at the noisy caprices of the crowd of roysterers. While he was expostulating and uttering dire threats of action, a policeman appeared, and clapping a firm hand upon the shoulder of the interfering person, threatened to arrest him for inciting a breach of the peace! The admonished resident, somewhat amazed at the turn of affairs, moved crestfallen away, and departed homewards. He omitted to look round at the emissary of the law, and ignored the guffaw of laughter which burst out at his discomfiture. Had he done so he would have observed a merry twinkle in the eye of the gendarme, who was a member of the party!

A company desired to secure a love scene between an engine-driver and a country maiden; so a small railway with the whole of its rolling-stock on the outskirts of a town was hired for a single day. Another firm, the Kalem Company, decided to picture a series of Irish stories. Instead of passing off American scenery as that of the Emerald Isle, the company and properties were dispatched across the Atlantic to the heart of the country which the author had selected as the scenes of his stories. Recently, the Gaumont Company, of London, dispatched its company to Scotland in order to stage Rob Roy. The Duke of Argyll graciously assisted in furthering the fidelity of the setting, by permitting scenes to be enacted upon his estate and extending invaluable aid, volunteering suggestions in order that everything might be as correct as was humanly possible.

The Vitagraph Company undertook the filming of Fennimore Cooper's "Leather-stocking" stories. They sent their company straightway to the scene of Natty Bumppo's adventures, and although the forest has disappeared long since, they pressed the lake into useful service. Williamson, the English producer, filmed a picture version of the tragic story of Lady Jane Grey, and the Tower of London formed the stage for some of the incidents in the sad story, culminating in the execution of the "nine days' queen."

Where do the moving picture producers obtain their plots? I have heard this question asked on many occasions, and the answer might be "everywhere." They have such an inexhaustible mine in which to delve that there is never any difficulty in finding an episode upon which to base a straightforward simple drama, comedy, tragedy, or farce. In this respect the cinematograph producer is far better off than his rival on the real stage. Situations, scenes, and episodes incapable of production by the latter, can be produced very simply on the film. Novels, short stories, plays, the Bible, Greek inscriptions, inventions, little episodes and incidents in everyday life—anything and everything is grist for his mill. Of course, fashions change just as in any other phase of our complex life. To-day there is a demand for subjects of mediæval English history; to-morrow the French revolutionary period holds the stage; three weeks hence there is a cry for Bible or ancient history subjects; or a demand for something modern. It is not difficult to meet each and every need. Most of the large producing establishments retain competent writers who know how to prepare plots for the picture producer, and in addition there is a staff to consider plots submitted from outside sources. The Edison Company receives 150 scenarios a week, and other companies as large or even a larger number. It will be discouraging but salutary to the beginner to hear that the chances of acceptance are very slender, the number of suitable scenarios being not more than one per cent. of those submitted. The remuneration varies according to the merit of the work. It may be taken merely for the title or one incident in the story, and may be worth only four shillings or a dollar to the producer; on the other hand, it may command £25 ($125). There is no fixed scale. The trained dramatist has realised that in the picture play he has a new and increasing source of revenue, and as he is the best fitted for the task, so he makes the greatest success in it. French writers were the first to take advantage of the market, and plays have been written and produced from the pen of many of the foremost dramatists—such accomplished men as Capus and others.

The entrance of the dramatist has precipitated a new situation. The suggestion has been discussed that well-known playwrights should decline to part with their work for a fixed sum, but that they should earn a royalty precisely as they do from their stage productions. It is an intricate question to solve, but there is no doubt that the time will come when such writers will receive a certain percentage upon the price realised from the sale of every film copy of a picture play from their pens.

A recent outcome of the development of the picture play has been the appearance of "independent producers," who are in evidence mostly on the Continent. These men enrol their own companies, rent or build a studio, paint their own scenery, and hire whatever properties are required from a theatrical costumier. The plays thus produced are sold to some recognised manufacturing firm. This "free lance" producer has an extensive market at his disposal, but his enterprise demands a large initial outlay. Yet it is a movement worthy of being fostered, inasmuch as such a producer is thrown entirely upon his own resources, and it is only the merit of his work from all points of view which secures him a market. The practice stimulates competition. Indeed, some manufacturers have found that in this manner they can secure work superior in character and treatment to that produced in their own establishments.

CHAPTER XIV

MOVING PICTURES OF MICROBES

DURING the past two or three years the cinematograph has entered a new field, which, fifteen years ago, would have been regarded as quite beyond its reach. With truly wonderful ingenuity the camera is attached to the microscope in such a way as to make possible the production of the actual processes of germ life.

The microscope is always a source of infinite interest. The thought of a whole world of organisms, existent, material, yet so small as to be invisible, has a peculiar fascination, and we are eagerly curious to get some conception of their structure and movements. But the possibility not merely of magnifying the red and white corpuscles of the blood till they appear like huge hoops, or the parasite of the sleeping sickness to a length of some two feet, to follow the attacks of these foes upon the human organism—such a possibility makes one feel that there is no limit to the power of man over the natural world.

Micro-cinematography is surely one of the serious triumphs of animated photography. Here again the latter offers itself as a coadjutor to scientific research, and proves its title to rank among the educational influences of the age.

Micro-cinematography may be divided into two broad classes—the study of bacteria, the most minute living organism which the scientific photographer has ever attempted to catch in motion, and popular microscopy, or the study of insects, plants, pond life, and so on.

Bacteriological micro-cinematography is an abstruse and difficult subject for investigation. The microbe is so sensitive to various influences, and so difficult to handle, that it is a formidable task to bring it within reach of the sensitised celluloid film and seize it in its normal condition and environment.

A French professor, Dr. J. Comandon, of Paris, has been for years absorbed in the study of the blood, its structure, functions, and the continuous warfare that is waged between the corpuscles, and a host of parasites as seen under the microscope and the ultra-microscope.

One supposes that the microscope is an ideal instrument for the investigation of those objects which are so minute as to be beyond the capacity of the human eye. This, however, is far from being the case. Briefly described, the microscopic investigation of bacteria is carried out by one or more of three broad processes, which are regarded almost as standardised methods. All three, however, possess numerous shortcomings. Often the bacteria has to be destroyed; and the slide has to be stained by means of aniline dyes, in order to bring up the details of the object sufficiently strongly for examinations; for the majority of the organisms under investigation are transparent, and their image stands out faintly against the brilliant light. Greater success is possible with the ultra-microscope than with the microscope. By its means objects so minute as to be invisible, even with the microscope, can be thrown as bright points upon a black background, not necessarily with sizes and forms clearly defined, but yet in such a way as to enable their positions and movements to be ascertained and followed.

The disadvantages of ordinary microscopic investigation are obvious. In many instances as the investigator has to kill the germ before he examines it, he has perforce to content himself with the study of coloured corpses of these infinitesimally small organisms.

It occurred to Dr. Comandon that possibly the microscope could be combined with the cinematograph in such a manner that the microbes could be photographed distinctly and brilliantly upon the film, and subsequently projected upon the screen with tremendous magnification, without the organisms suffering any distortion or other ill-effects. He realised that if this could be achieved, the scientist would be provided with a more powerful weapon for the examination of a particular microbe than hitherto has been available. Furthermore, if the object could be thrown on to the screen with perfect detail, then, owing to the tremendous magnification obtained, the study of the life, movement, and habits of the parasite would be possible under easy and congenial conditions.

The eminent French investigator approached Messrs. Pathé Frères, and unfolded his ideas. The technical difficulties in the way were prodigious, and the field was untested, both in microscopy and cinematography. However, as there was the possibility of some startling results being achieved, Pathé Frères decided to collaborate, and promised to provide Dr. Comandon with every facility he desired.

The work was commenced without delay, and the manufacturers proceeded with the construction of the special apparatus that was required. This had to be of an elaborate character, owing to the peculiar conditions; and exasperating failures attended the early work.

Although a cinematograph picture only measures approximately 1 inch in width by three-quarters of an inch in depth, the first magnification was considerable, ranging in the case of bacteria to 300 diameters or more. This had to be carried out with punctilious sharpness of detail, because when it came to projection, the magnification was multiplied enormously, and any error in the original picture or negative would be proportionately increased.

Bacteria are extremely sensitive to light and heat. Sunlight spells certain death to the microbe, and as a ray of electric light is the nearest artificial approach to the luminosity of our sun, its destructive component, the ultra-violet rays, had to be eliminated. Again, as the rays from the electric arc in the lantern focussed a strong heat upon the object, and as this likewise would bring about the sudden demise of the organism, the heat rays had to be mitigated as much as possible.

These two adverse factors were removed entirely by a novel arrangement. The illustration shows one of the apparatuses used by Dr. Comandon to secure his wonderful pictures. It is mounted on a rigid bench, and the parts which have to be moved to and fro to obtain adjustment, slide upon a horizontal triangular metal base, to which they are clamped in the requisite positions to secure rigidity. The lantern is mounted at the extreme end, and the light, supplied from an electric arc of 30 amperes, is concentrated into a thin ray, or pencil, which falls upon the object to be photographed, through which it passes to the film. The illumination may be either direct—that is, it may pass in a straight horizontal line from the lantern—or it may be reflected by means of a mirror in a direction perpendicular to the axis of the instrument, or at right angles, as in the ultra-microscope. The principle adopted varies according to the subject under observation. The organisms contained in a drop of blood, for instance, are dropped on to a carefully cleansed glass plate, which is inserted in the microscope in the usual manner.

At the opposite end of the bench is the cinematograph camera, which in this case is provided with extending bellows, as in the ordinary camera, for purposes of focussing. At the back of the camera is a small attachment whereby the bacteria, greatly magnified, can be focussed sharply and clearly upon the film. On top of the camera is mounted a small box containing the spool of unexposed sensitised film. When the contents of this are exhausted the box can be removed quickly and easily, and another charged film box substituted. The film drops from this box through the gate in the camera, and issues below into a second film box, which can be removed similarly when filled, to permit another empty case to be introduced. The mechanism of the camera itself is the same as that of the usual animated photographic camera, and it is operated in the same way, by the turning of a handle.

For the purpose of absorbing the heat rays, which in the

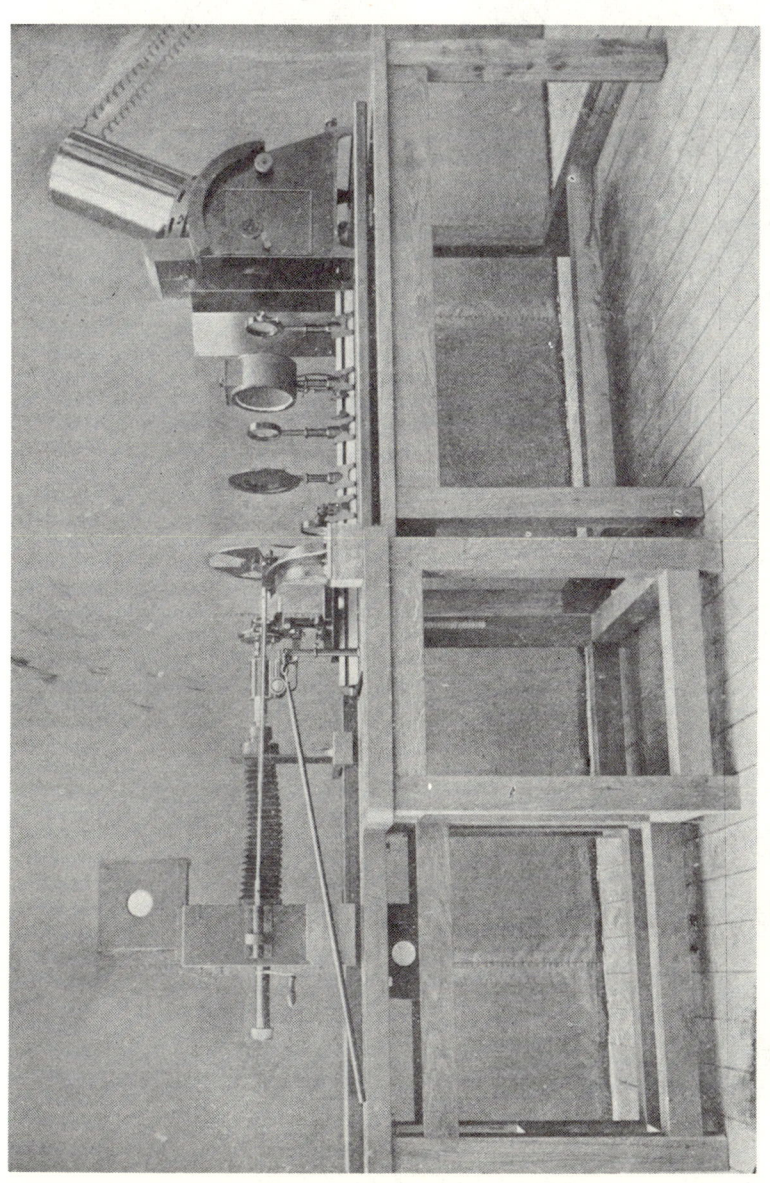

DR. COMANDON'S APPARATUS FOR TAKING MOVING PICTURES OF MICROBES.

The peculiar difficulties attending cinematographic work with germs demanded the preparation of special appliances. About twelve months were spent in experiments.

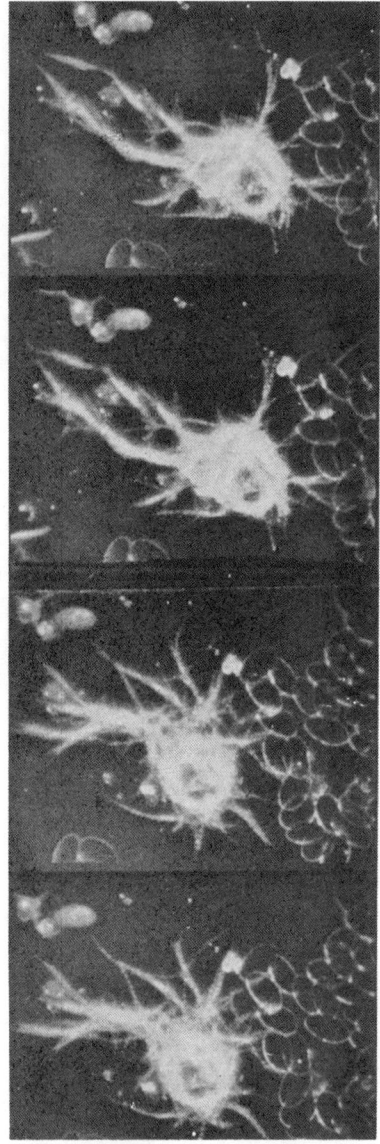 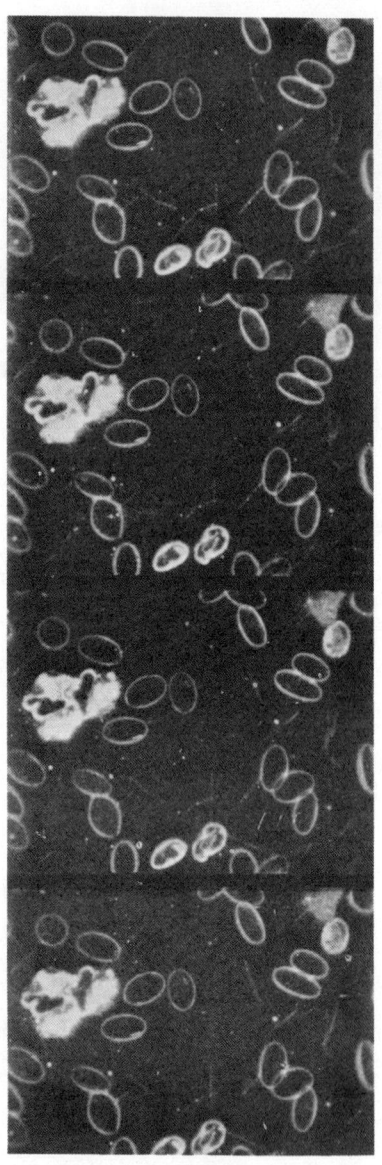

[Copyright, Pathé Frères.

CINEMATOGRAPH FILMS OF MICROBES.

1. The phenomenon of agglutination in a fowl's blood.

2. The blood of a fowl suffering from Spirochæta gallinarum.

concentrated beam of light would kill the microbes within a short space of time, a glass cell is inserted outside the lantern through which the focussed beam of light is passed. A stream of cold water is circulated continually through this water condenser, thus absorbing the greater proportion of the heat contained in the ray of light, without affecting its luminosity in any way. It will be observed that this is a reversion to the first projecting system evolved by the firm of Lumière for the cinematograph.

In order that the organism under photography should not be subjected to the action of the light any longer than is necessary, a revolving disc, or shutter, is placed between the microscope and the lantern. This shutter is fitted with opaque sectors or blades, corresponding to those in the camera, which at regular intervals eclipse the lens to enable the film to be jerked forward the depth of a picture intermittently after each exposure. This cut-off revolves with the camera shutter, so that when the lens aperture is closed, the light is also cut off from the organism slide in the microscope. By this arrangement the light passes through the slide of bacteria only during the fraction of a second that the celluloid film in the camera is exposed.

The evolution of this ingenious apparatus occupied several months of continuous work and hard thinking. Indeed, nearly a year was spent in experiments before a perfect film, suited to public exhibition, was produced.

As a result of the persevering and patient experiments on the part of Dr. Comandon and Messrs. Pathé Frères, a new and strange world has been revealed. The cinematograph, in conjunction with the microscope, has opened the gates of a kingdom long considered beyond the reach of all but the privileged few. Not only this; the bacteriological scientist is provided with facilities to study at ease intricate subjects which had hitherto baffled his skill. What the microscope is to the naked eye, the micro-cinematograph is to the microscope.

Some of the pictures obtained by Dr. Comandon are startling to such a degree as to be incredible. It was my privilege to see one of the first experimental films thrown upon the screen in the Paris Laboratory. It depicted the main blood stream of the frog magnified about 25,000 times. The corpuscles were plainly visible, being about the size of dinner plates. But most extraordinary was the form and movement of the parasite in the blood stream. This foreign organism resembled a tadpole in general appearance, and it darted with lightning-like rapidity to and fro, pressing home its attack upon the corpuscles of the blood with tremendous energy. One could scarcely believe that the eye was following the movements of an organism which under natural circumstances is beyond the scope of that organ. One had the sensation of gazing into a pond, where the spawn of the frog was in course of incubation, with specimens of the reptile in its first stages, darting hither and thither through the water.

Dr. Comandon introduced the spectator to still greater wonders in the under world. One may see in movement on the screen a drop of blood such as courses through one's own body. There are the red corpuscles, or cells of circular shape as large as saucers, and some are to be seen piled upon one another like coins. The extent of the magnification in this film may be seen when it is borne in mind that a cubic space measuring $\frac{61}{1000000}$ of an inch contains some 5,000,000 and 6,000 red and white blood cells respectively.

But the most fascinating spectacle to which we have been introduced by Dr. Comandon is the attack of the parasites upon the blood corpuscles, and the defensive tactics followed by the latter. There is one film showing blood infected with the trypanosome, discovered by Sir David Bruce, who was dispatched to Uganda by the Royal Society to investigate sleeping sickness. This malady is communicated by a species of the Tsetse-fly, which wreaks tremendous devastation among herds of cattle and horses in South Africa. For the purpose of this film Dr. Comandon inoculated a mouse with the parasite, and by the aid of the micro-cinematograph he shows the action of the disease germ through successive stages until the animal succumbs.

In the early part of the film the parasites are few in number; they are seen to dart to and fro among the blood cells with striking vigour and rapidity, jostling the corpuscles violently in all directions, and causing them to bounce against one another like india-rubber balls. As the film advances, showing the progress of the disease, the parasites are to be seen increasing rapidly in number. At last they appear to overwhelm the blood corpuscles, this multiplication continuing until death supervenes some four or five days after injection. The film was shown lately before a gathering of medical men, and created widespread interest, as it introduced them to a phase in the life of the parasite which hitherto had been beyond their comprehension.

Another film shows the "phenomenon of agglutination." The white cells of the blood act as the policemen of the stream and maintain a vigilant outlook for criminals in the form of parasites. When the microbe offenders come within the strong arms, or embrace, of this guardian, either they are seized, or serum substances are thrown out by the white corpuscles, which agglutinate, kill, and dissolve these enemies.

The film shows the blood of a fowl infected with spirochætes. In the first instance, the microbes are to be seen swimming about actively in the plasma—the liquid in which the red and white corpuscles are held. The bird is recovering from the malady; one sees the white cells engaged in their task of restoring law and order in the blood stream. The spirochætes commence to congregate, become sluggish in their movements, forming first strings, and then star-shaped groups. The white cell appears on the scene, and these enemies gather round him in a dense clump. The policeman grasps them in a sticky embrace from which they cannot escape, and in a short time all the spirochætes have joined one or other of the gatherings about a policeman. The latter continues to throw out the agglutinate, which locks the enemies as tightly together as if they were handcuffed. At first they wriggle and endeavour to escape, but the white blood cell is too powerful. Their struggles become weaker and weaker until at last they cease. The policeman completes his victory by devouring the corpses.

One must see these pictures in animation upon the screen to observe the wonderful definition, detail, and brilliancy which they reveal. The magnification is immense—the thousandth part of an inch is increased to three feet or more. When the picture on the screen measures some 16 feet in width, the organism is magnified as much as 50,000 or possibly 100,000 times; a flea is so increased in size that it represents a fearful prehistoric monster as large as an ordinary dwelling house. A magnification of 100,000 times the diameter of the original, however, by no means indicates the limits of the eminent French investigator's work. When the necessity arises, the enlargement can be carried to a far greater degree without any sacrifice of essential details.

Dr. Comandon's dogged perseverance in the face of disappointments has been crowned with complete success. Micro-cinematography is on the threshold of a vast field in which it has tremendous opportunities, the limits of which it is impossible to define.

CHAPTER XV

SOME ELABORATE PICTURE PLAYS AND HOW THEY WERE STAGED

THE first large film production, "The Passion Play," running to 3,000 feet, made its appearance, as we have seen, as far back as 1897—the result of unquenchable American ambition to be first in every field. It proved an amazing success; but it was regarded with greater favour by the public than by the manufacturers. They all acknowledged it to be a wonderful piece of work, but the prevailing opinion was that the public would tire of a picture lasting nearly an hour, and monopolising the greater part of the entertainment.

Moreover, such films were considered to be too speculative. The expense of staging them upon a scale suited to their length and importance was so heavy that the film-producers doubted whether the sales would be adequate to recoup the initial outlay. That fallacy, however, has been completely exploded. What was a marvel in 1897 is to-day a commonplace. The "Big Picture Play" is as much part and parcel of the cinematograph industry as the spectacular stage play is of the legitimate theatre. Every week records the appearance of an imposing subject from one or the other of the leading establishments.

The movement was established and developed by the firm of Pathé Frères. Having fixed their popularity upon a firm basis and developed their organisation to a high pitch of efficiency and resource, they decided to launch out upon a large scale into the new field. Striking historical subjects, especially of the French revolutionary period, offered them the greatest scope for gorgeous mounting; they had some apprehension about the attitude of the public toward such subjects, but their anxiety was quickly dissipated, partly, no doubt, because the plays were carried through with a vigour and sustained interest that defied the possibility of boredom.

French history has been a rich mine to the picture-play producer. The Reign of Terror and the Life and Times of Napoleon are the melodramatic episodes which offer such peculiar scope to the film play. They make an appeal to popular sentiment, especially to the French audience; the incidents in the career of the Little Corporal never failing to strike a strong emotional chord.

Such productions impose great responsibilities upon the producer, and demand a mastery of stage-craft, both in mounting the scenes and in handling the necessarily large companies of actors and actresses. There can be no consideration of expense; money must be poured out like water. Weeks and even months must be expended upon preliminaries; in order to achieve realism as many as possible of the scenes must be enacted in their natural surroundings, or else research must be carried out in order to stage the action with absolute fidelity—an exacting task, for the public is hypercritical.

In the first attempts the management of the crowds was perhaps the most troublesome factor. Large bodies of supernumeraries were enrolled, many possessed of stage experience. They had to be marshalled and put through their paces time after time, first without the principals, and then with them. Often days elapsed before the incidents in a scene dove-tailed tightly together, but the patience and perseverance of the manager were rewarded. Such scenes as the execution of Charlotte Corday, or the arraignment of the aristocrats before the Tribunal of Robespierre when thrown upon the screen stirred public enthusiasm to an extravagant degree.

Through this achievement, Pathé Frères became the first of picture-play producers. These elaborately staged films created a sensation, not only in France, but in England,

XV SOME ELABORATE PICTURE PLAYS 171

America, and other countries as well; and everywhere there followed emulation of the French success.

I have described in a previous chapter the disastrous effect of these films upon the American trade. American firms combined to keep them out of the home market as much as possible; and as a result of this combination American picture production, except in the case of a few eminent establishments, has never attained the technical excellence of the European studios. Two powerful manufacturing groups, the "Trust" and the "Independents" respectively, have the manager of the cinematograph theatre completely in their power. Each combination issues a certain number of films per week, which, through the "renter" or middle-man, are distributed to the theatres. The manager has no idea beforehand what he will be able to present to his patrons. Naturally this state of affairs does not stimulate excellence of production in the average studio, since the films have a market without regard to their quality.

The American producer cannot possibly court financial failure. He is certain of the sale of 80 copies of every film he makes; and as the sale of ten copies is sufficient to pay for the average expense of production, he is sure of a handsome profit on 70 copies or so—and this even if the picture is of the very poorest description.

The European method is quite different. An establishment produces a film, which is submitted to the "renter" or middleman. It is he who is the arbiter of success or failure. He buys the films which he considers will make a popular appeal, and rents them to the picture palaces.

Despite all I have said, it must not be thought that all the American films are inferior to the European productions. Such firms as the Edison, Selig, Vitagraph, the American Biograph, Kalem, Lubin, and one or two other companies have kept pace with European progress, and their films are in every way equal to the product of the leading European manufacturers.

The Vitagraph production of "A Tale of Two Cities" is a splendid example of the best American work. It tells

Dickens's story in three chapters, otherwise three reels, and from every point of view—photographic, staging, and acting—it is an excellent production. By the time the 3,000 feet containing 48,000 pictures reached the public £4,000 ($20,000) had been expended, while the preparations for staging occupied no less than three months. Curiously enough, although the Americans are keen admirers of the novelist who taught us how to laugh and cry, the demand for this film came from Europe, and it is in Europe that it has met with its greatest success. Within two or three weeks of its appearance over 300,000 feet of this film were sold in London alone.

The same firm produced another wonderful play on the life of Napoleon, which is probably the most costly film ever made in America. Mr. Stuart Blackton spent three months in France searching records and archives to secure unimpeachable historical accuracy of details. The country was ransacked also for furniture of the period, and for the staging of the interior scenes. No less than £6,000 ($30,000) were sunk in this enterprise.

Mr. William N. Selig, of the Selig establishment in Chicago, has recently made an astounding production depicting life in the jungle. He has been identified with many remarkable productions, but this is probably his most amazing feat.

For the purposes of these pictures a menagerie was acquired, complete enough to do credit to a large city. It consisted of 12 lions and lionesses, 9 lion cubs, elephants, 3 camels, 10 leopards, 7 leopard cubs, 5 pumas, 3 bears, 2 deer, 10 eskimo dogs, 8 grey wolves, as well as monkeys and other animals. As an investment the menagerie represents several thousands sterling.

The next matter in hand was the selection of the jungle. Would it be necessary to transport the actors and actresses, human and otherwise, to Africa in order to secure the natural surroundings? It was decided that Florida would suit just as well, because the flora near the coast is similar to that of some parts of the African jungle. The menagerie, together with the stock company of 30 per-

A REMARKABLE INSTANCE OF PICTURE-PLAY ENTERPRISE.

In order to obtain realistic and-dramatic films of life in the jungle the Selig Company transported a large company of actors and actresses, together with a menagerie, trainers, and operators, from Chicago to Florida.

The gigantic horse being hauled by the Greeks under the walls of Troy.

"THE FALL OF TROY."

The repulsion of the Greeks. Over 800 actors appeared in this scene.
An ambitious film produced by the Itala Company.—*See page* 175.

formers, as well as supernumeraries, travelled by special train from Chicago to Florida, a journey of several hundred miles. As African natives were impossible, Florida negroes were employed.

The production of the plays was naturally a thrilling affair, and many unexpected scenes were recorded. The animals were under the care of experienced trainers, but there was an occasional reversion to original habits under the influence of the familiar environment. In one scene the heroine was supposed to have lost herself in the dense bush, and to sink down from sheer fatigue. A leopard was to rush from the brush to spring upon her prostrate form. The scene was rehearsed time after time to secure the requisite dramatic effect; the operator was to stop the camera when the leopard was in the air springing towards the girl.

But when the picture was being taken the heroine did not accept her cue with sufficient alacrity. She was late in falling, and the leopard arriving exactly on his cue caught her in the act. The woman had the presence of mind to bury her face in her hands, but the animal's claws dug into her scalp. Had she made a movement, the leopard would have mauled her terribly, but she kept still, and when the trainer cracked his whip the animal scuttled off according to pre-arrangement. It was a narrow escape, but it gave the film a touch of vivid reality.

In another picture the heroine was protected by two tame leopards who mounted guard over her dwelling. The scene represented an attack upon her by a fierce lioness. The girl released her two leopards, and a terrific animal combat was the result. The beasts took the matter seriously, and fought until the lioness was killed by the two leopards. During the fray the operator, but a short distance away, kept the camera handle turning as unconcernedly as if the battling beasts were in a cage. Surely such an unusual spectacle is sufficient to meet the most querulous demands of the public for realism!

From the tropical jungle with its dense vegetation, to the Arctic circles with its monotonous wastes of snow and ice, is a far cry, but the Selig company dispatched its company northward to secure another powerful film play. The plot was slender, but the scenes portrayed the life of the frozen north with great fidelity and vigour, showing the Eskimo fishing through the ice, and hunting the polar bear and walrus by his primitive methods. A valuable polar bear was sacrificed to the desire for realism.

It is hard to estimate the educational service of scenes like these in broadening the outlook of an untravelled, perhaps unlettered, audience. And what they must contribute to the expanding imagination of the child, one would need to be a child again to know! An interesting attempt at a "big film play" was initiated by Mr. William Barker. He succeeded in persuading Sir Herbert Beerbohm Tree to let him film the Shakespearean production of Henry VIII. However, owing to the fact that the enterprise was bound by somewhat severe restrictions, the scope of the movement was defeated. If nowadays anyone can buy Caruso's voice on a gramophone record, why should not the interpretations of our greatest actors be brought within the reach of the masses? The truth is that the theatre manager still regards the moving picture in the light of a "penny gaff"—an attitude fraught with some danger to himself, for recent years have seen the cinematograph theatre encroach upon the successes of the legitimate stage to an extent that will force the manager to give it the respect due to a worthy foeman.

In the United States there are many theatres which can show bigger receipts at the box office from the presentation of moving pictures than from the staging of a play. Why are many of the foremost producers of stage plays forsaking the "legitimate theatre" to produce film plays, if not because they recognise the future of the latter and the scope offered for their technical ability.

Perhaps at this point I may be permitted to tell the story of the cinematograph in Italy, since its success there is very recent, and phenomenal in its completeness. Only six years ago the cinematograph was scarcely a feature of the Italian amusement world. It suffered from the hostility of the theatres, and there was but meagre enterprise enlisted in it. The example of other countries gradually caused increased popular demand, which was at first satisfied by French films. Then the Italians saw their opportunity, money and talent came to the service of the new development, and the languishing enterprise not only came to rank among the largest of Italian industries, but introduced its own wares with great success into other countries. Even the protected American manufacturers have not been altogether able to shut them out. There seems good ground for this state of things, and a special fitness in the Italian success. The average Italian is artist by temperament and a born actor; the Italian stage has long been famous for technique and stage-craft; and these factors, with the clear atmosphere, brilliant sun, and picturesque landscape, make Italy the natural home of the highest success in cinematograph production. Financially also the Italian producers have an advantage over all competitors. Luxurious picture plays can be staged in Italy for half the cost they would entail in France, England, or America. A French producer informed me that supernumeraries alone cost him from 10s. 6d. to 12s. 6d. a day, and that the salaries of the principals were rising to high figures. In Italy the remuneration is less than one-half.

A few months ago the Itala Film Company presented an historical film depicting "The Fall of Troy," undoubtedly the masterpiece of the establishment, employing 2,030 feet of film. It was lavishly mounted, carefully realistic, and the crowds in the big scenes aggregated over 800 actors and assistants. At the time of its production the films of the establishment were shut out from the American market, but the sensation created by it caused a demand among moving-picture enthusiasts in the United States, who saw no reason why they should be denied a film which was to be seen in every other part of the world. The Trust was compelled under public pressure to admit the film into the country—it forced its way into a rigorously protected territory sheerly by force of merit.

Another company, the Cines Societa Italiana, had long

been established in Rome, but its efforts were purely conventional. In 1908 new blood was infused into the undertaking, and its first ambitious effort was the pictorial representation of Alexander Dumas' famous novel, "The Three Musketeers," which lent itself admirably to handsome mounting, and fine acting in pantomime. The film ran to 1,500 feet. It made an instant success. In Great Britain alone over 50 copies of the film found an immediate sale, and a far greater number in Italy, France, Germany, and Russia. In Australia its reception was particularly enthusiastic.

Other most successful presentations were "Macbeth," which cost £2,000 ($10,000) to produce, Shakespeare's tragedy being condensed into 23,360 pictures, occupying 1,460 feet of film; "The Triumphant Hero," "Faust," "The Sacking of Rome," "Agrippina," and so on.

One might be inclined to suppose that some of these subjects were somewhat beyond British taste, but their success here has proved otherwise. As many as 80 copies of one of these big films have been sold in Great Britain alone, the total output for the world aggregating some 400 copies.

The experience of the Cines Company appears to confirm the theory that historical subjects make the strongest appeal. The public is fairly well acquainted with the milestones in European history, particularly those in connection with the rise and fall of Rome. Moreover, Italy is especially rich in beautiful landscape and historical sites, where the scenes can be re-enacted in their original setting—an advantage which the large companies realise to the uttermost.

The Cines Company is to-day one of the largest film-producing establishments in the world. It has three studios devoted to the staging of picture-plays, the premises in Rome having an area exceeding 128,000 square feet. Everything is installed upon a large scale—100,000 feet of film can be turned out every day. Six new subjects of travel, educational, and dramatic interest are placed on the market every week. The larger productions,

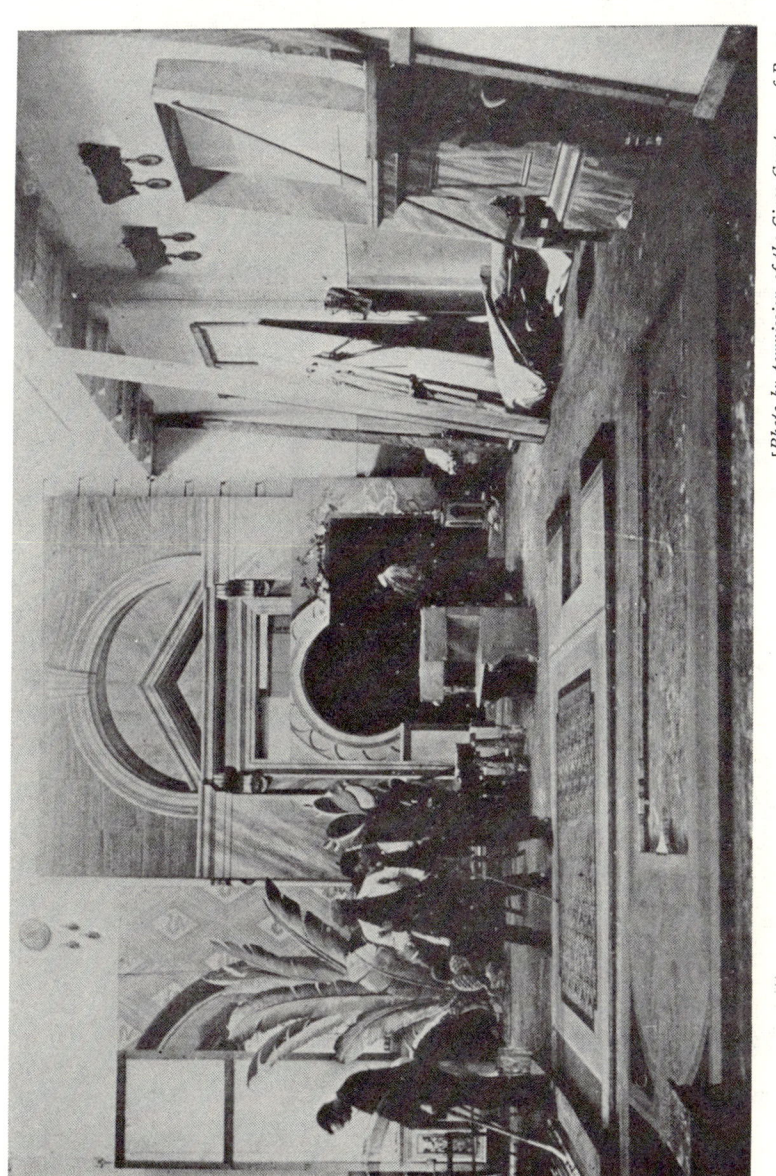

BUILDING AN ELABORATE INTERIOR SCENE FOR A PICTURE PLAY.

[Photo by permission of the Cines Company of Rome.

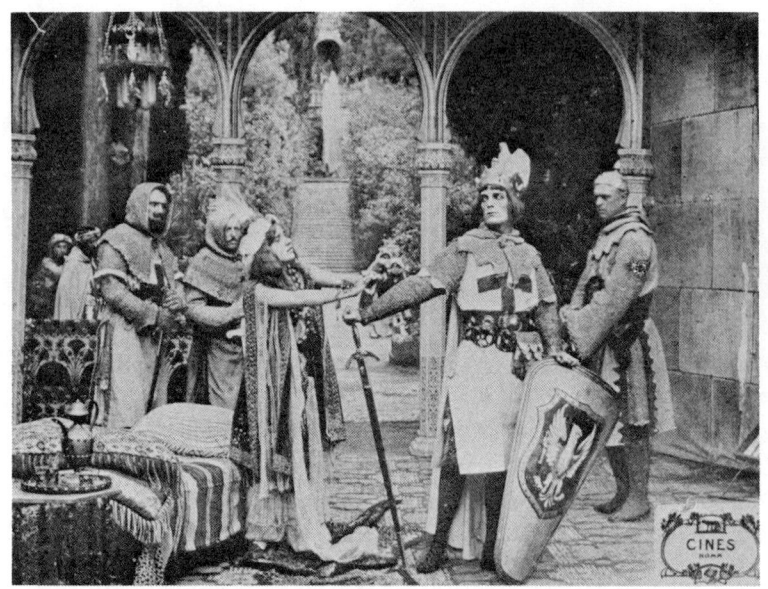

A scene from the picture-play representation of Tasso's poem, "Jerusalem."

An episode from "The Bride of the Nile."

TWO ELABORATE MASTERPIECES OF ITALIAN FILM PRODUCTION.

such as "Faust," "Judas Maccabæus," and so forth, appear regularly at intervals of about a month; the preliminary preparations are of such an extensive and elaborate character that they can scarcely be brought out at more frequent intervals. There is a demand in Great Britain, not only for "star" historical films from Italy, but also for those of a popular drama and humorous character.

The largest production of the Cines Company is undoubtedly the "Crusaders," a cinematograph version of Tasso's poem, which, it may be pointed out, is one of the longest films ever placed on the market, exceeding even the famous "Passion Play" of 1897. The film occupies nearly four reels, being 3,600 feet in length, and takes an hour and a half to project. This production required 600 players and 250 horses. When it appeared the film was sold exclusively to certain interests in different countries for a stated period, instead of being disposed broadcast among the "renters."

These big productions, however, entail a strong element of risk. The first difficulty is to select a subject which will make a world-wide appeal. The European manufacturers are not assured of 80 copies of each subject, irrespective of its character, as are their American contemporaries. When the negative has been obtained "sample" positive prints are prepared and dispatched to the great cities.

At each centre the firm attracts a certain number of patrons—possibly the aggregate of the first order may be only forty copies. Since a film running to 3,000 feet entails an outlay of £50 ($250) on the part of the renter, it is not surprising that he displays caution in making his purchases, because half-a-dozen copies of varied ordinary subjects can be acquired for the same money, with the additional advantage that the risks are spread over six subjects instead of being centred upon one. The initial order is fulfilled, and should the venture prove popular, a steady stream of orders may be expected to follow. However, the producer does not breathe freely until the two hundredth copy has been dispatched. Should the play fail to please the public, the manufacturer is faced with a heavy loss. The system has certain drawbacks, but it ensures the showman and the public being given the very best material, and causes very keen rivalry among the producers to eclipse one another's efforts.

There are certain subjects, however, which rarely fail of popular success, those of religious interest being foremost in the group. The "Life of Christ" was possibly the most successful venture of this description. It cost some £2,000 to stage. There were thirty-nine epochs, divided into four parts, and ranging from the "Nativity" to the "Crucifixion." Over 3,000 feet were required for their presentation. The film was largely purchased by religious societies. A certain "renter" is said to have amassed £30,000 from this single film. The story of "Cain and Abel," "The Trial of Abraham's Faith," "The Fall of Babylon," "Samson and Delilah," to name only a few, have proved powerful magnets. In the last-named the great scene was the destruction of the temple. The edifice was built of cardboard, and when Samson bent his strength in a final effort upon the columns, the whole structure came crashing to the ground.

Despite the antagonism of the "renter," the attitude of the public is distinctly favourable to the long film. Its production in Italy is being carried out with great vigour, one firm having been created expressly for the preparation of films having a minimum length of 3,000 feet.

CHAPTER XVI

PICTURES THAT MOVE, TALK, AND SING

When Edison invented the "Kinetoscope," his ambition was, not only to produce movement by the aid of pictures, but sound by the aid of the phonograph. But it proved a hopeless quest; and accordingly Edison confined his efforts for the time being to the perfection of animated photography.

In an earlier chapter I have described some devices for imitating sound. In this chapter I am speaking, not of imitation, but of reproduction. In order to secure perfect combination of movement and sound, it is essential to secure absolute synchronism in the actuation of the camera and that of the talking machine. This was Edison's insuperable difficulty. A single motor was utilised for both machines; but the phonograph was easier to stop and to restart than the camera, owing to the fact that the latter had to be driven at sufficient speed to secure 46 pictures per second.

The moving and singing picture machine known as the "Kinetograph," which worked upon the automatic "nickel-in-the-slot" principle, had a very brief existence. It was placed in cigar shops, railway stations, and other convenient public places, but it failed to interest the public, and was withdrawn in a short time.

Yet Edison did not relinquish his original plan. He cherished the idea that combined pictorial and audible records were feasible, and for nineteen years he devoted his energies to the consummation of the task. It was only a short time ago that the great inventor announced that he had succeeded at last. In the meantime, however, he had been anticipated by industrious and energetic experimenters in Europe.

In 1908 an attempt to produce motion and sound was made commercially with the "Cinephone." The solution presented in this apparatus is undoubtedly novel, but the results are very unsatisfactory, and its success is dependent entirely upon the skill of the operator. The "Cinephone" is designed to accompany the motions of acting with the sounds pertaining thereto. The pictures are fitted to the talking machine records—that is to say, the cinematographer merely takes a gramophone record and produces a film suitable thereto. Edison's plan was far more comprehensive. His idea was to prepare the phonographic record at the same time as the film pictures were made—for example, while a football or baseball match was being cinematographed, the phonograph was to record the applause, cheers, shouts—in short, make as complete a record for the ear as the camera did for the eye.

The principle governing the operation of the Cinephone is extremely simple. An ordinary talking machine is employed, without any modification beyond the addition of a small box with a governing dial, and a similar dial in the pictures upon the screen. The dial in each instance is fitted with a revolving hand, similar to that of a clock, and all that the operator is called upon to do is to keep the respective hands in relative positions by the manipulation of the projector.

The talking machine is mounted upon a baseboard, which is extended in front a sufficient distance to carry a small box the front face of which is fitted with the dial. The clock-like hand is transparent, and when an electric lamp, or other suitable illuminant, is placed within the box, it becomes illuminated, so that its rotation may be followed easily. The circle described by the hand is indicated at its four quarters by a small transparent point, through which passes the light from within the box. These four spots of light can be eclipsed and revealed by the movement of a shutter lever. When the lights appear the

XVI PICTURES THAT MOVE, TALK, AND SING 181

operator knows that the talking machine is ready. The hand of the rotating dial is actuated by mechanism driven by the motor of the talking machine, through a horizontal spindle.

In the bottom left-hand corner of each picture thrown on the screen is a duplicate of the talking machine dial. The position of the hand on each successive picture varies correspondingly with that on the gramophone, because in the preparation of the pictures the speaking or singing characters have accompanied the gramophone with their acting. When the picture is shown the speed of projection gives a steady forward motion to the hand on the picture dial.

When the apparatus is brought into play in the moving picture theatre the talking machine is placed on the stage in such a way that its illuminated dial is visible to the cinematograph operator. The latter's duty is to run the film through the machine at such a speed that the position of the hand on the picture dial keeps step with that of the talking machine dial. If this is done with precision, the action in the picture coincides with the sounds emitted from the talking machine.

This apparatus can be applied to any type of projector without any preliminary preparations whatever, and the mechanism of the latter has not to be modified or touched in any way. But, on the other hand, there are grave defects. Synchrony between picture and talking machine is dependent upon the operator, and until the latter has become accustomed to the combination, the results are disconcerting. It is no simple matter to keep the hands of the two dials rotating harmoniously. When the film lags behind the talking machine, a pronounced speeding up is requisite to bring the two hands into synchrony. The increased work thrown upon the operator is also far from being a negligible quantity. He has to watch the two dials intently, and cannot centre his mind upon the projector, as he should be free to do. More than once I have seen a film snap under the strain imposed in the effort to catch up with the talking machine, or the light has demanded attention, and the result has been far from pleasing. However, the appearance of the "Cinephone" served to stimulate inventive effort in this particular field, and proved to the public that the production of pictures that talked and sang, as well as moved, was by no means so forlorn a possibility as had been imagined generally.

The next attempt in the same direction met with better success—in the "Vivaphone," perfected by the Hepworth Manufacturing Company, Limited. In this machine the two dials were eliminated in favour of a single electric control or synchroniser.

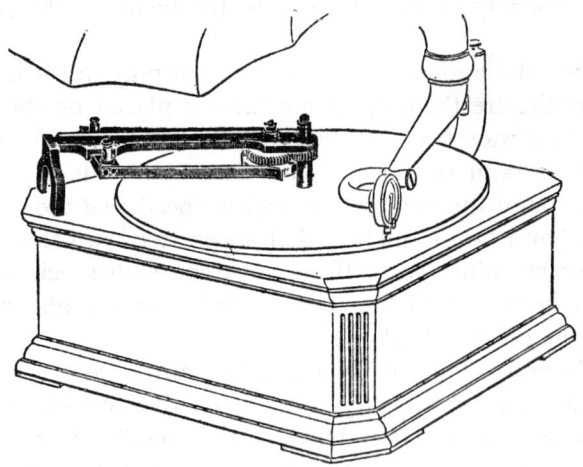

FIG. 14.—THE ELECTRICAL SYNCHRONISING ATTACHMENT TO THE TALKING MACHINE IN THE "VIVAPHONE."

In the projecting box by the operator's side is a small, compact case. This is the synchroniser, consisting primarily of a vertical needle, which can move to the right or to the left. The movement or deflection of this needle is effected by means of two electromagnets. One exerts a pull upon the needle towards the right, while the other draws it in the opposite direction. These two electromagnets are electrically connected to the cinematograph and to the talking machine respectively.

The attachments to the projector and the gramophone are very simple. The electrical contact device or commutator

XVI PICTURES THAT MOVE, TALK, AND SING 183

is attached to the handle to establish connection between the two parts of the apparatus. On the gramophone is another commutator (Fig. 14). It consists of an arm, one edge of which rests on the case of the talking machine, while the opposite end engages with the motor spindle of the gramophone projecting vertically through the turn-table.

The installation of this apparatus (Fig. 15) is likewise simple. The synchroniser *A* is placed in a convenient position in the operator's box, while the gramophone *B* is set upon the stage. From the projecting handle commutator *C* a pair of wires are run and attached to the connections *K* in the synchroniser, while similarly a pair of

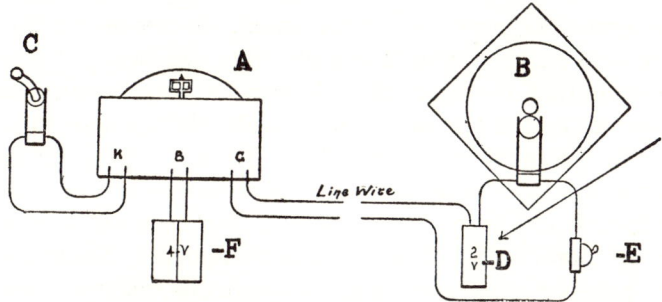

FIG. 15.—THE ELECTRICAL WIRING SYSTEM OF THE "VIVAPHONE."

wires are carried from the talking machine commutator to the connections *G* in the synchroniser. Two wires are led from the terminals *B* in the synchroniser to the battery *F*. Sufficient energy for the electric current is furnished from a 4 or 6 volt accumulator, such as is used in automobile practice, or from a dry storage battery. Ordinary bell wire suffices for the purposes of the connections. If the distance between the screen and the projecting box is very great it is advisable to introduce an auxiliary cell *D* in the gramophone circuit.

Behind the vertical needle of the synchroniser is a narrow transparent slot, which, when the synchrony is perfect, is covered by the needle itself. The upper end of the needle is fitted with two small glazed apertures or spectacle glasses, one on either side, fitted with red and green glass respectively. When the apparatus is in use the two electromagnets controlled by the cinematograph and the gramophone respectively exert a pull in opposite directions—the gramophone endeavours to draw the needle one way, and the projector electromagnet attempts to pull it in the other direction. If the projector is lagging, the needle moves over, bringing the red spectacle before the light aperture, and the red light thus shown warns the operator to accelerate the projector. On the other hand, if the projector is running too fast, the needle moves in the opposite direction and brings the green light into prominence. The degree of the deflection of the needle indicates how far the synchronisation is disturbed. When the opposing forces of the electromagnets are exactly equal, the needle maintains a vertical position, and shows absolute synchrony. It will be seen that the signalling system is very sensitive and accurate, and at the same time enables the operator to have complete control over projection. In fact this is the most perfect system of synchronising the pictures with the sounds emitted from the gramophone that has been yet produced in the combination of sound and movement. Some excellent subjects have been produced with this machine, one of the finest being the sound and movement reproduction of "Faust."

But, after all, these devices are far from representing the ideal singing and talking cinematograph. The drawback is this: the conditions prevent the pictures being secured at the same moment that the relative sounds are being recorded by the gramophone.

While Edison was striving with the problem, French investigators were active, and the first practical success in the field must be credited to Monsieur Léon Gaumont, the head of the French cinematograph establishment of that name. He succeeded where Edison failed; or rather, he anticipated the famous American inventor by several years. It was as far back as November 7th, 1902, that Monsieur Gaumont introduced his achievement for the first time before the French Photographic Society. The apparatus was not yet perfect, but it served to demonstrate that the synchronous production of sound and movement by the aid of the cinematograph and the talking machine was within measurable distance of attainment. The demonstration was held primarily to show how perfect a synchronising mechanism had been evolved. The great difficulty encountered was in regard to the sensitive character of the material required for taking the records of sounds from a distance. The ordinary process then in vogue was far from being suitable. By the aid of several interested friends and collaborators, however, Monsieur Gaumont was able to conquer this obstacle, and on December 27th, 1910, the "Chronophone," as the new invention is called, was submitted to the approval of the French Academy of Sciences and was regarded as eminently successful by that distinguished learned body.

Synchronism—both in producing and reproducing—between the cinematograph and the talking machine is secured by electrical connections between motors which furnish the requisite power for driving the two essential parts of the apparatus. In evolving such a combination as this the inventor had to bear in mind that portability and simplicity were two fundamental requisitions, so that resort to heavy, bulky, and intricate mechanism was quite out of the question. In comparison with the Cinephone and Vivaphone, the Chronophone appears somewhat complicated. But this is only relative. The apparatus is almost entirely automatic in its operation. Yet it can be operated by hand if necessary. If the latter method is adopted, the energy required to secure synchrony is derived from batteries or accumulators.

Synchrony is obtained by means of a patented system, which may be briefly described. The two motors required for driving the talking machine and the cinematograph respectively are of identical design, of approximately the same power, and are operated by the same direct current. The armatures of each motor are divided into sections, and the corresponding sections of the two armatures are connected together. By means of this arrangement the two armatures are rotated at the same speed, notwithstanding the slight differences in the mechanical resistance opposed to the machines.

The talking machine, driven by an electric motor, is of the disc type, fitted with two horns, so as to diffuse the sounds through the building. If the theatre is spacious the number of horns may be increased, while the sound waves projected into the hall may be intensified in volume by means of compressed air, as in the Auxetophone devised by the Hon. C. A. Parsons, which is also capable of considerable adjustment, so that the volume of sound may

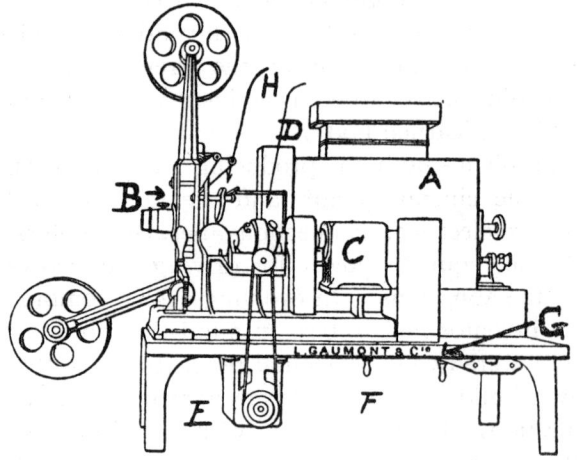

FIG. 16.—THE GAUMONT "CHRONOPHONE."

be accommodated to the acoustic properties of the building.

In comparison with the ordinary bioscope mechanism the Chronophone projector appears somewhat intricate, but here again everything has been simplified to a remarkable degree, while all adjustments are carried out automatically. The projector installation (Fig. 16), in addition to the lantern A and projecting mechanism B employed in the ordinary equipment, consists of a small motor C, which drives the projector mechanism proper and a differential D, whereby error between sound and movement is corrected, driven by a small motor E.

To start the apparatus, the first picture of the film, say

XVI PICTURES THAT MOVE, TALK, AND SING 187

that of the title, is placed in the film gate before the exposure aperture, and the needle of the talking machine sound box is placed on the first groove of the disc record. The talking machine motor is started, and the table carrying the record commences to revolve. Directly the needle reaches the point in the disc groove where the first sound wave has been recorded, an electrical contact is established, which is transmitted to the projector, and sets the latter in motion. But it may be that the speed is too much or not enough; the pictures move too slowly or too quickly, and the tone of the sound emitted by the talking machine is unnatural. In this case the operator moves the rheostat handle F over its contacts, this movement accelerating both the talking machine and the projector until the correct natural speed has been secured.

Again it may be that the pictures are slightly in advance of the phonograph, or *vice versâ*; the movements of the lips of the singer or actions of the performer do not coincide with the emission of sound. This error may be rectified instantly. There is a two-way commutator on the control board, which the operator moves in one direction or the other according to requirements. This instantly starts up the small dynamo E, the power of which is transmitted through belt and pulley to the differential gearing D, which works on the same shaft as that driving the projector. If the projector is lagging it is speeded up, so as to overtake the talking machine, or if the pictures are in advance of the sound, it is retarded until synchronism is restored. This device is particularly useful, inasmuch as the talking machine is somewhat sensitive to outside disturbance; if the machine is not set quite level, or receives a violent vibration, the needle jumps suddenly from one groove into another. By accelerating the projector this lead can soon be reduced without touching the talking machine in the slightest.

The operator need not follow the movement of the pictures upon the screen, or listen to the talking machine in order to ascertain that synchrony is perfect. He merely keeps his eye on an ingenious, simple "control board," which is set up in a convenient position beside the projector operator. It includes a starting gear, whereby the talking machine is set in motion, and which in turn actuates the cinematograph by the disc electrical contact, an electric switch, a volt meter, which acts as a speed indicator, its readings, in fact, having a constant relation to the revolving speed of the talking machine turn-table; and a two-way commutator, where the differential motor is started up.

The differential gearing is somewhat interesting. It belongs to the four-wheel type. There are two driven cog wheels 1 and 2 keyed to the ends of the interrupted shaft of the projector motor, and between these two wheels, and set at right angles thereto, are two satellite wheels 3 and 4, which mesh with the former wheels. If the cinematograph and the talking machine are moving in exact synchrony, the wheels 1 and 2 run at similar speed, but in opposite directions, and in harmony with wheels 3 and 4. To the short end of the interrupted shaft a needle is attached, and when synchrony is prevailing this needle maintains a vertical position. Now, if the phonograph runs away from the projector, this needle moves either to the right or to the left, and as it slides over a graduated scale the operator can detect in an instant how many pictures the projector is lagging behind the talking machine. The cinematograph projector accordingly must be speeded up, and the operator moves the commutator on his control board in the desired direction. Then instead of the two satellite wheels meshing evenly with the two wheels 1 and 2, they become displaced, with the result that the shaft driving the projector is rotated more rapidly, and overtakes the talking machine, the needle on the dial meanwhile moving towards zero, until, when it reaches its vertical position, the differential gearing and its motor are stopped. If the projector should have advanced before the talking machine, it is retarded, the needle deflecting in the opposite direction and requiring to be restored to zero. It will be seen that the speed of the talking machine remains constant. Any correction that has to be made is effected by means of accelerating or retarding the speed of projection.

As, however, the records of movement and sound are made in synchrony, and in view of the fact that both projector and talking machine run at the same speed, if started simultaneously no displacement of one in relation to the other should result. The differential, however, provides a means of correcting any accidental displacement of the phonograph needle when reproduction is carried out.

The Gaumont apparatus has proved highly successful, and has been turned to useful account already; we have excerpts from operas, ballets, recitations, and so forth recorded and projected with a perfect relationship between sound and movement. Through the energy and perseverance of Monsieur Gaumont the value of animated pictures has received a decisive forward impetus.

Edison has devoted his energies in the solution of the problem to the perfection of a more sensitive material than the wax hitherto employed. Naturally he has confined his attention to adapting to this work the phonograph or cylinder talking machine in preference to the disc machine, the former being his own invention.

What is the future of the phono-cinematograph? In the first place, until the peculiar nasal sound is eliminated from the talking machine it will not prove popular. It is well-nigh impossible, unless a speaker or singer has peculiar characteristics, to identify voices on this instrument. Furthermore expression in tone is practically nonexistent. Though the cinematographic world be flooded with talking and singing pictures, unless they are of some peculiar interest, the majority of picture-theatre lovers, after the first wave of excitement and curiosity, will patronise those establishments where they can see movement alone.

CHAPTER XVII

POPULAR SCIENCE AS REVEALED BY THE CINEMATOGRAPH

THE average audience before the micro-cinematographic film is very much in the attitude of the schoolboy in the natural history lesson. Scarcely any other subject holds such possibilities of interest for him; yet the instruction must be given in some vivifying form, or it fails to touch his latent sympathy, and becomes a tiresome repetition of formulæ and inexplicable processes. Similarly an audience will sit absorbed before a film displaying infinitesimal organic life; but only on condition that its human instincts are in some way appealed to. Science lessons must be humanised, when they rival the most dramatic films in interest.

Unfortunately the supply of this kind of film is extremely limited. Producers are not convinced of the heartiness of the demand; and the labour, expense, and anxiety attending the preparation of such subjects prevent their development upon any but a small scale.

An account has been given of Dr. Comandon's wonderful achievements in bacteriological micro-cinematography, through the firm of Pathé Frères. In popular science the world's market is practically supplied by an English company, Kineto, Limited.

This fact is due mainly to Mr. F. Percy Smith, who possesses the happy faculty of investing his subjects with a quaint fascination which compels appreciation. It is doubtful whether any film has stirred popular interest so intensely as that which he prepared for the purpose of illustrating the physical energy possessed by the common house-fly.

When this film appeared the newspapers far and wide associated the cinematographer with strange powers, and the capacity to train the bluebottle in much the same way as the lion tamer subdues the King of the Forest. Nothing was farther from the truth. The scientist merely devised unusual and novel devices to illustrate the points which he had in mind, and the fly was left more or less to follow its own devices. For instance, it was seen to walk again and again up the rim of a small wheel in a vain effort to reach the highest point. "Trickery!" was the verdict when the film was seen first, and it was hard to make people believe that the picture was genuine. As a matter of fact, the fly performed the operation quite naturally, though in order to induce it to do so the experimenter had to resort to an ingenious device.

A dark box was prepared with a very small door of thin glass at one end. This piece of glass was fitted with a narrow slit in which a small toothed wheel, similar to a watch escapement wheel, was fitted in such a way as to be free to revolve. The imprisoned fly, seeing the daylight entering through the glazed end of the box, attempted to escape in that direction, but found its passage obstructed by the glass. When it struck the latter, it received a smart tap on the head from a tooth in the wheel, which was caused to move through the fly's frantic efforts. Time after time the fly threw itself against the glass door, and on every occasion it received a rap on the head. At last frenzy gave way to tractability, and it came to the conclusion that the best means of escape was by walking up the wheel. Of course, as it advanced the wheel slipped round in the opposite direction. While the insect was walking like a criminal on a treadmill, the pictures were taken.

The results with the fly under restraint, however, were not entirely satisfactory, so the experimenter set up the wheel in the open, and withdrew a fly from its prison after it had become tractable. Time after time the blue-bottle would fly away directly it was placed on the wheel. The camera, however, was kept in readiness for exposure the moment a fly did attempt to walk along the rim, and at length it was successfully caught in the act. Again, the fly was laid upon its back beneath the wheel, and was seen to revolve the disc with its legs. The simple explanation of this seemingly clever juggling trick was that the fly thought it was walking in the same way that it walks up a wall or along the ceiling.

One fly in the same film was seen seated in a diminutive chair nursing a smaller fly, or balancing and juggling with articles such as tiny dumb-bells, but of large size in comparison with its own bulk. In this instance the fly was secured by a thin strand of silk passed around its body; but here again, in performing the apparent juggling feats, it was merely following its instinct. Being prevented from flying, it naturally endeavoured to make progress by walking.

The fly was to be seen endeavouring to balance a piece of cork, and intense amusement was caused when it was seen to wipe its feet, in the same way that a man rubs his hands together, preparatory to making some kind of effort. In reality, the fly found that the suckers on its feet, by means of which it secures a grip upon a surface when walking upside down, were somewhat dusty. The apparent preparation for a herculean attempt was nothing more than the fly cleaning its organs to achieve its purpose.

This film occupied several weeks in preparation. Extreme patience had to be exercised, and when a desired phase of movement had been secured, often it was found defective from the technical point of view, so that the wearying round had to be repeated. Recently Mr. Smith has continued his investigations, and has produced another fascinating film, demonstrating still more clearly the tremendous physical energy possessed by the bluebottle, and the wonderful powers of its proboscis, the movements of which, to assist the legs, are shown very distinctly.

Another of Mr. Smith's achievements is the film showing the hatching of a chicken's egg. The period of incubation is extended over 21 days—about 500 hours—and

NATURE AND THE CINEMATOGRAPHER—MR. PERCY SMITH AT WORK.

Great Britain has taken the lead in bringing the wonders of science popularly before the public.—*See page* 190.

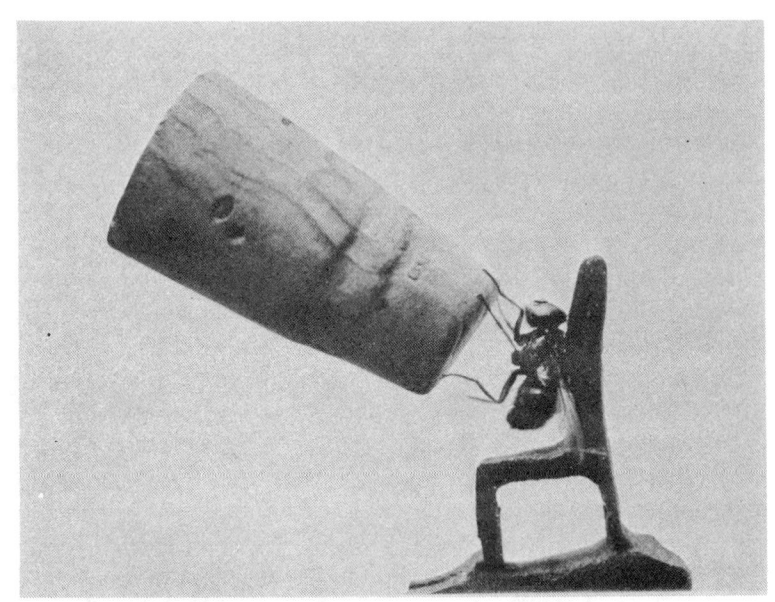

FLY SEATED IN A DIMINUTIVE CHAIR BALANCING A CORK.

AN UNFAMILIAR JUGGLER—BLUEBOTTLE BALANCING A PIECE OF VEGETABLE STALK.

the egg naturally has to be preserved at an even temperature the whole time, so some special means had to be devised to make the film without imperilling the life of the embryo. The opaqueness of the shell constituted a formidable stumbling-block. Moreover, in the initial stages the embryo is so small, and its movement so slight, that little difference is observable for the first 50 hours or more. Direct photography was seen to be out of the question.

An incubator was acquired, and the eggs were placed in it. At regular and frequent intervals during the incubation, some were withdrawn, and opened to ascertain the size and position of the embryo.

From these data diagrams of the early stages were prepared. They were drawn carefully to scale and accurate in every detail. This task had to be continued during the first 54 hours—the period when the movements of the embryo were unknown—and involved the preparation of no fewer than 1,000 diagrams, prepared in such a way that they resembled photographs. From the number of these records and the period occupied in incubation, it will be seen that they were prepared at intervals of about three minutes during both day and night. This consecutive series were then cinematographed upon the film, and thus a natural development lasting $2\frac{1}{2}$ days was reduced to a period of about one minute upon the screen.

The early part of the film is not so interesting to the public as that showing the chick coming out of the shell. Here again an initial difficulty was encountered. The hatching, of course, could not be cinematographed inside the incubator; and to remove the egg from the temperature of 103° in which it had been kept was to arrest the process at once.

Fortunately the experiment was being made in summer, and the thermometer read 103° in the sun. The camera was set up, and at the moment the chick gave signs of breaking through its shell, the egg was removed from the incubator and placed upon a table in the full glare and heat of the sun. In a few seconds the chick made further efforts to break down the walls of its prison, and very soon made the first breach in the shell. As the heat of the sun was exactly that of the incubator, hatching was continued under precisely natural conditions. It was not long before the hole in the shell was widened sufficiently to enable the chick to wriggle its way into the world. From the cinematographic point of view, the hatch was as perfect as could be desired, especially as the chick was strong and active after hatching.

Mr. Smith once ventured into the Sussex woods, to obtain some animated photographs of the British adder in its natural haunts. He succeeded in tracking down an excellent specimen, of which some first-rate pictures were taken. Then he proceeded to record on the film the methods by which this reptile may be caught and handled in safety. While holding a large specimen in his hand he provoked it to fury, and caused it to strike out savagely, so as to secure on the film some life-like pictures of an adder striking, as well as details of its mouth and fangs. As a contrast, he then decided to show how an adder should *not* be handled. He took the precaution to chloroform the reptile before mis-handling it, but the snake recovered too soon from the anæsthetic, and striking out with its fangs, caught the investigator a smart blow on the hand, leaving two minute punctures. The bite of the adder is seldom fatal, but, contrary to popular belief, it is far from harmless, producing delirium and precipitating collapse, recovery from which occupies several hours, or in some cases even weeks, as Mr. Smith found to his cost.

An unusually successful popular science film is the one showing the development of a flower from seed to blossom. It has been encored more than once on being presented.

The average plant demands several weeks from seed to blossom. Mr. Smith made an ingenious apparatus for securing a continuous representation of growth. The seed was shown first in the initial stages until the embryo burst from the protective or outer shell or husk; and then continuously from the moment the first sign of the shoot appeared above the level of the soil.

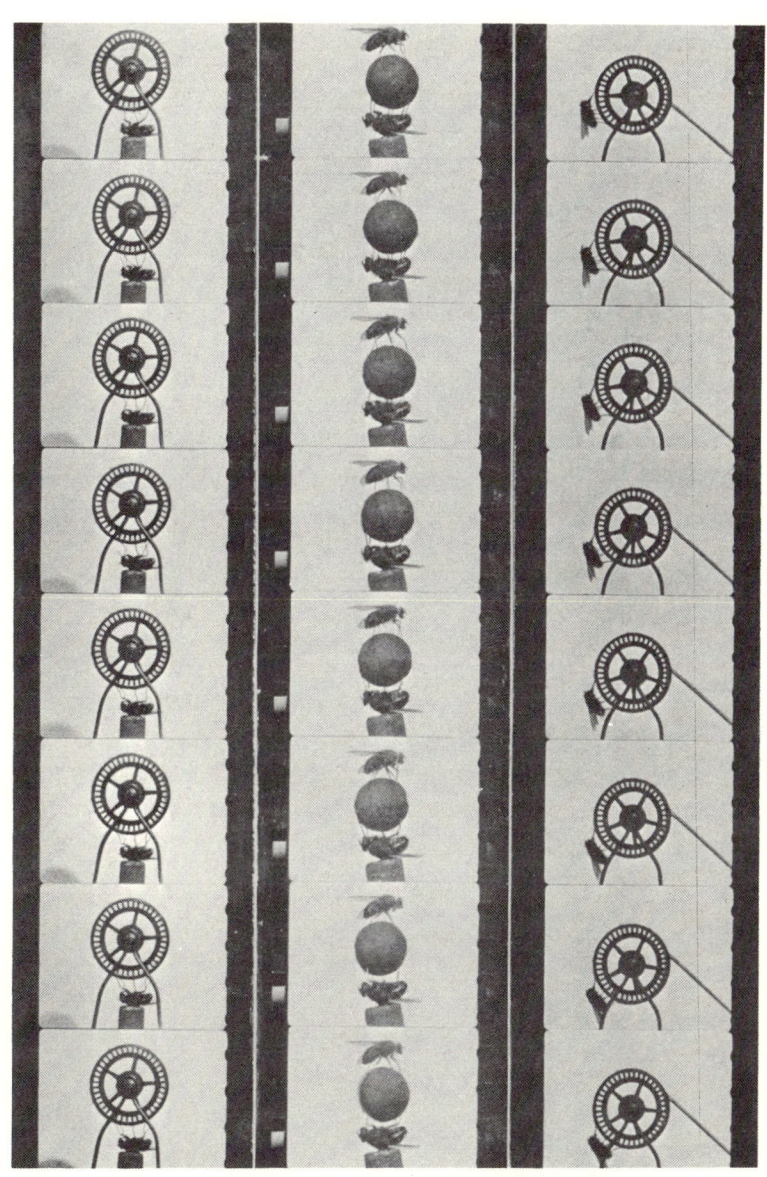

[Copyright, Urban Trading Co., Ltd.

DEMONSTRATING THE PHYSICAL ENERGY OF THE FLY.

1. Fly lying on its back spinning a wheel. 2. Juggling flies.
3. The fly walking up the turning wheel.

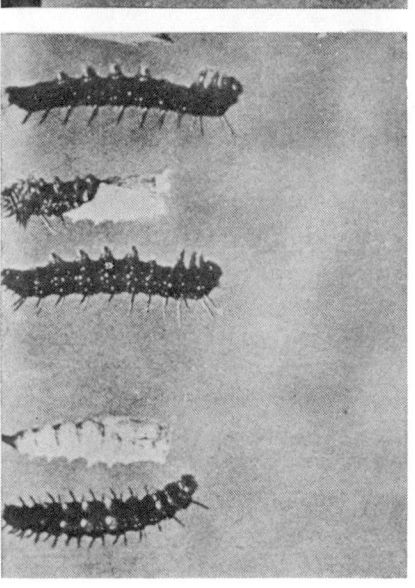

THE LIFE OF THE BUTTERFLY.

This remarkable film, prepared by the Ambrosio Company of Italy, illustrates the fascinating evolution of the butterfly from the caterpillar. It secured the premier award of 5,000 francs for the best natural history film in the cinematograph section of the recent Turin Exhibition.
—*See page* 324.

The camera was set up and an automatic apparatus attached thereto, which enabled an exposure to be made at predetermined intervals both during the day and night. The apparatus was driven by a curious motor which obtained its power from dripping water; and the arrangement was such that, after the exposure was made, the film was moved forward to bring the next area of sensitised surface before the lens. The receptacle containing the seed was placed at the correct distance to ensure a large picture, and for the purposes of illumination at night a special device was connected to the driving mechanism of the camera, whereby the subject was brilliantly illuminated at the instant of exposure. The exposures were made at average intervals of thirty minutes, giving forty-eight exposures at different stages of the growth in the course of the twenty-four hours. When projected on the screen at the normal rate of sixteen pictures per second, it looks as though the growth of the plant had been forced to about 30,000 times its usual speed, with the camera continuously in operation the whole time.

The great secret of Mr. Smith's success is the simplicity of the apparatus he employs for his work. Each subject demands special arrangements. His contrivances for the most part are extemporised from crude materials; even the microscope, which he sometimes uses, being of the simplest and cheapest pattern. He has found that elaborate apparatus often complicates his work without producing such good results as are procurable by the most primitive devices.

Work in this field is attended with some curious results. The eyes of some of the lower animals are extremely fine lenses, and unless care is bestowed some sorry tricks are played at the expense of the scientist. Mr. Smith related to me that on one occasion he secured an excellent series of pictures of the frog at close quarters; and congratulated himself upon his success. His dismay was great when he projected the pictures for the first time. Although the frog itself was beyond reproach, interest in it paled before the unexpected sight of the operator turning the handle of the cinematograph, reflected with great distinctness in the frog's eye.

There is one great difficulty attending the photography of the smaller organisms of Nature which is very difficult to surmount; that is, unnatural results arising either from the disturbance of the object under examination, or its photography in a false environment. This complexity is emphasised very strongly in connection with cinematography. If it is desired, for instance, to record garden pests engaged in their destructive work, it is trying indeed to convey a correct pictorial description of their methods. Troubles concerning illumination are particularly baffling of solution. Mr. Smith has devised a special apparatus, which is very similar in its general characteristics to a heliograph, mounted upon a tripod stand so that it can be revolved in any direction. With this parabolic reflector the sunlight can be brought into position and concentrated upon the subject under cinematographic observation without disturbing it. The photographs by this means of insects at work, no matter how unreal they may appear at first sight, are absolutely true to Nature, and are taken under incontestably natural conditions. In fact, the ray of illumination thrown upon the object by this means is so brilliant as to enable subjects to be photographed in their natural colours; which fact may in the future afford scientists a wonderful opportunity of studying protective colouring in insects.

It is probably beyond dispute that the popular scientific film, treated in such a manner as is indicated in this chapter, is certain to command the approval of the public in the end. At the present moment the popular scientific cinematograph picture is in its infancy. It will be only through the perseverance of the scientist who has the happy faculty of amusing as well as entertaining a general audience that this class of film ever will have a vogue. The tendency towards this state of affairs, happily, is improving every day, for the cinematograph is appealing more and more to the cultured classes, who, after all, constitute its most substantial support.

CHAPTER XVIII

TRICK PICTURES AND HOW THEY ARE PRODUCED

I.—The first attempts at cinematograph magic and the artifices adopted

As soon as the cinematograph had established itself firmly in popular favour, and there was every indication that it would become a permanent form of entertainment, it entered one field after another of popular interest. We have seen how the picture play was evolved from unrehearsed episodes in everyday life; and when the studio-stage became an indispensable acquisition to the picture play producer, another movement was created. This was the trick film. The pioneers realised that the intervals between the exposure of successive sections of film corresponding to an image offered extreme opportunities for the practice of chicanery, and the presentation of weird, fantastic, and mystifying effects.

The trick-film owes its inception to a well-known French prestidigitateur, Monsieur Méliès. He was among the first to embark upon the manufacture of film subjects, and it naturally occurred to him to impress magic into the service of the industry. His first attempts were of the simplest description. He confined himself to the performance before the camera of the same tricks that he offered an audience from behind the footlights.

Having by this means tested the public and found it responsive, he introduced all the devices known to the "Black Art." Furniture danced upon the screen, and moved hither and thither about a room; skeletons gambolled capriciously; weird displays of "Black Magic" were shown; all sorts of inanimate objects were imbued with life; dolls and toy animals and birds were given the semblance of natural action. The films amused and mystified the public exceedingly, and the Méliès trick films enjoyed a remarkable vogue.

Meanwhile, Robert Paul in England had been considering the feasibility of the same idea, but had feared that the personality of the magician would be missed. Seeing the success of the Frenchman, he decided to embark upon a similar line of activity. He saw the possibility of producing far more startling effects than even the most accomplished and dexterous magician ever could hope to achieve. But the task bristled with difficulties. The stage had to be overhauled and equipped with elaborate devices to facilitate sudden disappearances, apparitions, etc. A workshop also was necessary for the preparation of the properties, and the character of the work rendered indispensable the services of an expert magician.

Cinematographic knowledge was in its infancy; and accordingly some of the methods used in the late 'nineties seem somewhat involved as compared with those practised to-day. But it was upon these early struggles and failures that the present adequate equipment was built up. Indeed, from the point of view of the audience many of these first films have never been surpassed.

To describe the methods adopted in the production of every trick picture is obviously impossible in the compass of this volume, but I am able, through the courtesy of Mr. Robert Paul, to explain how many of the strange effects in his most striking trick films were achieved. The processes most generally practised were the "stop-motion" and "double printing," which are explained fully in the next chapter, but in addition to these methods he devised many others, some of which have been superseded by easier operations. For example, where gradual disappearances and appearances were desired, instead of using a rectilinear diaphragm stop in the lens as is now usual, Paul occasionally resorted to the chemical dissolution of the emulsion and image from the film—an intricate and delicate manipulation entailing considerable time and care, because if the dissolution process were carried too far or undertaken by unskilled hands, the film was spoiled and much labour fruitlessly expended.

Sometimes the desired result was brought about by means of two special detachable stops, which were placed in the lens. Each of these stops had a V-shaped opening of identical dimensions, and were set at right-angles to one another. As they were gradually drawn apart the aperture formed by the intersection of the V-openings through which the light passed to the film was enlarged, while, on the other hand, as they were moved towards one another, the aperture was decreased, until at last the film scarcely recorded any impression of the subject photographed. The gradual synchronous movement of these two V-shaped stops was somewhat difficult. To-day their place is taken by the rectilinear stop in the lens, whereby the same effect can be produced much more easily.

One of the best and most successful trick films Paul ever produced was the mediæval mystery entitled "The Magic Sword." It appealed to the grown-up because of the astonishing effects introduced, and to the children for the reason that it provided an intimate glimpse of fairyland with its giants, witches, good and bad fairies, and other strange beings not encountered in this world. It was sumptuously produced, and many of the tricks were introduced to the public for the first time.

The first scene shows a gallant knight meeting his ladylove on the battlements of the castle at midnight; a ghost appears, towards which the knight advances, but it melts from his grasp. A witch rides over the dark sky on her broom, and the knight in turn endeavours to seize her, but she eludes his attack and departs, shaking her fist in rage. An ogre no less than fifteen feet tall thrusts his head and shoulders over the battlements, seizes the damsel and bears her off through the sky. The lover is in the depths of despair, but a good fairy comes to his aid, gives him a flaming sword, and bids him go in search of his lady-love.

The battlemented castle gradually dissolves into a witch's cavern, to which the frightened lady is brought captive by the witch, and transformed into a second hag. Many adventures follow; finally the good fairy triumphs over evil, and the witch is converted into a roll of carpet, on which the lovers float through the air to fall from the sky upon the lady's parents while they are banqueting in the castle grounds.

The trick effects in this film were produced almost entirely by double printing, two negative films being superimposed to make a positive. The accompanying illustration shows how the appearance of the ogre was obtained. The scene with the two principal players, the knight and the lady, first was acted and photographed upon one film. The sky was a neutral back-cloth with a crescent moon painted on it. Then the second film was prepared bearing the ghost, the witch, and the ogre respectively. The spectral effect of the ghost named was realistically conveyed by under-exposing the second film, so that the stone of the battlements could be distinguished plainly through the form of the figure. The ogre was an actor of ordinary height, but as he was photographed with a short-focus lens from a point nearer the object than the characters in the first scene, when the print was made he appeared to be more than twice as tall as the other performers. In this scene the wall over which he reached was covered with black cloth.

In order to get the effect of the witch riding in the sky, Paul invented a novel movement in the camera, which is now in general use in trick cinematography. The lens was arranged to be raised or lowered in relation to the area of film in the gate, but still independently of the film itself. This was done with a small gearing device whereby, when the gear handle was turned, the lens was moved upwards or downwards. The witch astride her broom stood upon the floor of the stage, which was covered with black cloth, against a background of similar material. By turning the gear handle of the lens attachment the latter was raised, until the witch riding on her broom was lifted to

THE MAGIC SWORD: A MEDIÆVAL MYSTERY EXPLAINED.

Scene A was photographed first. The ogre was photographed against a neutral background upon a second film, B, the camera being brought very close to the figure. When the two films were superimposed and printed the startling picture, C, was obtained.

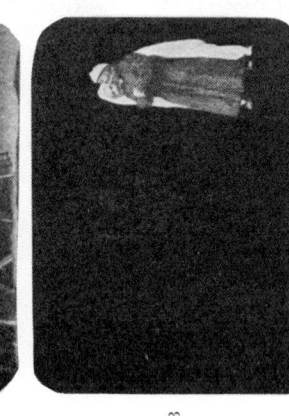

A CHRISTMAS CAROL: HOW SCROOGE SAW BOB CRATCHIT'S HOME.

The scene of the Xmas dinner, A, was photographed with the space at right. On the second film Scrooge and the spirit, B, were obtained. These two films were placed together for printing the complete picture, C.

the upper corner of the film and there photographed. Although she simulated the action of riding through space in the traditional manner, in reality she merely moved across the black-covered floor of the stage.

The strange effects produced in the witch's cave were obtained both by double printing and the "stop motion," as well as by the manipulation of the stop in the lens. The conversion of the captured lady into a witch was accomplished by stopping the camera; and while the lens was covered by the shutter, introducing a second actress, already made up, who stepped into the position occupied by the lady, while the latter quickly left the stage. The other actors maintained a rigid position while the camera lens was closed and the substitution took place. The conversion of the witch into a roll of carpet was effected in a similar way. When the "stop" call was given the witch disappeared from the stage, and a roll of carpet took her place.

The journey of the lovers through space upon the magic carpet was carried out by the manipulation of the rising and falling lens already described. When the solution of the baffling trick is given it appears absurdly simple, but the elaboration of the idea entailed several weeks' preparation, combined with hard thinking on the part of the producers, while the filming alone occupied several days.

Paul's studio was excellently adapted to producing strange variations in stature. He could make a giant or Lilliputian at will. The camera was mounted upon a special trolley, which could be moved forwards and backwards in relation to the stage over a pair of rails similar to a railway track. The closer the camera was to the stage the larger were the figures. A photograph at a distance of fifteen feet presented people of normal height. But when the camera was advanced close to the stage the players photographed were of immense stature, an effect emphasised still further when one film was printed over the other.

By varying the distance between the camera and the stage Paul produced some delightful results. One picture was called "The Cheese Mites," or "Lilliputians in a London Restaurant." A traveller entered a café and took his seat before a window. When he had finished his meal the waiter brought him a mug of beer, out of which, to the intense surprise of the traveller, a little sailor about six inches in height climbed and executed a hornpipe on the diner's plate. The sailor then went to the cheese, which was about his own height, and produced a lady therefrom. The sailor and the lass were engaged in an animated conversation when another little man appeared on the scene. The two men ultimately quarrelled and there was a spirited contest.

This introduction to modern Lilliput is simple to explain. On one film the diner and his actions were photographed, the camera being, say, fifteen feet distant. After this film was secured a second film was made of the Lilliputians, who, of course, were not midgets, but people of normal stature. They acted against a background of neutral tint; but the camera was set about 150 feet from the stage, and a long-focus lens was used. The consequence was that the figures appeared very tiny upon the second film, so that when the two films were superimposed for the purposes of printing the positive the contrast between the diner and the sailors was strangely impressive, the latter being no taller than the jug upon the table.

Some very astonishing results can be obtained by this superprinting operation, either straightforwardly or in combination with the variation in the photographic range as described in the previous paragraph. The soldier dying on the battlefield sees his home and mother in a dream which occupies the whole of one corner of the picture; there is the vision of Marley's Ghost, and so on. One of the earliest of Paul's simple trick subjects was a film illustrating the song "Ora Pro Nobis," wherein the starving, ill-clad orphan was seen to sink in collapse in the snow outside the church door, the climax being the death of the waif and the descent of the angel to receive and bear her spirit heavenwards. This was effected purely by double printing, the ascending and descending action of the angel being carried out by means of the gear-operated falling and rising lens of the camera.

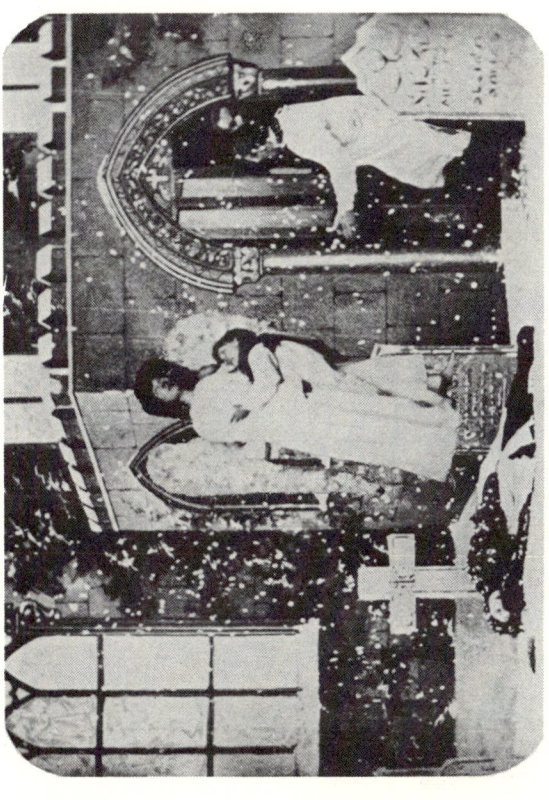

"ORA PRO NOBIS" AND HOW IT WAS PRODUCED.   [*By courtesy, R. W. Paul.*

The scene A was first recorded upon a film; then B was cinematographed, the angel and child being taken against a neutral background. A special device provided the ascending movement of the angel with the spirit of the waif. By placing B over A in printing the result C was obtained.

THE SECRET OF THE HAUNTED CURIOSITY SHOP. [*By courtesy of R. W. Paul.*

The scene, A, was photographed first, the black space representing the interior of a wardrobe. Another film, B, was made of the skeleton against a neutral background. When the two films were superimposed and printed the skeleton appeared to be imprisoned within the cupboard upon the positive, C.

"The Haunted Curiosity Shop" was a well-executed and startling trick film. A floating skull was transformed into the bust of a charming lady, while the second half of the body walked in and attached itself to the upper half. The dealer attempted to grasp his strange visitor around the waist with a view to stealing a kiss, but to his disgust the fair damsel changed into a grinning negress. In anger he thrust her into an old wardrobe, where she became white again. The outline of the fair prisoner could be seen through the woodwork of the cupboard; changing first into an Egyptian mummy, then a living Egyptian, and next into a skeleton. The dealer made a lunge at the skeleton with a sword, but the weapon struck the breastplate of a man in armour. The latter was then torn limb from limb, and the dismembered body was thrown into a huge jar, from which rose three gnomes, who finally resolved themselves into one. He was thrust back into the jar, and a dense cloud of smoke rose, from which the dealer fled in terror, while a large head appeared from the smoke and advanced towards the audience.

This picture was produced by recourse to "stop-motion" and double printing. The changes from white woman to negress, mummy, Egyptian, skeleton, and man in armour, were produced by substitution while the lens was closed by the shutter. The space indicated by the wardrobe was a recess having a black back-cloth, against which the skeleton was photographed, and which when the two negatives were superimposed was shown to be standing before the astonished dealer. The photographs of the girl were taken with the wardrobe doors open and well-exposed, so as to obtain a strong image, which could be seen through the other film showing the wardrobe doors closed. The dismemberment of the man in armour was carried out with properties, while the grotesque head was obtained by bringing the camera within a short distance of the stage so as to secure an enlarged photograph of an actor made up to suit the part.

"The (?) Motorist" was an extraordinary example of Paul's handiwork. The effects were so startling and the situations so unconventional that the spectators were sorely puzzled as well as vastly entertained. The picture opens with a motorist and a lady entering a small two-seated car. They set off, but presently a policeman attempts to stop them. He is picked up and dropped over the back of the automobile. The motorist continues on his way, with the offended emissary of the law in pursuit. Presently a public-house bars the road, but the car, on reaching the obstruction, runs up the wall, to the dismay of a large crowd, and shoots into space. Without a pause it speeds over the clouds, visits the sun, which it circles calmly, and once more swinging into space runs over the clouds until it reaches Saturn. The ring round this planet constitutes an ideal motor track, around which the automobile rushes in mad glee. Finally it shoots off this unusual highway and drops through space, to crash into a court of justice. After striking terra firma in this unconventional manner, the car continues its journey out of the building, followed by policemen, magistrate, and other officials. To their amazement, however, just as they are about to arrest the delinquent it vanishes, leaving in its place a countryman's cart, in which a smock-frocked farmer and his wife are seated. When the pursuers are at a safe distance, the cart changes back to the motor, and makes good its escape.

The point beyond the comprehension of the public was the journey of the motor across the clouds and round the sun and Saturn. It looked precisely as if the planets and the car were viewed through a telescope. To get this effect models were used. A suitable back-cloth was prepared painted with clouds, stars, the planets, etc. On the stage a large model was set up to represent Saturn with its ring. A small model of a motor-car was prepared, in which two dolls representing the motorist and his companion were placed, and propelled round the ring at increasing speed.

A model of the sun was suspended upon the stage before the back-cloth. The model of the car was attached to an arm, which was pivoted to the back of the sun, like a clock hand, so that the wheels of the model car

Motoring round the ring of Saturn.

The car circling the sun.

THE ? MOTORIST—A STARTLING TRICK PICTURE.

Both car and planets were small models.

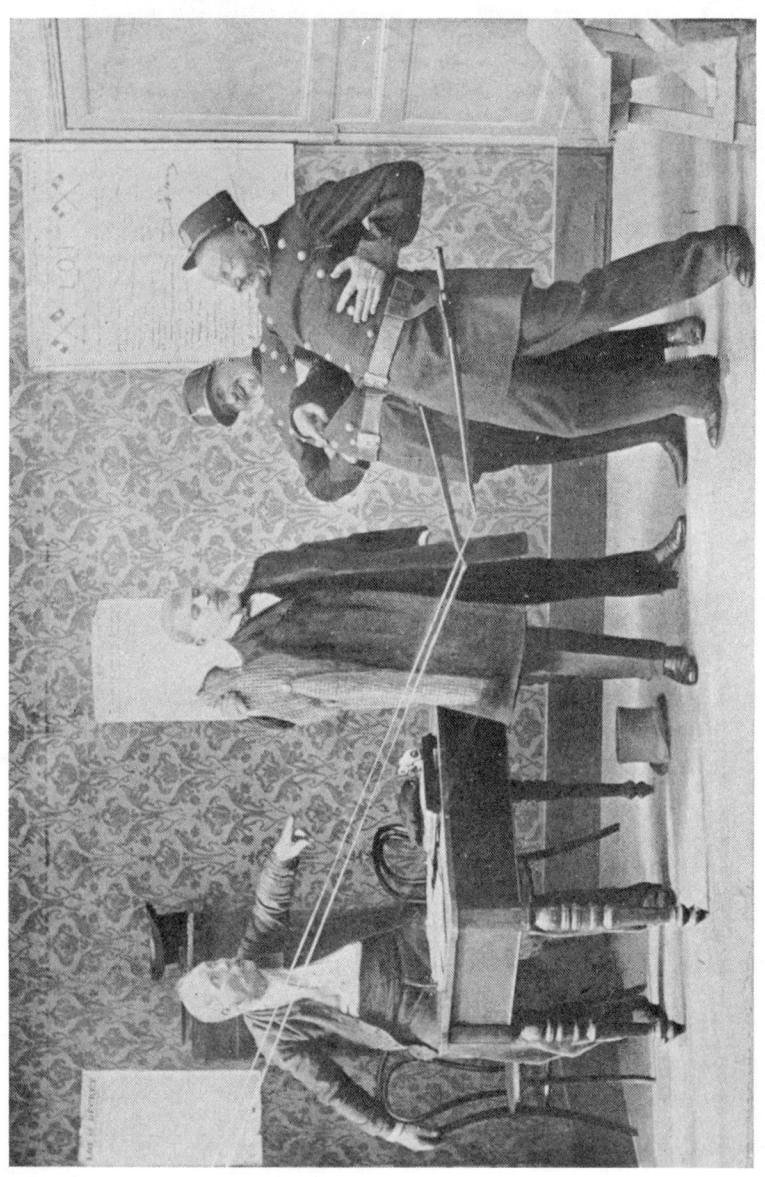

THE ANIMATED SWORDS.

The public is mystified by the manner in which inanimate objects apparently come to life. This picture shows one means of accomplishing this end. The swords are manipulated by invisible wires, indicated in this illustration to show method of application.—*See page 209.*

rested on the circumference of the model of the planet. This was revolved, thereby swinging the motor-car round and round, conveying the impression that the car was travelling round the sphere under its own power. For the journey through the clouds the model of the car was photographed against a back-cloth. The idea of falling through space was conveyed by the manipulation of the rising and falling lens. The success of this novel trick film prompted many imitations. Working with models, however, is by no means a simple operation, because, unless they are prepared and manipulated very skilfully, the deception is palpable.

Another of Paul's films was the representation of a railway collision. The scene represented a single railway line threading mountainous country. A goods train came in sight and overshot the danger signal. An attempt was made to back the train, but before it could reach safety an express dashed from the tunnel ahead and crashed into the stationary train, precipitating a scene of wreckage. Carriages, locomotives, and goods wagons were hurled down the embankment and piled upon one another by the force of the impact. Many people who saw this film marvelled at Paul's good fortune in being on the scene to photograph such a disaster. They were convinced that it was genuine. As a matter of fact, the scene of the accident was a field, in which the scenery was erected with considerable care, and a long length of model railway track was laid down, while the trains were good toy models. The film only measured forty feet, as it was designed originally for the kinetoscope; but its popularity was so complete that it was adopted extensively for the cinematograph. Certainly it produced forty of the most thrilling seconds it is possible to conceive, for the disaster was perfect in its swiftness and wreckage; and the cinematograph film images being less sharp and decisive than those obtained by a hand camera, the illusion was conveyed very convincingly.

Scores of trick pictures of infinite variety were produced by Mr. Robert Paul during his active connection with the cinematograph industry. In common with other producers of trick films, Paul found that the time involved in their production was out of all proportion to the financial results. It was no uncommon circumstance for a subject approximating 100 feet in length to absorb a week or more of continuous work. Moreover, his most successful subjects were seized by American houses and "duped"—as unauthorised reproduction is called in cinematographic parlance in that country : no copyright law existed on the subject. Some of the subjects thus exploited met with a phenomenal success, from which he never received the slightest benefit or even recognition.

CHAPTER XIX

TRICK PICTURES AND HOW THEY ARE PRODUCED

II.—Dancing Furniture: Strings, Cords and Wires: "The Magnetic Gentleman": The "Stop and Substitution": "The Automobile Accident": Reversal of Action.

THE achievements of Méliès and Paul set a very high standard of excellence in trick pictures. Their popularity precipitated a "trick film" fever. The market became inundated with so-called magic pictures, of which the majority were inane or conventional. The inevitable happened; the public appetite became satiated. Consequently, to-day, the popular taste demands extreme novelty. Unless the subject is original in theme, and the atmosphere of mystification is sustained, the effort is regarded with indifference, if not with absolute contempt. On the other hand, a first-class trick film commands the highest admiration, is regarded with as much satisfaction as were the products of the past masters in cinematographic magic of fifteen years ago, and when once seen is not frogotten very readily. There are certain producers who specialise in trick films with considerable success; but their number is small.

On the other hand, trick devices are introduced to a considerable extent into the ordinary picture play. I recall a film which depicted a scene at sea, where the vessel upon which the action took place was shown rolling and plunging in a truly appalling manner, and was swept from stem to stern time after time by the angry waves and scud. Wonder and admiration were expressed by the public at the daring of the producer in venturing upon a small boat under such terrible climatic conditions merely to procure a sensational picture.

That scene was produced in the serenity and quietness of the glass-covered studio under the glare of electric lights. The boat deck was a stage property, comprising a platform built to resemble the deck of an actual vessel, mounted upon rollers in such a way that when the latter were set in motion the boat was caused to rock, roll, and pitch in the most alarming manner. The angry waves seen on the horizon as the craft dipped its nose or rose upon a crest were no more than back-cloths and flats worked out by the scene painter, and set up by the stage carpenter, while the driving spray and water came from nothing more formidable than hydrants.

Behind the property boat deck, and disposed in concealed positions, were stage hands, equipped with hoses and nozzles. By manipulating these streams of water dexterously as the craft dipped, the jets of water were played upon its sides at varying angles, causing the foaming liquid to shoot into the air to produce the precise effect of a rolling boat dropping into the trough of the sea and smashing into an angry wave in its descent. The company suffered a severe drenching, it is true, and one of the actresses was afflicted with an acute attack of *mal-de-mer* provoked by the violent movement of the platform!

In another instance the public was shown a seaport town bombarded by a hostile cruiser. In the foreground were two big guns on the vessel's deck, while in the distance was the town. There was a puff of smoke, and the next instant the buildings struck by the projectile were observed to crumble into heaps of debris. The illusion was produced very simply. The big guns were fabrications of wooden laths and painted canvas, the smoke was a cloud of steam, and the buildings collapsed because they were built up with hinged sections, which were pulled down at the critical moment by means of concealed wires and cords, controlled from the back of the stage.

Through the courtesy of the Gaumont Company, of London and Paris, who are in the front rank of masters

THE TRAVELLING BED.

The progress of the bed down the public street provokes amusement to the pedestrians and consternation to its owner, but its movement is due to the fact that it is being pushed by concealed stage hands.

THE MAGNETIC GENTLEMAN.
The man-hole cover rises to pursue, and the lamp-post crashes over to strike the actor by the aid of wires, a common expedient in trick cinematography.
—*See page* 210.

in film magic, at all events as far as Europe is concerned, I have been allowed to go behind the scenes in their studio, and am in a position to explain to a puzzled public the secret of many an apparent miracle.

The film called "The Travelling Bed" is a typical subject of mystification. An aged tenant has fallen into arrears with his rent, and the long-suffering landlord at last commands his eviction. The bailiffs duly arrive upon the scene, but are spared all trouble by the fact that directly they appear the chairs, table, and other articles burst into life. They move about the room, and finally file out of the door, in the most methodical manner, to pass in a procession into the street. Meanwhile the unhappy tenant is reclining upon his bed in the depths of despair. He has no home and does not know where to search for one. The bed, however, promptly sets out to solve the problem. It bears its owner into the public highway. The owner is overwhelmed with fright and dismay at the unexpected development, and indulges in frantic gesticulations as the bed canters merrily down the centre of the road, with the passers-by pursuing the unusual spectacle. The mystery of the Travelling Bed is easily explained. It moves for the simple reason that it is pushed from behind by stage hands. These men are concealed from the camera, which merely records the movement of the bed, the alarm of the owner, and the excitement of the crowd.

This is the simplest and most usual means of imparting animation to a lifeless object. With such an article as a chair, which cannot hide a stage hand, recourse has to be made to wires or strings manipulated from a point in the wings, this being contrived in such a way as to be invisible to the public. For instance, a gendarme is astonished to see his sword whisked away from him. The accompanying illustration shows precisely how this is accomplished, the cords responsible for the action being made visible purposely to explain the mystery, whereas in the actual film these strings would be impossible of detection.

There is no limitation to the variety of effects which

can be produced by the invisible medium of cords, strings, and wires. Probably their possibilities are revealed to the most pronounced degree in such a film as "The Magnetic Gentleman." This unfortunate individual has been the victim of an attack by Paris Apaches, and forthwith vows never to venture through the streets again without a protective coat of mail beneath his conventional waistcoat. But he unintentionally comes into close proximity to a dynamo, with the result that his protective coat becomes highly magnetised. As he passes shops where metallic articles are displayed for sale, they jump towards him and cling tenaciously to his person. To one and all of these articles thin wires or strings are attached, the free ends of which are held either by stage hands or by the magnetic gentleman himself. At the critical moment the cords are pulled, and as the wires stretch across the path along which the magnetic gentleman is passing they appear to jump towards him. The articles which actually adhere to his person are connected to cords held by the actor himself, who merely pulls them to him as he passes the shops.

Presently the magnetic gentleman passes over a manhole cover set in the middle of the pavement. To the amazement of the audience, the cover is seen to rise up on its edge and to bowl along the street in pursuit of its disturbing factor. The cover is a stage property made of wood, manipulated by wires controlled by the actor. When the cover is raised there is a short "stop" while a stage hand enters the picture to give the cover its hoop-like impetus necessary to start it rolling, the actor then pulling it along by means of a wire, so that the cover follows hard on the heels of the luckless individual, until its career is arrested by two workmen, who struggle with the strange runaway.

But the magnetic gentleman's misadventures have by no means ended. He is passing a lamp-post, when suddenly the metal, attracted by the coat of mail, endeavours to jump towards him, with the result that the post snaps in twain. The lamp-post is a dummy or stage property, hinged at about half of its height so as to permit the upper part to

The pursuing man-hole cover is a wooden property.

The lamp-post is a stage article hinged in the centre.

HOW THE MAGNETIC GENTLEMAN TRICK FILM WAS PRODUCED.

TRICK PICTURE —THE AUTOMOBILE ACCIDENT.
The actor being replaced by the legless cripple with the dummy legs.

heel over like a flap. Wires are attached to the upper half, and as the individual passes they are given a sharp tug from the stage hands stationed outside the picture, or by the actor himself, and it falls over.

In such instances as these the deception is improved by the scenes being enacted in the public streets. Every action appears to be carried out so naturally, and the properties are designed so well and manipulated so carefully at the critical moments, that the spectators are led to believe in the actuality of the episodes.

Of course, a film of this character demands considerable preparation, and photographing it occupies a long time. The picture is built up incident by incident, in the same way that a picture play is produced, there being an interval of time between each series of exposures to permit the arrangements for the next episode to be made; and each phase is rehearsed over and over again before being filmed. When the pieces of film are connected to form a complete band, the continuity in action is so perfect that the public is unable to detect the points where the sequence was interrupted.

A film which created a sensation when it appeared was the "Automobile Accident." A workman, who has imbibed not wisely but too well, is homeward bound, and describes grotesque geometrical patterns as he advances along the thoroughfare. Presently he is smitten with an irresistible desire to sleep. Although the couch is hard and dangerous he lies down in the middle of the road, and in a few seconds is in the arms of Morpheus. While he is sleeping peacefully a taxi-cab comes along at a smart pace, and, not observing the slumbering form of the roysterer, the chauffeur drives over him, cutting off both his legs. The shock awakes the man rudely, and he is surprised to find his lower limbs scattered across the roadway. The chauffeur is horrified by the unfortunate accident; but his fare, on the contrary, a doctor, is not much perturbed. He descends from his carriage, picks up the dismembered limbs, replaces them in position, assists the afflicted man to his feet, and after shaking hands each proceeds on his separate way, the workman resuming his journey as if nothing had happened.

The requirements for this terrible calamity were very few. They consisted of three actors, to take the parts of the intoxicated workman, the driver, and the doctor respectively; a cripple who had lost both legs through an accident, and for properties a taxi-cab and a couple of artificial limbs. The legless cripple is, of course, the key to the whole situation. The great difficulty was to find such a luckless individual, and, when he had been discovered, to bribe him to participate in a picture play. Probably the unfortunate had never before found his misfortune so profitable to him.

In a trick film like this, success depends essentially upon what may be described as the "Stop and Substitution" action.

When the legless cripple was found, the leading actor was made up in such a manner as to be his exact counterpart. The company then proceeded to the scene of the accident, which was in the Bois de Vincennes. The camera was set up and the producer outlined the story to the participants.

In taking the film the operations were as follows: The leading actor, dressed like a French workman, ambled down the road simulating inebriation, and presently prepared his couch in the dust. While he was lying prone and asleep, the taxi-cab drove up quickly in such a way as to run over the sleeper's legs just above the knees. Of course, this did not actually take place, the chauffeur drawing up a short distance from the prostrate form. At precisely this point the camera stopped working, and the cab slowly continued its way until its front wheels touched the prostrate man's legs at the required point. The tracks of the vehicle's wheels were plainly visible on the road.

At this juncture the producer stepped forward with the legless cripple mounted on his self-propelled wheeled truck, from which he was lifted. The principal actor now got up and left the scene. The cripple took his place in the road, and the artificial legs were laid against his stumps in a

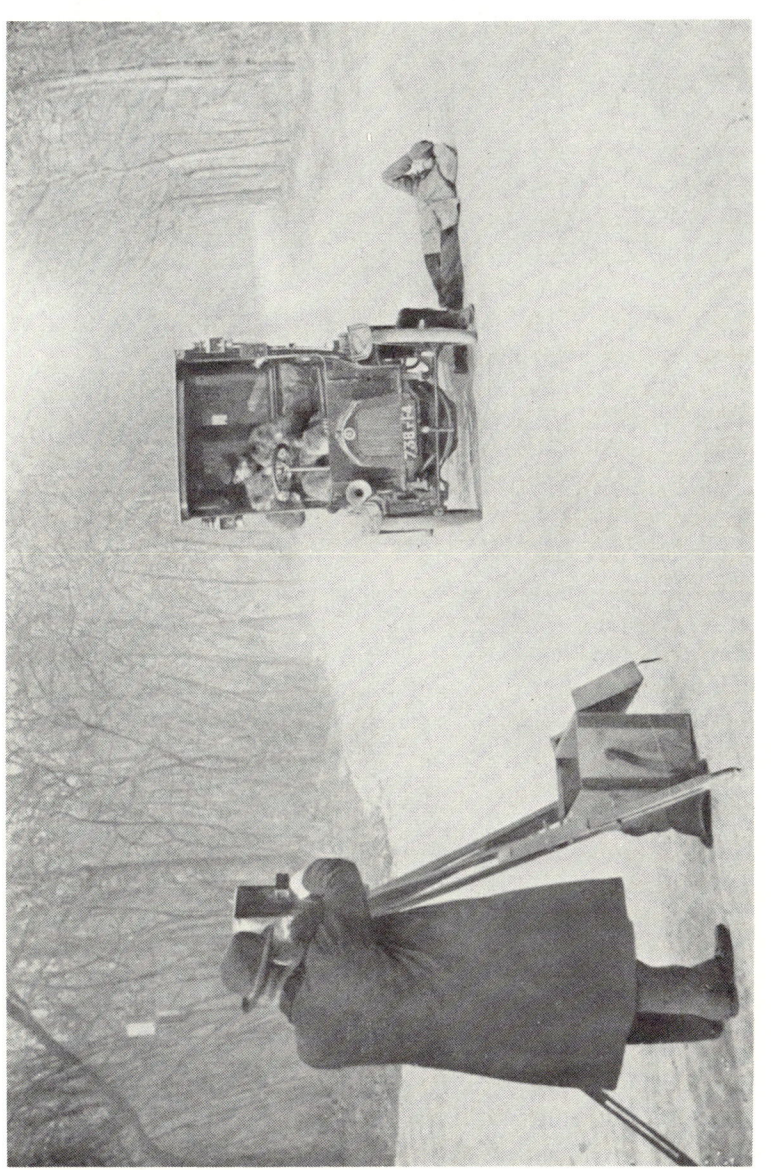

TRICK PICTURE—THE AUTOMOBILE ACCIDENT.

The taxi-cab running over the sleeper and apparently cutting off his legs, but in reality displacing the legless cripple's property limbs.

Observing the effects of the disaster, the doctor proceeds to replace the severed legs.

THE AUTOMOBILE ACCIDENT.

The limbs replaced, the patient and doctor shake hands.

natural position. Care had to be taken that the cripple occupied exactly the same position as that of the actor he had displaced, so that no sign of the substitution could be observed on the film.

The cab was now backed to its former starting point and then re-started, the chauffeur making it follow the tracks made by his wheels on the former journey. As the automobile reached the point where it had stopped in the previous picture, the camera started working again, and the cab ran over the prostrate cripple, cutting off both his legs—in reality displacing the dummy limbs and tumbling them across the road.

Suddenly awakened in this rough manner, the sleeper beholds his severed limbs with dismay, and then hops after the vehicle which had been the cause of his disaster. The cab stops, the doctor alights, picks up the severed limbs, and, while the cripple is seated on the ground, restores the displaced artificial limbs to their natural positions.

The camera now stopped working once more. The cripple was restored to his wheeled carriage and transported out of the picture, while the dummy legs were thrown on one side. In the place of the cripple the principal actor reappeared, and when the camera started again it photographed him sitting upon the ground. He is helped to his feet and resumes his journey.

In this picture we have seen two "stop and substitution" movements, once when the principal actor was withdrawn from the scene to make way for the legless cripple, and again when the reverse change was made. Owing to the neat and skilful manner in which the change from the actor to the cripple, and back from the cripple to the actor, is effected, the public fails to observe either the stop or the substitution, and thinks that one man acted the rôle throughout. The fact that the accident occurs on the high-road, and the possibility of a man being run over in this manner, helps in the deception.

The "stop and substitution" movement is probably practised more extensively than any other artifice in cinematography. In picture dramas where a situation is presented such as the throwing of the villain over a cliff, or before an approaching train, or some other scene impossible to picture without sacrifice of life, the camera is stopped immediately before the incident. The actors engaged in the scene become rooted to the spot when the "stop" call is given, signifying the fact that the camera has ceased its purring. At this juncture the villain disappears from the picture, a lay or dummy figure being substituted for him. When the camera resumes operation the episode is completed with the dummy.

Perhaps the best example of this expedient is that represented in the film illustrating the "Fountain of Youth," a version of the fable in which a beggar woman is transformed suddenly into a beautiful maiden by the kiss of a young gallant of good heart. A chivalrous young prince is strolling through a wood when he is confronted by an old and wrinkled witch, who makes supplication to him. In an instant the audience realises that her sombre garments have left her for brighter attire, and that the haggard face has been converted into youthful beauty. This wonderful transformation is worked by recourse to the "stop and substitution" action. After the "stop" call is given and while the lens is closed by the shutter the hag leaves the scene, a young actress, suitably attired, assumes her position, the actor retaining his position while the change is effected. As the new actress assumes the exact pose of the witch when the camera starts again, there is a complete continuity of action recorded, and the audience cannot detect that a pause and change has taken place between the two consecutive pictures.

The "stop" movement is, as a rule, the secret to all instantaneous disappearances. It enables people in the scene to vanish and reappear apparently from space. It explains the wrestling match, in which the audience is startled to see that the challenger has disappeared suddenly—leaving his antagonist wrestling with the air—only to reappear just as startlingly in another part of the

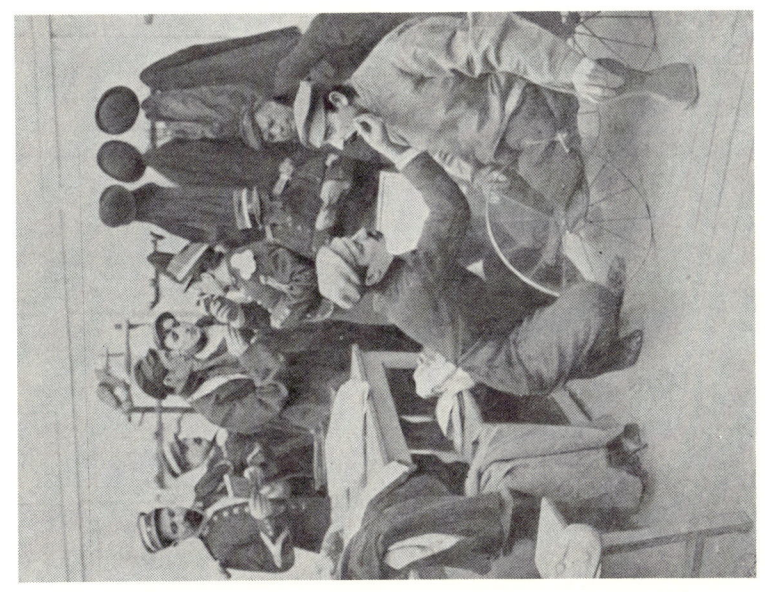

TRICK PICTURE—THE AUTOMOBILE ACCIDENT.

The roysterer after being run over by the the taxi-cab sitting up and brandishing his severed limbs.

The legless cripple being prepared for the act. The second artist is made up as the cripple's double.

THE FOUNTAIN OF YOUTH.
The film is stopped between pictures 2 and 3 to permit the actress to change her costume.

PUMPKINS RUNNING UPHILL.
This unusual effect is obtained by running the film backwards through the projector.

THE "STOP AND SUBSTITUTION," AND "REVERSAL OF ACTION" TRICK PRACTICES.

picture. When the time arrives the "stop" call is given. The disappearing actor slips out of the scene, while every other holds the position in which he has been caught by the last exposure. When the camera is re-started and the actors continue their movements, the wrestler proceeds as if gripping an opponent. When the "stop" call is given again a little later, the elusive opponent steps into the picture once more, assumes a suitable attitude, and his movements are continued when the camera resumes operation.

The power to stop the camera and arrest the action at any point provides the trick-film maker with boundless possibilities which are denied to his contemporary behind the footlights. On the legitimate stage the sudden disappearance and appearance has to be made through a trap door, and, no matter how smartly the operation may be performed, the public nevertheless sees the action taking place. In the moving-picture record not the slightest trace of the movement can be noted. The actor is seen in one picture and is missing from the next. He appears to have dissolved into thin air, and his reappearance is just as magically produced. This mystification of the public is rendered all the more complete by the environment in which the action is photographed. When performed by a magician or illusionist on the stage, the public naturally thinks that it has been effected by the medium of a trap door or some other artifice. When the magic takes place in the public street, where no such trick facilities exist, the natural surroundings lend the last touch to the illusion.

Another class of picture which causes considerable speculation as to how it is contrived is that in which all natural action becomes reversed. Horses, cabs, omnibuses, motor-cars, and cycles run backwards, pedestrians walk backwards, and smoke, instead of escaping from a chimney, appears to flow into it. Everything is topsy-turvy: the laws of gravitation appear to be defied. This novel result is produced by "reversal of action." The action may be photographed in the natural forward manner, but when the film is placed in the projector, the last picture taken by the camera is shown first, and consequently all movement becomes reversed.

Obviously the task could be simplified if the travel of the film were reversed through the camera during exposure, but in ordinary circumstances this would involve rotating the handle in the reverse direction, and cause unsteadiness in the picture. However, the camera manufacturer has solved this problem. When a reversed motion

FIG. 17—THE "EMPIRE" TRICK CAMERA.
It can be turned upside down while the film can be driven both forwards and backwards.

is required, the camera may be inverted upon its tripod, both top and bottom faces having facilities for screwing to the turn-table. When the camera is set upside down, the handle is rotated in the natural forward manner, but as the film is travelling backwards past the lens all movement is reversed. By this means the necessity to run the film backwards through the projector is avoided. It is not even necessary to turn the camera upside down now. Some manufacturers provide a second driving spindle, on to which the handle is slipped and rotated in the usual manner, the film being caused to travel backwards through reverse gearing.

Some astonishing and highly ingenious pictures can be obtained in this manner. For the purposes of illustrating the subject I have taken one of the most simple results. It depicts a "Pumpkin Race," in which the vegetables are seen to roll up a slope, to give one or two preliminary bounces, and then to fly into the air through an open window. When this film was taken the pumpkins were thrown out of the window, bounced and rolled down the declivity in the usual manner, but as the film for the purposes of the exposure was run backwards through the camera, when shown on the screen the opposite and apparently impossible effect is produced.

Some years ago Mr. James Williamson produced a subject of this class which provoked remarkable hilarity. It was called "The Workman's Paradise." A building was in course of construction, and the bricklayer duly arrived upon the scene to carry out his task, but he never stirred a hand. As he stood on the ground the bricks jumped by invisible effort into the hod and set themselves side by side in the most approved manner. Then the load rose through the air to the scaffolding; the bricks fell from the hod to the scaffold floor, and finally leaped into the air one by one to settle themselves in position upon the growing wall. Meanwhile the bricklayer surveyed the scene with his pipe in his mouth and an air of supreme satisfaction.

When the photographs of this picture were taken, the action was just the reverse of that seen upon the screen. The wall was standing, and the camera in reality photographed its demolition and the transport of the bricks to the ground. But the film was run through the camera backwards, so that the last picture made became the first projected upon the screen, and so on.

CHAPTER XX

TRICK PICTURES AND HOW THEY ARE PRODUCED

III.—Manipulation of the film: Apparitions and gradual disappearances by opening and closing the diaphragm of the lens slowly: "The Siren": Submarine effects.

THERE are many curious and bewildering trick effects which cannot be produced by recourse to the methods I have already described. It is impossible to detail every artifice employed; for every film possesses some individual characteristics. Only the broad outlines of the general processes employed can be described in the course of these chapters, but the information thus afforded will enable one to fathom how the majority of these miraculous pictures are elaborated.

We have all laughed and enjoyed the class of trick-film portraying frantic haste and its concomitant disasters or escapades. The scene may represent a public street, a park, a hotel, or even a private residence. The fact that the ordinary members of the public figuring in the scene move at the normal speed throws the frenzied haste of the principal performers into more striking contrast. I recall two excellent films of this character. In one case the story represented the operation of a wonderful little machine which, when its handle was turned, radiated a magical influence of acceleration upon everyone within a certain range, precipitating ludicrous incidents and situations. One saw the vehicles and pedestrians flying along the crowded Regent Street of Paris with terrible speed. The dawdling nursemaid was galvanised into life when the apparatus was brought within a few feet of her—she rushed her perambulator and charged along the boulevard with the velocity of a racing car; while the errand-boy completed his duties at the pace of an aeroplane, and so on. Mr. James Williamson was responsible for the second film of this character, which portrayed the British Workman "waking up" and becoming a "hustler" of the first water. The bricklayers ran up and down the ladders like squirrels racing up a tree, while the bricks were laid so rapidly that one could not detect the movements of the workman's hands, and the carpenter plied his saw so vigorously that it appeared to be a mere streak of light.

This peculiar effect may be produced easily by either of two methods. One is to turn the handle of the camera very slowly while photographing; but when the film is being shown to rotate the handle of the projector at a very high speed. The result is that the pace of every moving object in the picture is increased upon projection four, six, or eight times that recorded by the camera. In this case every moving object in the picture moves at the same pace. There are no contrasts between frantic movement on the part of some and slow, natural motion on the part of other people in the scene to enhance the ludicrous effect; moreover, the required result is left very much in the hands of the operator.

Accordingly, another and superior expedient was evolved and is now adopted universally. The picture is taken at the normal speed of sixteen pictures per second, but the film thus obtained after development is taken in hand, and its length is reduced by cutting out every other picture —or perhaps even more. If every alternate image is eliminated in this manner, and the remaining pieces of film are re-joined, the length of the film is reduced by one half, and when thrown upon the screen at the normal speed of sixteen pictures per second, the moving objects travel at twice the speed at which they were moving when photographed.

This removal of the images from the string of consecutive pictures is known as "manipulation of the film." It is a tedious and delicate process, because joining together properly a series of images measuring only three-quarters of an inch in depth demands skill and patience. By its means, however, some bewildering effects may be obtained, one of which is shown in the illustration. This film depicts a lad who has been hypnotised. When he enters a dwelling his presence sets the furniture dancing violently, while a circular table round which four people are seated, revolves at a dizzy pace. For the purposes of this film the table and those seated around were mounted upon a pivoted platform free to revolve, which was driven from beneath the stage or from some other convenient point. At the right moment the table commenced to spin around—at a comparatively slow pace, so as not to unseat the performers by the results of centrifugal force—the camera meanwhile recording the movement. After the film was developed images were cut out at certain points, these excisions being so made as to reduce the length of film devoted to the table-spinning incident from 100 feet as recorded by the camera to twenty-five feet or so for the projector. Accordingly, when the film was thrown upon the screen at a speed of sixteen pictures per second, the table appeared to whiz round at a fearful velocity.

If double printing be associated with this manipulation of the film far more mirth-provoking and astounding situations can be produced. For instance, such stories as that of the magical apparatus described above, which spurs into unwonted velocity the traffic in a crowded street, may be prepared as follows:—The camera is set up in a suitable position overlooking the thoroughfare, and one film is taken very early in the morning, when the traffic is either absent or very insignificant. Here and there may be a pedestrian or vehicle, but their presence only heightens the effect. Perhaps 125 feet of film are expended upon this subject. The camera is then left until later in the day, when the traffic is at its highest, and another film is secured of the now busy street from the same point of view. Thus the stationary objects—the shops, lamp-posts, and so forth—occupy the same relative positions in each film, with the

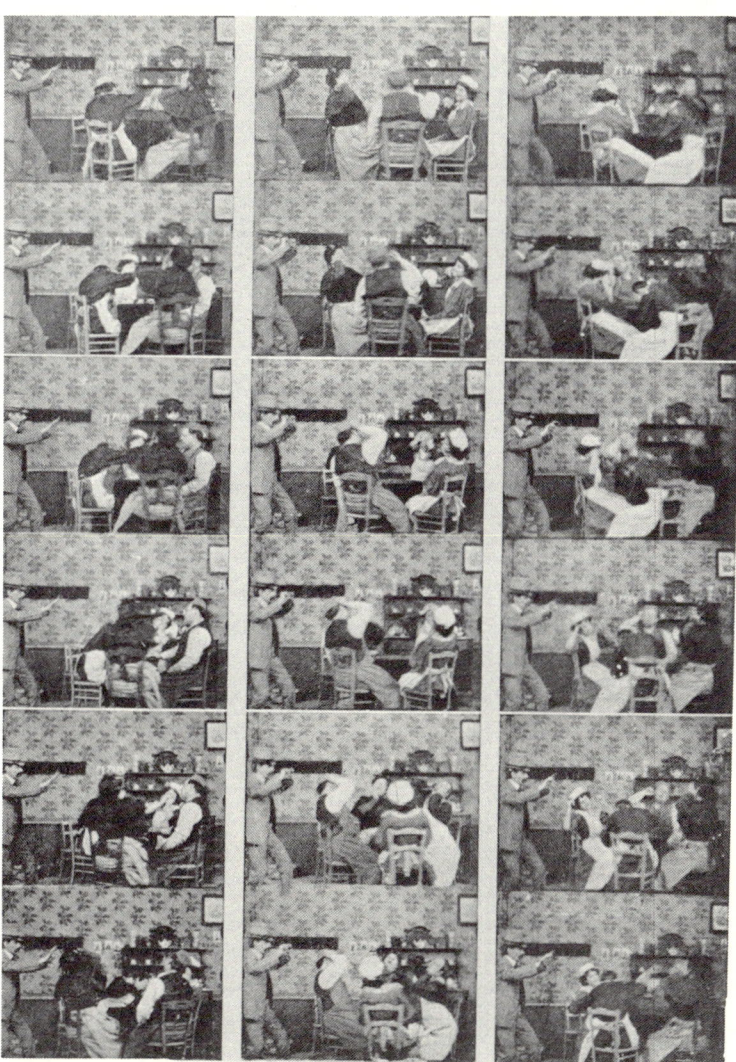

THE REVOLVING TABLE

The puzzling trick effect of a table rotating at dizzy speed is obtained by cutting out pieces of the film. The white lines show where excisions have been made.

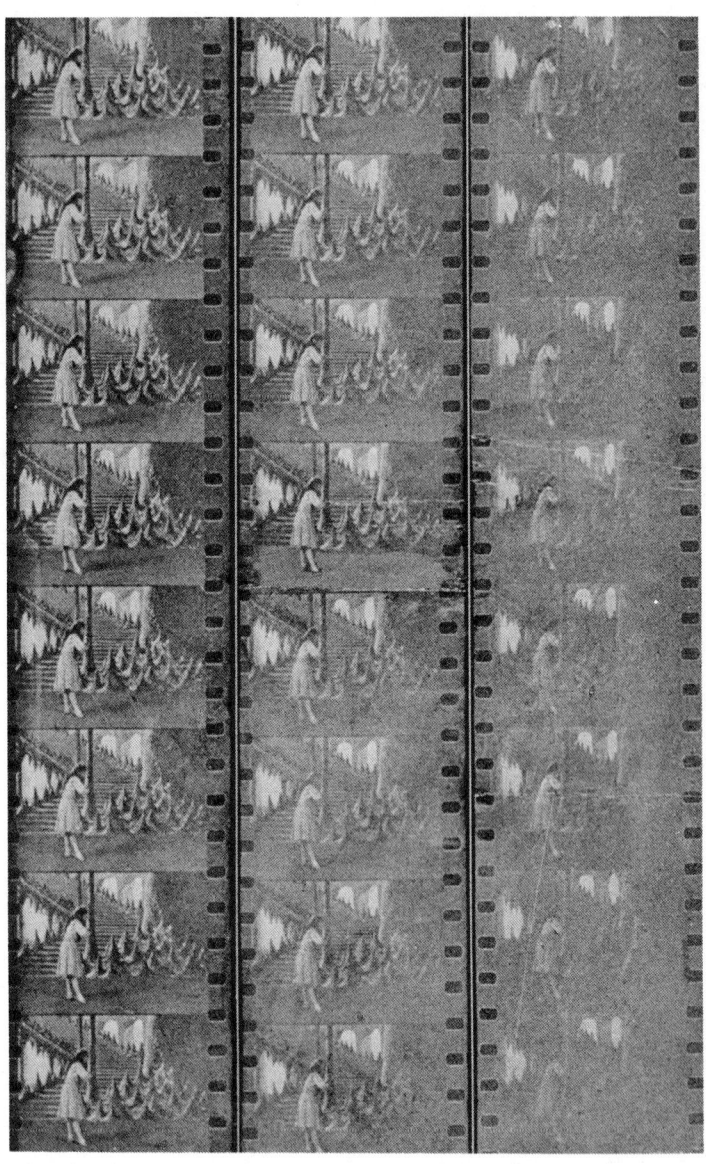

THE SECRET OF THE FAIRY'S APPEARANCE.

1. While a length of film is being exposed the diaphragm is closed slowly.

result that when they are placed one on the other a single impression of these fixed, inanimate objects is obtained. The second film, however, is longer than the first—perhaps it is 250 feet in length—but by cutting out each alternate image its length is reduced to 125 feet. The two films are now of the same length; one is placed on the other, and the positive print is made.

When the picture is thrown upon the screen the greater part of the wheeled traffic is observed to fly along in mad haste, while here and there a pedestrian or vehicle is seen sauntering in a very leisurely way—almost at a crawl by comparison. The latter are those photographed upon the first film which has not been touched, while the hastening vehicles and people are those photographed upon the second film, which has been manipulated into half its length.

If the excisions are made more heavily, and instead of every alternate picture being cut out, three out of four consecutive images are eliminated, the results are more ludicrous still. Suppose a man is being pursued, and runs as for dear life; if 100 feet of this episode are photographed, and the negative subsequently is reduced to twenty-five feet by manipulation, the man will not appear to be running when the picture is shown upon the screen, but will seem to be eluding capture by a series of long hops. In this instance two films and superprinting are requisite to give the most satisfactory result, the runaway being recorded upon one film and the pursuing crowd upon the second. Then while the man is shown to be leaping in a most extraordinary manner down the street, the crowd will be seen running in a perfectly natural manner.

Whereas the "stop" call is employed to effect sudden appearance or disappearance, a different method is essential for a gradual disappearance. Let us suppose the scene represents a magic cave in which the daring young hero is imprisoned by the wicked magician. Instead of the good fairy springing into the picture through a trap-door in the floor of the stage, as is the practice in legitimate pantomime, she is seen to materialise from nothing. The first sign of her advent is a slight nebulous haze in a certain part of the picture. This mist grows stronger and stronger, until at last it reveals the filmy outlines of the fairy, who in due course becomes as distinct and as clearly defined as the young hero she has come to assist. When the moment arrives for her disappearance she vanishes in the same mysterious manner, her body seeming to dissolve into thin air.

This apparition effect always provokes considerable interest and curiosity. It necessitates the use of a camera of such a design that the film can be driven both forwards and backwards, instead of in the first-named direction only. It must be fitted also with a special measuring indicator, and an easily adjustable diaphragm stop to the lens. The latter is of the rectilinear type, the results therewith being produced more easily and positively than by any other means. All these requirements are fulfilled in the "trick" camera, which is especially designed for work of this character.

For the purposes of explaining this operation I have obtained three films (see illustrations) by looking at which the process will be clearly understood. It is well known that as the aperture of a lens is closed, the quantity of light admitted to the sensitised surface behind is reduced, and if this action is carried out gradually by means of the rectilinear stop, without any variation in the length of the exposure, the image upon successive sections of the film will become fainter and fainter until nothing at all is recorded. The reverse action takes place as the lens aperture is increased in size by opening the diaphragm to admit a greater volume of light.

I will first explain the operation in its simplest form. The stop call is given and all the actors become stationary while the fairy stands alert to receive her cue to enter. The operator notes the point upon his indicator of the length of film used up to the time the stop call is given. For our purposes we will say it is 100 feet. The operator continues turning the handle at the same speed, but while so doing he gradually closes the lens aperture by means of the rectilinear stop, so that the images, owing to decreasing volume

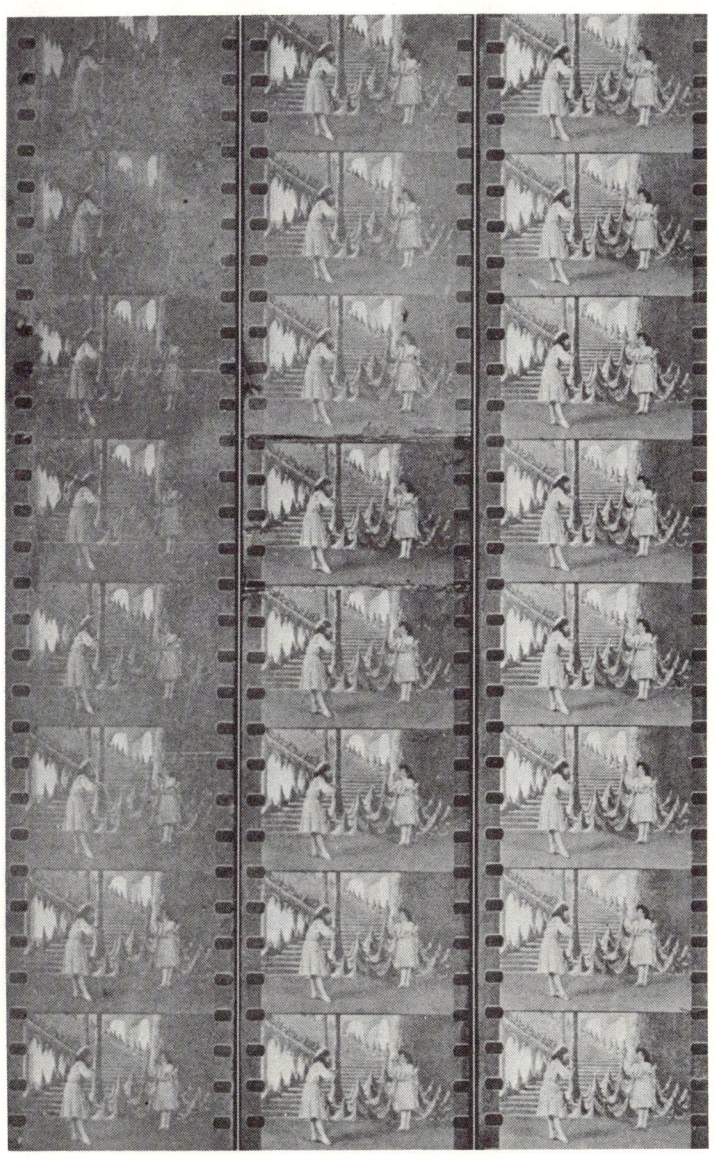

THE SECRET OF THE FAIRY'S APPEARANCE.

2. The same length of film is re-exposed after the fairy has entered the picture, under a slowly opening diaphragm.

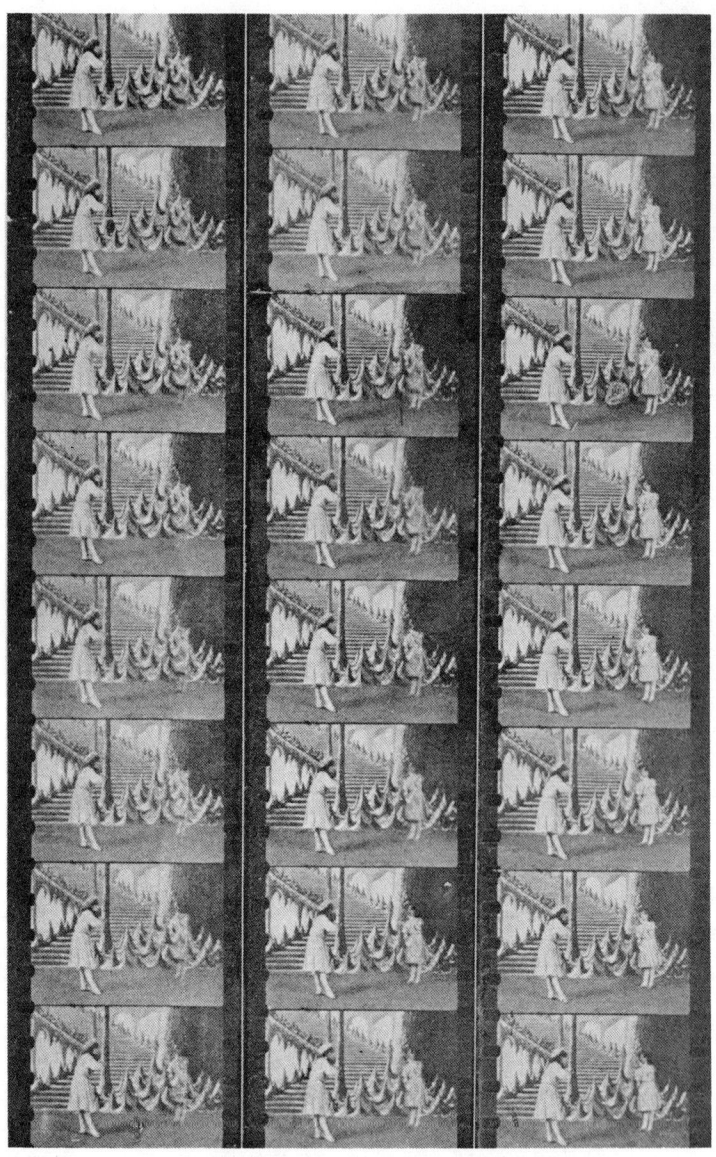

THE SECRET OF THE FAIRY'S APPEARANCE.

3. The effect of double exposure under closing and opening diaphragm. The subjects photographed twice upon the same length of film stand out with uniform distinctness, but the fairy being photographed only once gradually materialises apparently from thin air.

of light admitted through the lens, become fainter and fainter, until at last merely a haze is recorded. The effect of closing the stop in this manner is shown in the first film.

The operator consults his film register and finds that two feet of film have been consumed, representing thirty-two exposures, to carry the picture gradually to extinction, the indicator accordingly registering 102 feet at the conclusion of the operation. The fairy now receives her cue and steps into the required position in the picture. The operator resumes his turning, and during the next two feet of film, that is, another thirty-two exposures, he opens the stop just as gradually as he closed it, to its former aperture, the image upon the film thereby becoming stronger and stronger as increasing light is admitted through the lens.

The effect produced by this process is shown in the illustration. The first picture taken after the fairy has entered is scarcely discernible; then it becomes a slight haze in the next image, and as the aperture is increased her form slowly materialises until at last she is quite as distinct as that of the other actor in the scene, who meantime has retained his rigid position during the whole 64 exposures. When this second series of exposures have been completed, the film indicator registers 104 feet, two feet of film having been used in closing and another two feet in opening the lens aperture.

Now if the film is cut at the point representing 102 feet, and this second part of the film is superimposed upon the first in such a way that the second thirty-two exposures coinciding with the opening of the diaphragm are laid upon the thirty-two exposures representing the closing of the lens aperture, in the resultant positive the actor and the surroundings will stand out with uniform brilliancy throughout the superimposed section, and be equal in brilliancy and distinctness to the remainder of the film, for the simple reason that image 33—representing the first exposure under the opening of the stop and consequently the most indistinct picture—comes over image 1 in the stopping-down series of pictures, which is, of course, the most brilliant picture. Image 2 comes under image 34, and so on throughout the whole thirty-two pictures. As the pictures grow fainter on one film they become correspondingly stronger on the other film, with the result that when the two are overlapped and printed the sum of the two exposures produces a complete and fully-detailed picture, the second film supplying to the first precisely the complement of its incomplete exposure, in the case of each image.

But this action only affects the actor and scenery recorded upon the two sections of film. The fairy, having entered at picture 33, when the unstopping process was commenced, appears at first very indistinctly, like a small patch of mist, the nebulous haze resolving itself into her form slowly during the successive thirty-one pictures. The sum of this double exposure is represented by the third illustration, where the fairy is to be seen slowly materialising, the other parts of the picture under the double printing being of uniform brilliancy throughout.

This was the method adopted in the early days, but it was somewhat involved, and demanded recourse to double printing. The perfection of the camera mechanism has enabled the process to be considerably simplified. Now the operator makes a double exposure, with closing and then opening diaphragm upon the same length of film. When the "stop" signal is given he observes the indication on his film register. We will say it is 100 feet, as in the previous case. The actor becomes motionless and the operator resumes his turning while closing the stop slowly, until 102 feet of film are registered upon the dial, thirty-two exposures, or two feet of film having been made during stopping down. He now winds the film backwards into the upper film box until his dial registers 100 feet once more, the lens being capped during this operation. Thus he has regained the point upon his film where stopping-down commenced, and the two feet used in this process are ready to be exposed again.

At this point the fairy steps into position. The camera is re-started, and while the first thirty-two exposures are being made the lens aperture is opened, just as slowly and gradually as it was closed during the previous exposures. The result is that the portions of the films which in the first instance received a diminishing volume of light now receive a compensating increasing illumination, so that the effect upon this particular two feet of film, so far as the figure on the left and the scenery are concerned, is just as if they had been exposed once under a full aperture. The fairy, however, having been photographed only during the second exposure, appears at first very indistinctly. The result of the double exposure is shown in the illustration; and the gradual appearance of the fairy may be followed very easily. The outcome is exactly the same as obtained by double printing; but it is infinitely easier, and far more positive in its action than the delicate process followed by Robert Paul in the early days—the dissolution of the emulsion from the film by chemical action.

Exceedingly clever effects are obtainable under this double exposure process. Transformations from one scene to another are carried out in a manner that completely eclipse the handiwork of the stage-manager behind the footlights. Success depends to a great degree upon the skilfulness of the operator, because it is imperative that the stop of the lens should be closed and opened equally, in order that the combined exposures upon each successive image should be equal to a single exposure with a full aperture, so as to provide a uniform intensity and brilliancy throughout all the images.

The magic disappearances are worked in precisely similar manner, only in this instance the character leaves the picture at the moment the last image under the closing diaphragm has been taken. The film is wound back as before to the point where the "stop" call was given, and is subjected to a second exposure under an opening stop.

There are no limitations to the application of this form of trickery. Spirit forms can be produced to float in the air, recourse to the rising and falling lens front being made in conjunction with the manipulation of the diaphragm. Sylphs can be materialised from evening vapours; and articles of furniture can be transformed into human forms. Many of the pictures obtained in this manner are startlingly weird and magical. As a matter of fact, the manipulation of the diaphragm may be considered as one of the most useful weapons of trickery and magic in the hands of the cinematographic wizard.

Another miracle is performed when the public is introduced to the bottom of the sea to make acquaintance with the denizens of the deep, and the strange mermaid population. The audience is convinced that the pictures have been taken in the actual surroundings, because divers descend into the depths and they can see the air-bubbles rise from their helmets during respiration. The effect is certainly very realistic, and as the difficulties attending under-water photography are well-known, one wonders how these pictures can be obtained.

They can be produced by two methods. One is by using a large tank with a glazed front, in which the properties are distributed, while behind is a painted back-cloth to represent a submarine scene. The tank is filled with water, and fish are introduced to heighten the effect. Divers are employed to carry out their evolutions in the tank, which is brilliantly lighted, so that the sensitised ribbon in the camera disposed before the front window may be able to secure a well-defined image.

It is obviously impossible to introduce mermaids actually under water, since they could not breathe there; so for this part of the effect recourse to trickery is indispensable. A narrow tank with glazed back and front is set up on the stage, filled with water, and a few fish. The camera is brought as near as possible to this large aquarium and photographs the tank, the pictures being slightly underexposed.

The tank is then removed, and a scene depicting the floor of the sea is prepared upon the stage, with a back-cloth of a grey neutral tint. Perhaps a property ship to represent a sunken wreck is set up to enhance the effect. Actresses made up as mermaids disport themselves upon the sea-bed, and divers are observed to make their descent from the

THE MYSTERY OF "THE SIREN."

A beautiful woman is observed to be swimming gracefully in the depths of the sea, and the public is mystified as to how she can exist under water.

THE MYSTERY OF "THE SIREN" REVEALED.

The camera was placed in the flies with the lens pointing downwards upon the actress moving on the floor.

surface, which in this instance is the "flies" of the stage. The film which the operator has exposed already upon the stage tank is now exposed again before this scene, and the commingling of the two produces a very mystifying effect when shown upon the screen.

A fascinating film of this character was made by the Gaumont establishment under the title of "The Siren." A beautiful woman was observed to be swimming and diving in the watery depths with various fish as her companions. Her movements were so graceful and natural that it seemed impossible for them to have been produced while the actress was suspended from the "flies" by the aid of wires. How was it done? was an expression I heard on several occasions during projection in the picture palaces. The solution is very simple.

In the first place, a large aquarium was set upon the stage. It was stocked with fishes, which gambolled in a realistic manner, and the tank was photographed. When this exposure was completed the "Siren" had to be introduced.

The floor of the stage was cleared, and upon it, like a carpet, was laid a large back-cloth of a grey neutral tint, bearing faint designs of submarine growths, shells, weeds, and so forth, the work of the scenic artist. The operator carried his camera into the flies, and from a central point overhead set it up with the lens pointing downwards, and focussed the flat background spread out below. The actress then entered, and lying prone upon the back-cloth, carried out the movements necessary to simulate swimming and diving, moving the arms and legs and writhing the body to convey the correct natural impressions of under-water movement.

The rehearsals completed, the operator re-exposed the same film which had been previously exposed before the aquarium, and which had received a faint impression thereof. When the picture was projected the public was completely deceived; for the actress moved to and fro, in the company of fishes which darted from point to point, apparently unperturbed by the existence of the fair feminine form in their midst. In such operations as this, however, where a photograph has to be taken of an aquarium in the first instance, special attention has to be devoted to the lighting arrangements, so as to prevent the camera and the operator being reflected upon the film—since the water acts in the same manner as a mirror.

The audiences in picture palaces are sorely puzzled at the antics of motorists, cyclists, and others who, being pursued by an infuriated crowd whose anger they have raised for some reason or other, elude capture by turning their vehicles and running up the vertical walls of houses and buildings. The methods used in the presentation of the "Siren" are adopted here also. A cloth carrying a painted impression of the wall with its windows, doors, stack-pipes, and so forth, is laid upon the floor, and the camera lens is pointed thereon from a position in the flies. The vehicles are driven over this back-cloth, and the film conveys the idea that they have performed the impossible feat of riding up the wall. The effect is often improved by following the upward progress of the vehicle. This may be accomplished in two ways. Either the camera is moved horizontally along a track in the flies in synchrony with the advance of the vehicle, or else the rising and falling front of the lens is brought into use. Another means is to have resort to the "stop" action, the camera being rigid and the back-cloth moved across the floor a certain distance between each series of exposures.

For the production of elaborate trick pictures an extensive assortment of properties is demanded. When the episodes are accompanied by ludicrous catastrophes and smashes the public is moved to extreme mirth. In many of these pictures the performers are obtained from the vaudeville stage, being accomplished masters of knock-about, tumblers, cyclists, etc. Suppose a chase over house-tops is shown, accompanied by falls through the roof, the actors and actresses tumbling from floor to floor down to the basement. These pictures are prepared in sections. The first scene represents the roof, which is built up on the stage, while a back-cloth affords a vista of chimney-pots. At certain points in the roof are concealed trap-doors which, when the first actor brings his weight on them, collapse by the movement of the bolt or other support concealed beneath. The performers fall through the opening on to a soft mattress within, the extent of the fall being about four or five feet. In the next scene members of the company in turn fall through the ceiling of the sixth floor of the building. This scene is built up on the floor of the stage, the performers being stationed out of sight in the flies. The ceiling is represented by a piece of painted canvas with attached pieces of cardboard and canvas to resemble splintered woodwork and broken plaster. The ceiling is intact, but when the cue is given the leading actor jumps or falls through the painted canvas followed by a mass of débris and dust. The débris is merely properties thrown through the opening, while steam or smoke driven through the hole serves as dust. Perchance a party is dining in the room when the tumblers make their unexpected entrance through the ceiling, and the scene undergoes a complete disturbance as a result of the interruption. The next floor is reproduced in turn in the same manner upon the floor of the stage, and so on until the players come to a dead stop in the basement, when the cardboard and canvas débris produced by their hurried descent falls and practically buries them. The force of the latter is increased by men stationed in the flies, who hurl the material down pell-mell from their points of vantage through the hole the tumblers have made. As seen upon the screen it appears as if the house were cut in two from top to bottom, and the audience were permitted to follow the tumblers in their descent from floor to floor; instead of which, as we have seen, each floor is reproduced individually upon the stage. There is no indication whatever of this piecemeal preparation, although if the picture is followed closely it is readily apparent, because the performers in their descent do not comply with the laws governing the momentum of a falling body.

The laughable incidents showing men climbing laboriously through narrow chimney flues are attributable likewise to trickery. The chimney is merely a stage property, and generally is laid flat upon the stage, with the operator and his camera stationed in the flies, as in the production of the "Siren"; though, from the public point of view, the players appear to be crawling upwards through the narrow vertical brickwork passage, gathering an accumulation of soot in their advance. The latter is applied to their faces by the actors themselves as they move forward.

CHAPTER XXI

TRICK PICTURES AND HOW THEY ARE PRODUCED

IV.—Lilliputian figures: "The Little Milliner's Dream": the "one turn one picture" movement: how some extraordinary incidents are produced: "The Ski Runner."

IN Chapter XVIII. I made some reference to early methods of producing a class of films in which the principal performers were diminutive figures scarcely six inches in height. This kind of picture has never lost its hold upon the public. Indeed, experience has proved that it constitutes one of the most popular subjects which it is possible to throw upon the screen, especially when the tiny actors and actresses are introduced into a play having a well-defined plot carried to a logical conclusion.

I have related how Paul obtained the effect of pigmy actors by combining the possibilities of superprinting and photographing at varying distances from the stage. This method is practised nowadays in somewhat modified form. The stage is made so deep that there is no need to move the camera.

Two of the most attractive films of this description produced during recent years were "The Little Milliner's Dream" and "Princess Nicotine." Curiously enough, they represent two widely divergent methods of achieving the same result, as practised by French and American producers respectively. Both are associated with many features of interest in cinematographic magic.

In "The Little Milliner's Dream," a young and charming milliner's assistant is sent by her employer to deliver a creation to a customer. The girl sets out with the milliner's hat-box on her arm. On the way she pauses to admire the glittering array of precious stones and gewgaws in a jeweller's shop. While she is gazing at the articles longingly an old beau advances, makes himself known, and tries to force his company upon her. With a coquettish shrug of her shoulders she rebuffs him and resumes her journey, but presently, overcome by the heat, she sits down upon a seat in the street to take a rest. Presently she falls asleep.

In her dreams she sees the lid of the bonnet-box open, and from the interior steps the old gallant. At first he is no taller than a coffee-pot, but he grows until he has attained life-size proportions. Next, in the space occupied by the upturned lid of the bonnet-box, a bevy of dancing girls appear. They likewise are only a few inches in height, but they increase in size until they assume normal stature. To her astonishment each dancing girl proffers the apprentice a magnificent present. In an instant, as if under the magic spell of a fairy's wand, she finds herself attired in the rich clothes of a lady of rank, and taking the arm of her admirer—who, by the way, shoulders the bonnet-box—they march off together. The bonnet-box is suddenly dropped and instantaneously becomes a luxurious motor-car. The apprentice passes through many startling adventures in the world of fashion and gaiety, but the final scene reveals her still seated upon the seat, and being roughly awakened by a gendarme from her delightful dreams.

The first essential in such a picture as this is a deep stage, so as to secure the impression of distance. The Gaumont Theatre, from which this film emanated, is one of the best designed and largest in the world, and the preparation of such scenes as "The Little Milliner's Dream" offers them no difficulties. The street scene was merely a back-cloth painted to resemble one side of the street, with its shops, the roadway, and the kerb of the second pavement. Before this was set up an ordinary seat, such as is provided for the convenience of pedestrians along the highway, and it was upon this that the little milliner snatched her brief rest with the bonnet-box beside her, and but a few feet from the camera.

When she fell asleep the lid of the bonnet-box was opened by means of invisible wires, and the lid came to rest in a vertical position against the back of the seat, the top of the side of the box being level with the back rail of the seat. The inner surface of the lid was a dead black.

At this moment the "stop" call was issued. While the camera lens was closed the stage hands entered, took away the bonnet-box lid, and removed a panel in the back-cloth of the same shape and dimensions as the bonnet-box lid, and immediately behind it. This left a hole in the back-cloth, through which could be seen the stage behind. The lens of the camera, however, was on a level with the top of the bonnet-box, so that the floor of the stage behind the back-cloth could not be seen through the panel. At the extreme rear of the stage another back-cloth of black velvet was hung. Consequently, looking at the picture from the lens point of view, the black velvet, seen through the panel in the scenic back-cloth, appeared to be the inner surface of the bonnet-box lid; and the audience imagines that what follows takes place upon the inside of the lid, whereas it is, of course, seen through the back-cloth, and enacted upon the back or rear half of the stage.

The camera is started up again. Suddenly the diminutive figure of the old gallant is observed to rise from the interior of the bonnet-box. As a matter of fact, he is at the extreme rear edge of the stage, against the velvet back-cloth, but seated below the line of sight of the camera until he received his cue. The little milliner in her dream turns her head as if to gaze more closely into the lid of her box—in reality she is looking through the window in the back-cloth upon the scene taking place behind her. The old beau, having risen to his feet at the extreme rear of the stage, and six or more times as far away from the camera as is the milliner herself, appears, in accordance with the laws of perspective, to be no taller than a bottle, this peculiarity being accentuated by the distortion of the lens as in every camera.

The old beau lifts his hat and instantly commences to grow in size. This transformation was caused by his advancing towards the hole in the back-cloth, which, as the distance between him and the lens decreased, caused his stature to enlarge. At last the actor advanced to the limit of his forward movement, when his figure occupied the full depth of the opening, or of the supposititious bonnet-box lid. At this moment the camera paused to permit the actor to walk round the back-cloth, representing the street, and when the camera was re-started he was seen before the bonnet-box as if he had stepped out of that receptacle. Being as close to the camera as the milliner, he was now brought to life-size.

The spectacle of the dancing girls was carried out in the same manner. When the little milliner was urged to look into the lid of the bonnet-box once more, she peered through the back-cloth window. To her amazement she saw six diminutive dancing forms rise up as if from the interior of the box, but in reality from the floor against the black background, at the point where the beau had first appeared. They danced their way to the opening to a point marked on the floor of the stage behind the scenic back-cloth, thereby growing gradually in stature. Then the camera made pause to permit the girls to come round the back-cloth and to assume the required position before the milliner near the camera, where likewise they were brought to normal size. They presented their gifts to the delighted girl, and then there was another pause on the part of the camera.

During this stop the milliner changed her attire for that of a lady of fashion. At the same time the stage hands replaced the panel in the back-cloth, while the original bonnet-box lid was brought in and restored to its former position.

When the camera began again it recorded the beau closing the lid of the box, and while he picked it up with one hand he offered his other arm to his fair friend and escorted her along the street. Presently he dropped the box. Another "stop" call was given, during which the bonnet-box was taken away by the stage hands, and an automobile brought into position at the point where the hat-box was dropped. When the camera re-started it revealed the bonnet-box converted, like Cinderella's pumpkin, into an automobile. Entering the vehicle, the couple drive off to the ball. The process of "stop and substitution," which has been described already, is carried out from time to time to present sudden transformation effects; the audience sees only the continuity of motion as produced by joining the pieces of film together; and they marvel at the result. The film was produced very cleverly and skilfully, and it certainly ranks as one of the masterpieces of the Gaumont establishment.

Another favourite artifice, with which some truly bewildering effects can be produced, is known as the "stop motion," or "one turn one picture," movement. As may be imagined from the latter explanatory title, it resolves itself into a pause between each picture, instead of continuous exposure to record sixteen images per second.

This feature may be illustrated by reference to a popular film which appeared a short time ago, called "Animated Putty." A lump of this material was shown upon a table. Suddenly it was observed to become agitated, and to resolve itself gradually into statues and busts of well-known people, so cleverly wrought as to be instantly identified. In a similar picture a rose was seen to detach its petals, which became scattered over the floor; and just as mysteriously the petals came together once more and assumed their former positions. Another picture shows "Boots" going to sleep at his task, and the foot-wear cleaning itself while he dreams, brushes running to and fro to remove the dust, apply the blacking, and to give a vigorous polishing off. Upon waking, Boots gives vent to a self-satisfied smile upon beholding the completion of his work without any effort on his part.

In reality this is one of the simplest of trick effects; but it is at the same time one of the most tedious to perform.

The method can be best explained by taking the "Animated Putty" film as an example. The lump of material lies upon the table, to be fashioned into a bust of the King, of the American President, or some other illustrious personage. The camera is set up. The modeller advances to the table whilst the shutter is closed and moves the clay slightly towards the desired result. He then steps out of the picture, and the camera handle is turned sufficiently to expose one picture and to cover the lens again. The modeller comes forward once more and advances a little further with his work; after which he retires from the scene, and the second stage is recorded upon the next picture. Again the modeller approaches the material to mould it a further step, and upon his retirement the third picture is taken. This alternate process of shaping the putty a little at a time, and photographing every separate movement, is continued until the bust is completed.

It is essential that the progress should be very gradual, or else the material would look as if it took shape by spasmodic jumps, and the illusion would be destroyed. Some films of this character demand slighter movement between each exposure than others. It depends entirely upon the subject. It will be observed, however, that this magical effect is not produced in accordance with the generally accepted principles governing cinematography. It is merely a series of snap-shots taken at certain intervals, and could be produced just as well by a hand-camera if one had sufficient plates or film.

As may be supposed, the task calls for unremitting patience and perseverance, because it is so exasperatingly slow. Several hours and even days are often expended in producing a single film of this character. If, for instance, the film measures 200 feet in length, no less than 3,200 distinct operations have been carried out and photographed consecutively; yet when such a film is thrown upon the screen at the rate of 16 pictures per second, the successive snap-shots follow one another so regularly as to convey the impression of continuous motion.

The same operation is practised with the rose, the petals

being torn apart a little for each successive exposure, while to convey the effect of rolling along the table they are moved a minute distance between each exposure, and supported from behind in the requisite position while the shutter is opened and the film exposed one picture at a time between each movement of the rose. In the case of the "Boots" who has his work done while he sleeps, the brushes are manipulated by invisible wires. The interruption in exposure can often be detected unless the task is carried out with consummate skill, because the movement appears to be jerky in the picture.

An amusing film of this type appeared some time ago, in which cotton and wool appeared to be imbued with life. The cotton arranged itself into fantastic designs upon the table, while a stocking was knitted before the eyes of the audience by unseen hands. So far as the cotton designs were concerned this was the "one turn one picture" movement in its simplest form, the design being furthered little by little between each exposure. With regard to the mysterious knitting, this was achieved by a combination of the "one turn one picture" and the "reverse action" artifices.

While the picture was being taken the producer stood behind a table, concealed by a black cloth somewhat after the manner practised in "black magic." What the camera actually recorded was the unravelling of the stocking stitch by stitch, the needles being manipulated meanwhile in the opposite direction. As the stocking was unravelled the wool was pulled gently through a tube extending up the producer's sleeve to his back, where it was secured by a confederate and rolled into a ball. In this way the length of wool between the needles and the ball was kept fairly taut, as would be the case if a person were knitting. Each movement of the needles was photographed, the operator setting the needles in the requisite position and then withdrawing his hands from the scene. The task was continued step by step until the sock had been completely unwound, the last stitch pulled out and the end of the cotton and the needles were shown lying on the table. The film itself was driven backwards through the camera while the exposures were made, so that when the picture was printed and thrown upon the screen the movements were reversed—the destructive action recorded by the camera became constructive movement in the projector. The public first saw the loose end of the wool and the needles. They observed the needles rise up, form the first stitch, and then watched the sock grow at an amazing speed until it was completed, the needles moving in a perfectly natural manner to form the stitches. Further realism was imparted to the picture by the needles and work being jerked every now and again to release a little wool from the ball.

The Americans have brought the "one turn one picture" movement to a high state of perfection, and have produced some astonishing pictures as a result of its application. One is introduced to a magic carpenter's shop, where tools are manipulated without hands and where the wood springs from the floor to the bench, is planed, sawn, chiselled, and fashions itself into a box or whatever article is desired by an apparently mysterious and invisible force.

The apparently impossible is brought about in this instance by resort to a combination of the "one turn one picture," the "reversal of action," and manipulation by wires, strings, and threads. To secure the rising of the plank from the floor to the bench the camera is stopped when this incident is reached. The plank is laid on the bench and a string is attached to it. The camera operator runs his film forward a certain distance, say twenty-four inches, which is indicated upon the dial while the lens is covered. He then gives the signal, and the stage hand, by pulling the wire attached to the plank, causes it to fall to the floor. The operator of the camera meanwhile runs the two feet of film backwards past the lens, thus photographing the plank falling to the floor. But as he has advanced his unexposed film two feet forwards and runs it backwards during exposure, he has reversed the motion of the falling plank, and the first image records the plank, not as it moves off the bench, but as it strikes the floor, while the other images up to the thirtieth show it in the

TWO NOVEL TRICK EFFECTS.

A workshop in which tools move without hands.   A.—The skater approaching the factory chimney.

 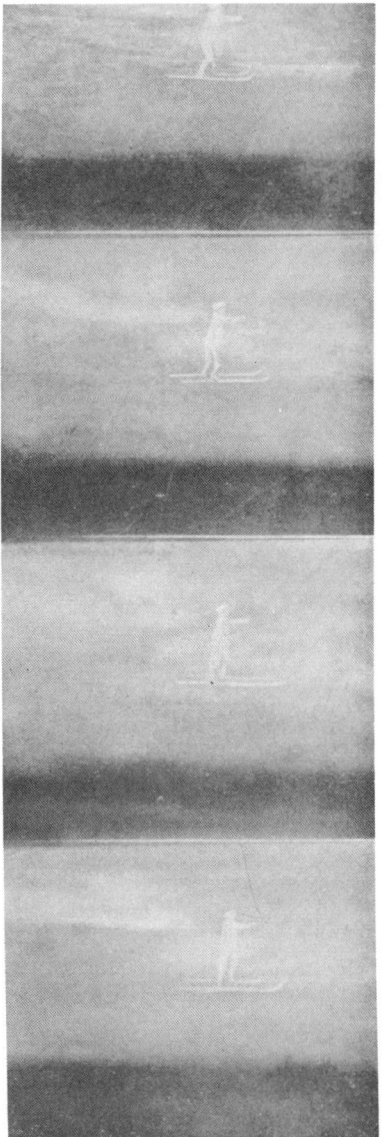

B.—The result of the collision with the chimney.   The ski runner disappears into space.

THE SKI RUNNER.

The methods adopted for the production of this novel trick film are described in the text.

air; and the last exposure displays it lying flat on the bench. Of course, when the film is thrown upon the screen the last phase of the action is shown first, and the first movement is the last image, so that the plank appears to rise from instead of falling to the floor.

The movements of the saw, chisel, and plane are carried out upon the "one turn one picture" principle, the tools being moved a slight distance between each exposure. In planing, when the shaving rises after the tool has reached the end of its stroke, a piece of thread attached to the shaving is given a sharp jerk to flick it out of the way, simulating the natural movement of the carpenter, who invariably, as he draws the plane back with his right hand, whisks the previous shaving out of the tool with his left. The hammer, chisel, and screwdriver can be manipulated by means of threads to give the varying positions of the particular tool in the driving process, and so on.

A film which appeared some months ago aroused a lively interest and speculation. It depicted a mysterious banquet where viands and liquors were consumed by unseen guests. The knife came suddenly into action to cut the bread, the various dishes were served and disappeared, while glasses of wine were filled and raised into the air by invisible hands; toasts were given, the glasses were tilted for the act of drinking, and became empty. The effect was somewhat uncanny, but it afforded a striking instance of the possibilities attending the utilisation of the "one turn one picture" movement, in conjunction with wires and threads. Each glass of wine was lifted into the air by two invisible threads, one being placed around the stem of the glass, while the other was connected to the bowl. These threads were controlled by stage hands on the overhead bridge. The glasses were lifted a slight distance between each exposure and photographed, and when the drinking act was demanded, while the thread attached to the bowl was held stationary, the second, attached to the stem, was steadily raised, giving the desired tilt. The liquid as it escaped from the glass fell to the floor, but its escape in this manner was not shown upon the screen, for the simple reason that the liquid fell out and was caught in a vessel held by a stage hand while the lens of the camera was closed, the exposure being made after the slightest quantity had fallen from the glass, this process being repeated until the toast was drained.

In the early days of the art superprinting was the favourite subterfuge used by the cinematographer magician to produce strange effects; as I have described already in regard to the pioneer work of Robert Paul. The composite construction of pictures has not been abandoned by any means, despite the advances in cinematographic magic. Indeed, some of the most startling productions seen to-day are prepared in this manner, two or even three films being used for the purpose. One of the most telling recent examples of this method is evinced in the pictures of the "ski-runner."

When first seen the actor is skating along a track in the usual manner. He approaches a towering factory chimney; but instead of avoiding the obstruction he crashes into it. The solid mass does not bring about the skater's extinction, but instead collapses to the ground. In the last picture the demon skater is seen ski-ing through the air, over the clouds, into oblivion.

The first part of the scene was taken in the vicinity of the Gaumont factory, and the chimney seen in film A belongs to the works of the company. The skater seems to strike the side of the chimney, but as a matter of fact he glides behind it, as might be supposed, and the film is cut short at this point. If one examines the film B closely it will be observed that the chimney there shown under collapse is not the same as that depicted in film A. As a matter of fact, the scene was changed. When this film was taken in hand the producers had heard that a chimney was to be felled in a certain place by the method of cutting away the masonry base, and supporting the structure temporarily upon wooden members, which are afterwards burned through to raze the chimney to the ground. Accordingly a camera and operator were dispatched to the scene to film this interesting operation, and a striking picture of the falling chimney was secured.

The combination which presented the illusion that the chimney was knocked over by the ski-runner was carried out as follows:—A special back-cloth of a neutral grey tint was prepared for the studio stage. When the ski-runner ran across the stage before the camera only the actor himself was seen in the resultant film. When this film of the ski-runner was superimposed upon that showing the demolition of the chimney, the former was seen to be forging ahead through the air after apparently knocking the structure out of his way. It will be observed that the idea is so worked out that the ski-runner appears to pursue the chimney as it crashes over, conveying the impression that he is continuously pushing the crumbling mass out of his way.

For the final disappearance of the skater into thin air two similar films were prepared. One was exposed to a cloudy sky, the lens being stopped down very severely to give a small aperture and an under-exposed result. In the studio the skater once more rushed across the stage before the neutral-tinted background, the lens stop in this instance being more open so as to secure a stronger image, but when the end of his mad career was required, the closing diaphragm was adopted. The first film was superimposed on the second to print the positive, and the result on the screen is of the ski-runner moving like a spectre through the clouds, to disappear finally into a haze. This film proved a conspicuous success owing to its novelty and realistic appearance.

CHAPTER XXII

TRICK PICTURES AND HOW THEY ARE PRODUCED

V.—" Princess Nicotine " and her remarkable caprices

"Princess Nicotine" ranks as one of the finest trick films ever made in the United States, and was the handiwork of two producers who rank as the leading American exponents of this strange craft—Messrs. J. Stuart Blackton and Albert S. Smith. In its production, all the subterfuges known to the cinematographic trick art were pressed into service, rendering it completely mystifying from beginning to end.

Some years ago these two artists were responsible for a trick-film, "The Haunted Hotel," which was so puzzling and so cleverly worked out that it was regarded as a masterpiece of cinematographic chicanery. It was a prodigious success; some idea of its widespread popularity may be gathered from the fact that over 150 copies of the subject were disposed of in Europe alone, while its total sales were well over 400 copies; for its success in the land of its origin was quite as marked as that which it scored in the Old World. For a long time it ranked as the finest trick-film the United States had produced, and it precipitated a "boom" in "haunted" subjects. The success of that film, however, threatens to be surpassed by "Princess Nicotine," which, in addition to being a distinct novelty, is dainty in its conception, fascinating in its theme, and finished in its production.

The story of the play may be briefly related. The scene opens with a young bachelor reclining in an armchair at a table. Before him are scattered the indispensable adjuncts to a bachelor's comfort—a box of cigars, a tobacco-box, a corncob pipe, a box of matches, a square white bottle standing upon the cigar-box, a bottle of whisky and a syphon of soda-water. In addition, there is a large, round reading-glass with a handle. The bachelor fills his pipe, lights it, leans back and dozes. Suddenly the lid of the tobacco-box is opened and a small fairy, Princess Nicotine, jumps out and falls over the pipe, which arrests her attention and gives her a brilliant idea. Laughingly she returns to the tobacco-box and helps out a second and smaller sprite, whom she leads to the pipe and unfolds her scheme. The fairies are no larger than the man's hand, and the contrast between their diminutive figures and the bachelor is decidedly grotesque. At first sight one might think the two tiny forms were dolls, but their movements are so graceful, steady, and natural that this idea is quickly abandoned.

The two wee plotters pull out the tobacco, and the smaller fairy jumps into the bowl and is buried beneath a layer of the shredded weed, which is pushed in by Princess Nicotine, who afterwards hides in the tobacco-box.

The bachelor wakes up, and after yawning turns to his pipe once more. To his amazement the tobacco will not light, and he looks at it closely. He starts in amazement and picks up the hand-magnifying glass to examine the contents. He reveals what he sees to the public, for the magnifying-glass is held up as it were before the spectators, who see the elfish face of the fairy peeping from the tobacco and enveloped in wreaths of smoke.

The startled bachelor then inverts the pipe and raps out the contents in true smoker's fashion upon the table, emptying the fairy in the process. She struggles to her feet from the tobacco débris, and rushes to the tobacco-box, into which she jumps, pulling the lid down after her. Princess Nicotine thrusts her arm out of the box, which the bachelor grasps, but instead of withdrawing the fairy, he seizes a rose, which he proceeds to smell; but he is seized with a violent fit of coughing caused by a cloud of smoke which issues from the flower. He examines the rose through the magnifying-glass, this view as it appears to him being held before the audience as before, so that it sees the form of the fairy embedded among the petals, smoking a cigarette. The man drops the rose and rushes out of the room. The rose falls to pieces gradually, the petals accumulating on the table and turning into a cigar. The bachelor re-enters, picks up the cigar, lights it, the smoke rises and whirls round rapidly, and presently rushes into the white bottle. Startled at the extraordinary action of the smoke, the bachelor picks up the bottle, examines it and sees the fairy imprisoned within and vainly endeavouring to escape. The man breaks the bottle, and the fairy is seen standing on the tobacco-box. She picks up a packet of cigarettes, proffers one to the bachelor, and dances before him on the table.

The bachelor commences to tease Princess Nicotine. He lights a match and holds it towards her. She shrinks from it in fear, and in revenge she approaches the match-box, extracts the matches, stacks them in a pile, and lights them. The magnifying-glass is held up as before, and the audience sees the pile of matches burning like a big bonfire. The last scene shows the man, somewhat terrified at the blazing pile on the table, picking up the soda-syphon and endeavouring to quench the outbreak, at the same time deluging himself in the process.

Through the kindness of Messrs. Blackton and Smith I am able to explain how this apparently miraculous picture is produced, and the various tricks employed. In describing the "Little Milliner's Dream" I have shown how the appearance of a fairy can be produced, by placing the performers fulfilling the *rôle* at the very back of the stage, a long distance from the camera, whereas the principal actor is caused to carry through his part but a few feet away from the lens. The same effect can be produced by the aid of a mirror placed at the back of the scene; when the players fulfilling the *rôles* of fairies enact their parts on a stage placed beside the camera, the film records simply their reflection in the mirror, and the impression of extremely small stature is conveyed. By pressing the mirror into service a great saving in stage space is gained.

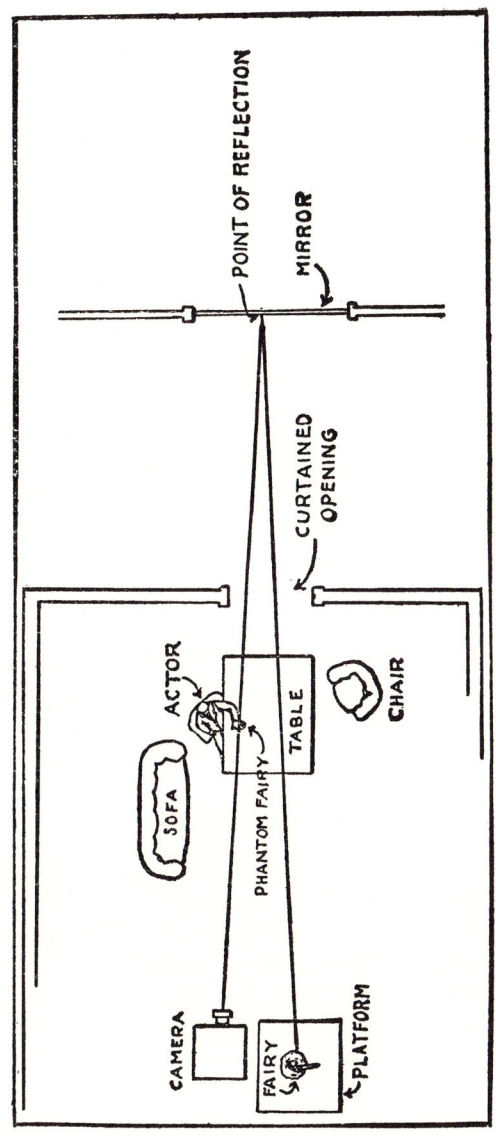

Fig. 18.—How the Stage was Set for Taking the Trick Film "Princess Nicotine."

Two stages are required for the effect: the set stage on which the scene is built up, and on which the bachelor figures, and a temporary stage placed beside the camera, whereon the fairies carry through their parts. The diagram, Fig. 18, shows the setting of the stage. The mirror is placed some distance behind the back-cloth of the stage scene, immediately behind a curtained window, which is really an opening in the back-cloth. As the action takes place at night all is darkness outside the window. The lens is exactly flush with the top of the table in the scene, so that when the reflections of the fairies are caught they appear to be moving upon the top of the table. The mirror at the back of the stage is so disposed as to appear to be the glass in the window of the back-cloth behind the actor, and is arranged so skilfully as to betray no evidence of its existence. The stage set up beside the camera is of such dimensions that it keeps the actresses taking the parts of the two fairies within the limits of the centre of the table; while its floor is marked accurately for other purposes, which will be described later. If the principle adopted for presenting the diminutive players in "The Little Milliner's Dream" had been followed in this instance instead of using a mirror, the fairies would have had to carry out their work at a point equal to twice the distance between the camera and the mirror to present the same effect. It may be pointed out, in passing, that during the whole play the actor fulfilling the part of the bachelor sees nothing upon the table in front of him beyond the articles placed there for his own comfort.

The *rôle* of Princess Nicotine was fulfilled by an actress of average height, while her companion was a little girl of about twelve years of age. In addition, certain properties were required, all of which were enlarged facsimiles of objects in daily use. These comprised a cigar-box of huge dimensions capable of permitting the fairies to stand upright within it; a huge corn-cob pipe, the bowl of which was as big as a barrel; a property match-box containing matches measuring about thirty inches in length, with paper rolled round one end to convey the impression of phos-

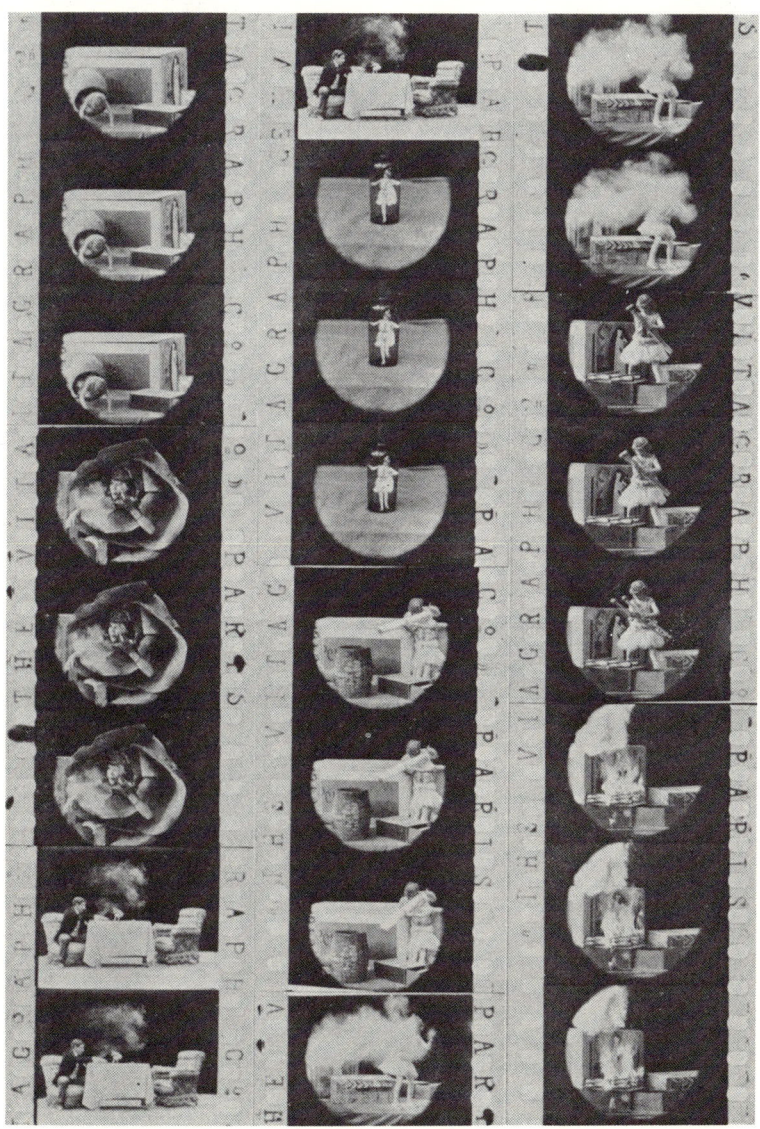

PRINCESS NICOTINE—A DAINTY TRICK FILM.

This subject, produced by the Vitagraph Company of America, has proved to be one of the most popularly successful subjects of this description seen during recent years.

The fairy, buried in the heart of the rose, smoking a cigarette. The blossom is a large paper property flower.

PRINCESS NICOTINE.

The diminutive form of the fairy on the table. The bachelor, although astonished, in reality sees nothing.

phorus heads; a property packet of cigarettes nearly six feet in height, containing cigarettes thirty-six inches long formed of rolls of paper stuffed with straw, and more straw to represent the tobacco. These properties had to be prepared carefully to scale, while the actresses themselves had to be accomplished performers. The play demanded searching rehearsals, as in a trick picture of this character the slightest slip in the acting destroys the illusion.

The properties were used on the second stage beside the camera operator, and when reflected in the mirror they appeared no larger than the smoker's companions lying upon the table. Behind the fairies' stage a back-cloth of black canvas was stretched, so that all their movements were against a black background, and this served to sustain the impression of darkness behind the back-cloth window of the scene, beyond the window in which the mirror was placed.

In addition to these properties stage hands were required at various intervals to complete certain operations, but were concealed out of the sight of the lens of the camera. Their tasks also will be described in due course.

In the opening scene the bachelor uses his own materials lying upon the table. The camera stops, and in the interval their place is taken by the properties, which are placed upon the second stage to produce a reflection in the mirror. When the fairy appears to jump out of the bachelor's cigar-box on the table she actually steps from the property cigar-box on the second stage, the lid of which is opened by means of a thread pulled by a stage hand concealed behind. The antics of the fairies, which appear to take place on the table before the bachelor, are carried out upon the second stage, beside the camera, the smaller fairy climbing into the property pipe.

When the bachelor wakes up and tries to light his pipe the fairy stage properties are removed from the fairy stage, and those of the bachelor replaced upon the table. Accordingly, the audience see him vainly endeavouring to light his own pipe, which finally he examines with the magnifying-glass. When the scene revealed to the smoker is flashed to the public on the screen in such a way that the audience appear to be looking through the magnifying-glass, they are not looking at the bachelor's pipe, but at the property one. To produce the effect of magnification the second stage is photographed directly from a short distance instead of by means of the reflection in the mirror. The smoke curling lazily about the smaller fairy and issuing from the pipe is produced by steam, there being a tube carried beneath the table and connected to the bottom of the bowl of the property pipe.

When the scene is flashed back once more, and the bachelor is again seen seated at his table, photographing is resumed of the mirror's reflected image.

The second stage is cleared again, and we see the man empty the ashes of his pipe upon the table. The débris containing the fairy is again thrown upon the screen in an enlarged form, as if through the magnifying-glass; that is to say, the second stage and its properties are being photographed once more to show the little lady laughing and running among the smoking, half-burnt tobacco. The tobacco is straw and the smoke is steam.

The scene reverts to the table showing the man. By reflection the fairy is observed to jump into her property cigar-box, leaving an arm protruding. This is a property arm built to scale in the same manner as all the other properties used on the fairies' stage, and when the man seizes it, in reality he grasps the stem of a paper property rose of natural size protruding from the cigar-box standing on his own table. He turns the rose over to smell it, but beneath the table is a stage hand, who puffs a stream of smoke through a flexible pipe connected to the stalk of the rose which the bachelor is holding; the smoke provokes a fit of sneezing and coughing, and the bachelor has recourse to his magnifying-glass to examine the rose. Again the second stage is brought into play, a large property rose lying thereon, revealing the head of the fairy within smoking a cigarette.

Every time the audience is permitted, as it were, to see what the bachelor discovers beneath his magnifying-glass the second stage is photographed direct, the camera being placed about eight feet away. The fact that the properties used are of large dimensions does not strike the public, as they put themselves in the position of the bachelor at the table and look through the magnifying-glass at the articles lying upon the table, which naturally would undergo tremendous magnification. This "flashing" to and fro, as it is called, is so cleverly accomplished that the public does not realise the fact that it is being deceived. Everything that the bachelor handles on the table is of natural size; every duplicate article which the audience sees through the magnifying-glass belongs to the large-sized properties upon the second stage.

In the next scene the bachelor is seen to drop his rose and flee from the room. The rose instantly falls gradually to pieces, petal by petal, each of which runs across the table to roll into and form a cigar. To produce this effect recourse has to be made to the "one turn one picture" movement described in the previous chapter. Each petal is displaced by hand and moved a slight distance by the stage-manager between each exposure. This destruction of the rose and fabrication of the cigar from the petals occupies hours, but it passes across the screen in the course of a few seconds.

When this strange act is completed, and while the camera is not working, a real cigar is substituted on the table for that apparently made from the rose. When the bachelor returns he picks it up and lights it. Thenceforward various tricks, the principle of all of which has been described already, are practised in rapid succession. For instance, the bachelor as he puffs the smoke into the air is astonished to see it whirling rapidly, instead of curling slowly in the usual way. The film is manipulated to produce this effect, as explained in Chapter XX. The actor retains a fixed position, puffing while the operator runs a few feet of film to record the smoke. After development several images on the film—perhaps fifty per cent. of the movement obtained—are cut out, and thereby the smoke is accelerated in its motion so as to become a whirl upon the positive.

While smoking the bachelor is somewhat astonished to see the smoke disobey natural laws by rushing into the square bottle beside him. This illusion is produced by reversal of motion. The operator placed the cap upon the lens and ran the film forward a certain distance, observing the length of its travel on the measuring device. The camera action was reversed, and the film run backwards the length of the unexposed section. The smoke in the bottle was supplied from beneath the table, there being a hole in the base connected to a pipe, through which steam was driven. Naturally the steam flows from the mouth of the bottle, but by turning the film backwards the smoke is made to appear to rush into the bottle. When this incident has been recorded the lens is capped, the film run forward the distance it was reversed, and everything is ready for the next episode.

The bachelor, somewhat puzzled by the behaviour of the smoke, picks up the bottle and looks at it. To his astonishment he sees the fairy within dancing and endeavouring to escape. He picks up his magnifying-glass and examines it closely, and the bottle containing the girl, as seen through the glass, is seen by the audience. The illusion is produced by double exposure, a process fully described already. The bottle was stood against a dark background and photographed. Then the reflected image of the fairy was photographed upon the same film. The stage upon which she acted was marked out, and she had to keep within these limits while making her assumed efforts to escape. Thus the whole of her movements are brought within the area of the image of the bottle already secured upon the film, so that when the latter is developed she appears to be imprisoned within the bottle. If she should step outside the limits during this incident, the reflection would be shown outside the bottle and the illusion would be lost.

The man breaks the bottle with a hammer, and the released fairy is seen standing upon the cigar-box. The "stop motion" has been requisitioned to produce this

The fairy imprisoned in the bottle. This effect is obtained by double exposure.

PRINCESS NICOTINE.

The fairy, after coquetting with the bachelor, is driven away by the smoke from his cigarette. The smoke effect is produced with steam.

Enraged, the fairy proceeds to build a bonfire with matches. The property matches are used for this purpose.

PRINCESS NICOTINE.

The fairy, her accomplice, and properties, which are enlarged reproductions of the actual articles.

effect, the camera being stopped when the bottle is broken to enable the fairy to assume her position upon the property cigar-box on the second stage, the box and bottle on the table in the meantime having been removed. Gratified at her release, the fairy stoops down and draws out a packet of cigarettes—the property package concealed behind her property cigar-box on the second stage—and withdrawing one of the cigarettes she offers it to the bachelor. Although the cigarette she holds is three feet long, the reflection in the mirror representing her standing apparently on the table, brings the cigarette down to the natural size. The bachelor holds out his hand to receive it, and at this point the "stop" is called to enable the bachelor to place a real cigarette in the position of the property one, the stage-manager informing the actor when the real article covers the reflection, because the actor himself can see nothing. The property cigarette is withdrawn, and the camera resumes. The bachelor places the cigarette in his mouth, and as the audience cannot detect the "stop" it appears as if he had taken the cigarette from the fairy.

The smoker lights the cigarette and takes a fiendish delight in blowing the smoke at his diminutive companion, meanwhile coquetting with her. The little lady resents the smoke; and as the bachelor again takes up the magnifying-glass the public apparently looks through it at her plight. The fairy is surrounded with cigarette smoke, coughing and sneezing and shaking her fist furiously at the bachelor, who is out of the picture, because in this instance, as before, the actual scene is photographed direct, and not its reflection in the mirror.

The magnifying-glass is laid down and the audience sees the bachelor strike a match, from which his tiny visitor shrinks in fear. The man laughs heartily at her discomfiture. The fairy is bent upon revenge, and steals stealthily towards the match-box. The bachelor follows the fairy's operations through the magnifying-glass, and the scene is flashed to the spectators. They see the infuriated fairy tearing out the matches and stacking them into a pile. Of course she is handling the property matches, which, as I have already said, are good-sized sticks. She strikes a match and fires the pile upon her stage.

The scene is flashed back to the table, but in the meantime the real matches have been taken out of the smoker's box and arranged in a pile, which is burning upon the table, so that they appear to have been fired by the fairy. The bachelor picks up the syphon of soda-water and directs a stream upon the burning mass of matches. A final glimpse of the fairy is given through the magnifying-glass as a stream of water, this time from a hose, plays upon the blazing property pile, and she falls over and disappears.

The preparation of a film of this character involves the utmost care in stage management, so that there may be no disconcerting interruptions in the continuity of the action. The greatest difficulty is to obtain exact overlapping of the reflected and the real articles upon the bachelor's table; moreover, as the actor cannot see anything, but has to act to an imaginary diminutive person on the table, his every action has to be guided by the producer. The actresses must be faultless in their movements. A film of this description requires days to prepare, especially since it entails resort almost to every subterfuge known to trick cinematography.

It will be observed that the work resolves itself into two essential parts—the photographing of the bachelor in his sitting-room when in company with the fairies, as shown by the mirror reflections, and the photographing of the fairies and their properties. Whenever the latter have to be taken, the idea of looking through the magnifying-glass is adopted, and is artfully conveyed by the circular mask of the picture. The magnification explains the apparently abnormal proportions of the articles used; but the public do not realise them as properties because they have been watching the little ladies on the table. Naturally, when the magnifying-glass is turned upon them, the audience thinks that the fairies and their attributes have been enlarged proportionately, whereas, as a matter of fact, they are not enlarged at all, but are photographed direct from a distance of only a few feet. In such a film as this the producer, having sketched out the work and arranged the scenes, photographs all the incidents pertaining to the reflection one after the other, and subsequently photographs the views apparently taken through the magnifying-glass upon either the same or another stage. The trick effects, such as the conversion of the rose into the cigar and so forth, are taken at other times. When the numerous strips of film are developed the various sections are sorted out and placed in rotation, to be connected up to form one continuous subject showing the natural progress of the play.

Such is the story of the production of one of the prettiest and apparently most miraculous trick-films that has ever been seen. It should be said that such charming and mystifying productions as "Princess Nicotine" appear only at very long intervals, but their rarity is compensated fully by their fascination and novelty, which, it may be pointed out, is a salient feature of the productions of the Vitagraph Company in this particular field.

CHAPTER XXIII

TRICK PICTURES AND HOW THEY ARE PRODUCED

VI.—Some Unusual and Novel Effects

AT times a trick picture cannot possibly be produced by any of the methods I have so far described. Accordingly, the producer has to rely upon his own ingenuity and inventiveness to cope with an unusual situation or effect.

Some years ago an extraordinary film was produced by Mr. James Williamson which created no little astonishment. It was entitled "A Big Swallow," and was decidedly startling in its effect. It depicted a man to whom the sight of a cinematographer acted as a red rag to a bull. On this occasion he was goaded to such desperation that he advanced towards the camera with open mouth. Upon reaching it he gave a terrific bite, and swallowed the whole apparatus and operator, the final scenes showing him retracing his footsteps apparently enjoying his strange meal, and satisfied that he had disposed of one cinematographic fiend at least.

Curiously enough, although the idea adopted in this instance offers illimitable possibilities, it apparently has never been exploited since. This particular film never failed to arouse the enthusiasm of the public, and there was considerable speculation upon all sides as to how it was carried out. Through the courtesy of Mr. Williamson I am enabled to unravel the mystery.

It is well known by amateur photographers that when a person is focussed a certain distance from the camera, if he steps towards the instrument the focus is immediately upset. When the individual is taken in motion, and in such a way that he comes right up to the lens, this difficulty is enhanced. It is impossible to keep adjusting the focus of a cinematograph camera while the subject is advancing, because the focussing tube is obstructed by the passing of the film through the gate.

Accordingly, Mr. Williamson resorted to a combination of the cinematograph with the racking bellows of the ordinary camera. The latter, of special design, was attached to the front of the cinematograph instrument, the bellows attachment carrying the lens. The camera was set up, and the distance between the apparatus and the actor was measured and marked off upon the ground. Observations were made to ascertain at what points the actor in advancing should be re-focussed, and these points were indicated upon the ground. The camera bellows was then racked out until the figure was focussed sharply once more, and this point was indicated upon the base-board of the bellows. The figure then advanced still closer, until a similar result was observed, when the bellows was racked out a little farther, focussed, and a second mark was placed on the base-board corresponding to that on the ground. The process was continued until the figure had advanced right up to the camera.

The picture had to be taken under the "stop motion" principle. At the word "Go!" the actor advanced to the first mark, where he stood stock-still, while the camera bellows was racked to the point indicating the correct focus. The second picture was taken under the same conditions, and so on, until the actor's face almost touched the lens of the outstretched bellows. In the first photo the actor was seen at full length, with the lens set in a horizontal line with his mouth. As he approached the camera, less and less of the lower part of his body was to be seen in each successive picture. Presently only his head was recorded; then nothing but the open mouth and teeth; and at last, when he almost touched the lens, nothing but a black cavity was revealed upon the film.

The actual swallowing operation had now to be carried

out. For this purpose a large window opening into a darkened room was required. The window was covered with dead-black material, leaving only the opening. The camera was set upon a stage, and the window cavity focussed in such a way that the opening occupied the whole of the picture. On the inside of the building a thick mattress was placed with stage hands in readiness. The camera and operator were set up before this cavity as if photographing the approaching irate individual, and were photographed by a second camera. This was intended to represent the former scene from the moment where the man's mouth only was visible upon the picture in the form of a black space, and for which the opened window sufficed.

At the critical moment the camera was pushed gently over through the window opening, and immediately afterwards the operator dived into the chasm, the last sign of him being his upturned feet as he fell downwards head first into the interior through the window, to alight upon the mattress placed below to receive him.

When he had disappeared in this manner the third scene had to be taken. This represented the actor stepping back from the camera after he had devoured his antagonist. When he retreated to the mark on the ground nearest to the camera, the bellows was racked in to its corresponding mark on the base; then the second backward step was made by the actor to the next mark on the ground while the bellows was racked back to the next mark, this succession of stop-motions being in the reverse direction to the advance. As the actor retreated, his teeth were seen to close with a snap, and the look on his face as it came into view revealed intense satisfaction with his strange feast. Retreat was carried out in this series of steps until the actor had regained his original position.

In this film the difficulty of keeping an advancing and retreating figure in focus was solved very ingeniously; and when the pictures were projected upon the screen the illusion was perfect, not the slightest sign of a stop between the exposures being detected. As a matter of fact, the advance and retreat series of pictures were produced at one time, the disappearance of the camera and operator being taken later; and upon the development of the negatives, the last episode was introduced between the other two at the correct point. As the area of the open mouth when close to the lens more than covered the sensitised picture, the opening in the blackened window as it appeared upon the screen gave no intimation as to the manner in which an ordinary individual contrived to swallow a camera, tripod, and operator at one gulp.

During a recent General Election infinite amusement was provoked by the display upon the public screens, which appear to have become an inseparable feature of such political events, of a film depicting "The Dissolution of the Government." The dissolution was complete in the fullest sense of the word. A picture—a conventional portrait—of one of the members of the Cabinet was thrown upon the screen. Slowly it was observed to undergo a strange and ludicrous transformation. An eye slipped down into the collar, the chin fell away, the nose was lengthened abnormally, and the forehead narrowed to nothing. The conditions presented were the most extraordinary to conceive, and the manner in which the features melted into oblivion leaving a transparent surface, or only a series of indecipherable streaks, aroused indescribable merriment in the crowd. It is certain that no "election" film ever has proved such a diversion as this trick picture.

The idea was worked out by Mr. F. Percy Smith. Like many other displays of cinematographic magic, its success was due to its simplicity. Every amateur photographer in his earliest days has endeavoured to force the drying of a glass plate after development by placing it before the fire. Invariably the effort ends in disaster. The gelatine melts and causes the emulsion to run all over the plate, producing grotesque results.

In order to produce this bizarre film a primitive apparatus was contrived, consisting of a small tank the back and front of which were cut out to admit pieces of glass. This tank was filled with water and placed upon an ordinary spirit stove. The cinematograph camera was placed in front, and at the rear a powerful electric light was arranged in such a manner that the illumination was diffused equally over the rear glazed part of the tank. A transparency portrait of the politician was then copied upon a small glass dry photographic plate, developed and fixed. It was then suspended in the small tank between the camera lens and the electric light, so that the illuminating rays passed through it, throwing the features in the picture up brilliantly. The water was heated by the spirit lamp beneath, the rise in the temperature being followed closely with a thermometer; and when the requisite degree of heat was obtained, the features upon the transparent plate, owing to the melting of the gelatine emulsion, commenced to slip and slide about over the glass surface, and were caught in the act by the camera.

Although the process appears absurdly simple, considerable time had to be expended upon the subject to secure the most grotesque results. One portrait frequently had to be prepared and boiled in this manner six or more times before a sufficiently ludicrous effect was secured. Owing to the capriciousness of the gelatine emulsion, occasionally the whole coating would slip bodily off its glass support. The temperature of the water had to be judged to a nicety, and suitable arrangements had to be made to prevent the boiling water from marring the photographic effect upon the celluloid film by the interposition of bubbles. Our illustration shows a member of the Government under photographic dissolution in this manner. The treatment has almost infinite possibilities, for no two plates are affected alike. This film appealed to the American taste. After the British Government had been dissolved in this manner, a second film had to be prepared, in response to the demand from the United States, dealing with the dissolution of the American Government at the time of the last Presidential Election, the portraits subjected to this drastic and peculiar treatment being those of members of the United States Cabinet. This film created

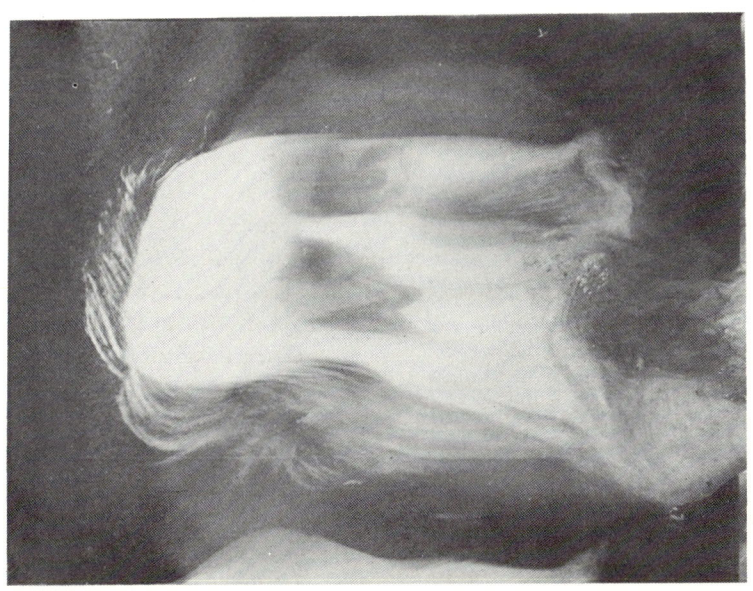

THE DISSOLUTION OF THE GOVERNMENT.
One of the most mystifying and amusing trick films ever produced.

[Copyright, C. Armstrong.

THE LATEST CRAZE IN TRICK CINEMATOGRAPHY.

Silhouettes with models.

just as great hilarity in the United States as attended its exhibition in this country.

During the past two years the silhouette trick film has come to the front owing to the novelty of the fundamental theme and the successful combination of humour with mystery. We all know the old shadowgraph play, wherein the actors carry through their parts behind a white sheet before a powerful light, which casts their shadows upon the screen. The idea is now applied to cinematography. One or two films of this character made their appearance some time ago from foreign sources, but it has been left to an English experimenter, Mr. C. Armstrong, to reduce this ingenious trick subject to an exact science.

In an American attempt in this direction, living actors were used, but the outcome was scarcely happy, inasmuch as the trick effects were very limited, being confined mostly to weird contrasts in the sizes of the figures thrown upon the screen, arising from the proximity of the actor to the light. If he stood near the illuminant his stature was that of an immense giant, while if he enacted his *rôle* near the screen, his shadow was just life-size. Mr. Armstrong has improved upon this method by resorting to the use of models, constructed of flat material, with jointed limbs, like dolls, in order to secure ludicrous poses and situations and impossible statures.

Seeing that only silhouette figures are required, it seems a very simple and easy matter to fashion the models and move them through their parts to obtain the desired effect; but such is far from being the case. Both preparation and manipulation demand unremitting care and patience. It may be pointed out at once that exclusive use has to be made of "the one turn one picture" movement, the models being shifted a small fraction of an inch between each exposure. When one has a group of figures to move in this manner, the work is exceedingly tedious, weeks often being spent upon the production of a single film.

When Mr. Armstrong embarked upon this enterprise he concluded that the work could be accomplished without any great effort, but he was soon disillusioned. Moreover, he found, to his dismay, that in order to produce really striking trick effects, combined with complex movements, perfect in every detail, it was not only the construction of the models which presented many difficulties and required great mechanical skill, but that the most intricate part of the work, involving a vast amount of patience and extremely delicate manipulation, proved to be the actual taking of the negatives. Innumerable failures attended the first attempts. It was only after months of practice, and after he had devised numerous special accessories, that Mr. Armstrong gradually brought his methods to perfection. The outcome of his perseverance was seen at the Palace Theatre, London. The film was entitled "The Clown and his Donkey," and it provoked the audience to unrestrained mirth.

Such work not only demands the conception of a suitable subject, its adaptation to technical requirements, and the preparation of the negatives to express humour and produce movements portraying distinct traits of character and temper; but, as I have said, the construction of the models presents singular difficulty, in view of the complexity of the movements. It is indispensable that the person who takes the negatives should also construct the models, the mechanical peculiarities of which must be understood to a nicety.

The supplementary devices necessitated by the work seem to be without limit; and to overcome the constantly recurring technical obstacles, it is essential that the operator should be endowed with quite exceptional mechanical resourcefulness; otherwise he will be baulked time after time. Frequently he will find himself faced with a difficulty, successful extrication from which, without compromising the subject upon which he is working, will tax his ingenuity to the last degree.

The most lucrative field for silhouette trick cinematography should lie in its application to the production of animated advertisements and caricatures; for the idea

[Copyright, C. Armstrong.

THE POSSIBILITIES OF TRICK SILHOUETTE CINEMATOGRAPHY.

1.
A quaint advertisement film.

2.
Mr. Asquith in cartoon.

3.
A novel curtain idea.

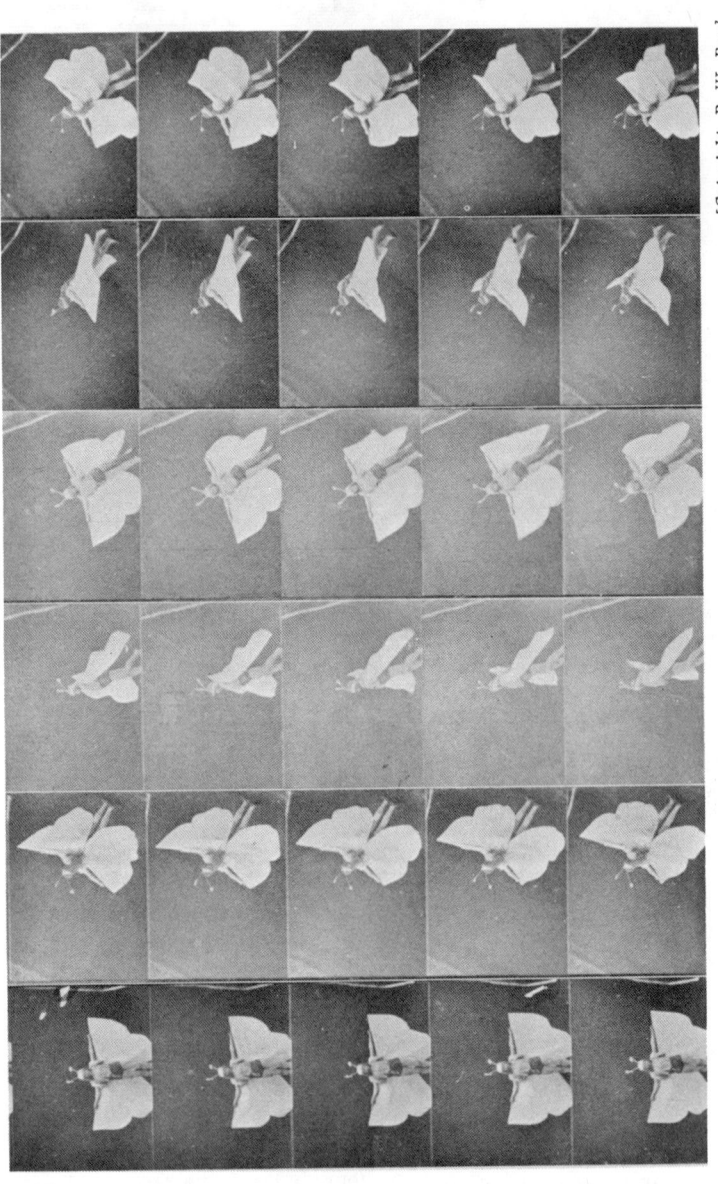

THE HUMAN BUTTERFLY: HOW ARE THE EFFECTS OBTAINED?

[*Copyright, R. W. Paul.*

The search for novelty in trick cinematography is very keen. This illustrates a new idea which so far has never been exploited. *See page 263.*

possesses the indispensable attribute of novelty, which is the mainspring of commercial success.

As for caricature, despite the promising look of the field, there are certain practical obstacles to success: first, the time occupied in production, and second, a hostility on the part of the theatres to political films of a party character—an attitude easily explainable, as it is the aim of such establishments to appeal to one and all.

We give a few illustrations showing, in caricature, Mr. Asquith speaking. The various attitudes clearly show the wonderful possibilities of silhouette trickery, and also demonstrate strikingly what can be done by a skilful operator with finely executed models. The ones in the illustration are made of metal.

In regard to advertising, the innovation is unquestionably of real importance, and I am told that use has been made of it with conspicuous success by a prominent European cigarette manufacturing company. This concern acquired a film measuring 300 feet in length, which figured continuously in the programmes of the picture palaces. It was most ingeniously conceived and worked out, the actors being a large burly figure endowed with a movable nose, which changed from snub to aquiline, a baby boy, and a chimpanzee, all of which characters are shown in the illustration. The movements were carried out with perfect realism. The burly figure is at one side of the stage, while the words, "The Best Cigarette is———" appears at the top of the picture.

The chimpanzee and the baby come forward from opposite sides, each picks up a rod from the ground, by means of which the letters forming the name of the firm are jerked up alternately. They then drop the rods; a box comes flying along, and is caught by the monkey, who tenders it to the baby. The latter takes out a cigarette, which he throws across the stage straight into the burly figure's mouth; he then does a somersault across the monkey's back, steps on to one of the hands of the large figure, and after he is raised to the requisite height, the baby produces a match and lights the cigarette. The burly man puffs away, demonstrating his satisfaction with the quality of the cigarette by facial contortions. In the meantime the baby has descended, and the large figure having lowered the hand holding the cigarette leisurely, the baby seizes it, and, placing it in his mouth, sends forth a big puff of smoke.

The effect of this absolutely novel advertisement seems to have been extraordinary in Germany. One company after another is being formed in that country, systematising publicity in the picture halls, affiliating a number of them under contracts involving sole rights for showing advertising films on terms of payment according to the length of film shown. The halls seem, naturally, to prefer humorous and trick films to sober industrial subjects. Things seem to move more slowly in this country. Many halls would no doubt welcome good trick advertising films. which would yield them an additional substantial income, and at the same time would amuse and mystify their audiences.

Finally, we would refer to the excellent purposes to which this invention is being applied in the matter of announcement films, to replace the conventional lantern slides. A typical subject of this description, "Ta-Ta, Come Again," is illustrated. The actors comprise a baby elephant, a jackdaw, a chimpanzee, and a tiny monkey.

The elephant and jackdaw alternately draw letters from a box and throw them into the air to form the title. The last letter, N, while being slowly raised into position by the elephant, is snatched up by the jackdaw, who flies away to set it in position. The tiny monkey then appears, carrying an exclamation sign, which he balances on the tip of one of his feet, and finally tosses into its place. He then steps on to the tip of the elephant's tail. The chimpanzee now advances, seizes the elephant by the trunk, and pulls him sliding off the stage.

Silhouette trick films, the production of which has become the speciality of this manufacturer, lend themselves to vast development. I have seen some subjects produced by European and American firms which represent possibly the high-water mark of this form of magic cinematography. But the enterprise has one distinct disadvantage. The preparation of the films is slow, and the process is unavoidably expensive.

Novelty in trick cinematography, which is essential to popular success, is difficult to hit upon. Some years ago Mr. Robert Paul experimented with a new idea, the result of which is shown in the illustration. The strange poses of the actor will occasion interest and speculation as to how they were obtained. The camera, while the exposures were being made, was revolved, the actor on the stage meanwhile maintaining his feet. The resultant pictures conveyed the impression that the subject photographed was rolling over and over, and flying through the air. This idea does not appear to have been exploited, although it should offer opportunities to produce some highly bewildering effects.

Time and cost are the most adverse factors in this ramification of moving pictures. The market could absorb four times the number of trick subjects that are produced at present, so long as they were comparable with "The Little Milliner's Dream" and "Princess Nicotine." But their popularity would not always compensate the producer for the time and expense of the preparation. Under the present conditions governing the manufacture of trick films, distinct arrangements and facilities must be provided for their manufacture, so as not to disturb the routine preparation of ordinary subjects. These are the main reasons why to-day trick films worthy of classification in the first rank are so rarely seen—the majority of so-called trick films are pure inanities. In fact, the trick film of the highest order is in danger of extinction, because for every trick film that is produced half a dozen ordinary film plays can be placed on the market.

CHAPTER XXIV

ELECTRIC SPARK CINEMATOGRAPHY

ALTHOUGH we commonly think of the human senses as very acute, yet in reality they possess many imperfections. For instance, our vision is too slow to follow the excessively rapid and brief movements of insects. Strive as one may, one cannot detect the flapping motion of a fly's wing, or follow the different methods of flying practised by the dragon-fly and the bee. I have spoken early in this work of Marey's wonderful researches, which were spread over a prolonged period, and carried out with the express object of extending our knowledge of animal motion.

Marey's experiments, however, were limited in their scope, as he soon realised. The dry glass plate was not a convenient medium for recording the impressions of rapid motion, while extreme difficulties were encountered in connection with the illuminant and the exposure. These drawbacks became baffling when it was attempted to record the movements of insects. He endeavoured to solve the problem by concentrating a pencil of brilliant sunlight upon a condenser, so as to secure such a powerful luminous cone of light as to enable an exposure to be made in 1/42,000th of a second.

Marey wrestled with the task in a most determined manner, and his efforts were supported by eminent physiologists in other countries; but the obstacles were so formidable and the available resources so limited that they could not arrive at any practical result. It has been left to Monsieur Lucien Bull, the accomplished assistant director of the Marey Institute, to overcome the difficulty. Through his courtesy I am enabled to describe his fascinating researches, as well as the peculiar and efficient apparatus he has evolved for the purpose. The beautiful and highly interesting results he has achieved are shown in the accompanying illustrations.

It was obvious at the outset that the familiar cinematograph camera and its system of operation were unsuited to recording such excessively rapid movements as take place in the oscillation of a fly's wing. Intermittent motion was quite out of the question. No device working on this principle was capable of enabling one hundred exposures or more to be made in the short space of one second. If it were attempted the film would only be torn and twisted before it had moved twelve inches. In its place continuous motion on the part of the film was imperative, and finally this requisite was supplied in a decidedly novel manner.

The general characteristics of the apparatus conceived and fashioned by Monsieur Bull may be gathered from the illustrations. As the usual illuminants were unsuited to photography of extremely rapid motion, recourse was had to the electric spark, which is of tremendous luminous intensity. These sparks are generated at uniform intervals and as rapidly as the exigencies of the experiment demand. In order to grasp the details of the installation a vertical sectional diagram, Fig. 19, is given, and by its means the design and operation of the apparatus may be gathered.

Instead of the ordinary camera there is a cylindrical wheel R, mounted rigidly upon a shaft supported on brackets at either end. The flat rim of this wheel carries the sensitised film, which, as the wheel is $13\frac{1}{2}$ inches in diameter, is $42\frac{1}{2}$ inches in length. This band is of the standard width and is sufficiently long to receive fifty-four pictures of the ordinary cinematographic dimensions during one revolution of the wheel. As the pictures are only three-quarters of an inch in depth, the deformation arising from the impression being made upon a curved surface is so slight as to be unworthy of consideration. The arrangement adopted has the advantage of enabling the wheel to be rotated very rapidly, so that consecutive pictures may be taken at very brief intervals of time.

266 MOVING PICTURES CHAP.

As the work is carried out in the laboratory in full daylight, the wheel carrying the ribbon of sensitised film is enclosed in an octagonal light-tight box *B*, the upper half of which is hinged so that when the box is dismounted

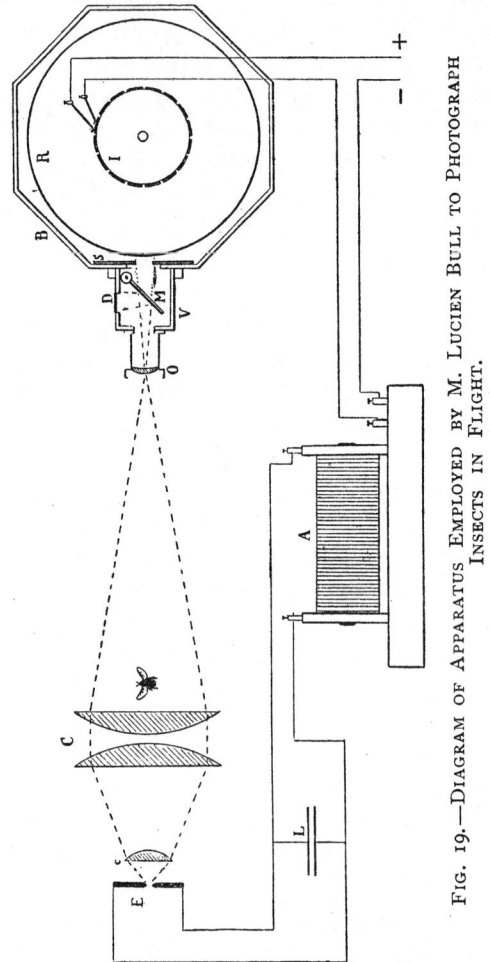

FIG. 19.—DIAGRAM OF APPARATUS EMPLOYED BY M. LUCIEN BULL TO PHOTOGRAPH INSECTS IN FLIGHT.

and taken into the dark-room it can be opened easily to permit the exposed film to be withdrawn and a new strip inserted.

The shaft upon which the cylinder revolves is fitted with

an interrupter I, whereby the primary circuit of the induction coil A may be broken at regular intervals during the revolution of the wheel. If desired, as many as 2,000 interruptions can be made in one second, by rotating the wheel at a very high speed, if the necessities of the experiment demand such a high number of exposures; each interruption producing an electric spark in the spark gap E placed behind the condenser C. This condenser converges the luminous rays into the objective O, which is mounted in front of the travelling sensitised ribbon.

The lens is mounted in a small box V attached to the front vertical face of the octagonal box, the latter being pierced at this point to permit the light to pass from the objective to the film behind. In this lens box, between the back of the objective and the exposure aperture, there is a mirror M, attached at its top to a horizontal rod having a milled screw head. When the mirror is in the position shown in the diagram, the image reflected therein through the lens is thrown on to a ground-glass screen D, set in the top of the lens box. This serves consequently as a view-finder. When the exposures are to be made the screw controlling the mirror is turned, and this swings the mirror upwards like a flap until it lies flat against the under side of the ground-glass D, forming a light-tight joint.

The wheel carrying the sensitised film is driven by an electric motor, the shaft of the wheel being extended beyond the box on one side to carry a small grooved pulley, the drive from the motor being transmitted through a small belt. The motor may be driven at varying speeds, so that the number of exposures per second may be varied according to the revolutions of the box completed in that period of time.

The interrupter—also mounted outside the film-box—whereby the make and break in the primary circuit of the induction coil is controlled, and consequently the frequency of the spark between the points E in the secondary coil circuit, is a disc of ebonite, into which are compressed fifty-four strips of copper spaced equidistantly—each strip corresponding to a picture on the film—which are pressed by two metal brushes as in the commutator of the ordinary dynamo. As the copper strips in the ebonite disc pass beneath these two brushes the electric circuit of the induction coil is opened and closed, thereby producing an electric spark in the secondary circuit of the coil. The intensity of the spark is augmented by means of a small condenser L, which is placed in parallel in the secondary circuit.

The sparks are produced between two pointed magnesium electrodes, less than 1/12th of an inch in thickness, while the spark is about 1/25th of an inch in length. The spark is very rich in the ultra-violet rays, which possess a powerful photographic quality. In order that these rays shall not be absorbed during their passage through the condensers C, the latter are made of Iceland spar. To secure improved results, a small condenser c is sometimes placed immediately in front of the spark-gap E. The general arrangement of the apparatus for operation is shown on page 266, the whole being mounted upon a bench with the induction coil upon a shelf beneath.

The photographs obtained in this manner, however, are purely of a silhouette character, and often it is very difficult to interpret correctly the movement of the wings of an insect from such a result. In order to obviate this drawback, Monsieur Bull introduced a stereoscopic system, wherein two lenses are mounted side by side before the film box, with two spark-gaps in the same circuit. This enables two sparks to be produced simultaneously with each interruption of the primary circuit, to give two images of the object upon the sensitised celluloid films.

In order that the two exposures should be made upon the films exactly at the same time, a special type of shutter had to be evolved, whereby the exposure apertures were opened simultaneously at the critical moment when the cylinder commenced to revolve, and which closed in concert when the rotation was completed, because, as the films were travelling continuously, there was no necessity for an alternate closing and opening shutter movement, as is required in ordinary cinematography working upon the intermittent motion principle. The interval between the sparks acts in the same manner as a shutter swinging across the lens, and serves to secure a succession of instantaneous pictures upon the films. The images are obtained in such rapid succession that there is no possibility of the films becoming fogged through the objective apertures being open the whole time the wheel completes a revolution. The two sparks being in the same circuit, they must be produced in absolute synchrony.

The crucial question was how to open and close the shutter simultaneously at the critical moments. This was solved in an ingenious manner. The shutter itself is made of brass and is placed close to the film. There are two

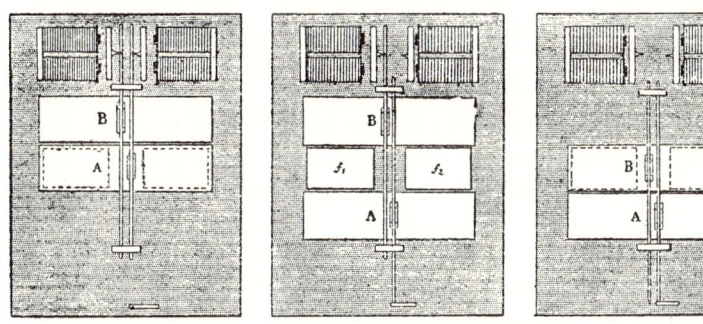

FIG. 20.—THE INGENIOUS STEREOSCOPIC SHUTTER TO THE BULL CAMERA.

apertures, side by side, corresponding to the size of the image upon the cinematograph film.

The operation of the shutters is shown in Fig. 20. When the cylinder is at rest, the exposure holes are closed by a single curtain A, consisting of a thin sheet of steel of sufficient length to cover the two holes. It is held in position by means of an electromagnet controlling an extended spring. When the cylinder commences to revolve the spring connected to the shutter is released under an electric impulse discharged through the electromagnet. The shutter falls, exposing the two apertures f_1 and f_2. When the cylinder has completed its revolution, another electric impulse releases a second steel curtain B, held in position by a second spring, controlled by an electromagnet, so that it drops also and falls over the exposure holes. This system is both simple and positive in its operation, and it may be pointed out that this control is quite independent of the interrupter, which works in conjunction with the electric spark.

The interval of time elapsing between each picture is determined by means of a tuning fork making 50 double vibrations per second, which operates an electric signal. This tuning fork is set up in such a manner that the ends of its vibrating tongues are photographed upon the film throughout the experiment. As the vibrations of the tuning fork are known, it is only necessary, in order to determine the interval of time between each exposure, to count the number of photographs taken successively during a complete vibration of the tuning fork. As a result of experiment, however, it has been found that the ear can be trained to determine with astonishing accuracy the speed at which the apparatus revolves—and consequently the number of pictures taken per second—by the succession of sparks produced by a tuning fork the vibrations of which are known. This means that in conjunction with the photographic record, the speed at which the exposures were made can be determined without effort, and this velocity can be varied very easily. In addition, a measured scale, engraved on glass, is placed in the field of the lens, whereby the investigator is enabled to determine the exact displacement of the insect in the field of vision within a given period. Such is the apparatus, devised so far back as 1904, with which Monsieur Lucien Bull has accomplished some remarkable work of incalculable value to science, and with striking precision.

I will now proceed to explain how the photographs are taken. In the first place, in order to obtain natural and conclusive data regarding the flight of insects, it is imperative that they should be cinematographed while in full liberty, but the point arose as to how to control the instrument so that the camera and film did not commence to revolve until the moment the insect entered the field of the lens. The habits of insects vary greatly. Some fly

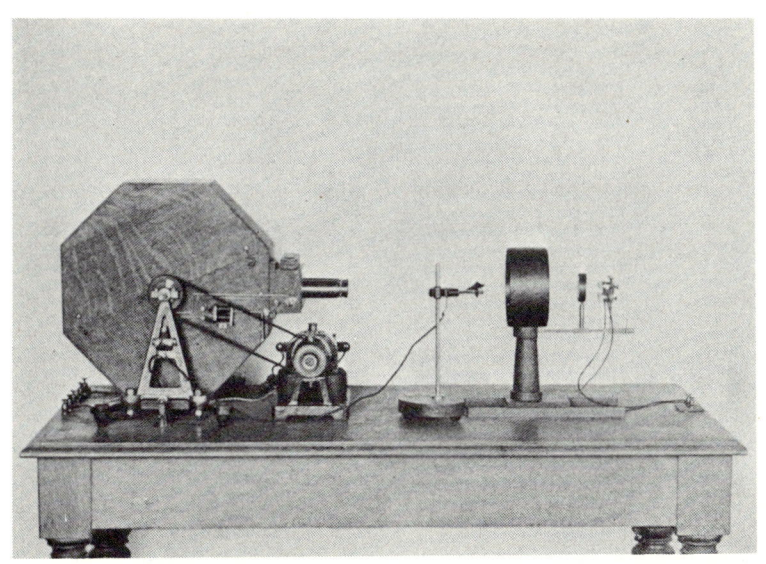

M. LUCIEN BULL'S COMPLETE APPARATUS.

THE NOVEL CAMERA SHOWING STEREOSCOPIC LENS.
Taking 2,000 moving pictures per second.—*See page* 265.

A BEE CINEMATOGRAPHED IN FULL FLIGHT.

At the left is the glass tube from which it has escaped.—*See page 273.*

off immediately they are released, while others hesitate for a minute fraction of a second. As the apparatus makes only one complete revolution at a time, and that in the fraction of a second, the control has to be of such a finely adjusted character that the record obtained is of movement purely and simply, and not of the insect in a quiescent state preparatory to flight.

Another question was how to induce the insect to cross the field of the lens. All insects instinctively fly towards a light. The apparatus therefore was set near a window, the insect being released from the side away from the window, so that in order to reach the light it had to traverse the field of the lens. As the latter is very small, it was essential that the release should be carried out in such a way that the insect did not fly above or below the field of the lens during exposure of the film.

At first sight these obstacles appeared insurmountable. It was obvious that the release of a fly from the hand would be too slow and uncertain, while the movement of the insect after securing its liberty would be unnatural, because no matter how delicately it might be handled, there would be the liability of injuring its fragile frame. The governing point was to devise ways and means of opening the shutter just at the moment the insect started to fly from one side of the lens field to the other, under completely natural conditions.

This delicate problem was resolved by Monsieur Bull in an ingenious manner, but not before he had carried out innumerable experiments attended by dispiriting failures. At last he succeeded in evolving means whereby the insect automatically and instantaneously opened the shutter of the camera at the moment it started to fly. The artifices by which this end was achieved are shown in Fig. 21. The system, however, had to be modified for different types of insect. That marked *A* was used for the ordinary house-fly and for dragon flies. It comprised a small pair of pincers, or clamp, which held the fly firmly captive by means of a small electromagnet, but in such a way as not to inflict the slightest injury. This clamp was introduced in the stereoscopic shutter electrical circuit. The two legs of the clamp have a natural tendency to fly apart under the action of a spring, but are held closed by a tooth at the end of a rocking arm, mounted on one leg, engaging with a fixed tooth on the second leg of the clamp. The latter is placed in an electrical circuit with the shutter of the camera. When all arrangements are completed, the experimenter closes this circuit. This action causes the electromagnet of the clamp to pull down the projecting end of the toothed arm; the two legs are allowed to fly

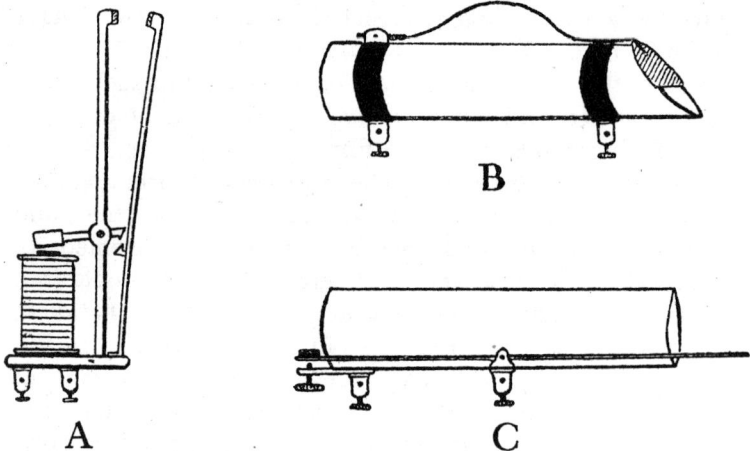

Fig. 21.—The Ingenious Devices Employed by M. Lucien Bull to Release the Insect at the Critical Moment.

apart, liberating the insect, and as the clamp releases the fly the stereoscopic shutter is opened.

This system, however, was of no avail in connection with the *Hymenoptera* group of insects, since wasps, bees, and similar insects hesitate slightly before they seek safety in flight. Consequently the device B was evolved. This consists of a small glass tube, in which the insect is introduced at one end. The opposite end is cut obliquely, and is fitted with a very light hinged shutter of mica, having a fragile spring, which covers about one-half of the opening. The spring closes the electric circuit operating the stereoscopic shutter of the camera.

Let us suppose a bee is to be cinematographed in flight. It is pushed head foremost into the free end of the tube, which is large enough to carry it comfortably, and the half-closed mouth is pointed towards the window. The insect naturally endeavours to approach the light, and accordingly crawls along the tube until at last it reaches the mica shutter, beneath which it endeavours to escape. As it crawls out of the tube it lifts the mica flap, and the circuit is broken. But the shutter does not open, because at this moment the operator himself closes the contact. By this time the insect has emerged a sufficient distance from the tube to complete its final preparations preliminary to flying away. Just as it springs from the tube the mica shutter falls, the electrical circuit is closed once more, the shutter is opened, and pictures of the bee on the wing are recorded upon the celluloid film.

For the *Coleoptera* group of insects—beetles—where there is still a more marked hesitation before flight, the device C was prepared. In this instance Monsieur Bull compels the weight of the insect, which is relatively heavy, to establish the necessary contact to operate the shutter. A glass tube without an oblique mouth is used for this purpose, and instead of the mica flap, a very light horizontal plate of aluminium, balanced by a counterweight at one end, is passed through the tube. This plate is mounted on a central pivot, and extends a certain distance from either end of the tube. The counterweight is slightly lighter than the weight of the insect, and rests in contact with a platinum point. The beetle is introduced into the tube at this end, and crawls along the rod towards the opposite end. When it has passed about half-way through the tube, and has crossed the fulcrum of the beam, it causes the contact end to rise like a see-saw, thereby breaking the electrical contact. In this case, as with the device B, the operator recloses the break in the circuit. The beetle continues its journey, and finally emerges from the tube upon the flattened end of the beam, on which it completes its arrangements to fly away. Directly it leaves the platinum beam, the latter, under the action of the counterweight, falls upon the platinum point, re-establishes the contact, the circuit is closed, the shutter is opened, and the flight is caught upon the sensitised band.

Monsieur Bull has devised a wide variety of these ingenious appliances, whereby he is able to secure the flight of any insect, and by the employment of which the chances of failure are reduced to the minimum. Indeed, when the apparatus is set up correctly, is in the hands of a skilled operator, and every arrangement has been completed satisfactorily, failure can only result from one cause —the refusal of the insect to fly away. The best results are obtained from insects which are in a fresh, healthy condition. If they have been imprisoned for too long a period, or are fatigued, the chances are that the results will be very disappointing. The records which Monsieur Bull has secured, showing insects in flight, illustrate some very interesting facts, and are of far-reaching value from the scientific point of view. At the present moment they are of additional interest owing to the absorbing fascination of aviation, inasmuch as they enable us to study with ease the movement of the wings of powerful, speedy fliers, which hitherto has been impossible under natural conditions, owing to the excessive velocity with which the wings move, and the brief character of the motion. With such an apparatus as I have described, any very rapid motion can be cinematographed, for the system is very elastic, and capable of very extensive application.

Another vast field of research which has been opened by the cinematograph is the study of the flight of projectiles. This subject has occupied earnest attention among military authorities for some time past. A few years ago Professor Vernon Boys carried out some wonderful experiments in this direction, and produced some very striking results. His work has been continued recently, by cinematographic means, by an eminent German investigator, Dr. C. Cranz, professor at the Berlin Military Academy. He has succeeded in accelerating the exposures of the film to such a degree that 500 consecutive pictures can be taken in 1/10th of a second, the exposures varying from

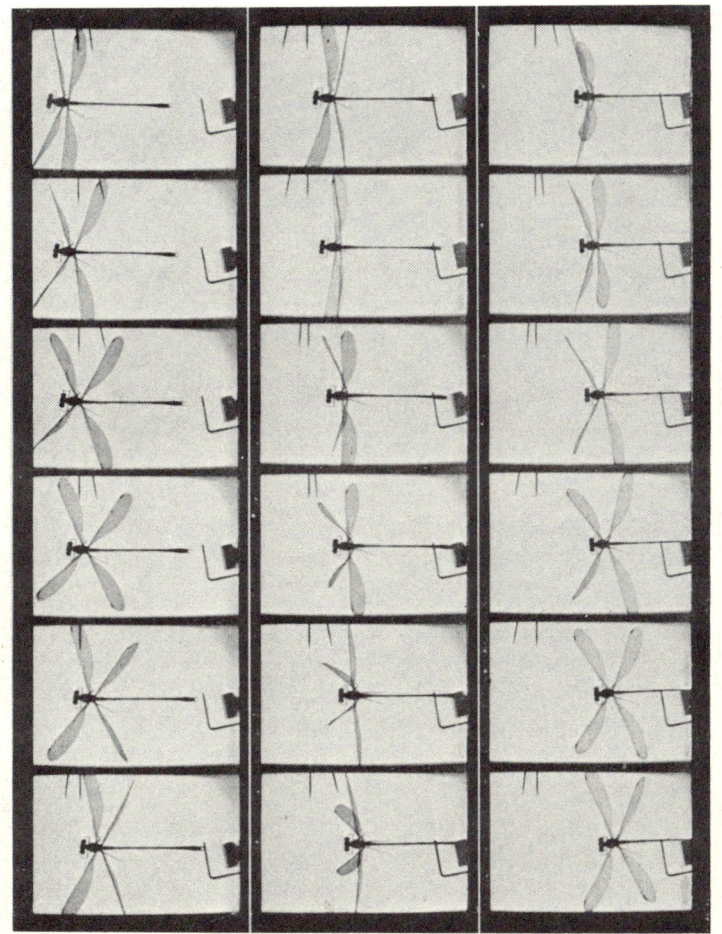

A DRAGON-FLY IN FLIGHT.

At left is the electric clamp from which the insect has been released, and at right the tuning fork to determine the interval of time between successive pictures.

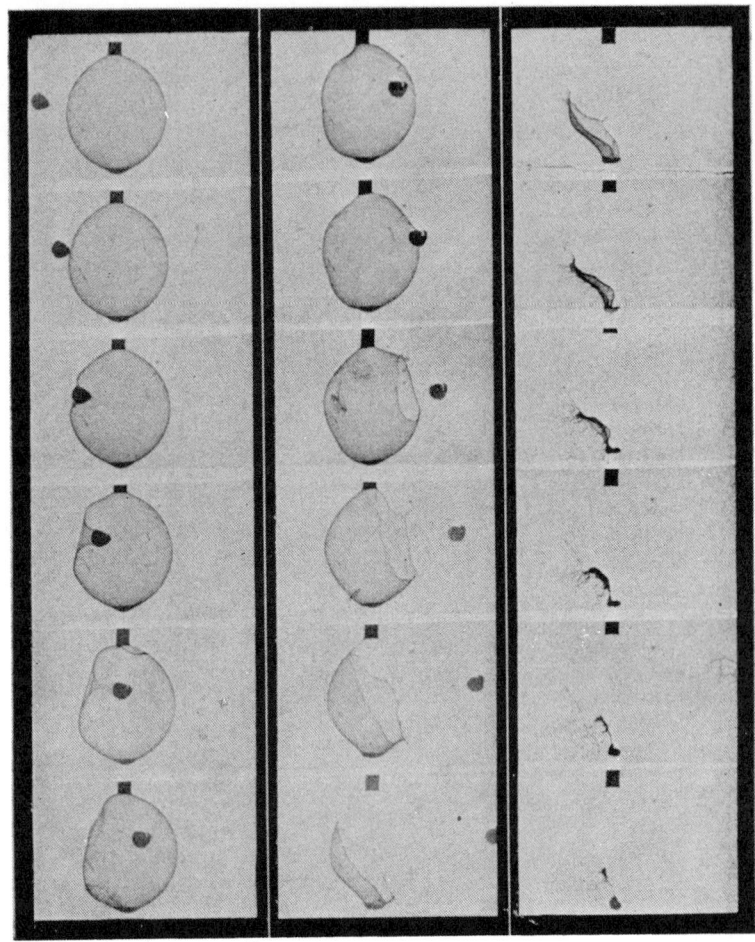

CINEMATOGRAPH FILM OF A BULLET FIRED THROUGH A SOAP BUBBLE.

The flight of the missile may be followed easily. It will be seen that the bubble breaks, not when the bullet enters, but when it emerges.—*See page* 276.

1/1,000,000th to 1/10,000,000th part of a second, the last-named period being such an infinitesimal fraction of time as to be beyond human comprehension. The pictures obtained are of the standard dimensions, and a striking feature, despite the tremendous speed at which they are taken, and the extremely brief exposure, is the clearness and definition obtained.

In this instance, also, the electric spark is called upon to serve as the illuminant to enable the images to be recorded upon the sensitised band, but the means whereby the interruption of the primary circuit of the induction coil is secured differs materially from that practised by Bull. Obviously the film travels with a continuous, instead of with an intermittent, motion, the sensitised band in this instance being run over two steel cylinders. The tremendous speed at which the film moves may be gathered from the fact that, at the rate of exposures made, over 280 feet of film must pass before the exposure aperture in the short space of one second—more than $2\frac{1}{2}$ miles per minute.

The apparatus evolved by this German investigator is more complicated than that of his French contemporary, and the method of operation is widely dissimilar. The arrangements, too, for preventing the film receiving more than one series of pictures—the film is rotated before the exposure aperture in the form of an endless band—demanded a special electrical contact control system, while the manipulation of the apparatus varies according to the character of the experiment.

The results obtained are startling. Although taken at such a tremendous speed, the pictures when thrown upon the screen under normal conditions enable every motion to be followed quite easily because everything moves slowly. For instance, one can see the hammer of an automatic pistol fall, and follow exactly what takes place during the whole firing operation, and the ejection of the spent cartridge. Similarly, when the pistol is fired, and the bullet is photographed as it emerges from the muzzle or when it strikes, passes through and emerges from a steel plate, the movement can be followed with complete facility, as it appears to move across the screen no more rapidly than a person walks, because, although the exposures are made at the rate of 30,000 pictures per second, they are projected at a speed of only 16 pictures per second. By this means analysis of extremely rapid motion in all its details can be effected—a result of far-reaching possibilities to the study of ballistics.

Facilities are provided to enable the progress of the missile, both vertically and horizontally, to be measured, so that the speed of the projectile may be determined with unimpeachable accuracy. Fluctuations in the speed of a missile can be ascertained and investigated. Suppose the speed of the projectile is measured as it emerges from the arm, and again as it reaches the end of an extensive free trajectory; losses in velocity due to resistance of the air and other causes can be calculated. Individual pictures, when enlarged—and the sharp, well-defined character of the images on the band enables this enlargement to be carried out to a very wide limit—supply a ready means to investigate any particular phase and phenomenon at close quarters.

It is not generally known that about twelve years ago the British Government set up such an installation at Devonport to investigate the phenomena of bullets in flight. Here also illumination was carried out by means of the electric spark, but the rate of exposures was considerably slower. The results of the work of Monsieur Bull and Professor Cranz, however, has opened up another and more wonderful province for the cinematograph, and the investigation of rapid motion. The efforts of these two scientists prove conclusively that motion photography is capable of recording the most rapid movements known with perfect success, although the circumstances may demand such extraordinarily short exposure as the $1/10,000,000$th part of a second.

CHAPTER XXV

THE "ANIMATED" NEWSPAPER

WE have seen how the topical picture has developed into one of the most attractive and extensively appreciated phases of the art. Events of annual occurrence like the Derby or the Grand National, or those which have been advertised widely on all sides, such as an aeroplane race, are always anticipated with a keen curiosity.

At the same time, however, there are many incidents of daily occurrence which are of absorbing passing interest, such as the launch of a battleship, a railway collision, a big fire, or a public demonstration. Such subjects are not adapted to presentation as individual films of great length, being insufficiently momentous to grip the public for several minutes in the same way as the International Yacht Race, or some other dramatic item in our complex social and industrial life.

For some time occurrences like these were ignored. Sometimes weeks slipped by without any public event being presented on the screen, owing to lack of opportunity.

At this juncture one or two enterprising firms conceived a brilliant idea of turning these events to interesting and profitable account. Why not secure short lengths of film on various subjects of passing interest, and join them together to form one film between 200 and 350 feet in length, to provide a regular weekly topical feature? These little "topicals" were secured—a few feet of this, and a few feet of that, subject depicting the most striking or interesting phases in each news feature—and joined to form a continuous miscellaneous moving mirror of the world's happenings.

When the idea was first carried into execution the film could scarcely be described as "topical." There was no attempt to serve up the pictures to the public in a "red-hot" condition. The incidents portrayed in many instances had passed beyond the allotted nine days of wonder, and having been almost forgotten, aroused but a flicker of interest. The experiment recalled the days when newspapers first resorted to photographic illustrations; when the pictures were published often two or three days after the occurrence of the event to which they referred.

Yet the results achieved sufficed to prove that a new and promising field in cinematography had been tapped. Great possibilities awaited enterprise and energy. All that was required was to supply the pictures while the events were still fresh in the minds of the public. Haphazard methods promised only failure; a special organisation was essential to cope with the situation. In order to emphasise the motive of the undertaking, the topical film, which presented in tabloid form an assortment of news, was given a newspaper title; the animated "Chronicle," "Gazette," and "Graphic" appeared; while to render the newspaper idea more pronounced, the exteriors of the picture palaces were emblazoned with placards drawn up in the most approved newspaper style.

In the course of a few weeks, as the operators displayed keener competition to outstrip rivals in securing the first pictorial representation of something of importance, and the pictures assumed a more and more up-to-date aspect, the moving picture newspaper established its significance. Showmen were tempted to assist in the enterprise by being able to purchase the newspaper film at a lower price than the ordinary subject. Although the animated newspaper has been amongst us for only a few months, yet it has already developed into an institution. Many people would as soon think of missing the "newspaper" item as they would think of overlooking an opportunity to see the Derby re-run upon the screen.

From a cursory view no difficulty appears to be attached to the preparation of a film of odds and ends of topical interest; but as a matter of fact the task is quite as exacting and strenuous as the production of the morning newspaper.

The work can be handled successfully only by a firm having an extensive organisation, and with better chances of success if it has specialised in the ordinary "topical." There must be an editor to direct operations and to prepare the film. He must possess a large and scattered staff, so that no part of the world is left uncovered by a cinematograph. His scouts must be active and keen, always on the alert, and ready to secure on the instant a few feet of any incident of importance in their respective localities. In the offices a number of skilled operators must be ready to hurry off at a moment's notice to any desired spot.

The first-named emissaries constitute the special foreign correspondents, while the office staff feed the film in the same manner that the newspaper staff reporters supply the columns of the morning newspaper with material.

There is one feature in which the man with the camera holds an undisputed advantage over his *confrère* armed with notebook and pencil. He gives a truthful pictorial account of what takes place, not the garbled product of a vivid imagination. As a result the editor of the animated picture newspaper is spared the menace which hangs always over the head of the newspaper director. He is immune from the pains and penalties of the libel law!

In order to secure a more intimate impression of the work of the moving newspaper, we will go behind the scenes of one of the most flourishing and successful of these animated news-sheets—*The Gaumont Graphic*—and follow it through its successive phases of production. When the proprietors of this pictorial record embarked upon this new development, they had the experience of some twelve years' work in the "topical" field, and their machinery and staff had acquired the instinct to "get there first."

There is, of course, the editorial sanctum in which the

presiding genius holds autocratic sway, and directs the many threads which control the acquisition of news. At his elbow the tape machine ticks merrily the livelong day. The telegraphic ribbon reels out the bald announcement that a big fire is raging in the City, that a devastating explosion has spread death and ruin somewhere in the north of Scotland, or that a Transatlantic liner has run on the rocks off some remote part of the coast. An operator is rushed to the scene, and there left to his own devices to secure a sensational few feet of film. He may succeed or he may not; it all depends upon the circumstances and conditions. Maybe he may have to wait four or five hours perched in an uncomfortable position, but if a few feet of film can be exposed to advantage he will not have failed.

The country is divided up into districts where cinematographic reporters are retained in readiness for any emergency, and they have command over a certain radius around that centre. For instance, if an accident happens in northern Scotland a telegram to the operator responsible for that locality hastens him to the spot. The editor of the *Gaumont Graphic* has branch offices at Newcastle—which covers the north-east of England—at Glasgow for Scotland, and at Liverpool and Manchester for the northwest of England, the Liverpool operators being ready to proceed to Ireland or the Isle of Man should the necessity arise. In addition, there are what might be described as sub-offices at Bristol and Birmingham, whence any point in the Midlands and the west of England can be gained, as well as another at Scarborough, so that the whole of Great Britain may be said to be mapped out and covered cinematographically.

As far as the foreign areas are concerned, owing to offices being established in all the large centres from China to Peru, no difficulty is experienced in gathering items of interest from all parts of the world. Operators are searching constantly for films of general interest from the industrial, commercial, scenic, travel, or some other point of view, and in the course of their work secure pictorial snippets of topical interest. As a result a steady stream of items recorded in animation pour in constantly from all parts of the world. The European and Asiatic items in the form of lengths of film pass to the French headquarters in Paris, while those of Canadian and Australian interest flow to London. A daily record of the films of a news interest received from foreign correspondents is received from France for the London editor to sift and select what he considers of interest. When this has been done, he telegraphs to Paris for what he requires—so many feet of this and so many feet of that film.

In addition, he has a tabulated statement of what may be described as "fixed" functions, such as a race meeting, a motor competition, a flying-machine test, a society wedding, and what not, to which operators are dispatched.

In due course the small lengths of exposed film filter in by train and post. So soon as they arrive they are developed and printed. Proofs are handed over to the editor to be scanned and revised, sections which he considers the most suitable and likely to interest the public being snipped from each film-proof, by the aid of the indispensable scissors. Possibly much of the material when it reaches the editor's eye fails to win his appreciation, and meets an inglorious and premature end in the editorial waste-paper basket. A certain amount of wasted effort is unavoidable; for space, that is to say, length of film, is limited, and when the *Graphic* appeared only once a week, sifting was of a searching character. When a considerable amount of incident has occurred and has been cinematographed during the week, the selection process is by no means easy; many interesting items find themselves crowded out to be held over until the next issue, or destroyed.

As the pieces of each film are selected, they are "pasted" together, and each incident receives its full explanatory title and sub-title. These revised proofs are connected up so as to form a continuous length of film, and copies are reeled off in the printing, developing, and drying rooms at tip-top speed, the operation corresponding with the printing machine room of the newspaper. The first complete proof is submitted to the editor's approval by being projected on the screen just as it will be submitted to the public. Further revision may be requisite, in which event the film undergoes another trimming process with the scissors, or possibly some late news has been received, and space has to be found for its inclusion at the expense of some other item.

The "composition," or, as it is called, the "make-up," of the animated news film is just as complex as that of a newspaper or magazine. It is essential that it should be diversified in its contents so as to appeal to the tastes of all classes of the community. There are the big items which stand pre-eminent, and which range from London to South America, and from Paris to China. Around these have to be disposed various other features of lesser importance.

Seeing that the length of the film newspaper is limited to between 500 and 650 feet, and is built up of from ten to seventeen subjects which vary in length according to their respective importance, careful discrimination is necessary. The public has become hypercritical in regard to animated pictures, and the appeal has to be made to the great majority. As a rule, endeavour is made to incorporate regular features in each issue. Sport is represented by some one or other of the many branches of athletics and racing; society finds itself displayed in a wedding, garden-party, ball, or other fashionable function; the woman's page has its equivalent in the animated portrayal of the latest Paris fashions as displayed by the manequins —generally in order to give an enhanced effect this section is reproduced in colour—and so forth. Effort is made also to incorporate, if possible, a special function of some description performed by some personage looming prominently in the public eye. Variety is the keynote of success as much in the successful cinematograph newspaper as in its ink-and-paper contemporary.

The *Gaumont Graphic* has an extensive and influential foreign and colonial circulation, and accordingly special attention has to be devoted to the requirements of these readers, or rather spectators. The special topical films are ransacked, and little excerpts made. For instance, in the Coronation number of the *Gaumont Graphic,* two or three of the greatest features of the long Coronation film were cut out and pasted together to form a prominent item of news; the same applies to the inter-University boat race and other sports, the Derby and great race meetings, the Football Final; in short, to every important annual event. This procedure is necessary, for the animated newspaper reaches remote parts of the world, where perchance the complete film of an individual event may never find its way.

One noticeable feature is the friendliness extended to the cinematographic news-gatherer, who often meets with greater appreciation than his *confrère,* the Press snap-shotter. The latter, armed with his small camera, often allows his zeal and enthusiasm to overstep his discretion—a fact that is particularly noticeable with regard to society and royal events. The cinematograph operator, on the contrary, being burdened with a somewhat cumbrous apparatus, is forced to remain at a fixed point. The apparent drawback is really a blessing in disguise, because special care is invariably taken to afford him an advantageous position. The outcome is that cinematographic portraiture ninety-nine times out of a hundred is far better than that secured by the snap-shotting fiend, who thrusts himself forward and catches his quarry, perchance, in an unhappy moment.

Yet the editor of the film newspaper is not relieved from worries and anxieties. Cinematography is dependent mainly upon a bright light; thus the success of a film, at least in Great Britain, is never certain beforehand. When the elements are adverse it is difficult indeed to collect the news. The operator may wait for hours to film a subject, or perhaps he makes his exposures in despair, and with a blind trust in luck. When heavy fogs hang like blankets over the great centres, passing events of importance defy recording, and it is a sheer waste of film to endeavour to secure pictures. As a result the film newspaper is much easier to produce in summer than in winter, and this climatic influence probably constitutes a unique feature in newspaperdom.

The animated newspaper even has its stop-press feature; that is to say, it can deal with pictorial records of events which occur after the paper is being printed off or has been circulated. A short film of some great incident trickles into the editorial room. It cannot be delayed until the next issue—by that time public interest in the item will have vanished. Consequently it is rushed through, and all subscribers scattered throughout the country are advised by telegraph that a record of such-and-such a topical subject has been obtained, and can be dispatched at once for display in the form of supplement to the animated newspaper now being shown. The late item is sent out, and upon arrival at the picture palace is attached to the end of the newspaper film already received, its inclusion perhaps necessitating sacrifice of some other item of less importance.

When the *Gaumont Graphic* first appeared, it was issued weekly, and accordingly corresponded to the weekly illustrated newspaper. Now it is published twice weekly, and with increased success. Indeed, the pictorial news film reaches its subscribers in the colonies and foreign countries contemporaneously, or even prior to the arrival of the illustrated weeklies, which are dispatched by mail.

In Australasia, Canada, India, and the smaller British colonies, the idea of giving the week's news in animation has met with a remarkably hearty reception, inasmuch as it serves to bring the world's happenings far more vividly before the public in those remote parts of the world than can be done in a brief newspaper cablegram or a single photograph published in the pages of the illustrated weeklies. The history of the world is re-enacted before them; they are brought to the localities where the episodes occurred—a miracle of transportation not to be effected by any other known scientific means.

How does the film newspaper affect the cinematograph theatre? What is the attitude towards the idea? Does the showman regard it with favour? These are questions which naturally occur to the mind. Opinion is best reflected by the success of the enterprise. Now that the picture paper is published twice a week, the expenditure of the showman is doubled; but this fact does not appear to have exercised a deterrent influence. When the *Gaumont Graphic* was published weekly, its circulation approximated 200 copies per week. In other words, 200 showmen subscribed towards this feature. This, by the way does not represent its full circulation, as a single subscriber may control two or more halls in one city, and very often the one film suffices for several picture palaces under one control. These 200 copies of the film newspaper, then, were seen, at a modest computation, by several millions of people weekly. Seeing that the subscriber is unable to hire the film newspaper for the week, but has to purchase it outright at a uniform price of $2\frac{1}{2}d.$ (5 cents) per foot, and that its average length is 600 feet, his outlay amounts to £6 ($30) for a subject, the exhibition life of which is restricted to three or seven days. As the average showman is a keen and shrewd business man, it is not to be supposed for a moment that the investment of such a sum every week is otherwise than remunerative from his point of view.

Will the cinematographic newspaper ever supplant its printed rival? By no means. It acts rather as an illustrated supplement to printed details; it renders the latter more comprehensive by bringing scenes and actors vividly and naturally before the eye, thereby causing a more living and detailed impression than can be obtained through the medium of words. On the other hand, it is beginning to rival the illustrated paper, which depends upon photographic contents, and this competition will be felt more keenly as time goes on.

The day is probably still far distant when a man, instead of giving a penny for a printed daily newspaper to see what has happened during the previous twenty-four hours, will spend the same sum to enter a picture palace, and devote a quarter of an hour to seeing in full animation what paper and ink merely describe. The modern business man acknowledges that he only has time to glance through the staring headlines of his morning newspaper; and surely comprehensive titles and a series of excellent pictures would perform the same service for him, and more besides. Producers would aid the development by giving careful attention to titles and headlines.

Thus the era of the daily cinematographic newspaper is not so remote as may be thought at first sight. The *Gaumont Graphic* is quite ready to appear daily if the demand should arise. The organisation is perfect so far as the news-film collecting, printing, developing, and other technical details are concerned. A complete paper could be turned out in four hours. That is to say, films could be received up to about ten o'clock at night, and the newspaper could be ready for projection by two o'clock in the morning. The early special trains which now leave the great cities at express speed for the delivery of printed newspapers to remote parts of the country may yet be called upon to carry small boxes of daily news-film for similar distribution. The manufacturing cost of the film is being constantly reduced; and once this essential is brought to a very low figure, enterprising showmen will not hesitate to spend a few shillings per day to reproduce in animation before the general public the chief episodes of the preceding twenty-four hours.

CHAPTER XXVI

ANIMATION IN NATURAL COLOURS.

THE perfection attained in the projection of animation upon the screen in black and white naturally stimulated efforts towards the achievement of similar results in natural colours. As a matter of fact, experiments in this direction were undertaken long before monochrome cinematography was perfected. W. F. Greene indicated the development when he produced his instrument in 1889; while as far back as 1897 Frederick E. Ives, celebrated for his efforts to solve the problem of still-life natural colour photography, outlined a means of applying his process to cinematography with glass plates, the celluloid film not having appeared at that date. No doubt he was urged to this development by the wonderful results achieved in chronophotography with glass plates by Dr. Marey in Paris.

Since that year experimenters without end have grappled with the problem; but little material success has been achieved. Indeed, commercial cinematography in the *true* colours of Nature appears to be as far from realisation as a simple process of still-life colour photography. Nature defies the photographic investigator to capture and reproduce the myriad tints and hues in which she is garbed.

We see colour pictures upon the white screen, but with one or two exceptions the tints are the result of the artist's handiwork. An ordinary black and white film is taken, and then coloured, in the same way that the photographic artist tints his portraits. If the work is skilfully performed the results are distinctly pleasing and effective. After one has been watching brilliant black and white pictures, the introduction of a coloured film comes as a restful interlude to the eyes. The coloured cinematograph film was introduced by Robert Paul, shortly after he established his studio. As lantern slides could be coloured by hand with brush and paints, he saw no reason why a film 40 feet in length should not be treated in the same way. Accordingly he enlisted the services of an expert artist to make the experiment. But it was a laborious undertaking. A picture measuring only 1 inch wide by $\frac{3}{4}$ths of an inch in depth is a base of operations quite different from a lantern slide measuring $3\frac{1}{4}$ inches square. A magnifying glass had to be used, and a considerable length of time was needed to treat a whole film.

One of the earliest colour effects to which the public were introduced was a film produced by James Williamson, in the 'nineties of the last century. It depicted a fire. The conflagration was enacted realistically, an abandoned house being used for the purpose. The flames and the entire scene were coloured, giving additional sensationalism to the picture. At that time the coloured film was very rarely seen, owing to the expense involved in its production, and when Williamson put his handiwork on the market it received an extraordinary reception. The lurid tinting of the flames caught the public fancy.

When the film measuring 400 feet or more came into vogue it was recognised that hand colouring was no longer feasible. The method was too slow and costly. Accordingly a stencil process was evolved, and is in use to-day, giving many of the beautiful effects seen in the moving picture theatres. A mechanical method of tinting the films by means of these stencils was next taken in hand, and finally, after prolonged experiment, was perfected. In this development the French firm of Pathé Frères played the most prominent part, and to-day, despite the strides made in natural colour cinematography, their productions still rank first in popular estimation, owing to the delicacy of the colouring. This Parisian firm has made the colour film a prominent feature of its business, and laid down

PREPARING THE PATHÉ COLOUR FILMS.
The colour system perfected by this famous French firm produces beautiful effects.

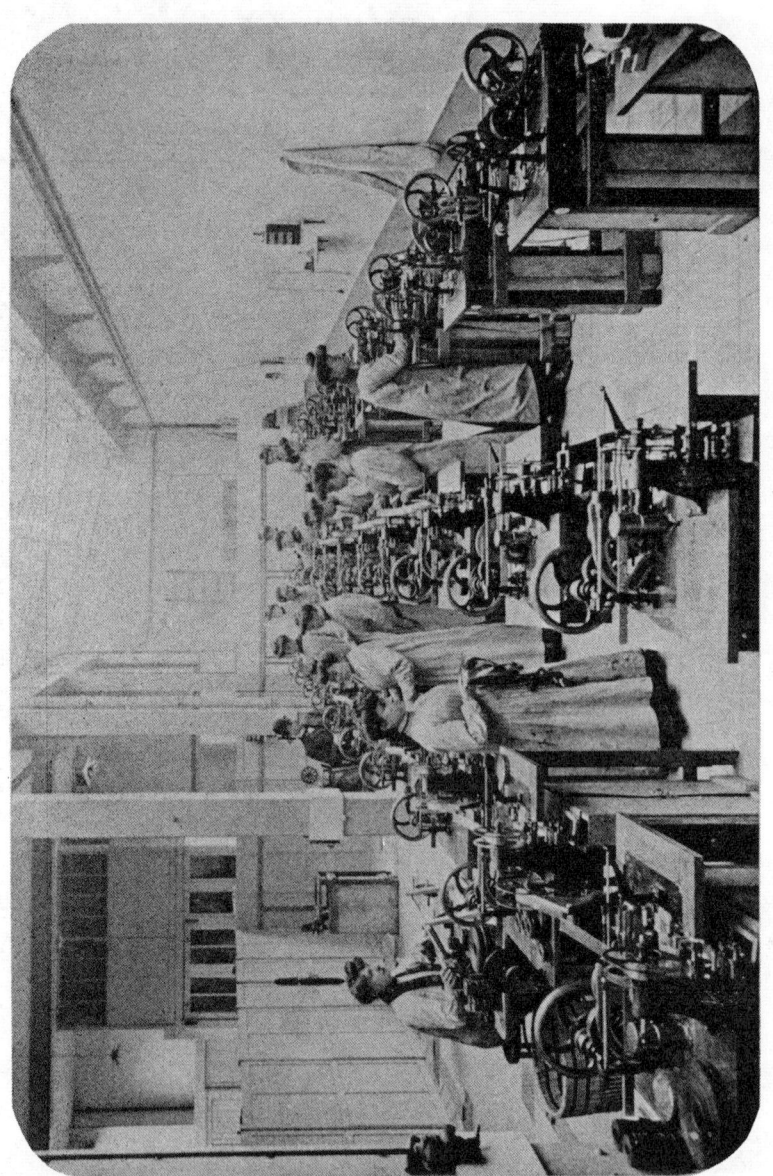

THE PATHÉ COLOUR MACHINE-PRINTING ROOM.

an extensive and well-equipped establishment especially for colouring operations.

Probably everyone knows what a stencil is. It is a pattern cut out of a solid thin flat surface, which is afterwards laid upon the subject to be treated, and paint applied by means of a brush or some other medium. The colouring only can reach the surface beneath the cut spaces in the plate, and consequently is applied just where it is desired. The process is practised freely in the printing of wall-papers, and in applying designs to other surfaces, as it is both cheap, rapid, and highly effective.

Cutting the stencils for a moving picture film is a long and exacting task. Three stencils have to be prepared for each subject. In the first the spaces corresponding to the red tones in the picture have to be cut; in the second, those for the yellow; and in the third stencil, those for the blue. By putting one over the other the various mixtures and tones are obtained. The process may be likened to the preparation of the three process blocks for heliochromic illustrations in letterpress printing. Since each picture measures only 1 inch wide by $\frac{3}{4}$ths of an inch in depth, we may gather some idea of the labour involved for the treatment of, say, 8,000 pictures contained in a film 500 feet long. It follows that unless a film is likely to have a large demand, colouring is not attempted. In one case which I have in mind, the firm will not attempt colouring unless they are certain of the sale of 200 copies of the subject. The colours—aniline dyes—are applied successively by means of rollers, the film to be coloured being passed through special machines contrived for the purpose.

In view of the expense and time entailed, it is not surprising that many inventors have devoted their energies to devise ways and means of taking colour pictures direct from Nature. Greene evolved the first cinematographic process for taking and projecting moving pictures in natural colours, and his patent constitutes the base upon which all other experimenters have worked, just as to-day in America the kinetoscope is regarded as the progenitor of the cinematograph. Six months later another process working upon the same broad principle was patented by Lee and Turner. But Greene's process was premature; at that time it was unworkable. The Lee and Turner system, fundamentally the same, suffered from a similar defect, as I shall explain a little later.

Natural light is the result of waves oscillating at a tremendous speed per second, just as other waves, heavier and travelling far more slowly in comparison with light waves, produce sound. Our familiar conception of natural light, or daylight, is that it is white; but we also know that when a narrow beam is permitted to fall upon a length of glass of triangular section, known as a prism, the light which on the outer side appears white is found to be resolved into colours on the opposite side. In passing through the prism the beam of light has been deflected from a straight path, and the result is that the waves of varying length, of which white light is composed, have been sorted out. The shortest rays are red, while the longest rays have a violet tinge. The analysis of light, as revealed by the spectrum in a dark chamber, is performed for us by Nature in the rainbow.

If we examine that phenomenon we shall see that the innumerable tints constituting it fall into three broad groups—red, green, and violet. These therefore are regarded as the primary colours. By combining any two, or all three, of these, the multitudinous hues with which we are familiar may be produced. The average person, when he hears red, green, and violet described as the primary colours, is inclined to remonstrate. At school or when using his box of paints, he was taught to regard yellow, red, and blue as the primary colours, and green, a mixture of blue and yellow, as a secondary or complementary colour. But the two instances deal with totally different forms of light. The former is transmitted, and the second is reflected, light. This confusion of thought led to the undoing of many early experimenters in colour photography. They took their images through successive screens of red, yellow, and blue, and when projecting used the complementary coloured screens—orange, green, and violet. The results were startling. It was not until Greene took his pictures through the red, green, and violet screens, and subsequently projected them through screens of the same colours—that is to say, the picture taken through the green glass was projected through the green glass, the red through the red, and the violet through the violet—that any tangible progress was made.

When the celluloid film came into vogue the experimenters lost no time in commercialising a system of natural-colour cinematography. The idea was to take a picture through each successive screen. In other words, the first picture was taken through the red screen; the film was jerked forward, and the second picture was taken through the green screen; lastly, a fresh area of sensitised surface was brought before the lens and third or violet screen. Thus three consecutive pictures, taken through three different screens, were secured. The screens comprised sectors of red, green, and violet respectively, each colour screen being succeeded by an opaque sector. Thus the shutter was divided into six parts—three colour screens and three opaque sectors alternately. After exposure through one screen, as the following opaque sector flitted across the lens, the film was jerked into position to bring a fresh surface of sensitised surface before the next screen in the revolving shutter.

When the red screen is brought into position before the lens, the colours in the object are filtered, as it were, only the red rays being permitted to pass through the screen to the film. The picture on the film, therefore, is a photograph of the red tones in the subject. Similarly the green screen absorbs all but the green rays, and photographs a record of the green tones in the subject. The same is true of the violet screen. The developed film possesses no tinge of colour in itself. It is merely a black-and-white image. Close examination of three consecutive pictures, however, reveals varying densities according to the filtering action of the respective screens. In projecting, the picture taken through the red screen is thrown through a red screen, the green image through a green screen, and the violet though a violet screen. Thus the lantern reconstructs upon the sheet what the camera dissects when photographing the object. Experimenters anticipated that, in virtue of the law of visual persistence, if these pictures were projected at a sufficient speed upon the sheet, the three images taken through the red, green, and violet screens would be superimposed one on the next, thereby conveying to the eye a faithful colour record of Nature.

It sounds feasible and seems attractively simple to perform; but Nature has not been caught yet.

At the very outset the investigators were baffled. The sensitised emulsion on the film was too slow to render the application possible. Every photographer knows that the red light is non-actinic—he uses it for the illumination of his dark-room while developing his plates. Obviously, therefore, it was hopeless to endeavour to take a photograph through the red screen in 1/100th part of a second. For this reason Greene's process failed, as did also that of Lee and Turner.

Then another miscalculation was revealed. With black-and-white pictures a speed of sixteen pictures is the minimum capable of conveying the impression of continuous motion to the brain. As the pictures are in monochrome, the perfection of the illusion is facilitated. But when it came to projecting the pictures taken in three different colours, one after the other, this law was seriously upset. When only sixteen pictures per second are shown, the eye and brain are able to single out the respective colours. The pictures do not run together to give a natural colour-effect, but are merely successive flashes of red, green, and violet light. Accordingly, the rate of projection had to be increased three times at least—forty-eight pictures per second—and the strain of this speed upon the film was so great that often it succumbed.

Consequently, before colour-cinematography could advance beyond the year 1899—when the first patent was filed by Greene—the chemist had to be called in once more to accomplish a miracle and make possible the dreams of inventors. The sensitised emulsion had to be speeded up to such a degree that it was sensitive even to red light. By this means the film is made "panchromatic," as it is called; that is to say, it becomes so sensitive that it will permit an exposure to be made as rapidly through the red as through the green screen. But "panchromatism" brought its own drawbacks. The film could no longer be handled in the dark-room illumined with a ruby lamp, for fear of becoming fogged.

It has not been found practicable to impart panchromatism to the film at the time it is manufactured. I do not mean to say that it cannot be done at that stage, but the demand for such a film is so small that it is not worthy of present consideration on the part of the manufacturer. Until colour-cinematography becomes generally practised, those engaged in its exploitation will be compelled to render their film panchromatic preparatory to exposure.

This means that the film as it arrives from the manufacturer must be submitted to a preliminary operation to augment its sensitiveness to light. For this purpose it is passed through a "colour-sensitising" solution. The precise constitution of this sensitising bath is jealously guarded, though the materials employed in the process are well known, and several formulæ which will render a film panchromatic have been published. Any one of three chemicals can be utilised to render the ordinary film so sensitive to light that the ruby lamp will fog it. These are pinachrome, pinacyanol, and ethyl-violet. The proportion of these fundamental chemicals varies, the majority of investigators having evolved a particular formula which they have found to be the best suited to their own requirements. The published formulæ, however, have proved quite reliable, and have been productive of some excellent results; and they provide the experimenter with a basis upon which to carry out his work. Recently a further development has been recorded. W. F. Greene, the pioneer, has successfully employed a new colour sensitiser, which is faster than either of the three above-mentioned mediums.

Panchromatising is a tedious operation. The work has to be carried out practically in total darkness, or at the utmost in the faint glimmer of a blue-black light. Even this slight illumination has to be used very sparingly, being switched on only for a few seconds at a time. After being passed through the colour sensitiser the film is wound upon a large drum and dried, this operation being accelerated by rotating the drum at a high speed in a current of warm air. When dry the film is wound upon the spool ready for use. As may be supposed, the operation is somewhat slow, about three hours being occupied under the most favourable conditions in the process of sensitising and drying.

It is imperative that the film, after being sensitised, should be used as soon as possible. It deteriorates rapidly; the sensitiveness of the emulsion to red light becomes impoverished through keeping, the life of stock so treated being, as a rule, one of only a few weeks.

Another objection to colour cinematography is the expense. When the three primary colours—red, green, and violet—are used, demanding a photographing and projecting speed of forty-eight pictures per second—sixteen per second through each screen—as compared with sixteen pictures per second with black and white work, three times the quantity of film has to be used. Accordingly, the expense of the film alone is three times as heavy. The further necessity for panchromatising the film before use increases the cost of the material still more. By the time the "stock" has been treated with the colour sensitiser its cost is increased from $1\frac{1}{2}$d., or 3 cents, to about $3\frac{1}{2}$d., or 7 cents, per foot.

When tricolour cinematography is attempted, three feet of film are required to record the movements of the subject during the space of one second, as against one foot for black and white work. With a view to reducing this heavy cost, inventors concentrated their attention on the possibility of securing *approximately true* natural colours by the aid of two screens only—the green and the red. In this way a third less film was required and the cost was reduced by an equal proportion.

This development was led by W. F. Greene. Realising the disadvantages of the three screens, he abandoned that system—although it has since been exploited—and in 1905 perfected the first practical method of natural-colour cinematography through two screens—red and green. A demonstration was given in the Library of the Royal Institution on January 26th, 1906. This was not Greene's first demonstration in two-colour work, as in 1900 he devised a machine for achieving the same object, which was exhibited before the Royal Photographic Society in that year.

Another diligent investigator in this field was Mr. Albert Smith, who was striving towards colour cinematography at the same time as Greene, but independently of him. The art fascinated him in the early days; and although he prosecuted his experiments first in black and white, the result of Ives's efforts in still-life colour photography prompted him to wrestle with the problem of producing natural colours in moving pictures. The elimination of the third or blue screen was his special study, and years were expended in researches to this end, involving countless experiments with the red and green screens, varying in density and intensity from the colour point of view, and in relation to one another. For instance, one screen, say, of emerald-green and the other of orange-red would first be used. This proving unsatisfactory, the proportion of the red in the one screen was increased, the green remaining untouched. Then the green would be varied, and then the red again, the process being continued until a satisfactory result was obtained. The search was rendered all the more exasperating when the screens which produced satisfaction on one day with a subject, failed altogether with another subject the next day, owing to variation in the light. At last, in 1906, Mr. Smith's patent, known as "Kinemacolor," made its appearance some eighteen months behind that of Greene; though it was not perfected sufficiently to be introduced to the public until 1908.

Undoubtedly "Kinemacolor" is at present the best-known commercial natural colour system. The appearance of this process has stimulated the movement in colour cinematography to a pronounced degree, and its improved appearance in 1911 created a sensation. Some of the effects produced have been very beautiful, and although they are far from perfect, as those identified with the process will readily admit, yet it constitutes an excellent stepping-stone for further improvement.

The statement that the blue screen has been eliminated will doubtless provoke discussion as to how the hues of a pronounced blue or purple effect so common in nature can be obtained. If one picture is photographed through the red screen and the second through the green screen, this alternation of exposure being continued throughout the film, it seems certain that the result will be pictures wherein only green and red tones exist, since no combination of these colours will give purple. This, in fact, is the case, and it constitutes the foremost imperfection in "Kinemacolor"; the pictures do have a prevailing green or red tone. But these tints become modified slightly. The essential blue tone is partially supplied in two ways. In the first place there is a certain proportion of blue associated with the green screen; secondly, when the electric arc light is used there is a pronounced blue tone in the light. The combination of these factors, to a certain but very small degree, compensates for the absence of the blue screen.

On the other hand, resort to the two screens serves to emphasise the direct colours. The red and green tones do stand out with startling purity—"unnaturally vivid" is a criticism that I have often heard—but the intermediate tones, particularly those of the browns, are strikingly soft. Some of the pictures are assailed as being unnatural in tone; and to a certain extent the criticism is a just one. In some instances, however, it is due to the fact that the spectator has never actually concentrated his attention upon colour effects in Nature. His eye has never given him a faithful report of their quality.

XXVI ANIMATION IN NATURAL COLOURS

That "Kinemacolor" has severe limitations cannot be denied, especially when it comes to dealing with Nature direct. Fidelity to the myriad hues of Nature, ranging from one extreme end of the spectrum to the other, cannot possibly be obtained by recourse to two screens.

One searches in vain for the true blue and the rich, deep purple, while the pure yellow also is absent, being represented by varying tones of orange. So far as the blues and purples are concerned, they never can be obtained by resort to the two screens—red and green respectively—because what is known as the lower end of the spectrum is lost entirely by "Kinemacolor." The hues stop short at the boundary where green meets blue.

The public has sometimes drawn attention to another defect in colour cinematography. It appears to photograph the subject in a brilliant sunlight, regardless of the fact that sunlight kills colours. Every amateur photographer knows that if he exposes his plate upon a brilliantly lighted subject the tones are hard, everything being practically resolved into an intense white and black, while the leaves of trees appear to be covered with snow. When such a disadvantage afflicts the black and white worker, what can be said of a colour subject taken under the same conditions? The brilliantly lighted points are lacking in tone, and some very bizarre effects are produced in consequence. When an essentially scenic subject is thrown upon the screen these defects are very manifest, but when it is applied to such a subject as the Coronation of the King the flaws are overlooked, because public interest is concentrated upon the principal actors.

It cannot be denied that from the popular point of view the Kinemacolor records of the Coronation, the Investiture of the Prince of Wales, and other Royal subjects of the same time left little to be desired. They brought the scene before millions with a wonderful realism and gorgeous blaze of colour such as never before in the history of moving pictures had been witnessed upon the screen. The excellence of these portrayals established "Kinemacolor" firmly in the mind of the public.

Another disconcerting feature which has aroused considerable comment in the public mind is the apparent duplication of the outlines of figures near the camera. The most uninitiated observer cannot fail to see the outlines in green and red, as if the superimposition were out of register. "Fringing," as this defect is called, is difficult to eliminate in many instances, and although often it is only momentary, it is decidedly distressing. It is due to diffraction, the glass screen as the light passes through acting somewhat as a prism, and splitting up the light into its component parts or groups of wave-lengths.

"Kinemacolor" has vast possibilities in the presentation of picture-plays; indeed, this may be said to be its true province. Here one can prepare the scenery and costumes to come within the limitations of the two screens adopted; the drawbacks can be eliminated by proper staging, and all those colours omitted which cannot be faithfully reproduced. Even if the latter expedient is not practised, the colour-distortion is not seen upon the screen. The audience cannot see that a rich purple cloak has turned to a whitish-green, or a brilliant yellow become reddish-orange.

In justice, however, it must be said that Kinemacolor is only in its infancy; it occupies the same position to-day that black-and-white cinematography did in the early 'nineties. The combined efforts of several independent investigators will eliminate the defects one by one and effect steady improvements. Black-and-white cinematography has passed beyond the formative period and reached an advanced stage of development; natural-colour cinematography must go through the self-same ordeal. Operators have not become accustomed to the new order of things, and have not realised the many new factors that have to be taken into consideration. The sooner they do so, the more profitable will the art become.

A new rival, "Biocolor," has recently made its appearance. This process is based upon the Greene patents, and the results achieved so far, in combination with this indefatigable experimenter's latest discoveries, represent a marked advance in the art. Not only are the tones purer to Nature, but "fringing" and other defects have been eliminated, while the process is much simpler and cheaper.

Considerable attention has been centred upon a new natural-colour cinematographic process which has recently made its appearance. The three primary colours are used, and are projected upon the screen simultaneously to present merely one image before the public, as in the Ives system of lantern-slide colour-projection. The pictures are projected at the rate of sixteen per second in groups of three, and the lighting arrangement is carried out upon different lines. Instead of a revolving shutter eclipsing the red image to permit the green picture to be brought into place, the light is extinguished, projection being carried out upon a flash system, whereby a powerful beam of light is thrown momentarily through the three images and screens, the pictures being changed in the period of darkness. The flashing must be carried out with uniformity, which is assured by electric-mechanical means, independently of the operator. The results, it is stated, show the most distinct advance so far made in natural-colour cinematography.

Although colour-cinematography has made remarkable strides, the monochrome picture has become established more firmly than ever. The appearance of the new rival has stimulated perfection in the technical excellence of the latter process. The monochrome possesses one overwhelming advantage over its competitor—it is far cheaper. A subject which in black and white requires, say, 500 feet of film, demands, as we have seen, 1,000 feet, or twice the quantity of material, for the two-colour record of the same subject. At present also the monochrome film possesses finer and more brilliant detail, is clearer, and, from the photographic standpoint, leaves little to be desired.

It is becoming quite a common practice to relieve the monotonous black-and-white by the introduction of colouring effects. For instance, the impression of a bright moonlight night is conveyed by giving the pictures a prevailing blue tone; for other scenes brown or red tones are given.

These effects are secured by steeping the film in a chemical solution in precisely the same way as platinotype and bromide papers are tinted after development.

"Toning," as it is called, is coming into extensive use, especially in connection with the most artistic films. The treatment imparts a solidity to the figures in the picture, and gives a pleasing softness, so that the pictures upon the screen possess a quasi-stereoscopic effect highly pleasing to the eye. The beauty of this treatment is revealed very significantly in the films of Italian manufacture, and especially in the "art" productions of the Cines Company, of Rome. There is no limitation to subsequent improving processes such as these, and their effect is to implant the monochrome pictures more and more firmly in public estimation. Consequently, the black-and-white picture is far from being eclipsed by its new rival; in fact, such a contingency is more remote to-day than it was ten years ago.

CHAPTER XXVII

MOVING PICTURES IN THE HOME

WILL the cinematograph ever enter home life? Will the world and his wife ever become wedded to a camera with which they can secure life in motion by some simple and easy method, just as now they can obtain still-life pictures by the aid of the hand-camera? Will the cinematograph become as popular as the ubiquitous Kodak?

There is no doubt that the widespread favour extended to cinematography has brought about a popular desire to follow the art in an amateur manner, as is possible in ordinary photography. Hitherto certain obstacles have stood in the way of the amateur enthusiast; but these difficulties have been broken down in an ingenious manner. The desire to practise the new cult has been increased by the number of firms engaged in the making of topical pictures and by the increasing demand for such subjects. Occasionally pictures command a high value, fluctuating in proportion to public interest. For instance, the dramatic manner of Blériot's flight across the Channel caught the professional cinematographers by surprise. Elaborate arrangements had been made to secure pictorial records of this journey, but only one man, a wide-awake amateur, obtained a film of the embarkation. Although his film was deficient in technique and photographic quality, it commanded a high price; and the enterprising photographer never had occasion to regret his enterprise, for his initial expense was recouped several times over.

The cost of the camera and the expense of the film are the chief drawbacks to the popularisation of cinematography; the bulkiness of the apparatus has also militated against its adoption by the amateur. Recently, however, these admitted drawbacks have been overcome, and by methods which claim the distinct merit of ingenuity and resource.

About 1886 a novel device known as the "Kineograph" appeared. It was an anticipation of the "Mutoscope," which made such a bold bid for public appreciation in the early 'nineties and, like the Kineograph itself, failed to make its mark. A number of instantaneous photographs were printed and mounted upon separate leaves. The pictures were placed in consecutive order and bound at one side to form a kind of book. When the leaves were turned over rapidly, giving fleeting though distinct glimpses of the successive pictures, the idea was conveyed that motion was being represented.

Recently this idea has been revived in the "Kinora" motion photography system. This likewise made its first appearance some years ago, but failed of success, although it was distinctly ingenious. It offered to the home in pictures just what the phonograph provides in regard to sound—the capture of a particular incident to be reproduced at leisure. In a highly improved form the same device has recently reappeared, and its reception augurs well for its future.

The amateur is provided with facilities for taking his own photographs, a special camera having been evolved for the purpose of simple design and operation. In general appearance it resembles the ordinary hand-camera, measuring $9\frac{1}{8}$ inches in length by $6\frac{5}{8}$ inches wide by $7\frac{5}{8}$ inches deep. When loaded it does not weigh more than $7\frac{1}{4}$ pounds. Externally it possesses few fittings. There is the lens, which can be focussed by moving the lens tube to and fro in an outer sleeve, as in a telescope; the viewfinder, placed on the top, and the actuating handle at the right-hand side. At the rear is the dial, whereby is indicated the length of film exposed, a focussing tube and the device whereby focussing is carried out.

The mechanism of the camera is very simple. The

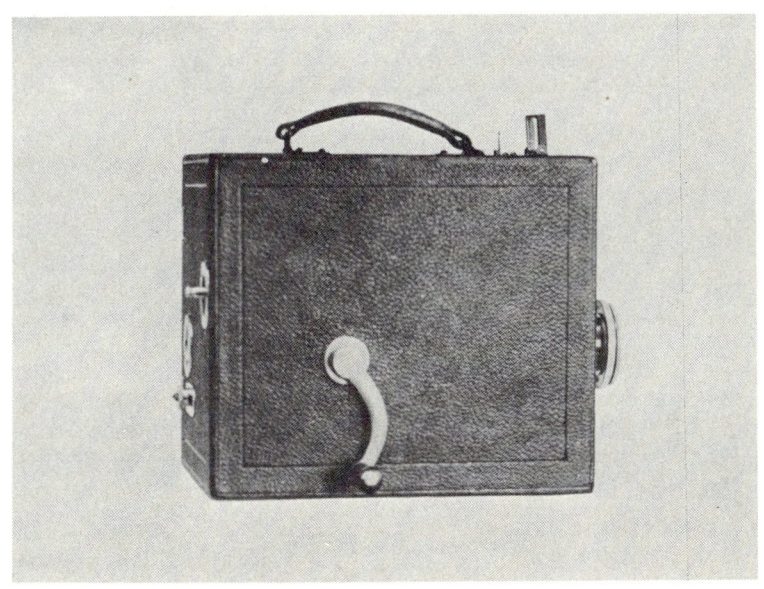

The Kinora camera.

The mechanism of the Kinora camera showing paper negative film in position.

MOVING PICTURES AT HOME.

The reel of positive prints. The pictures are mounted separately upon leaves fixed to a core.

MOVING PICTURES AT HOME.

The Kinora reproduction instrument. It resembles a stereoscope, and the pictures are exposed singly by rotating the handle.

sensitised ribbon is placed in a circular spool box and then is threaded through the film-gate and the intermittent gear, to be taken finally in a second circular spool-box. The intermittent gear differs entirely from that in the ordinary camera, which works upon a claw or finger system with the film running over sprockets. In the Kinora camera below the gate there are two eccentric rollers, mounted side by side, acting in the same way as the rollers of the domestic mangle. These rollers are split at one point through their entire length, and when these two edges, rotating synchronously but in opposite directions, come together and in contact with the film, which is fed between them, they grip and pull it down the depth of one picture. It may be pointed out that a similar movement was adopted in the very earliest cinematograph cameras built by Greene and other experimenters, in order to secure the requisite intermittent motion. Their imperfection was the uncertain motion of the rollers; but in the Kinora camera this defect has been completely overcome.

The apparatus can be used either with a paper negative or the celluloid film. The former is very satisfactory and inexpensive, and it may be stated that this is the first occasion in which the paper negative has been applied successfully to motion-photography. The camera is adapted to carry forty feet of ribbon, which is sufficient for 640 consecutive pictures, the latter being precisely of the same dimensions as those obtained upon the ordinary celluloid cinematograph film—one inch in width by three-quarters of an inch deep. Paper is suited to ordinary work, although the grain destroys sharpness to a slight extent; however, as such sensitised ribbon costs only 1s. 6d. (36 cents) per length of forty feet, the drawback is slight. If desired, celluloid film can be used, in which case the ribbon is one inch in width—three-eighths of an inch narrower than the standard cinematographic film, although there is no variation in the size of the image, since the necessity of perforating the edges has been obviated. Celluloid film printed in this manner cannot be used for the purposes of projection upon a screen. Moreover, the celluloid film is expensive; the paper sensitised ribbon is more suitable for homework.

The paper negative is developed in the ordinary manner, but as the operation is somewhat delicate, the exposed ribbon should be sent to the manufacturers, who also prepare the positive for a modest outlay. In any case, the positive must be prepared by the manufacturers, as it is a somewhat intricate process, demanding resort to special machinery; the pictures have to be printed one by one, on successive leaves in rotation, and attached by one end to a bobbin so as to present a circular reel for use in the Kinora projecting apparatus, as shown in the illustration. The pictures are printed upon bromide paper in such a way that the image stands upon a black background. The latter is obtained by exposing the sensitised paper surrounding the negative image to the light at the same time that the negative is printed; and as it becomes thoroughly exposed, development brings it out perfectly black. It looks as though the positive were printed upon paper and afterwards cut out and mounted upon a black background.

The positive has next to be submitted to a treatment whereby the back of the paper is coated with a dead black. The strip of paper carrying the images is then cut to the requisite size by means of special machinery, so that each picture forms a leaf about $3\frac{1}{2}$ inches long by 1 inch deep. The blank end of each leaf is attached to a central core or reel, some 640 leaves being mounted edge-wise in this manner, and the positive is then ready for projection.

The apparatus by means of which the motion is reproduced varies slightly in the different types. In its simplest form it recalls the stereoscope in design, only instead of two lenses it has one large rectangular magnifying-glass. The reel is mounted upon the opposite end of the instrument in a horizontal manner so that the pictures stand vertically and parallel to the lens. There is a small handle at one side whereby the reel of pictures is rotated through simple gearing, while a metal finger rests lightly upon the extreme outer edge of the leaves in such a way as to permit only one picture to turn over at a time. When this handle is turned and one is looking through the magnifying-glass, the leaves fly over in rapid sequence, producing a vivid illusion of animation. In the second type of machine the reel is mounted in a cabinet, which is fitted with two or more lenses, so that two or more people can follow the movement of the pictures simultaneously. The actuating mechanism is driven by clockwork, as in a gramophone.

Endless pleasure can be obtained with this instrument in the home. Pretty little incidents of domestic life, such as children playing, animals gambolling, and so forth, can be photographed and reproduced upon the reel! If one is more ambitious one can cinematograph great events, such as a horse race, a boxing contest, an express train at full speed—in short, anything in motion. It is only necessary to set the camera upon some rigid foundation, if a tripod is not carried, to secure steadiness during exposure.

There is one great benefit accruing from the use of this apparatus. Unless wanton carelessness is displayed, one need not worry about under- or over-exposure. The paper negatives are coated with an exceedingly rapid emulsion of considerable orthochromatic quality, so that true colour-values are ensured.

A very noticeable feature is the ingenious focussing device. Instead of opening the camera and removing the film from the gate, as in the ordinary cinematograph camera, one has merely to slide a stop projecting from the back of the camera to the length of its slot. By so doing the whole of the internal mechanism is moved bodily to one side to bring a small square of ground glass attached to the gate into position before the lens-tube, when focussing can be carried out very easily and readily.

As already pointed out, if celluloid films are employed with this camera, they cannot be used for projection purposes, because positives cannot be printed from them upon the standard perforated positive film. Consequently, the amateur who wishes to take motion pictures for projection on the screen will find the Kinora system valueless. It was designed especially for the production of positive bromide prints mounted upon a reel to be used with the special viewing machine.

The true future for this ingenious development of the art undoubtedly lies in the possibility of purchasing at a reasonable price reels of "star" events and subjects of general interest or picture plays, in the same way that one can purchase talking-machine records. In this way motion-photography can indeed be brought to the fireside.

The amateur who wishes to invade the new field so as to be able to find a market for his work, or even to project his own pictures, has his requirements fulfilled by two excellent cameras, each possessed of striking individual features, in both of which great inventiveness has been displayed to achieve the desired result without recourse to complicated mechanism or intricate operation. These machines are respectively the "Tak-kos-Kope," perfected by Captain Thomson, and the "Aeroscope," devised by Mr. Prozynski. In each instance the apparatus resembles the ordinary hand-camera, and is about the same size. Both use the standard perforated celluloid cinematograph film, so that after exposure it can be run through any projector.

The mechanism of the "Tak-kos-Kope" is exceedingly simple. The film-box contains two spindles. The unexposed film is slipped on the upper spindle and threaded through the camera mechanism to be rewound upon the lower spindle. The film as it is withdrawn from the velvet-covered mouth of the box is passed round the detachable pair of cog-wheels A mounted on a common shaft, the teeth meshing with the perforation on either side of the film, so as to move the latter forward. This sprocket is then slipped into position, one end, which is square, being inserted into the bevel cog-wheel B, while the other is held by a bayonet-jointed catch C, which by means of the milled screw can be pulled out slightly to enable the spindle to be placed in position. When released, this catch closes to grip, under the tension of a spring, the spindle of the sprocket drum.

A loop is now formed in the film, as shown in the illustration (depicting the mechanism closed), and the film is then led through the gate H, which is hinged to permit it to be opened so as to bring the film into position. The aperture in the gate H may be adjusted within certain limits by the screw I. Emerging from the exposure gate, the film passes through a second gate, wherein is the propelling mechanism, by means of which the film is jerked forward with an intermittent motion to bring successive areas of film before the lens while the light is eclipsed by the shutter. In the back plate supporting the mechanism are two toothed wheels D, which engage with the perforations on either side of the film. The gate itself, G, is fitted with two rollers, at the top and bottom, which ensure the film being kept in position to mesh with the teeth when the gate is closed. Passing through this second gate, another loop is formed in the film, and then the latter enters the bottom plate F, which is fitted with rollers, which ensure the film meshing with the toothed sprocket wheels E. From this gate the film passes through a velvet-protected slot into the film-box to be wound upon the lower spindle.

The driving mechanism is very simple, and employs the three-slotted Maltese cross, the properties of which Paul was the first to discover, as related on page 94. The smooth-running characteristics of this mechanism are displayed afresh in the Tak-kos-Kope camera. When the film is threaded through the mechanism, and the gates are closed, it presents the appearance shown in the illustration, where the upper and lower loops are plainly discernible. The whole is then slipped into the camera case and pushed home, as in the illustration, which shows the coils of unexposed and exposed film. The film-box is closed by means of a detachable panel, held in position by a spring, and when the camera is shut, two other flat springs pressing against this box serve to hold it rigid. The three gates in the mechanism are likewise held closed by spring catches.

The travel of the film is very regular and positive; I have seen films taken with this ingenious little camera which are as steady as those taken with the ordinary apparatus. The mechanism is operated by a handle in the usual manner, there being two pulleys, to secure the requisite gear ratio, mounted on the exterior of the camera, the drive being transmitted through a thick rubber band. The camera is completed by a view-finder mounted on the top.

If it is desired to use the camera for time exposure or snap-shot work with quarter-plate glass plates or pack films, the cinematographic mechanism is removed from the box, the back lens in the camera is taken out, and its place taken by the outer lens—there are two lenses for cinematographic work—which is unscrewed from the external face and re-inserted inside the camera, only one lens being required for snap-shotting. At the back of the camera is a hinged door, which when opened reveals a ground glass, while the front of the camera is provided with a short bellows to admit of racking for focussing purposes. The film or glass plate is carried in a dark slide in the ordinary manner. The handle pulleys and rubber belting, not being required in snap-shot photography, are also removed.

This camera is a small, compact, and handy cinematographic instrument. In the ordinary size it will carry 100 feet of film, but if it is desired to use a spool having 350 feet of film, it is only necessary to insert the mechanism in a larger external case. When loaded with 100 feet of film the camera weighs $6\frac{1}{2}$ pounds. For travelling and exploring expeditions it is all that could be wished; and it certainly brings cinematography within the reach of the amateur in a most practical manner.

The "Aeroscope" is a camera quite different in type. It may be said to represent "press-the-button-and-we-do-the-rest" cinematography, for there is no need in this case to turn the handle, because the operation is automatic,

The cinematograph attachment removed from camera, showing mechanism.

The interior of the camera showing film threaded ready for use.

AMATEUR CINEMATOGRAPHY.

The Tak-kos-Kope which can be used for taking moving pictures or ordinary snapshots.—*See page* 306

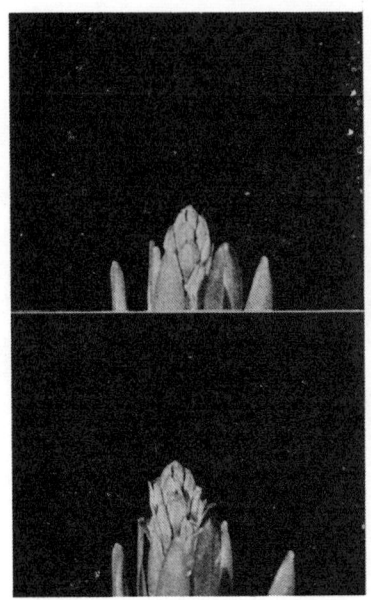 

THE BIRTH OF A FLOWER.

A wonderful Kinemacolor film. The pictures represent the stages of growth on the second, fourth, sixth, and eighth days respectively.—*See page* 194.

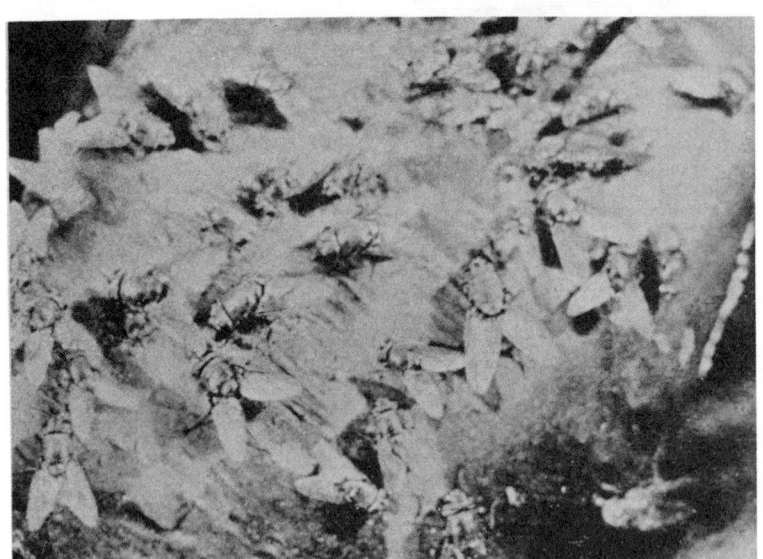

[*Copyright, Kineto, Ltd.*

WAGING A HEALTH CAMPAIGN BY MOVING PICTURES.

This film, representing flies upon putrid meat, was used in the United States in the war against the house fly with conspicuous success.

XXVII MOVING PICTURES IN THE HOME

exposures being made the whole time a button is pressed. This camera carries 450 feet of film, and the mechanism within is driven by a small air-engine worked by compressed air stored in a small reservoir, and which is charged by means of an ordinary bicycle-pump. One charge is adequate to expose 450 feet of film.

On the outside of the camera is a small lever, by means of which the rate of exposure can be varied from ten to twenty-five or more pictures per second, while on the top is a small gauge, which indicates the pressure of the air in the reservoir. The operator merely has to view his picture and press the button. The exposures being made automatically, a better uniformity is obtained than is possible by means of the manually operated handle. The mechanism is of the simplest character, so that the liability of derangement is reduced to the minimum.

One great advantage is that the camera does not necessarily require a rigid support such as is demanded imperatively by the ordinary camera. It can be held in the hand in any desired position without suffering any disturbance from movements during exposure, such as those produced by respiration, which are so disastrous with the hand-camera. This end is ensured by a novel device described as an equilibrator, which is in reality a small and powerful gyroscope, the revolutions of which counteract completely any slight oscillating movements. The task of the operator is enormously reduced. He merely has to keep his finger on the button and his eye on the view-finder, so that the moving object under record is kept within the range of the lens. The moment the button is released exposure ceases. The "Aeroscope" is the acme of simplicity in cinematography, and its greatest field of application will be in regard to topical pictures.

The amateur, although fascinated by the possibility of taking his own moving pictures, may hesitate on account of the cost of the projector. No apprehensions on this score, however, need now be entertained. Many photographers possess efficient stereopticons, and the projector mechanism for attachment thereto can be purchased very cheaply. One of the most efficient and simple projectors adapted to home use is the "Empire," which is stoutly built and very cheap, considering the excellence of its construction. Attachment to an existing lantern is very simple, the fitting occupying only about half an hour. A simple arc light and resistance has been devised for use with such a lantern, but other illuminants may be used with equal facility. Thus at a small outlay one can acquire a complete installation for projecting pictures, either at home or for exhibition purposes in outlying villages, where the professional cinematographic showman is never seen, and where the inhabitants are denied the pleasure of the ruling modern form of entertainment.

The next question which occurs to the budding cinematograph fiend is the cost of the film.

The negative and positive stock costs $2\frac{1}{2}d.$ per foot in the British Isles, and more in the United States—a price which may be considered prohibitive for the amateur. This objection was raised when Captain Thomson first introduced his idea to the public. He realised the significance of the obstacle, and immediately endeavoured to meet the situation. He met with no assistance—in fact, with hostility—on the part of the film manufacturers. But opposition made him all the more determined to succeed. Learning that the manufacture of films was about to be taken in hand by a well-known Continental firm, he approached them on the subject. As they had no market and were faced with powerful opposing interests, they saw in Captain Thomson's proposition an excellent opportunity to force their product before the public. They seized it. Captain Thomson was so successful in his efforts that he has brought the cost of the film down by nearly 70 per cent. He informs me that it is to be sold at $\frac{3}{4}d.$, or $1\frac{1}{2}$ cents per foot. It is equal in every way to the films already on the market. Even this price is not to remain constant for a great length of time. Captain Thomson is confident that he will ultimately be able to retail the film at $\frac{1}{4}d.$, or $\frac{1}{2}$ cent a foot. The new Continental manufacturers contemplate an extensive plant to capture the coming market, for once such a price becomes available to the amateur, the larger picture-producing establishments will be certain to adopt the cheaper commodity, especially those engaged in the production of topical subjects. The price of the stock has been forced down steadily and persistently for some time past, but this indicates the biggest reduction effected so far. Truly the day of the "cinematograph fiend" may be said to be dawning.

CHAPTER XXVIII

MOTION-PHOTOGRAPHY AS AN EDUCATIONAL FORCE

There remains no doubt whatever that the cinematograph has completely won over the great public—the many millions who are constantly seeking fresh fields of amusement and diversion. Of all the classes that patronise the moving-picture entertainment, the children form the one most open to its influence and most responsive to what it offers them; and it is this well-known impressionableness of the young mind that has set people thinking of the educational responsibility of the moving-picture show. From this it is but a step to the question, May not the cinematograph be brought into the schoolroom?

The subject has several aspects that are worth treating somewhat at length. The firm of Pathé Frères has here, as in so many other directions, been first in the field. Let us examine some of its educational films.

The peculiar properties possessed by the magnet are profoundly mysterious to the child. Text-books may be written in the simplest language and freely illustrated with diagrams, but the points still remain somewhat obscure. This French manufacturing company has prepared a film, "The Magnet," in which the well-known subject-matter of the school book is illustrated, and the phenomena described therein are demonstrated in a simple manner by visual records of the peculiar properties possessed by the magnet.

The familiar experiments with the magnet and iron filings are treated simply and with endless variety. If the pupils see the teacher perform the manipulations with filings and magnet in the usual way, the experiment conveys no tangible idea, and interest is not greatly aroused. But when the same magnet is thrown upon the screen in movement, and is ten feet or so in height, while the iron filings are so magnified that they resemble not dust, but thorns or long pins, a more convincing and indelible impression is conveyed.

One may have seen many diagrams showing the lines of force, as they are called. But no diagram can produce the unforgettable impression gained by the sight of the phenomenon itself occurring before the eyes. The iron filings may be seen resolving themselves into the two distinct groups about the poles, as if imbued with life, and the process may be followed from beginning to end with perfect ease, owing to the size to which the filings are magnified in projection.

The operation of natural laws is indelibly impressed upon the schoolboy when he is shown some novel experiment in physics carried out upon the screen. Physiology and anatomy can be taught by producing pictures taken by X-ray photography.

History ought surely to be a successful field for the educational cinematograph. The portrayal by Pathé Frères of episodes during the Reign of Terror and the Napoleonic era; the representation of the Normans landing in England, the discovery of America by Columbus—these and similar pictures have already shown the wide possibilities of the historical film. Of course, great care must be taken to adhere to strict historical truth in fact and setting; when they will greatly serve to fix in the pupil's mind events and historical atmosphere, and aid him in distinguishing various periods.

A film worthy of introduction into the class-room is that described in Chapter XVII., showing the birth of a flower. The fact that this film is produced in natural colours enhances its effect; a schoolboy would be hard indeed to impress if he failed to appreciate the wonderful significance of this evolution of the hyacinth from the bulb to the flowering stage. Again, he is enabled to witness upon the screen the birth of the common house-fly, and its entire span of existence. He can see how ants work and live, and how the bee manufactures its honey. As a corollary to the matter-of-fact and uninteresting text-book the cinematograph film cannot be excelled. It presents in actual movement what mere words, which have to be committed to memory, seek to convey without any durable result. Indeed, there is not the slightest doubt that a thousand pictures will impress themselves upon the schoolboy's mind, and impart to him more definite knowledge of their subject in one minute than hours of hammering with the aid of text-book and blackboard. Even actual ocular demonstration fails to be so convincing as a projection upon a whitened sheet, where everything immediately concerned is magnified to an extreme degree.

The inventor of the Kinetoscope, Mr. Thomas Alva Edison, is of opinion that the cinematograph will displace all other methods in the schoolroom for the teaching of geography. Both teachers and pupils will be inclined to agree with this dictum. A teacher may talk for hours about the tremendous height of the peaks in the Andes, the racial characteristics of the natives of Abyssinia, or the manner in which rivers are born on the flanks of mighty glaciers. But words sometimes convey very little to the immature mind. Throw upon the screen a series of pictures of an actual journey, and the youngster gleans the facts without the slightest effort. He sees the towering, snow-capped rocks with their precipitous flanks; the melting snow and ice flowing down from the mighty glacier and forming a tempestuous, rushing river; he sees in their natural surroundings the folk of a hundred strange and distant tribes. Perhaps he is transported for the time to the deck of a steamer driving its way up through the St. Lawrence River and the Great Lakes. Books and pictures have given him but a faint idea of these noble waters; but when he sees their beauty, and witnesses the enormous traffic carried upon their broad bosoms, figures and facts take on new significance, and are never forgotten.

CINEMATOGRAPHING AFRICA FROM A LOCOMOTIVE.

In order to secure scenes along the Cape to Cairo Railway a special platform was erected over the cow-catcher of a railway engine for the convenience of Mr. Butcher and his cameras.—*See page* 125.

Looking into the Crater of the Volcano.

[*By permission of Jury's Imperial Pictures, Ltd.*
MOUNT ETNA IN ERUPTION.

The plumes of smoke as seen from the Observatory.
One of the most daring and striking cinematograph films ever taken.

Whatever scene he sees, from the Atlantic to the Pacific, from the Arctic to the Antarctic circle, that scene becomes henceforth not a mere spot on the map, but a living reality.

One of the most remarkable series of pictures worthy of inclusion in this category is that obtained of Mount Etna in eruption. The cinematograph operator displayed wonderful daring in venturing to the verge of the crater of this vent to internal fires. The reward for his intrepidity certainly conveys a more realistic and vivid impression of a belching volcano than the most imaginative flights of description in text-books.

The success of the educational campaign of the cinematograph depends upon the suitability of the film. The cinematographer has roved through all the fields of science securing interesting pictures in metallurgy, natural history, manufacturing industries, electricity, agriculture, horticulture, and so forth. The educational value of the films now produced is beyond dispute; but it may be that they are somewhat too old for children. The film manufacturers have, up to the present, chiefly consulted the tastes of adults; and the films of a distinctly educational character which they produce appeal to the mature rather than to the child mind. On the other hand, it should not be at all difficult to produce films which, like the one already described, representing experiments with the magnet, would give regular instead of incidental instruction upon subjects actually treated in schools—animated text-books, in short. But as yet the picture producer has not received sufficient encouragement from the educational authorities to warrant him in preparing such films.

Unfortunately, the feeling against the moving picture has not been entirely eliminated, despite its tremendous popularity. Once an energetic Board of Education realises the possibilities of cinematography as a supplement to the information conveyed by text-books and manuals, the film manufacturers will hasten to supply the demand thus created. The last obstacle will have been removed; for the field presents no special mechanical difficulties, the only serious one having been removed by the discovery of the non-inflammable film. The perfecting of this film has obviated the necessity of confining the installation within an iron box—a requirement which militated very appreciably against the introduction of the cinematograph into schools.

A striking illustration of the educational value of moving pictures is revealed in the beautiful series of "Empire" pictures which are being secured by Messrs. William Butcher and Sons. They are completing what may be described best as a cinematographic encyclopædia of Greater Britain—its peoples, resources, industries, sports, and scenic beauties. Every corner of the Empire is being searched for entrancing pictorial contributions to this project.

As might have been expected, others beside educational institutions have seen in the moving-picture show a powerful instrument of propaganda. Political, charitable, municipal, and numerous other organisations have pressed the celluloid ribbon into service to aid them in their crusades. It has been of far-reaching utility in preaching the gospel of sanitation and prosecuting the war against disease, for the films convey their lessons in a terribly realistic manner. The Americans have produced a striking film for the dissemination of information as to how to combat advantageously the ravages of the great "White Plague" of consumption. The various American hygiene associations also have pressed home their campaign against the common house-fly with commendable vigour by means of the cinematograph. Other photographs of a similar character have been produced in various places for the purpose of initiating the public into the causes of certain diseases and maladies, and the best means of prevention or treatment.

Medical science has profitted materially from the perfection of the art and its application to surgery. It is not always possible for students to be present at a peculiarly delicate and abnormal operation. Although the subject may be described at length in the technical papers, words fail to be so emphatic as a pictorial reproduction of the feat. Not only can the operation be followed closely when reproduced upon the screen, but, if desired, any particular phase in the achievement can be selected, and by enlargement upon photographic paper it can be subjected to closer and more minute investigation at leisure.

Even the Government has not failed to recognise the power of the cinematograph. Some years ago Mr. Robert Paul applied to the War Office for permission to film scenes in a soldier's life. The facilities were granted, and some first-class pictures were obtained. They proved immensely popular with the public, and were far more potent as a means of inducing enlistment with the colours than the most glowing word-pictures painted by glib, persuasive recruiting sergeants. This idea has been copied by other nations, and to-day the cinematograph is regarded as an indispensable weapon for attracting recruits to the land and sea services.

Religious institutions have not been backward in realising the value of animated pictures in preaching the gospel of faith. The producer, by means of the stage and actors, can present any episode from the Creation to the Resurrection. The world before the Deluge, the toil of the Israelites in the land of the Pharaohs, the Sacrifice of Abraham, the Passage of the Red Sea, with the destruction of the Egyptian hosts, the story of Samson and Delilah, the Fall of Babylon, scenes from the Life of Christ—all these and many others help to familiarise both old and young with the Bible stories, and add wonderfully to their convincingness, as the following episode shows:—A teacher was describing the Passage of the Red Sea. The children followed his words intently; and his peroration was accompanied by a piping voice exclaiming:

"Yes, teacher, I know that is right!"

"Why?" asked the somewhat startled teacher.

"Because I saw it!"

The teacher was perhaps prepared to chide at this flight of imagination; but the child soon explained that the previous evening she had been to a picture theatre and had seen the Israelites crossing the Red Sea.

Among the American preachers the significance of the cinematograph is beginning to be recognised. Ministers see in the projector a valuable adjunct to their teaching, and are disposed to introduce it into their churches. I am at liberty to quote in this connection a letter from one of the leading luminaries in American church circles, which was received by Mr. Richard G. Hollaman. The divine wrote: "My opinion is that the moving picture is the coming great educator. This I believe to be true, not only in the education of the youth, but in the church. I believe in a very few years every well-equipped church will have a moving-picture apparatus, so that the minister will appeal to the eye more than to the ear."

CHAPTER XXIX.

RECENT DEVELOPMENTS : THE GROWTH AND POPULARITY OF THE CINEMATOGRAPH : SOME FACTS AND FIGURES : CONCLUSION

In the opening chapter of this book cinematography is described as an *illusion* : that the eye believes it sees continuous animation in the pictures thrown upon the screen in accordance with the law of visual persistence. I referred also to the fact that an effort had been made to remove this illusory effect, and to produce upon the white wall by photographic agency results identical with those obtainable by the aid of the *camera obscura*. The outcome of these investigations, which have been pursued patiently for many years by one whose name is associated inseparably with the art from its earliest days, W. F. Greene, is a new type of camera and projector.

The camera is fitted with two lenses mounted side by side. It is as if two cameras of the usual type were clamped together to form a single instrument, the two film-moving mechanisms being driven by one handle, and a single shutter, mounted centrally, serving to open and close each lens in turn.

In this system two spools of film are required, one for each half of the camera, and an image is recorded upon each sensitised band alternately. The shutter with its opaque sector, being mounted between the two lenses, eclipses one while the other is exposed. The result is that two different cinematograph film records of the same subject are obtained. The left-hand camera photographs those incidents which are lost while the film is being moved in the right-hand camera during the fraction of a second the lens of the latter is covered, and *vice versâ*. If the camera is run at a speed of thirty-two pictures per second, representing sixteen pictures for each lens, either of the two films when run through the ordinary projector gives a faithful representation of the event photographed. At the same time, however, each film gives a different record, for the simple reason that one film carries the moving incidents which the other has lost during the regularly intermittent closing of the lens.

The projector works upon a similar principle. There are the two objectives with attendant mechanisms driven by a single handle, mounted side by side, and with a common shutter mounted centrally between. Projection is identical with recording. The picture is thrown from the right-hand objective, while the left lens is covered, and *vice versâ*.

At first sight the advantage of such a double system might seem somewhat obscure, but a little explanation will demonstrate its advantages. With the single camera and projector the pictures shown on the screen are isolated incidents—some phase of motion must be lost while the lens is closed to permit a further area of unexposed film to be brought into position behind the lens, although the interval of eclipse is very short indeed. With the double and alternating system complete continuous motion is photographed and projected.

As a matter of fact, this double camera and projector actually records and throws on the screen more than the eye sees. The human organ works upon the same principle broadly as the single camera, because the periodical eclipse of the eye by the lid, which is known as "blinking," interrupts continuous vision, in just the same manner as the shutter of the lens in its eclipsing action. Although the lid falls and rises very quickly so that the interruption of sight is exceedingly brief, a certain phase of movement is lost. This is apparent when a very swiftly moving object passes before the eyes. In order to lose no part of the movement the eyes are strained, and the periodical action of the eyelid is postponed so long as possible. With the double cinematograph, therefore, as a section of sensitised surface always is exposed during the running of the machine, either through the right or left-hand lens, it follows that the whole of the movement must be photographed. In fact, the action is exactly the same as if the eyelids closed and opened alternately. It might be explained in connection with this physical action that no apparent interruption in the sight is conveyed to the brain, because the movement of the lids is very rapid, and owing to the principles of the law of visual persistence.

The pictures thrown from this double projector produce an effect upon the screen precisely similar to that of the *camera obscura*. There is only one difficulty attending its use. Unless the instrument is used in a large hall, and the picture is thrown from a great distance, the images do not superimpose correctly. They are thrown upon the sheet at converging angles to one another, and the rays of light accordingly from each lens do not strike the sheet at right-angles to the longitudinal axis of each objective. The result is that the picture is narrower slightly at one end than the other, and the position of the narrow end flits from one side of the sheet to the other, according as to whether the picture is being thrown from the left or right-hand lens. At short range and with a small picture this peculiarity is very pronounced, but as the length of the throw—the distance of the lantern from the sheet—is increased, it becomes less and less observable, until at last it escapes detection.

Although the mechanism requires two spools of film, the total length needed to record faithfully a particular event is no greater than with a single camera and projector. In the latter case a minimum speed of about sixteen pictures per second is required. With the double instrument a similar number of exposures suffices, for the simple reason that each lens records one half the movement while the other photographs the second moiety of the movement. This means eight pictures per second for each lens, making sixteen pictures per second for the two—the same as by the ordinary instrument. The disadvantage, of course, is

y

that two rolls of film are required to give a complete picture, and care has to be displayed to keep the positive films in pairs for the projector, while threading up the latter is a somewhat longer process. Again, should one film break and it become necessary to cut out a few pictures to obtain a perfect joint, it would be necessary to remove the relative pictures to an equal extent upon the second film. Under these circumstances, therefore, it would appear that the di-optic projector would be reserved to the more delicate phases of cinematography, such as scientific research.

The development of cinematography in the past has been attributable in a very great degree to the enterprise of the French nation, and that country still remains ahead of all others in this peculiar work. The valuable investigations of Dr. Marey never have been forgotten, and the work with which he was identified is continued still by enthusiastic investigators in cinematographic science. The "Marey Institute" is unique, in that it is the only establishment of its class devoted to what might be termed the higher branches of the art in the world. It is fitted with special and complete apparatuses for the prosecution of any especial research in which an experimenter may be interested, so that he can carry out his work under the most favourable conditions. The foremost scientists of the world, who realise in moving pictures more than a means of amusing the public, are members of the Institute, and the results it has achieved are of far-reaching value.

A typical illustration of the work carried out at this institution is described in Chapter XXIV. M. Lucien Bull, the assistant director, is one of many indefatigable workers in the particular field of operations with which the establishment is identified. Pioneer investigation is fostered, and accordingly often follows highly interesting lines, not only in regard to cinematography in its most popular form, but also in its collaboration with science in one or other of its varied branches.

For instance, M. J. Carvallo embarked upon a series of investigations to combine the Röntgen rays with the cinematograph so as to obtain an absolutely reliable

THE "CRADLE OF CINEMATOGRAPHY":
THE MAREY INSTITUTE IN PARIS.

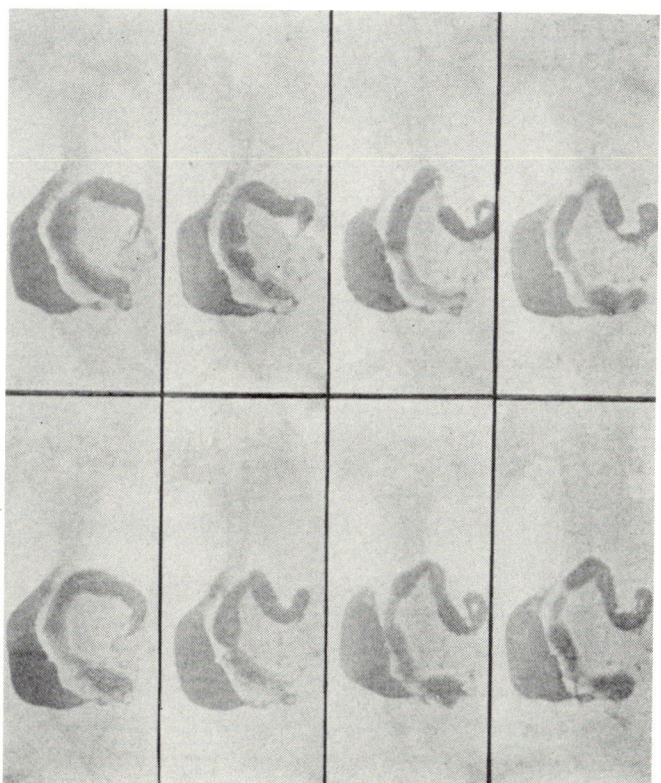

[*By permission of the Director of the Marey Institute*]
THE LATEST MARVEL IN MOVING PICTURES.

Combining the X-rays with the cinematograph. One of Monsieur Carvallo's remarkable films.

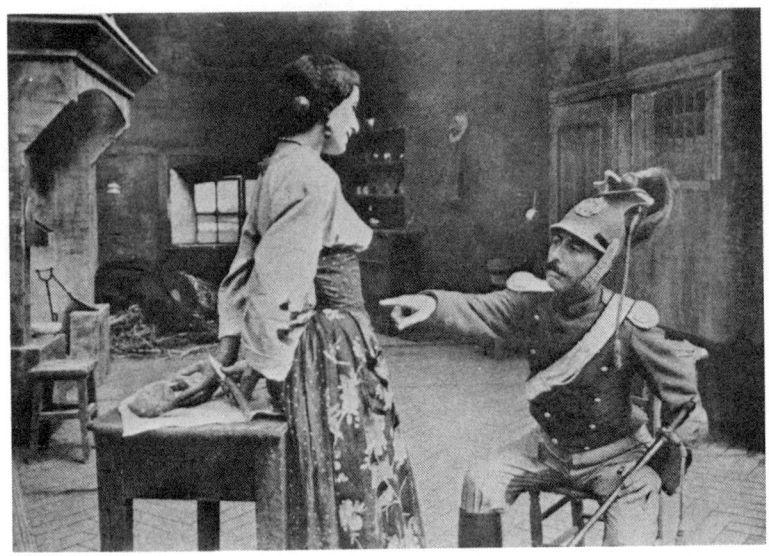

A sensational incident. The heroine gashing her hand to explain the presence of blood on her sleeve to the Austrian soldier.

A mimic fight in the public street to produce a realistic battle scene between the Italian and Austrian forces.

AFTER FIFTY YEARS

This film won the first prize of 25,000 francs for the Ambrosio Company at the recent Turin Exhibition

moving-picture record of what takes place in the organs of the human body. It was a difficult undertaking, owing to the peculiar problems associated with the task. Many experimenters had endeavoured to work with the X-rays, but had failed. In the first place, M. Carvallo had to evolve and construct a special type of apparatus for his purpose. It is of a complicated character, more especially as the exposures had to be made at a high speed per second. Unlike M. Lucien Bull, whose apparatus I have described already, M. Carvallo resorted to the familiar intermittent motion, and in such a way that the number of exposures may be varied from every twenty seconds to one per hour, according to the character of the subject under investigation. The camera is driven by an electric motor, and the arrangement is of such a nature that once set in operation it demands no further attention, even if the experiment is prolonged over several days.

He found also that the standard cinematograph film, giving a picture one inch wide by three-quarters of an inch deep, was not suited to his purpose, so a special film was prepared to yield pictures of larger dimensions, while the sensitiveness of the emulsion was also augmented very appreciably. This was essential, inasmuch as the discharges in the X-ray bulbs are of variable duration, ranging, in fact, from 1/1200th to 1/1500th of a second.

By means of his apparatus he obtained some very interesting and instructive pictures, such as showing the process of digestion in the frog, mouse, chicken, etc. The subjects were fed with a peculiar paste, or the usual food combined with basic bismuth nitrate. As a result of these successful experiments a further application of moving pictures has been revealed. In combination with the X-rays the apparatus should prove highly useful for ascertaining what actually takes place under certain conditions in the various organs of the human body.

The Marey Institute undoubtedly is the cradle of cinematography, and similar institutions should be founded in every country for the prosecution of scientific research. Moving pictures have long since issued from the purely amusing stage, and although they will never lose their popular appreciation, the sterner phases of work open to this craft should not be neglected, for there is no science in which cinematographic records of certain phenomena would not serve to widen our knowledge, and at the same time offer conclusive evidence for the refutation of many popular fallacies, or enlighten us regarding the mysteries of others.

So far as the popular picture is concerned, every effort is being made to elevate what may be termed the cinematograph drama. Sensationalism is in keen demand, and is likely to maintain its measure of appreciation so long as it is free from demoralisation. An interesting illustration of the manner in which this movement may be fostered has been offered this year in connection with the International Exhibition at Turin. Prizes exceeding 40,000 francs were offered for the best films in a cinematograph competition, the subjects to include popular drama, science, and education. The Grand Prix of 25,000 francs was awarded to the Ambrosio Film Company for the subject entitled "After Fifty Years." This concern has been responsible for many striking and magnificent productions, which have compelled attention as much for photographic quality, stage setting, and technical excellence as for dramatic force. Indeed, Signor Ambrosio, who was formerly a well-known Italian portrait photographic artist, and consequently was able to bring valuable knowledge and technique into the Italian cinematographic industry, forced his way into the closed American market by sheer merit, and forcibly impressed upon the American picture palace public the high standard of the films produced in his native land. "After Fifty Years" is a film of powerful dramatic intensity, full of that exciting incident, carefully blended with sentiment, which appeals so strongly to the picture palace *clientèle*, especially the vivid scenes of fighting in the streets between Austrian and Italian forces in the troublous times of 1859.

The Ambrosio Company also carried off the first prize of 5,000 francs for a popular science film dealing with "The Life of the Butterfly" and "The Bee." This is one of the best natural history films that has been seen yet, for it illustrates the marvellous metamorphosis of the caterpillar into the butterfly in an attractive manner. The first prize of 5,000 francs for educational films was given to the Cines Company of Rome for a film entitled "The Little Sardinian Drummer," which company also secured a prize of 4,000 francs for a dramatic subject, "St. Francis of Assisi." There is no doubt that the example of the Turin Exhibition authorities will be followed in subsequent expositions of such an international character, and this tendency should promote a healthy competition and friendly rivalry between the various producers of all countries to excel.

Although the picture palace, with its attractive façade and brilliantly illuminated entrance, is a familiar building in our towns and cities, few people can form any idea of the grip this form of amusement has secured upon the public, of its commercial proportions, or of its rapid expansion. Fifteen years ago there was not a single theatre providing a complete entertainment with a programme of moving pictures purely and simply.

The picture palace had its birth in France, and the Parisian public extended such a warm greeting to the new diversion, which offered a welcome and novel relief to the prevailing forms of amusement, that it developed into a rage. In a short time the craze spread throughout the world, and moving-picture theatres sprang up like mushrooms in every civilised country between the two Poles.

At the present day there are some 4,000 picture palaces of all descriptions scattered throughout the British Isles, and these are patronised by the public in their tens of thousands daily. The money expended upon this form of entertainment is incalculable, but it rolls continually into the coffers of the theatres throughout twelve or fourteen hours every day, the larger proportion of these establishments offering a continuous show, with a programme lasting $1\frac{1}{2}$ hours. The remaining theatres give two performances, afternoon and evening respectively, providing about three solid hours of recreation and education in each instance. The prices of admission for the most part are very low, though in the better class theatres they approach somewhat closely to those prevailing with the modern music-hall.

On the Continent the picture palaces aggregate several thousands, and are supported by the public with equal enthusiasm. Curiously enough, Germany has been the most lethargic nation. For many years an attitude of complete indifference was maintained towards the cinematograph. That country is now waking up, but so far as the manufacturing aspect of the industry is concerned, it is far behind the more progressive countries. The German picture palaces depend for their programme almost exclusively upon foreign films. Strange to say, the English productions appear to make the strongest appeal to Teutonic fancies, although the French, American, and Italian producers are striving hard to capture this highly promising and expanding market.

In the United States the development of the movement has been phenomenal. I have described already the wondrous boom in "store shows." The greater majority of these "palaces" enjoyed a brief meteoric career, as they became superseded by more pretentious buildings with perfection in comfort and luxury. To-day there are about 14,000 moving-picture theatres appealing for support between the Atlantic and Pacific seaboards. It is computed that these establishments are visited by nearly 5,000,000 men, women, and children every day. Although low prices for admission rule, it is estimated that about $130,000,000, or £26,000,000, are spent by the American public upon this form of amusement in the course of twelve months.

The coming of the picture palace has created a new race of playgoers who find infinite delight in the varied programme offered upon the screen. At the same time, however, the legitimate and vaudeville theatres have been deprived of much of their support. This effect is reflected by the number of buildings originally built for dramatic presentations which have had to close their doors for lack of patronage. When converted and re-opened under the magic sway of the projector, film, and sheet, however, they have embarked upon a remarkably prosperous new lease of life.

The stage in Great Britain is threatened in a similar manner. A few years ago, when the music-hall entertainment was overhauled and an entirely new era was created, the legitimate theatre suffered severely. Bitter antagonism developed and has prevailed between the two caterers for public amusement. Now both are being threatened by a common enemy. The picture palace, which has been despised for so long, is making its influence felt. In London the competition is not experienced so keenly, perhaps, as in the provinces, where many theatres have succumbed to the attack of moving pictures.

There is no indication that the movement has gained the height of its success. Moving picture palaces are being built and opened on all sides every day. The irresistible force with which the cinematograph is sweeping forward is proved by the enormous quantity of film which is produced. Great Britain is an open market for producers throughout the world, and at the present day something like 150,000 feet of new subjects are offered to the picture palaces every week. If the present demand is maintained together with the rate of production, this volume will be doubled within the next five years. The output in America likewise is enormous, although in that country it is confined for the most part to the productions of home firms, the foreign film being allowed to enter only in small quantities. The Motion Picture Patents Company, composed of the largest members in the United States' manufacturing industry, and swearing allegiance to the Edison patents, has an aggregate output of about 1,500,000 feet per week, each producer contributing from three to five new subjects to this total.

This community of interests, which was formed primarily to eliminate the objectionable pictures which were being shown extensively throughout the country, and which were responsible for considerable obloquy being hurled against the cinematograph, arranged on its formation to pay

Mr. Edison a royalty of half-a-cent, or one farthing, upon every foot of film which they printed in the United States. On the above total output, therefore, it will be seen that the famous American derives a revenue of $7,500, or £1,500, per week from the American moving-picture loving public.

The financial investments in the industry in all its complex branches—film manufacture, play producing, machine making, picture palaces, etc.—represent several millions sterling, while tens of thousands of men, women, and children find employment in different capacities. Although it might appear that there are sufficient producers in operation at present for the world's needs, this is far from being the case. New markets are being opened up constantly, while others are in the early stages of development. When the industry in these new centres commences to move forward in a manner characteristic of the expansion in the older countries, the demand for film will become twice or thrice what it is to-day. Consequently there is ample room for doubling the existing manufacturing facilities. The promise of the future is shown conclusively from the fact that the foremost film-play manufacturers in France, Italy, and the United States are extending and enlarging their plants to meet the increasing demands for their particular products.

One might naturally ask: How is Great Britain benefiting from this wonderful expansion? So far as film-play production is concerned, there is every indication that this country will profit now that conservatism is being abandoned. The fiscal position places the English manufacturer somewhat at a disadvantage, but this handicap can be removed entirely by the display of more financial confidence in the film-play producing business, where the law of the "survival of the fittest" is waged to its logical conclusion. A few years ago the British product was distinctly inferior to the foreign films, whether considered from the acting, dramatic, photographic, or any other point of view. Even to-day the British films are not quite up to the technical standard of the foreign manufacturers, while the histrionic quality is deficient. The plays likewise lack that grip incidental to the foreign picture dramas, and there should be excellent scope in this country for competent and imaginative picture-playwrights.

The British producers have failed also to recognise the merit of the stock company, on the plea that the public tires of seeing the same faces time after time in successive plays. The fallacy of this contention has been recognised at last, because the public now has its film idols on the screen, in just the same way as it has its footlight favourites on the stage. It is doubtful, however, whether the English producers will ever rise to the same plane in this respect as their contemporaries in the United States, who gamble practically for the exclusive services of actors and actresses. Some of the American cinematograph stars receive fabulous salaries, while even the smaller and more obscure members of the companies receive wages far in advance of what they would obtain for similar work on the legitimate stage. The protected nature of the American industry, however, favours such tactics, which probably will prevail only for a time.

There is every evidence that the British producers are making up leeway. The Hepworth Manufacturing Company, for instance, which is probably the foremost producing company in this country, recently has produced several powerful and excellent film-plays. They have extended the stock-company practice, and the increasing popularity of the "Hepwix" films offers convincing testimony to the value of this procedure. The Colonies have become satiated with the American products, and turn with relief to the English films, but the supply is not equal to the demand. Even the American public is nauseated with its home productions, and as it appreciates the work of British dramatists, so it approves of the British film play.

If England is behind her foreign rivals in the production of picture plays, it cannot be denied that London is destined to become the world's clearing-house for films. Every large foreign manufacturer has his representative in the British metropolis, where the transactions in this article aggregate a large sum every week. The Colonial picture palace proprietor, film renter, or middleman retains a purchasing agent in London, who scans the new productions as they appear, to discover their suitability for the particular corner of the world for which he is acting. These agents are autocrats, and consequently the subjects have to be brought direct to them for approval. The manufacturers realise the situation, and as the Colonial market is highly promising, spare no effort to secure its capture.

The suggestion has been made that records of the most important events of to-day, such as the Coronation of King George V., the Unveiling of the Victoria Memorial, the Durbar, and so forth, should be preserved in a museum for the benefit of generations a century or more hence. Impressions of the voices of our greatest singers are being preserved for posterity, and the question has been asked why historical cinematographic films should not be treated in the same manner. This is by no means a new idea. Robert Paul advanced the same plea in the early days of the art, but there were many objections against the proposal which are just as acute to-day. The greatest is the perishable character of the celluloid film, and also of the photographic image upon the emulsion. Both would deteriorate, even if preserved in hermetically sealed cases, with the flight of time, and the chances are if a film were held for one hundred years that it would be found useless when opened at the end of that period.

The question often arises: What becomes of the films? Bearing in mind the thousands of feet of new subjects which are introduced to the market every week, it is but natural to think that there must be an immense accumulation of old subjects. When a new subject sees the light it passes through its first "run" among the foremost picture palaces of the country. Then it is returned to the renter, who dispatches it upon a second journey among the smaller halls. Once more it comes home, otherwise to the shelves of the renter, as a rule bearing sad evidences of its service. If of sufficient interest, the film undergoes a third run among the cheapest halls, and upon the completion of this round it is either shipped abroad to the smaller colonies, or, scratched and torn, it is offered for sale at a bargain price. The end is tragic: the film slips from sight in flame and smoke.

INDEX

ABRUZZI, DUKE OF, cinematography, 128
Acetylene, as illuminant, 98
Acres, experimenter, 16
Actors and Actresses, 149–151; accidents, 156, 157, 173; special companies, 151; kinemacolor, 151
Advertisements, moving, 261, 262
Aeroscope, 306; description, 308 foll.
"After Fifty Years" (film), 324
Alhambra Theatre, London, 4; Derby film, 116
Allefex, sound producer, 140; special sounds, 141, 142
Amateur operators, 87; Aeroscope, 308; Blériot's flight film, 301; cost of stock, 310; "Kinora" system, 302 foll.; projectors, 309; Tak-koskope, 306
Ambrosio Film Company, 324
American Biograph Company, 155
—— Kinetoscope Company, 35
—— Mutoscope Company, studio described, 105
Aniline dyes, 289
Animated advertisements, 261
"Animated" newspapers, 277 foll.; circulation, 284; compared with printed newspaper, 285; effect on picture theatre, 284; length of film, 282
Animated photography (see Cinematography)
"Animated Putty" (film), 235
Animatograph, 33 foll.; at Alhambra Theatre, 116
Announcement films, 262
Anschütz, Ottomar, 20
Anti-firing devices (see under Fire)

Apparitions, 222–225
Armstrong, C., 259–60
Asquith, Right Hon. H. H. (film), 261
Austin-Edwards Co., 50
Automatic safety cut-off shutter, 95
"Automobile Accident" (film), 211
Auxetophone, 186

BACK CLOTH, in trick pictures, 241, 228
Ballistics, 276
Barker, William, 174
Base, definition, 25
Baucus (American agent), 35, 49
"Bee, The" (film), 324
"Best Cigarette, The" (film), 261
"Big Picture Play," 169
"Big Swallow," A (film), 254
Biocolor, 298
"Black Maria" (studio), 105
Blackton, J. Stuart, 172; trick pictures, 242
Blair, roller photography, 28
Blair Company, 29
Blériot's Channel flight (film), 301
Blinking, compared with action of shutter, 320
Blockless Motiograph, 99
Blue-black light (in panchromatising), 294
Blue screen, 295; compensation for absence, 296
Boys, Prof. Vernon, flight of projectiles, 274
Bull, Lucien, 264; experiments, 265 foll.; Marey Institute, 322
Bull Camera (illus.), 269–270
Butcher and Sons, 316

333

334 INDEX

CALL-BOARD, in theatre, 152
Camera, 65 foll., 107; double camera, 319; electric spark apparatus, 265 foll.; for explorers, 73; preparation for exposure, 69, 70
—— obscura, 7, 321
Cannock, Frank, 49
Capus (picture playwriter), 160
Carvallo, M. J., 323
Celluloid film, 24 foll.; accidental discovery, 28; Blair's experiments, 28; development of industry, 51; Eastman and Walker, 26 foll.; effect of climate, 53; inflammability, 54; length, 55; manufacture, 52; manufacturers, 50; non-inflammable, 55; waste product, 56, 330
Cellulose-acetate, 55
"Cheese Mites, The" (film), 201
Chemist: instantaneous photography, 2; colour cinematography, 292
Chevreul's black, 20
"Chronicle" (animated), 278
Chronophone, 185; differential gear, 188; Green's apparatus, 107; projector, 186
Chronophotography, 16; development, 322 foll.
Cinematograph (C i n e m a t o-graphe), 43-49
"Cinematograph fiend," 11, 310
Cinematograph plays, 146 foll.; dress-rehearsal, 153; production, 152; realism, 155
—— Theatre, 130 foll.; in remote districts, 132; development, 133; electrical equipment, 136 (see also Picture Palace)
—— Trust (American), 110; effect on British trade, 111
Cinematography (or Animated Photography) :—
(1) *General:* Amateurs, 301; army recruiting, effect on, 317; action of brain in connection with, 5; educational value, 312 foll.; effect on theatre, 174; expansion of industry, 327; litigation, 110; optical principle explained, 90; scientific value (*see* Scientific Research); various uses, 316-318; waste in the industry, 86
(2) *History and Development:* Instantaneous photography, 1-3; early attempts, 10-22; kinetoscope, 30-33; animatography, 33 foll.; cinematograph, 43-49; micro-cinematography, 161 foll.; in Italy, 174; phono-cinematography, 180; electric spark cinematography, 265 foll.; natural colour cinematography, 287 foll.; recent developments, 319 foll.; growth and popularity, 323 foll.
Cinephone, 180
Cines Company (*see below*)
—— Societa Italiana, 175, 176; "Crusaders" (film), 177; toning, 300; Turin Exhibition films, 325
"Clown and his Donkey" (film), 260
Collins, Esmé, 107
Collodion process, defects, 24
Colour pictures, 287; "A Fire" film, 288; aniline dyes, 289; colour sensitiser, 293; compared with monochrome, 299; Coronation records, 297; stencil process, 288
Colour-sensitising solution, 293
Comandon, Dr. J., 162; investigations, 166
Commutator, 182
Composition of news film, 282
Continuous motion, 32; for excessive speed, 265
Control board of chronophone, 187
"Coronation" film, kinemacolor, 297
Coronation films, competition for, 119
Cranz, Dr. C., 274
"Crusaders" (film), 177

DAGUERRE, exposure experiment, 1
Daily cinematograph newspaper, prospects of, 286
Dancing furniture, 209
Daylight projection, 142
Demeny, Georges, 21

INDEX 335

Derby film, 116, 117
Desvignes, 16
Detaille, 15
Developing apparatus, 85, 86
—— solution, 79
Development of pictures, 76 foll.; long films, 79, 80
Diaphragm, manipulation in trick pictures, 226
—— stop, in trick camera, 222
"Dime Show," 131
Di-optic projector (*see* Double Projector)
"Dissolution of the Government, The" (film), 257
Dog-movement, 93; in Gaumont chrono, 100
Donisthorpe (experimenter), 16
Double camera, 219 foll.; disadvantage of, 321
—— exposure process, 225
—— printing, 200
—— projector, 320 foll.
Drying operation, 79
Dumas, Alexandre, interest in Muybridge's experiments, 15
Du Mont (experimenter), 16
"Duped," 206

EASTMAN AND WALKER, 26
Eastman Dry Plate Company, 26
—— Kodak Company, 26, 50
Ebonite disc in electric spark apparatus, 267
Eden Musée—"Passion Play," 106
Edison, Thomas Alva, 29; educational films, 314; film production, 113; the kinetoscope, 30; litigation, 110; projector, 100; royalty on films, 328; studios, 105, 112
Edison Company, 151; riot scene, 157
Edison's First Kinetoscope, 31
Edison standard gauge, 57; drawbacks, 59
Educational film, 312 foll.
Election films, 257, 258
Electrical tachyscope, 20, 21
Electricity as illuminant, 98
Electric spark, 268
—— spark apparatus, 265; copper strips, 268
—— spark cinematography, 265 foll.

Electrodes, magnesium, 268
Empire Film Mender, 138
Empire Film Winder, 137
Empire projector, 101; for amateurs, 310
"Empire" series of pictures, 316
Empire Trick Camera, 216
Equilibrator (in aeroscope) 309
Essanay plant, 112
Ethyl-violet, 293
Exposure of film, 274
Eye, as camera, 4

FAIRY, production of, 244
"Fall of Troy, The" (film), 175
Faust on the Vivaphone, 184
Film, 23 foll.; American, 171; British, 328; European, 171; exposure, 274; firing of, 95; "Hepwix," 329; for kineto, 305; length, 149; manipulation in trick pictures, 220; non-inflammable, 316; repair, 137; waste product, 56, 330; weekly output, 327
—— gauge, 33, 57
—— punch, 72
—— tinting, 288, 289
Film-trap, 100
Film-winder, 137; illus., 77
Financial investments, 328
Finsbury Technical College: Theatrograph, 39
Fire, protection against, 136; anti-firing devices, 95, 96; in Empire projector, 101
First Moving Pictures, 14
Fixing solution, 79
Flashing: in trick pictures, 249
Flicker, cause of, 7
Flight of projectiles, 274 foll.
"Fountain of Youth" (film), 214
Fox, William, 145
Free-lance producer, 160
Fringing, 298; elimination, 299

GAEVERT FIRM, 50
Gate, 38
Gaumont, Leon, 184 foll.
Gaumont Chronophone, 186
Gaumont chrono projector, 100
—— Company, 110; "Automobile Accident," 211; chronophone, 185; Coronation films, 119, 120; Rob Roy, 158; The Little Milliner's

Dream, 231; The Magnetic Gentleman, 210; The Siren, 227; The Travelling Bed, 209
Gaumont Graphic, 279; bi-weekly issue, 284; branch offices, 280; circulation, 282; Coronation number, 283
"Gazette" (animated), 278
Geissler tube, in Anschütz tachyscope, 21
Gelatine, proposed use, 23
Gelatino-bromide process, 24
Gerome, interest in Muybridge's experiments, 15
Goupil, interest in Muybridge's experiments, 15
Grand Central Palace, New York, roof stage, 106
Grand Prix film, 324
"Graphic" (animated), 278
Green screen, 291; Smith's experiments, 295
Greene, W. F., 17, 107; biocolor, 298; colour sensitiser, 293; double camera, 319; natural colour cinematography, 289; three- and two-screen systems, 295
Greene and Evans, 22

Harris, Sir Augustus, and the Theatrograph, 40
Harris Safety Shutter, 96
"Haunted Curiosity Shop, The" (film), 203
"Haunted Hotel, The" (film), 242
Hazelton Picture Palace, 132, 133
"Hepwix" film, 329
Hepworth, T. C., 98
Hepworth Company, 151
—— Manufacturing Co., Ltd., 329; Vivaphone, 182
Himalayas, scenic films, 128
Hollaman, Richard G., 47; production of Passion Play, 106
Hove Camera Club, 107

Iceland spar, for condenser, 268
Illuminant, 98; electric spark, 265
Imperator projector, 100
Independent or "free-lance" producers, 160
"Independents," American film manufacturers, 171
Insects, flight of, 270; apparatus for photographing (illus.), 266, 272; Coleoptera records, 273; Hymenoptera records, 272; scientific value, 274
Instantaneous photography, 2; analysis of movement, 13
Intermittent motion, 32; Lumière's camera, 43; Paul's camera, 38, 92; for excessive speed, 265
International Exhibition, Turin, film competition, 324
Interrupter, electric spark apparatus, 267
Inventor's fiddle, 21
"Investiture of the Prince of Wales," Kinemacolor, 297; monochrome, 120–122
Itala Film Company, 175
Ives, Frederick E., 287; Ives's system, 299

Jansen, Astronomer, 17

Kalem, manufacturing firm, 171
Kelvin, Lord, film perforation, 58
Kinemacolor, 295 foll.; apparatus, 135; Coronation films, 297; "fringing," 298; limitations, 297; picture plays, 298; scenic films, 125; stock company, 151; studio-theatre, 108
"Kinemacolor Special," 126
Kineograph, 302
Kineto, Ltd., 190
Kinetograph, 179
Kinetoscope, The, 30; heat absorbent, 46; Edison's studio, 105
Kinora, 302 foll.
Kramm projector, 101

Lantern Room (see Operating room)
Latham, apparatus, 47
Laurrilard, Mr., of Marble Arch Electric Theatre, and "Investiture of the Prince of Wales" film, 120
Lee and Turner, natural colour process, 290
"Life in the Jungle" (film), 172
"Life of Christ" (film), 178
"Life of the Butterfly, The" (film), 324

INDEX

Lilliputian figures, 231 foll.; explanation, 202
"Little Milliner's Dream, The" (film), 231–235
"Little Sardinian Drummer, The" (film), 325
Loew, Marcus, 144
Lubin, of Philadelphia, 158; studio, 112
Lumière and Sons, 43 foll.; manufacture of film, 50; perforation of film, 44; projector (illus.), 45;

"MACBETH," picture play, 176
"Magic Banquet" (film), 239, 240
Magic pictures, 207 foll.; explanation, 209 foll.
"Magic Sword, The" (film), 199–201
"Magnet, The" (film), 312
"Magnetic Gentleman" (film), 210
Maguire, American agent, 35, 49
Make-up of news films, 282
Mallez, Dr., 15
Maltese Cross movement, 92, 101
Marey, Dr. E. J., 17 foll., 322; camera, 18, 19; experiments, 18, 264
Marey Institute, 322, 264
Marey's Camera showing Shutter with Radial Slots, 19
Mask, of printing apparatus, 81
Medical science and cinematography, 316; micro-cinematography, 161
Meissonier, interest in Muybridge's experiments, 13, 15
Méliès, French conjurer, 197
Microbes, moving pictures of, 161 foll.
Micro-cinematography, 161 foll.; Dr. J. Comandon, 162; difficulties, 163; experiments with blood, 166; magnification, 168; "phenomenon of agglutination," 167; popular science, 190; shutter, 165; sleeping sickness, 166
Mirror, in trick pictures, 244; in electric spark apparatus, 267
Monochrome cinematography, 299
Moorhouse, A. H., 140
Motion, records of, animal motion, 13; flight of insects, 273; flight of projectiles, 274 foll.
—— Picture Patents Company, 327
"Motorist, The (?)" (film), 203–205
Moul, Mr. (of Alhambra Theatre), 41; picture plays, 104·
Mount: for projector, 99
—— for sensitised emulsion, 23, 24; Eastman's experiments, 27
"Mount Etna in Eruption" (film), 315
Movement, illusion explained, 6; illustrated, 8
"Movement," record of Marey's experiments, 20
Movement and sound combined, Edison, 179; Gaumont, 184; Hepworth Company, 182
Moving picture circuits, 143
—— Pictures: (*see* Cinematography)
Mutoscope Company, 105
Muybridge, 12–16; demonstration in Paris, 15; studio, 13

NATURAL COLOUR CINEMATOGRAPHY, 287 foll.; "Biocolor," 298; expense, 294; Greene's process, 289; "Kinemacolor," 296; Lee and Turner, 290; new process, 299; three screens, 291; two screens, 295
—— light, 290
New Guinea, films, 128
Newman and Sinclair Camera (illus.), 73
Newman-Sinclair Printing Apparatus, 81
Newman-Sinclair Reflex Moving Picture Camera, 74
Nickel show, 131
N.S. Film Perforator, 63

OLYMPIA: First picture palace, 40
"One turn one picture" movement, 235–240; by Americans, 238; in silhouette trick films, 259
Operating room or lantern room, 136; law relating to, 135
Optical principle of the Cinematograph, 90
"Ora Pro Nobis" (film), 202

Z

INDEX

Oxy-hydrogen limelight as illuminant, 98

"PANCHROMATIC" film, 293; deterioration, 294
"Panchromatism," 293; process, 294
Paper, as base, 24, 303; Eastman, 27
—— negative, 303
Parkes, A., 26
Parkesine, 26
Parsons, Hon. C. A., 186
Passion Play, 106
Pathé, Charles, 35
Pathé Frères, 109; colour pictures, 288; development of picture play, 169; film, 312, 171; "The Magnet," 312; micro-cinematography, 163; projector, 101; village scene, 158
Paul, Robert W., 34; camera, 37, 66–69; colour pictures, 288; intermittent gear, 92; mount for lantern, 99; "Ora Pro Nobis," 202; "Railway Collision," 205; "Scenes in Soldier's Life," 317; "The Magic Sword," 199; "The Cheese Mites," 201; "The (?) Motorist," 203; topical films, 116 foll.; trick pictures, 198
Paul's Improved "Cross" Driving Mechanism, 94
Peep-hole machine, 33
"Penny gaff," 131
Perforating machines: "N-S" perforator, 63; Rotary perforator, 61; Urban-Joy, 64; Williamson perforator, 62
Perforation gauge, 57; Edison standard, 57; Lumière's, 59
—— of film, 33; necessity for mathematical precision, 60; Lord Kelvin's suggestion, 58; Lumière's method, 44
Phenaktiscope, 11
Phono-cinematograph (*see below*)
Phonograph, with cinematograph, 180, 181, 189
Photographic gun, 17
—— revolver, 17
Picture House at Briggate, 134
—— Palace, 144; effect on legitimate theatre, 326; British Isles, 325; France, 325; Germany, 326; U.S.A., 144, 326; facts and figures, 325 foll.
—— plays, 103 foll.; development, 109 foll.; the "Big Picture Play," 169 foll.; educational service, 174; financial risk, 177; historical subjects, 170; Kinemacolor, 298; Pathé firm, 110; playwright, 147; plots, 159; popular subjects, 176; religious subjects, 178; staging, 103 foll.; studio (*see under* Studio); "After Fifty Years," 324; St. Francis of Assisi, 325; The Passion Play, 106, 169; "The Soldier's Courtship," 103
Pinachrome, 293
Pinacyanol, 293
Poch, Prosper, 142
Polar exploration films, 127
Political films, 257
Popular science, 190 foll.; films, 324
Portraiture, cinematographic, 283
Praxinoscope, 11; records, 12
Primary colours, 290
"Prince's Derby," 117
"Princess Nicotine," 242–253; illustration of staging, 245; trick explained, 244
Printing, 80; Newman-Sinclair apparatus, 81–82; Williamson printer, 82–84
Projection: kinetoscope, 8; praxinoscope, 11; rate of monochrome films, 6; colour films, 292
Projector, 37, 88 foll.; for amateurs, 309, 310; double, 320, 135; driving system, 99; intermittent motion, 38; rate of projection, 6, 292; second lens, 99; shutter, 94, 95; "B Underwriter," 100; Gaumont Chrono, 100; "Imperator," 100; Lumière, 45
Provincial Cinematograph Theatres, Ltd., 134
Prozynski, 306
"Pumpkin Race" (film), 217

QUENTIN, daylight projection, 142

INDEX

RACKING BELLOWS, 255
Rainbow screen, 142
Realism, in picture plays, 155 foll., 172
Red screen, 291; failure, 292; panchromatic film, 293; Smith's experiments, 295
Religious institutions and cinematography, 317
Renter, or middleman, 171
Reversal of action, 215
Reynaud's praxinoscope, 11
Rheostat handle, 187
Rhumkoff coil, in Anschütz tachyscope, 21
Roller-photography, 26; Blair, 28
Roosevelt, T., and cinematography, 128
Rostand, picture plays, 160

SAFETY SHUTTER, 95–98
"St. Francis of Assisi" (film), 325
Sample prints, 172
"Samson and Delilah" (film), 178
Scenery (see Realism)
Scenic films, 125–129; Polar exploration, 127; Victoria Falls, 126
Scientific research, 161 foll.; electric spark cinematography, 265 foll.; explorations, 73, 127; medical science, 316
Scott, Capt. R., 127
Screen, 138; daylight projection, 142; in natural colour photography, 291
Selig, William N., 172
Selig organisation, 112; company, 151; fire-rescue film, 155; at Los Angeles, 112; studio, 112; wardrobe, 114
Sensitised emulsion, 2; in colour photography, 292
Shackleton expedition, 127
Shadowgraph play, 259
Shutter, 94; automatic safety, 95; electric spark apparatus (illus.), 268, 269
Siemens and Halske, 47
Silent Knight, projector, 101
Silhouette trick films, 259; advertisements, 261; in America, 259, 263; "The Clown and the Donkey," 260

"Siren, The" (film), 227
"Ski-runner," 240–241
Smith, Albert, 242; Kinemacolor, 295 foll.
Smith, F. Percy, 190; apparatus, 195; experiments, 191–195; magic film, 257
"Soldier's Courtship, The" (film), 104
Soret, M. L., 20
Sound effects, 139; production, 141
—— and movement combined, 179 foll.
South America, progress of cinematography, 145
Spool box, 91
Sprocket, use of, 33
Stage, 104 (see also Studio)
Stage properties, 204, 208; for "Princess Nicotine," 246
Stanford, Governor, interest in Muybridge's experiments, 15
Steinheil, interest in Muybridge's experiments, 15
Stencil, 289
Stereoscopic shutter (illus.), 269
—— system, in electric spark cinematography, 268
Stereopticons, projector attachment, 309
Stern, inventor, 22
Stock, 294; cost, 310
Stop, of lens, 199
—— and substitution action, 212–215
—— call, 215, 222
Stop-motion, 201; method illustrated, 236
Stop-press news, 285
Studio for picture plays, 103 foll.; American Mutoscope Co., 105; Edison, 105, 112; equipment, 113; Kinemacolor, 108; Lubin, 112; Muybridge, 13; Pathé Frères, 109; Paul, 104; Selig, 112; Vitagraph Co., 112; J. A. Williamson, 107
Submarine effects, 240
Superprinting, 240
Synchroniser, 182 foll.
Synchronism, 185

TACHYSCOPE, electrical, 20, 21
Tak-kos-kope, 306–308

INDEX

"Tale of Two Cities, A" (film), 171
Talking machines, 180 foll.
"Theatrograph," 39
Thomson, Capt., 306; cost of film, 310
"Three Musketeers" (film), 176
Three-roll film, 106
Three-screen cinematography (tricolour), 291; cost, 294; latest process, 299
Toning, 300
Topical pictures, 116 foll.; dangers, 123; competition, 118; Coronation of King George V., 119; East End battle with anarchists, 124; Investiture of Prince of Wales, 120; prize-fights, 122
Transformations, 225
"Travelling Bed, The" (film), 209
Travelling show, 130
Tree, Sir H. B., picture play, 174
Treuwé, Professor, 130
"Trick" camera, 222
Trick picures, 197 foll.; manipulation of film and camera, 219; M. Méliès, 197; R. Paul, 198; miscellaneous, 228–230, 237; two stages, 246; wires and threads, 238 foll.; "Animated Putty," 235; "Automobile Accident," 211; "Boots," 235; "The Cheese Mites," 201; "The Dissolution of the Government," 257; "Fountain of Youth," 214; "The Haunted Curiosity Shop," 203; "The Haunted Hotel," 242; "The Little Milliner's Dream," 231; "The Magic Carpenter's Shop," 238; "Magic Knitting Needles," 237; "The Magic Sword," 199; "The Magnetic Gentleman," 210; "The (?) Motorist," 203; "The Mysterious Banquet," 239; "Princess Nicotine," 243; "Railway Collision," 205; "The Siren," 227; "Scene at Sea," 207; "The Travelling Bed," 209; "The Workman's Paradise," 217

Tricolour cinematography (see Three-screen cinematography)
Tripod, for camera, 72, 73
"Trust," film manufactory, 171
Tuning fork, in Bull camera, 270
Two-colour work (see below)
Two-screen cinematography, 295
Tyler-Ernemann "Imperator" projector, 100

UNCLE TOM'S CABIN" (film), 156
Union Square Theatre, New York, 144
Urban, Charles, 48, 49
Urban-Joy anti-firing device, 96
Urban-Joy-Harris Anti-firing Device, 97
Urban Trading Company, 125

VINCENT, JOHN, 106
Violet-rays, 268
Violet screen, 291
Visual persistence, 3; "blinking," 321; in colour photography, 292; in monochrome, 8
Vitagraph Company, 112; "Leather Stocking" stories, 159
Vivaphone (illus.), 182–184
V-shaped stop, 199

WAR OFFICE AND CINEMATOGRAPHY, 317
Warwick Trading Company, 49
West, T. J., 130
Wheel, cylindrical, of electric spark apparatus, 265–267
"Wheel of Life," 10
"White Plague" pictures, 316
Williamson, James A., 107 foll.; colour picture, 288; "A Big Swallow," 254–257; "The Workman's Paradise," 217
Williamson printer, 82
"Workman's Paradise" (film), 217
Wright, Wilbur, flight film, 72

X-RAYS, and cinematography, 322

ZOETROPE, 10
Zoopraxinoscope, 11
Zoopraxiscope, 15

R. CLAY AND SONS, LTD., BRUNSWICK ST., STAMFORD ST., S.E., AND BUNGAY, SUFFOLK.